ALL THE TRADES AND OCCUPATIONS OF THE BIBLE

ALL THE TRADES AND OCCUPATIONS OF THE BIBLE

A Fascinating Study of Ancient Arts and Crafts

by
HERBERT LOCKYER

"What is thine occupation?"
Jonah 1:8

ZONDERVAN PUBLISHING HOUSE

OF THE ZONDERVAN CORPORATION
GRAND RAPIDS, MICHIGAN 49506

ACKNOWLEDGMENTS

Grateful appreciation is expressed to the following for their permission
to quote from their copyrighted material:

Wm. B. Eerdmans Publishing Co. for the quotes from
The International Standard Bible Encyclopedia, ed. by James Orr.
Copyright © 1930 by Wm. B. Eerdmans Publishing Co.

Oxford University Press and Cambridge University Press
for the two verses from *The New English Bible: New Testament*.
Copyright © 1961 by The Delegates of the Oxford University Press and
The Syndics of the Cambridge University Press.
Also to Oxford University Press for the quotes from
A Dictionary of Life in Bible Times by W. Corswant.
Copyright © 1960 by Oxford Press.

Charles Scribner's Sons for the quotes from *Daily Life in Bible Times*
by Albert E. Bailey. Copyright © by Charles Scribner's Sons.

Zondervan Publishing House for quotes from *The Amplified Bible*.
The New Testament copyright © 1958 by The Lockman Foundation.
The Old Testament copyright © 1964 by Zondervan Publishing House.

Printed in the United States of America

86 87 88 89 90 91 92 / 18 17 16 15 14 13 12

CONTENTS

Male Occupations (In the Spiritual Realm)

Female Occupations (In the Secular Realm)

Female Occupations (In the Spiritual Realm)

ALL THE TRADES AND OCCUPATIONS OF THE BIBLE

INTRODUCTION

Occupations in the Bible, as we hope to prove, is a most fascinating and fruitful aspect of Bible study, and also reveals how rich and practical a Book the Bible is. Pre-eminently a spiritual Book, it is at the same time, down to earth in its historical record of how those of ancient times lived and labored. While many of the trades and professions mentioned in the Bible differ from those of the same in our time and land, yet the Bible presents for our enlightenment an insight into the way those of old worked to live and lived to work. As we shall discover there are characteristic distinctions in the attitude of Gentiles and Hebrews toward manual labor. Under Gentile monarchies daily labor had little dignity. It was more like slavedom. The ancient Greeks regarded manual tasks as unworthy of a free citizen. The Hebrews, however, came to hold arts and crafts in high esteem.

John Milton describes God as, "The Great Work-Master," which the creation of the world and of man reveal Him to be. Fashioning man in His own image He ordained him to work. "Every art," said Seneca, "is an imitation of Nature." Charles Lamb, in his essay on *Work* asks the question —

Who first invented work and bound
the free,
And holiday—rejoicing spirit down?

When God provided for the rest of the Sabbath, He provided also that man should labor during six days of the week. For this purpose, God placed Adam, not in a dormitory, but in a garden, where he had to till the ground and pursue his task as a gardener. Thus the state of original *innocence* was not a state of *indolence*. God purposed that man must be like his Creator, a worker (John 5:17).

ARTS AND CRAFTS — THEIR NECESSITY

Going back to the institution of manual and mental labor, these facts are clearly defined —

Adam worked according to divine direction (Genesis 2:15; see Matthew 26:19);

Adam labored without painful fatigue, which came as the result of the Fall. Because of transgression, harder labor was imposed upon Adam. "In the sweat of thy face shalt thou eat bread" (Genesis 3:19).

Adam, by working, accomplished what was useful and necessary, bringing to himself a personal recompence in the fruit he cultivated (Genesis 2: 15, 16. See II Thessalonians 3:10-12; Titus 3:14).

Adam combined manual labor with intellectual effort. He not only tilled the ground but also gave names to all cattle, fowl and beasts (Genesis 2: 20).

In all true work for God, the Christian must give heed to "his work" — "good work" — "the work of God" — "fruitful in every good work" — "labour . . . with hands" — "with the mind I serve" — "your labour is not in vain" — "the fruit of my labour" (Mark 13:34; John 6:29; Romans 7: 25; I Corinthians 15:58; Ephesians 2: 10; 4:24; Philippians 1:22). Labor is necessary for man's maintenance. The apostolic dictum is still universally true, namely —

"If any man would not work, neither should he eat" (II Thessalonians 3: 10). An old couplet reads —

No bees, no honey,
No work, no money.

Human society, however, is filled and plagued with those who have no occupation, and little desire for one. Like certain parasites, they live upon

11

others. Those sailors who took Jonah on board felt that such a healthy full-grown man would be sure to have some occupation, and so asked, "What is thine occupation?" (Jonah 1:8).

John Stuart Mill in his essay *Liberty* was bold enough to say —

> The bad workmen, who form the majority of the operatives in many branches of industry, are decidedly of the opinion that bad workmen ought to receive the same wages as the good.

While this assertion might have been true in the essayist's day, it is to be hoped that present-day industry has more *good* workmen than bad. The question does arise, however, as to whether workmen give the full return of brain or brawn, or both, for the wages they receive. Employers are not against good wages, as long as their employees give a good day's work for a good daily wage. Faithfulness in the discharge of our obligations brings its own reward.

> Seest thou a man diligent in his business? he shall stand before kings; he shall not stand before mean men (Proverbs 22:29).

In these days of aggressive trade unionism, when the cry is for larger wages and shorter hours, the old time command—"Six days thou shalt work" (Exodus 34:21) — appears to be outmoded. Certainly, no one desires a return to the almost slave conditions which Pharaoh imposed upon the Israelites when, rejecting their cry for easing of their burden, he commanded, "Let there more work be laid upon the men, that they may labour therein" (Exodus 5:9); or to the fearful conditions of child and adult labor, such as was characterized in Britain in the day of Charles Dickens. What we are saying is that, no matter

what our occupation may be, it is our responsibility to give honest work in return for the wages received.

We cannot read Paul's epistles without realizing how practical he was even when it came to working for a master. The Thessalonians were exhorted to *work*, as well as *walk* honestly, "to do your own business, and to work with your hands" (I Thessalonians 4:11). The tireless apostle himself never did "eat any man's bread for nought" (II Thessalonians 3:8). He gave more than a full measuse in labor for the material things he received. It was this example that gave his appeal to the Thessalonians to do their work quietly and efficiently, and eat the bread they had earned, such mighty force (II Thessalonians 3:12). An ancient proverb has it — "Of all crafts to be a honest man is the mastercraft."

In writing to young Timothy, Paul says that it is incumbent upon all who profess and call themselves Christian to "learn to profess honest occupations" (Titus 3:14, asv margin). *The New English Bible* translates the passage thus —

> Our own people must be taught to engage in honest employment to produce the necessities of life; they must not be unproductive.

Distaste of regular and faithful work is utterly foreign to the Christian ideal. It would seem as if our urge is unchristian in its attitude to general depreciation of necessary labor. The Bible is hard on idleness. What a stinging rebuke Solomon has for sluggards (Proverbs 6:6, 9)! Christians, above all others, should work in such a way as to attest to their genuine Christian integrity. To them, work should be a phase of worship. No matter how menial their task may be, grace can be theirs to invest it with "the glory of the celestial." If the occupation is *honest,* then it is important to realize "the dignity of good work." Ruskin reminds us that, "Fine art is that in which the hand, the head, and the heart go together."

> Ye servants of the Lord,
> Each in his office wait:
> Observant of His heavenly Word,
> And watchful at His gate.

Carlyle, in his *Inaugural Address* given in Edinburgh, said that —

> "It is the first of all problems for a man to find out what kind of work he is to do in this universe."

Once an occupation has been decided upon, whether one has a natural gift for it, or has acquired training to pursue it, it adds to the zest of honest labor to recognize how interdependent our occupations are. Voltaire once said that "All the arts are brothers; each one is a light to the others." The philosopher Cicero gave us a similar sentiment when he wrote, "All the arts appertaining to men have a certain common bond, and are, as it were, connected by a sort of relationship." The motto of *The Surgeon's Company* is, "The arts which profit all men."

To name all the occupations each of us are dependent upon would be almost impossible. Then have you thought of how your own task fits in with the general scheme of things? Take a simple illustration — When you sit down for breakfast tomorrow morning, try to think of the many all over the world who contributed to that one meal e.g. sugar, tea, coffee, cereals, bread, bacon and eggs — how many hands and processes they represent! How dependent we are upon each other! If a wildcat strike paralyzes all forms of transportation, people in all walks of life suffer. As we engage in our daily work, then,

it is necessary to understand that we labor, not only for a personal living, but that others may also live. "Each for all, and all for each."

ARTS AND CRAFTS — THEIR NATURE

Under this heading there are interesting introductory aspects of Bible trades and professions to consider, the range of which, as our alphabetical classification reveals, is surprisingly large. While we have listed well over 150 of them, with an ever-increasing population and a progressive development of arts and sciences, we have an imposing list of arts and crafts unknown in Bible times. The last few years, have provided us with scientists, technologists, astronauts, mechanics, specialists and offices which our forebears knew nothing about. Our rapid strides in automation and nuclear science provide us with new trades almost overnight.

Artisan Designations

Various general terms are used to describe those who labored with hand and mind. As far as specific trades were concerned, in the majority of cases, the name given to the worker was qualified by the name of the material he handled and wrought with.

CALLING

This term was employed in both the secular and spiritual realms, but principally in the latter. In writing to the Corinthians, Paul said —

> "Let every man abide in the same *calling* wherein he was called" (I Corinthians 7:20).

God does not only *call* preachers. Bezaleel, the son of Uri, was as divinely *called* to make hooks and rods and shovels for the Tabernacle. In the spiritual realm, our calling is a holy, heavenly one (Romans 11:29; Philippians 3:14; II Timothy 1:9; Hebrews 3:1). We should be content if we know that we are exercising the calling we are called to. Carlyle said, "Blessed is he who has found his work: let him ask no other blessedness for those who serve God, as well as man. In his study of *call* or *calling*, W. E. Vine says that the word suggests "either vocation or destination, the context determines which."

OCCUPATION

As used in the Bible, this term implies what a person does for a living. It is employed in this sense by Joseph of his brethren (Genesis 46:32; 47:3), by the sailors of Jonah (1:8), of Paul and others (Acts 18:3). In the latter reference the Greek word for *occupation*, given as "trade" in the ASV is *techne* from which we have technique, technical, technology. This same word is used of *craft* in Revelation 18:22. Having an occupation means serving others, as well as laboring for our own needs. An occupation means that you help me and I help you. Seneca gave us the adage that, "Nothing is so certain as that the vices of leisure are dispersed by occupation." When Jesus urges us to "Occupy till I come," He means that we are "to do business," as the word *occupy* means. Whether our occupation is spiritual or secular, or both, it must have the very best we can give it. Cowper has reminded us that —

> Absence of occupation is not rest,
> A mind quite vacant is a mind distressed.

ARTIFICER

Related to *artizan*, artificer comes from a word meaning "to cut" (I Chronicles 29:5). This general term

for a skilled worker is akin to *craftsman* (II Kings 24:14), and is one covering various arts and crafts. The New Testament word for craftsman is *technites*, from which we have technical. Perhaps Erasmus was only partially right when he said, "No one is born an artificer." There are some areas in which it would seem as if a few are born with natural gifts. We call them *prodigies*. Years ago, when working in the Woolwich Arsenal, I had friends who were known as artificers because of their skill in metal work. Some were like those who prepared the metal and stone work for the Temple David planned (I Chronicles 29:5).

CRAFTSMAN

Generally used throughout the Old Testament, this expressive term usually means one who plows, carves or engraves. It can cover, however, any handicraft. Paul lodged with Aquilla and Priscilla in Corinth "because he was of the same craft," namely *tentmaker*. (See Deuteronomy 27:15; II Kings 24:14-16; Jeremiah 24:1, ASV; Hosea 13:2; Acts 19:24-25; Revelation 18:22). Craft, or Craftsman are from *technites*, and Archbishop Trench suggests that "this word brings out the artistic side of Creation, viewing God as moulding and fashioning . . . the materials which He called into existence" (See Hebrews 11:10 where the word is given as "builder," also I Corinthians 3:10). The term before us must be distinguished from *craftiness* and *crafty*, both of which are related to unscrupulous conduct, fraud and deceit (Luke 20:23; II Corinthians 4:2; Ephesians 4:14). The chief priests sought how they might take Jesus "by craft," that is, by cunning or guile. When the Bible speaks of "a cunning workman," it means one that is skillful with his hands. An old proverb has it, "Be not ashamed of your handicraft." Plantus, the Latin philosopher wrote —

> Those who are poor live wretchedly in every way and especially those who have no means of getting a living, and who have learnt no kind of handicraft.

Depicting the tragic destruction of prosperous Babylon, John declares that "no craftsman, of whatsoever craft he be, shall be found any more," in the city (Revelation 18:22). Monarchs, merchants, mariners and musicians are mentioned as being among those whose loss will be great when judgment falls.

TRADE

An axiom has it, "A useful trade is a mine of gold." A Japanese proverb expresses it, "Better be proficient in one trade than a smatterer in a hundred." In the ASV *trade* has taken the place of "craft," as a more modern term (Genesis 34:10, 21; Ezekiel 27:12-17; Revelation 18:17), for those who bought and sold various products. Our Lord's use of the term, both in a secular and spiritual sense is illuminating (Matthew 25:16; Luke 19:13, 15). The word James uses for trade is the one from which we have "emporium" — a place where all kinds of goods are traded in (James 4:13). As used by Luke, it is the word *techne*, an art, or technique (Acts 18:3).

WORK

When used in a secular sense, work means to labor in any given trade. The Bible employs it to include different manual occupations (I Chronicles 22:15; II Chronicles 2:18; 24:13; Psalm 37:1; Isaiah 40:20; 44:11; Hosea 8:6, etc.). Spiritually, the term is used to describe both good and evil deeds (Job 31:3; Psalm 6:8; Matthew 10:19; Luke 13:27; John 5:17; 9:4). When Paul said that the saints are God's workmanship, he used the word *poiema,* from which we derive "poem" (Ephesians 2:10). It is found elsewhere only in Romans 1:20 "the things that are made." God's two creations are the world and the believer. We are all familiar with the saying attributed to John Wesley that although "God buries His workmen, He carries on His work."

PROFESSION

Although, in our modern times, we use this further term to describe what one may work at for a livelihood, in the Bible the word is always related to our witness for Christ. Proclamation and confession are usually implied (I Timothy 2:10; 6:12, 21; Titus 1:16; Hebrews 3:1; 4:14; 10:23).

Artisan Guilds

We have much evidence that in Bible days, those of the same craft grouped together as fraternities, corporations or guilds, just as they do today in many large cities. These associations are seen in phrases like, "A son of the apothecaries," meaning, a member of the Guild of Perfumers (Nehemiah 3:8); and "A son of the goldsmiths" (Nehemiah 3:21); the expression "Sons of" denoting membership of an association, goes back to the days when trades were hereditary in particular families. Thus we have "The sons of the porters" — "The sons of the prophets" (Ezra 2:42). There is mention of a corporation of linen-weavers, and of potters (I Chronicles 4:21, 23). In Ephesus, there was a guild of silversmiths (Acts 19:25). Doubtless those old-time guilds were formed to preserve and protect the secrets, rights and privileges of the trade represented.

Artisan Quarters

It is also interesting to note that another characteristic feature of the more important crafts and trades was for those who followed them to live together as a colony in one street, or part of the city, to which they gave the name of their particular occupation. Thus we read of, "The valley of craftsmen" (I Chronicles 4:14; Nehemiah 11:35); of "The baker's street" — "The fuller's field" — "The cheesemaker's valley." Josephus mentions, "A smith's bazaar," a "wool market," and a "clothes market" as operating in Jerusalem during his days. Probably there was more than one tanner in that part of Joppa where Simon lived (Acts 9:43). In large cities those of the same foreign nationality grouped together in one part of the city.

Artisan Variety

Later in the book notice that we have endeavored to deal with all Bible occupations, mentioned or implied, in alphabetical order. In the section before us, we have grouped together those trades which are more or less related. For a full treatment of each particular trade, reference is made to its place in our alphabetical treatment of the trade.

CRAFTSMEN IN WOOD

Mention is made of "workers in timber" and of "carpenters" (I Chronicles 22:15; Matthew 13:55; Mark 6:3). Dr. A. R. S. Kennedy says that the productions of these skilled tradesmen, "probably surpassed in variety those of any other craftsmen for they comprised not only those of the modern carpenter and cabinet maker, but also of the ploughwright, woodcarver, and other specialized arts and crafts of today." While a carpenter's tools

are more highly developed today, perhaps they do not differ very much from those of Bible times. Mention is made of various axes or hatchets with iron head and wooden helve (Deuteronomy 19:5; II Kings 6:6; Psalm 74:6, ASV; Jeremiah 10:3). Hammers were more like wooden mallets (Judges 4:21; Jeremiah 10:4). As for the carpenter's saw, reliefs and excavations indicate that they were made of bronze, were single-handed with holes bored with a drill worked as in the present day by a bow and string (Isaiah 10:15). Then we have the rule, or measuring line — the plumbline — the line, or sharp metal pencil or stylus for tracing the work — chisels and compasses (Isaiah 44:13; Amos 7:7).

CRAFTSMEN IN METAL

The principal metals used in Old Testament times were gold, silver, brass, iron, tin, and lead (Numbers 31:22). By brass, which is now a manufactured composition, we are to understand "bronze" — a mixture of copper and tin, except where pure copper is mentioned (Deuteronomy 8:9). We have references to goldsmiths, silversmiths, coppersmiths and ironsmiths (Genesis 4:22; I Samuel 13:19; I Kings 7:13, 14; II Chronicles 24:12; II Timothy 4:14). The smiths which Nebuchadnezzar took captive were probably skilled craftsmen in weapons of war (II Kings 24:14; Jeremiah 24:1). Among the tools these particular tradesmen used we have the hammer, anvil, tongs and bellows (Isaiah 41:7; 44:12; Jeremiah 6:29).

CRAFTSMEN IN STONE

Many of the temples of the Nile, still in a state of wonderful form and beauty, reveal how skilled those ancient workers in stone or masons, were (II Samuel 5:11; I Chronicles 14:1; 22:15). The various processes of preparing stones for building are referred to. For instance, we have —

The hewing out of stones from the quarry (I Kings 5:17; 6:7, ASV).

The hewing out of winevats, and tombs in the solid rock, the cutting and dressing of hewn stones for different buildings (Exodus 20:25; I Kings 5:17; II Kings 12:12; Isaiah 5:2, ASV; 22:16; Amos 5:11).

The stonebuilders, or squares, worked to a prepared plan or model (Exodus 25:9; I Kings 5:18; I Chronicles 28:11; Psalm 118:22), and used the measuring-reed; the plumb-line or plummet; stone-cutter, axe or pick (Exodus 28:11; I Kings 6:7; II Kings 21:13; Jeremiah 23:29; Ezekiel 40:3).

CRAFTSMEN IN CLAY

Pottery, it would seem, is the oldest of all crafts. As an artificer, the potter is first brought to light in II Samuel 17:28. Workers in clay, which was the building material among the Jews, also made bricks for vessels, kilns and houses. Walls were plastered with clay or lime (Leviticus 14:42; Daniel 5:5; Matthew 23:27; Acts 23:3). The clay was usually kneaded with the feet (Isaiah 41:25).

CRAFTSMEN IN LEATHER

Although the Jews regarded tanners and their trade with much disfavor because of the unclean accompaniments of such a trade, they yet took advantage of the tanner's products. A tanner (Acts 9:42) was a craftsman who not only prepared and supplied leather from animal skins but also manufactured articles like shields, helmets, shoes, bottles for liquids, and girdles (Exodus 25:5; Leviticus 13:48).

CRAFTSMEN IN TEXTILES

While we have witnessed a gradual development of all the companion trades of those who work with cloth, the fashioning of garments goes back to ancient history (I Samuel 2:19). Tailors, weavers, embroiderers, dyers were all required to prepare the magnificent curtains of the Tabernacle, and the garments of the priests (Exodus 35:25; I Samuel 17:7). The work of the dyer, or fuller comes in for frequent mention, as he labored with vegetable and animal dyes (Exodus 35:25; Isaiah 7:3; Malachi 3:2; Mark 9:3). The tentmaker was also a clothworker seeing the material for tents was linen or strips of native goats' hair cloth sewed together (Exodus 26:2; Jeremiah 4:20).

CRAFTSMEN IN FOOD

As we shall see more fully when we come to itemize respective crafts, there are many employments connected with food and drink. We have references to cooks, bakers, millers, cheesemakers, vinedressers, fishermen, shepherds and farmers, all of which are related to what people ate and drank.

Among unconnected occupations we have barbers, perfumers, physicians, scribes, etc.

Artisan Wages

Trade unions, or standard rate of wages, which came in with the Industrial Revolution some years ago, have no place in the Bible. In fact, it is difficult to assess what wages were paid to workmen, skilled and otherwise. From the time of the Egyptians of Moses' days down until a century or so ago, the majority of laborers received just about enough to keep body and soul together. Over half a century ago, when my wife and I set up housekeeping, we had to start our wedded life living on my evangelist's wage of about two pounds, or six dollars a week. The fabulous wages paid today for an ever-shortening week, seem a fortune when compared with Bible wages, or with what our grandparents were paid for longer hours than people work today.

The first reference to wages in the Bible is found in Laban's assessment of Jacob's value —

> Because thou art my brother, shouldest thou therefore serve me for nought? tell me, what shall thy wages be? (Genesis 29:15).

Apart from food and shelter, Jacob served Laban seven years for Leah and another seven years for Rachel. Jacob was further paid by "The speckled shall be thy wages" (Genesis 31:8).

When, after the passage of some twenty years, Jacob decided to leave Laban's employ and return to his native Canaan, he complained to Laban that he had changed his "wages ten times" — being made less each time (Genesis 31:7). Agreeing that all the unspeckled cattle should be Laban's Jacob took all the speckled and spotted cattle as his hire or wages. Through his schemes, in which Jacob's wives had a share, he became very rich. Laban, of course, had openly violated the terms of the hiring-bargain. When all the spotted kids and lambs increased beyond expectation, although they were rightfully Jacob's ten times over, Laban went back on his bargain and robbed Jacob of the speckled cattle (Genesis 31:41).

The next interesting reference to wages is when Jochebed was paid for nursing her own child, Moses, for Pharaoh's daughter who had adopted him (Exodus 2:1-11). "Take this child

away, and nurse it for me, and I will give thee thy wages" (verse 9). How much was the customary wage the Egyptian paid for the nursing occupation we are not told! The mother of Moses must have been grateful to God, not only for the preservation of her child, but also for the pay she received for lovingly caring for him.

As work on the land was the chief occupation at all times in Palestine, slaves and hired servants, who were mainly aliens, received little more than their keep for their labor. A hireling cost the farmer twice as much as a slave who only received food, clothing and shelter. The hireling earned the equivalent provision and over and above a wage (Deuteronomy 15:18).

A definite engagement with stipulated wages was made by Micah who hired the Levite as his domestic chaplain for ten shekels a year, plus a "suit of apparel" and his "victuals" (Judges 17:10). Under the Mosaic Law there were yearly engagements and instructions as to daily payment of wages in cases of poverty (Leviticus 19:11, 13; 25:53; Deuteronomy 24:14, 15. See Job 24:11; Jeremiah 22:13; Malachi 3:5).

From the Code of Hammurabi information is available as to the wages of different occupations among the early Babylonians. Meissner writing on the wages of hired workers says that —

> The early introduction of a *standard wage* did not lead to a rise of wages for only on a very rare occasion do these exceed 6 shekels a year in addition to food and clothing. It was customary to give a sum, probably a shekel, as earnest-money, the remainder being paid at stipulated intervals, daily or monthly, or in a lump sum at the expiration of the engagement.

It would seem as if Saul, David and Solomon had a permanent wage-earning bodyguard. Amaziah, King of Judah, enrolled for a hundred talents of silver a hundred thousand Israelite warriors (II Chronicles 25:6). The hirelings Isaiah mentioned were possibly soldiers whose hire contract was for three years (Isaiah 16:14; 21:16).

Coming to the New Testament we have the familiar instance of the vineyard laborers who received a denarius for their day's labor (Matthew 20:1). Jesus declared that the laborer is worthy of his hire (Matthew 10:10; Luke 10:7. See I Timothy 5:18). The Bible is cognizant of the hard work of those who are hired, and expresses concern about the wages he should receive. Judgment is pronounced on those employers withholding just wages from their workmen (Leviticus 19:13; Deuteronomy 24:14; Job 7:1, 2; Isaiah 16:14; Matthew 20:12; James 5:4). John the Baptist admonished the Roman soldiers to be content with their wages and to be violent to no man (Luke 3:14; Hebrews 13:5). The word used for wages and Paul's word for charges (I Corinthians 9:7), imply that provisions were part of a soldier's wages. Paul himself received material support from some of the churches he established (II Corinthians 11:8).

The term wages is used metaphorically of the reward which faithful laborers receive in the Master's harvest of souls (John 4:36); and of the result of winnings (Romans 6:23; II Peter 2:15). Too many in these modern times who work hard for their wage forget the rebuke of Haggai of those who put their earned wages into a bag with holes (Haggai 1:6), which symbolizes wanton waste of earnings. Money, out of the pay envelope, spent on drinking and smoking and gambling is money put in a bag with holes.

Do you recall the lines of Charles Dickens in *The Chimes?*

Oh, let us love our occupations,
Bless the squire and his relations,
Live upon our daily rations,
And always know our proper stations.

In conclusion, there are two aspects of employment we must draw attention to, namely *Its Choice* and *Its Loss.*

The Choice of a Trade

Young children have visions of what they want to do when they grow up, and often their early choice is fulfilled. A girl who loves to bandage her doll, wants to be a nurse, and turns out to be a most devoted one. A boy who never tires of playing with his toy soldiers, makes up his mind to be a soldier, and grows up to be a courageous one.

Young people, devoted to Christ, in their college days prayerfully wait upon Him for guidance as to a future calling, and a choice is made. Then, when school days are over, out into the world they go to labor with their hands and heads, or to be set aside for the service of God at home or abroad. But how important it is to make the right choice. Too often parents choose a profession for their children which they have no aptitude for whatever.

Why was the trade of carpenter chosen for Jesus? Who made such a choice? Seeing His foster-father, Joseph, was a carpenter, was it by chance Jesus followed the same trade? Further, why did He follow a trade at all? It was stated in the Talmud as one of the duties of a Hebrew father to his son that he must be apprenticed to a trade. So, like every Jewish boy, Jesus was taught a trade and chose to be known as a carpenter, although He knew that His claim to be the Messiah would not be enhanced by His being identified with a trade for which He had received the conventional training and equipment (Mark 6:3).

Working with His hands at a humble trade until He was thirty years of age, when He entered His brief but dynamic ministry, He still labored with His hands. Skilled in working with wood and nails, and strong and hardened by rough toil, those same hands healed all who came to Him in need. Having been a laboring man, He was the best Friend of those who labored and were heavy-laden.

What a difference there was between Jesus and John the Baptist, His cousin. From the day of his birth, John — coming from a priestly family — was not associated with the working class, and became a prophet along conventional lines. He never knew the toil and struggle of years, such as the One he baptized had experienced.

What governed the choice both for John and Jesus? Why did John live in the desert and preach all the time, and Jesus worked hard at the bench for some fifteen years? Is there not a deeper reason for the occupation of John than the priestly heritage he was heir to; and for the trade Jesus followed apart from the laborer's home in which He was born? Behind any human choice was there not an Omniscience directing the career of both?

It was according to divine purpose and plan that Jesus was trained at a carpenter's bench. Giovanni Papini in his *Life of Christ* says the craft of the carpenter was one of the four most ancient and sacred.

> That of the ploughman, the mason, the smith, and the carpenter, are among the manual arts, those most closely connected with the life of man; the most innocent and religious. Whilst the soldier may degenerate into a highwayman, the sailor into a pirate, the merchant into an adventurer — the ploughman, the mason, the smith, and the carpenter cannot change, do not become corrupt.

Jesus became a carpenter by the guidance and grace of God, because such a trade is symbolic of deep spiritual truth. When men were to ask the undying question, "What is God like?" Jesus was to answer: "He that hath seen Me, the hard-working Carpenter of Nazareth, hath seen the Father." Carpenters work with wood coming from a living tree. But before they can shape it, it must be cut down, or suffer and die, before it can take on the plan of the craftsman. The life, teaching and sacrifice of Jesus always proclaims that we must die in order to live the higher life.

Because a person's occupation has a profound bearing upon his own life and character, and often upon the lives of others, how necessary it is to know that whether he pushes a pen or a plough, he is in the will of God, laboring as He has appointed. If you are facing life, and deliberating upon the niche you are to fill, let your prayer be, "Lord, what wilt Thou have me to be and to do?" Leave the choice with Him.

The Loss of a Trade

The lack and loss of work is a scourge. Fitted, able and willing to toil in a given area, but forced to be idle so often breaks a true man's spirit. While there are tramps, thieves and scroungers who loathe work, the vast majority of men have pride in their trade and toil, and are at a dead end when it is taken from them.

The Bible is critical of those who prefer idleness to work —

> Slothfulness casteth into a deep sleep; and an idle soul shall suffer hunger.
> (Proverbs 19:15)

She . . . eateth not the bread of idleness.   (Proverbs 31:27)
Through idleness of the hands the house droppeth through.
                    (Ecclesiastes 10:15)
. . . the abundance of idleness, was in her.   (Ezekiel 16:49)
They learn to be idle.
                    (I Timothy 5:13)
If any would not work, neither should he eat.   (II Thessalonians 3:10)

The Israelites were charged with extreme idleness when all the while they were toiling as slaves (Exodus 5:8, 17). For those who are purposely workless, we have nothing but contempt.

What concerns us is the army of those who are unemployed through no fault of their own — a section of society which the Bible also mentions. Zechariah predicts the time when there will be "no hire for man" (8:10). Our Lord describes those standing idle in the market place, where laborers were hired, but who were downcast because no farmer hired them (Matthew 20:3, 7). How pathetic it is to see able-bodied men unable to secure work!

Contributing factors of massive employment are manifold. The termination of a war finds unwanted craftsmen and workmen until the economy of the war-torn country rights itself. During the First World War, the British were told that their land would be fit for heroes to live in, but crowds of discharged soldiers found themselves facing beggary. What sad homes followed in the wake of such disillusionment!

Many find they cannot work any more because of sickness, or some crippling disease. Then accidents or disaster incapacitate others. Jesus spoke of eighteen men who were killed when the tower of Siloam fell. Doubtless others were crippled for life by the falling masonry (Luke 13: 4). National monetary crisis, fluctuating markets, and falling prices, as well as industrial strife, swell the ranks of the unemployed.

Enforced idleness, however, does not spell hunger as it used to when there were no social security benefits. But even with such, it is humbling for a good workman to go on welfare. Alas! the ever-increasing demand for wage increases, less working hours, and more leisure time, often result in protracted serious strikes and hardship at home as mothers and wives try to make ends meet on the pittance of strike pay. Before we had trade unions and wage boards, employers could do as they liked with their own. Now, they are often dictated to, and are compelled to pay up. Many of them are prepared to give good pay, if only they could get a good day's work.

An aspect that we greatly admire is the way several organizations have come to the aid of the blind, the crippled and handicapped, and are teaching them how to earn their own living in some useful trade. Is it not amazing what some afflicted people are able to do in spite of their disability?

Where does all this bring us? Well, if we have health and strength, soundness of mind, a worthwhile profession or trade or work, with an income sufficient to meet our obligations, how grateful to God we should be. Further, no matter what our task is, whether conspicuous or menial, may grace be ours to labor, not merely as men-pleasers, but as in the sight of Him who doeth all things well.

MALE OCCUPATIONS

MALE OCCUPATIONS

Although an endeavor has been made to give as complete a coverage as possible of Bible occupations, it may be felt by some readers that other callings might have been included. For instance, there is no listing of occupations represented by family life, simply because certain relationships are not financially remunerative, as ordinary trades or professions are. Many a wife, or mother deems her lot as a keeper-at-home a full-time occupation — and rightly so! Not for her more pay for shorter hours. Her work is never done. Husbands may clamor for a five or four day a week job, but for the housewife it is always seven days a week. She does not watch the clock and quit when the schedule time is up. On she toils, even when the rest of the family is in bed for the night. She does not labor for a wage.

> Dusting, darning, drudging,
>   nothing is great or small;
> Nothing is mean or irksome,
>   love hallows it all.

IN THE SECULAR REALM

While we are to deal with the arts and crafts of the Bible in alphabetical order so that the reader can more easily identify any occupation he desires knowledge about, it is recognized that Bible occupations increased in number and nature with the development of the human race. The trades of mankind varied at different periods of history. Our first parent, Adam, was a gardener, placed in the Garden of Eden to dress and keep it (Genesis 2:15). As a result of his fall from innocence harder labor was imposed upon him, and he received the edict — "In the sweat of thy face shalt thou eat bread" (Genesis 3:19).

With the birth of Cain and Abel, two further kinds of livelihood which the land offered came into being, namely, *agriculture* — which has been called, "Fair Queen of Arts from Heaven itself who came"—and *Sheep-Feeding*. "Abel was a keeper of sheep, but Cain was a tiller of the ground" (Genesis 4:2). Jabal, one of Cain's descendants, became the first nomad or camper. He was the first herdsman — "The father of such as dwell in tents, and of such as have cattle" (Genesis 4:20). Jubal, the brother, was "the father of all such as handle the harp and the organ." This genius had hands more suited to being humanity's first musician than to becoming calloused by hard manual toil. The discovery of the mechanical arts is assigned to Tubal-Cain, "an instructor of every artificer in brass and iron" (Genesis 4:22). This half-brother of Jabal and Jubal, was earth's first craftsman. The advance of mechanical skill is evidenced by the building of the Ark (Genesis 6:14-16), and of the Tower of Babel (Genesis 11:1-5).

After the Flood, when the three sons of Noah separated to different parts of the then known world to become the progenitors of different and mighty races, arts and occupations multiplied in number and variety, with agriculture leading the list. With each new phase of the growth of civilization, trades hitherto unknown would appear. Coming to our own highly industrialized and scientific age the introduction of air travel, nuclear weapons and automation have created a multiplicity of new crafts not dreamed of a half a century ago. Dictionaries have to be enlarged to include the definitions of an ever-

growing number of skilled and un-
skilled professions. Our purpose, however, is to consider the occupations
of Bible days, and to such a task we
now devote ourselves, hoping to discover from the example and teaching
of laborers of old that —

An idler is a watch
    that wants both hands;
As useless if it goes
    and when it stands.

The Actor

It is most interesting to find that
the severe word Jesus used of the
Pharisees when He called them *hypocrites* means "play-actors." W. E.
Vine reminds us that the term *hypocrite* denotes one who answers, thus,
a stage-actor. It was the custom for
Greek and Roman actors to speak in
large masks with mechanical devices
for augmenting the force of the voice.
So *hypocrite* has a history of its own,
meaning one taking part in the dialogue, acting a part in a play, or one
who plays a part. In Job, the word is
used in a figurative sense of one who
feigns a virtue which he has not (36:
13 LXX). The same connotation of
playing or feigning the hypocrite was
used by our Lord (Luke 20:20).

Hypocrite occurs only in the first
three gospels, being used fifteen times
in Matthew, and is a word implying
a deliberately played part (Matthew
6:2, 5-16; 22:18, etc.). There are occasions when the word indicates a deception of which the actor himself is
unconscious (Mark 7:6; Luke 6:42;
12:56). Jesus taught that a hypocrite
is one who plays the part of religion
whether consciously or unconsciously,
without being religious. This term is
apropos of those Pharisees who appeared before men what one ought
to be, but is not before God! John
Milton wrote —

For neither man nor angel can discern Hypocrisy, the only evil that
walks Invisible, except to God alone.

Hypocrisy, as used in the epistles
(Galatians 2:13; I Timothy 4:2; I
Peter 2:7) carries the same idea of
pretense, play-acting as actors spoke
in dialogue. Without mercy, Jesus un-
masked the practical falsehood of the
Pharisees under saintly show. "A bad
man is worst of all when he pretends
to be good," says the proverb, and
the religionists whom Jesus scathing-
ly condemned were "inwardly base
though with an outward appearance
of good." Their vice deceived, under
the shadow of virtue. But their acted
contrition, for example was exposed
(Matthew 6:16). "The *show* of contrition is as dangerous as the reality
is helpful."

To act means to feign — to play or
imitate the part of — and the Bible
introduces us to some superb actors.
We are not speaking of the Pharisees
who, although they appeared as
whitened sepulchres were full of dead
men's bones. Jacob played his part
well when he imitated his brother
Esau and stole his blessing (Genesis
25:28; 27). Joseph was another, who
when he made himself "strange unto
his brethren" (Genesis 42:7), proved
himself to be a good actor. Perhaps
the most effective piece of acting in
the Bible was that of David when, before Achish, King of Gath, he changed
his behavior, and feigned himself to
be a madman. So perfect was the assumed guise that Achish, completely
deceived, ordered the madman removed from his presence (I Samuel
21). Judas made a poor show at acting when, with the betrayal of Jesus
on his conscience, he approached Him
as a true disciple, giving the Master
a kiss, the token of affection.

Centuries ago, when religious dra-
mas were prominent, the church culti-

vated an acting fraternity, forgetting that Christianity is not to be acted but *lived*. Hollywood, for purely financial gain, has wantonly exploited several Bible events and characters. It is to be deplored that actors and actresses of unsaintly character have been made to represent Bible saints. Bible stories have been distorted and given a sexual slant for the sole purpose of box-office appeal. To depict our Lord in surroundings so foreign to Biblical narratives is sacrilege of the worst order.

The only theater mentioned in the Bible is the one at Ephesus, the imposing ruins of which still remain (Acts 19:29, 31). While the Israelites knew very little of dramatic art, both the Greeks and the Romans had their vast open-air structures for the staging of dramatic plays. These ancient theaters, which were also used as assembly centers, were usually semi-circular in form with seats ranged in tiers one above another. Access was by means of entrances and stairways around the half circle. The stage was raised up on a stone platform, open to the audience and closed on the other three sides. That these theaters were admirably fitted for public gatherings can be seen from the riot at Ephesus. Paul's travel companions, Gaius and Aristarchus, had fallen into the hands of a tumultuous mob, and rushed "with one accord into the theater" as the most fitting place to discuss the subject concerning them. It was in a similar "theater" that Herod Agrippa I made his self-glorifying speech which brought about his miserable death.

The Greek word for theater meant the spectacle itself, as well as the place in which it was exhibited. It is in this sense that Paul uses the word spectacle which is the same word in the original for theater. *The Amplified Bible* translates the phrase, "We have become a spectacle to the world — a show in the world's amphitheater — with both men and angels (as spectators)" (I Corinthians 4:9). In his *As You Like It*, Shakespeare, in describing the seven ages of man reminds us that —

> All the world's a stage,
> And all the men and women merely players.
> They have their exits and their entrances;
> And one man in his time plays many parts,
> His acts being seven ages . . . .

The Advertiser

The English word *advertise* occurs twice in the Bible. Balaam counseling Balak of the future of Israel and its influence upon his kingdom said, "I will advertise thee" (Numbers 24:14). Here, the term means to counsel or advise and is the same one given as advice. "Then Amaziah king of Judah took advice" (II Chronicles 25:17). A different word, however, was employed by Boaz in speaking of the nearer kinsman of Ruth, "I thought to advertise thee" (Ruth 4:4). The actual meaning of the word here is "to uncover the ear," and the thought implied is most captivating. Commenting on I Samuel 9:15 and how God uncovered Samuel's ear, Ellicott observes —

> The image is taken from the action of pushing aside the head-dress, in order the more conveniently to whisper some words to the ear. This is one of the few more direct intimations in the sacred records of one of the ways in which the Spirit of God communicated Divine thoughts to the human spirit. Here the Eternal Spirit is represented as whispering in the ear of man.

In our modern usage of the Biblical term advertise, two aspects are prominent —

1. To inform, notify or to warn as in advertising a person of some loss or trouble.

2. To announce publicly by means of newspapers, printed notices, or by TV and radio broadcasts. Here, public attention is drawn to the desirable qualities of properties or goods, and pressure brought to purchase or invest.

Evidently it pays to advertise, otherwise advertisers would not spend the colossal sums they do on the various avenues of advertisement. Forceful and attractive advertisements compel people to buy the products presented. But there are times when the quality of the product is far below the glowing description given of that product. Samuel Johnson once wrote — "Promise, large promise, is the soul of the advertisement." All the Bible advertises for the benefit of mankind, however, can be relied upon. God is never at a fault as an advertiser.

The Advocate

By profession, an advocate is one who pleads another's cause, instructs, exhorts, comforts and intercedes for another. Ellicott says that the word has "two meanings; one, as in Job 16: 2 — he who comforts, or exhorts; the other, as in I John 2:1 — he who is appealed to — a proxy, or attorney." In present day law there are two kinds of advocates. There are those who appear before a court and plead, and then those who are only consulted and give advice, or who prepare the case and make it ready for the pleading advocate.

The original meaning of the term advocate is "one called in" or "called to one's side to give advice." Another name English-speaking nations have for advocate is "counsel." A British advocate with the letters "Q. C." after his name means that he is Queen's Counsel. In law courts, "Counsel for the defense" or "Counsel for the accused" are constantly used. Christ is our Counsel, pleading our cause before the Father, while the Holy Spirit is the advocate here below who prepares our case. Convincing us of sin, righteousness and judgment the Spirit helps us in our case. Not knowing how to plead as we ought, He intercedes on our behalf.

Our Advocate with the Father is His righteous Son, our Saviour (I John 2:1). The Advocate within our heart is the Holy Spirit. When the term is applied to Him it is always translated Comforter (John 14:16; 15:26; 16:7). All of the ideas expressed by the word apply both to Christ and the Spirit. Thus, in the goodness of God we have two effective intercessors. There is the Holy Spirit within us that we might not sin (Romans 8:26, 34).

> In us, for us, intercede
> And with voiceless groanings, plead
> Our unutterable need,
>   Comforter Divine.

Then there is "Jesus Christ the Righteous" who is the Advocate above to plead His efficacious blood if we do sin (Hebrews 7:25; I John 1:8-10; 2: 1).

> Before the throne of God above
>   I have a strong, a perfect plea;
> A great High Priest, whose name is Love,
>   Who ever lives and pleads for me.

Tertullus, the only advocate in an ordinary court mentioned in the Bible (Acts 24), is an example of a counsel usually employed by clients in the Roman provinces. The Jewish leaders engaged him to speak against Paul before Felix, the Roman governor. Tertullus is called an orator. Although

Paul often appeared before a judge, he never employed an advocate. Listen to the promise of Jesus —

> Ye shall be brought before governors and kings for my sake . . . . But when they deliver you up, take no thought how or what you shall speak; for it shall be given you in that same hour what ye shall speak (Matthew 10:18, 19).

When Jesus Himself was arrested and tried, He not only did not employ an advocate to plead His case, He did not even speak for Himself, and the surprised judge came to the conclusion that Jesus was innocent. Now in heaven, the One who would not speak on His own behalf appears in the presence of God for us, and no one can lay anything to our charge as He pleads His merit and shed blood in our defense.

> There is a way for man to rise
> To that sublime abode;
> An Offering and a Sacrifice,
> A Holy Spirit's energies,
> And Advocate with God.

The Ambassador

The original significance of this occupation is that of one who is an interpreter, a messenger, an agent (II Chronicles 35:21; Isaiah 30:4; 33:7; Ezekiel 17:15). When Paul spiritualizes the word and uses it for himself, ambassador means an "elder or senior," and is from *presbeus,* which is the root of "presbyterian." Those referred to as "messengers" (Numbers 20:14; 21:21; Deuteronomy 2:26; Judges 11:12, 19; II Samuel 5:11; II Kings 19:9) were practically "ambassadors" or diplomatic agents of sovereigns, and any insult to their persons was a sufficient cause for war (II Samuel 16:4). Their persons were regarded as inviolable (II Samuel 12: 26-30). An "ambassage," describing the mission of an ambassador, is used as a collective for ambassadors themselves (Luke 14:32; 19:14; ASV). Gideon feigned an ambassage (Joshua 9: 4).

Usually those chosen as Israel's infrequent embassies — an infrequence her isolation from other nations produced — were men of high rank as Sennacherib sent his chief captain, chief cup-bearer and chief eunuch, Tartan, Rabsaris and Rabashakeh to meet Hezekiah's chief men of the kingdom, namely Eliakim, Shebna and Joah (II Kings 18:17, 18; Isaiah 18:2; 33:7). "Ambassadors of Peace" were those earnestly soliciting peace from the Assyrian monarch. In our modern times, with their highly organized international associations and upsurge of Nationalism, those chosen for ambassadorial rank are persons of integrity, wisdom, tact and skilled diplomacy. An ambassador is supposed to personate the authority he represents. Thus, in ordinary parlance an ambassador is one who represents his sovereign or nation in a foreign country, and who has all the authority and power of his own State behind him. Knowing the mind, will and purpose of the nation he represents, he must present the same without a bias. Reception accorded, or denied him, is necessarily regarded as virtually given or withheld in respect to the nation whose representative he is. If war should be declared between his nation and the one he temporarily resides in, then he is immediately withdrawn.

How full of spiritual application all this is as we think of ourselves as ambassadors! Such a designation speaks of the nature and dignity of the ministry of all those called to witness for Christ. Gravity, fidelity and spiritual wisdom must be theirs. They must "bear their great commission in their look." As citizens of heaven (Philippians 3:20), as they witness in the world they must always remember that they are in a foreign country. "They are not of this world" (John 17:16). Beseeching men on Christ's behalf to be reconciled to God, they have behind them all the authority and power of the King they represent (II Corinthians 5:20). Our part is to send prayers, as our ambassage, to meet God's ambassadors, desiring His conditions of peace (Luke 14:32; Isaiah 27:5). As war is declared between heaven and earth, as it will be when the Great Tribulation overtakes the world, the heavenly King is to withdraw all His faithful ambassadors. All are to be caught up to meet Him in the air (I Thessalonians 4:16, 17). Because the King's business requireth haste, how imperative it is to obey His command and declare His claims on a hostile world.

I am a stranger here within a foreign land;
My home is far away upon a golden strand;
Ambassador to be of realms beyond the sea,
I'm here on business for my King.

This is the King's command, that all men everywhere
Repent and turn away from sin's seductive snare;
That all who will obey with Him shall reign for aye,
And that's my business for my King.

The Apothecary

That the mixers, or compounders of perfumes and spices had many secrets all their own, is evidenced by the fact that the six references to apothecaries speak of their art (Exodus 30:25, 35; 37:29; II Chronicles 16:14; Nehemiah 3:8; Ecclesiastes 10:1). The ASV renders the word apothecary as "perfumer." The word confection is derived from the Latin *con*, "together" and *facere* "to put" and literally signifies, "something put together or com-

pounded." The margin of the ASV gives us "perfumers" for "confectionaries" (I Samuel 8:13). In Britain, a "confectionary" is a shopkeeper who sells confections, or sweets and candies; but in the Bible a "confection" means merely a compound or mixture, and a "confectionary," a person who compounded drugs, medicines and perfumes.

A generation or so ago we also called chemists or druggists, apothecaries. The apothecary of the Bible, however, could scarcely be called a chemist, although some of the oil he compounded had a healing virtue. His main art consisted in taking various gums extracted from trees, mixed with oils or liquid to make ointment which was used for anointing purposes. These gums, once hardened, would be crushed into powder, and burned as incense. Priests would throw this powder into the hot censer and the smoke would send out a strong odor or perfume. God would smell the sweet savor and be pleased with such an offering. The Psalmist prayed, "Let my prayer be like incense." John speaks of an angel with a golden censer offering incense which represented the prayers of saints. The Apocrypha speaks of the apothecary as one who "makes mixtures . . . through him well-being is spread abroad over the earth" (Ecclesiasticus 38:8).

While the compounds of Bible Apothecaries were used in many ways, generally there were three chief uses of their art —

Perfume

Because of the climate and the heat we can see in a large measure the Oriental liking for odoriferous substances. This rendered the functions of the perfumer an important one. Perfumes in great variety, from antiquity onward, gave rise to an important trade (Genesis 37:25). Nehemiah speaks of a guild, or corporation of perfumers (Nehemiah 3:8). A Jewish tradition affirms that the preparation of cultic perfume was entrusted to a family which specialized in the art and which kept to itself certain technical secrets. The ascending smoke from the family's perfume courted universal admiration.

Perfumes were used in great quantities by the Egyptians in worship and for embalming the dead (Genesis 50: 2, 3, 26). Dead flies cause the perfumer's oil to stink (Ecclesiastes 10: 1). The Queen of Sheba brought camels laden with spices to Solomon (I Kings 10:2).

Solomon received perfumes as annual gifts from his subjects (I Kings 10:25).

Hezekiah displayed among other things, "spices" and "precious oil" (Isaiah 39:2).

Esther had to perfume herself with spices and ointments (Esther 2:12).

The Song of Solomon gives an important place to various perfumes (1: 3; 3:6; 4:10; 5:1, 13; also Psalm 45).

Harlots used perfumes to gain their sinful ends (Proverbs 7:17; Isaiah 57: 9).

Amos reproached Israel's leaders for perfuming themselves while being indifferent to the stench of national sin (Amos 6:6).

Perfumes and spices played a prominent part in funeral ceremonies and in burials (II Chronicles 16:14; Jeremiah 34:5; Mark 16:1; Luke 23:56; 24:1; John 19:39, 40).

Choice perfumes were used in both idolatrous and divinely ordained worship (Exodus 30:8; Leviticus 10:1; 16: 12, 13; Numbers 16:6, 7, 17, 18, 37, 46, 48; Psalm 141:2, etc.).

A signal of honor was to pour aromatic oil on the head of a visitor as he entered a house (Psalm 23:5);

Jesus said to Simon, "My head with oil thou didst not anoint" (Luke 7: 46).

The house was filled with a captivating odor when Jesus was anointed with the precious spikenard (Psalm 45:8; John 12:3).

The materials used by those ancient perfumers were gums, resins, roots, barks and leaves, which were variously combined according to the skill and fancy of the perfumer. The secrets of Arabian perfumes, all of which Shakespeare said could not "sweeten this little hand" stained as it was by blood, died with Bible apothecaries. In this scientific age of ours, wonderful research has given us many synthetic scents. Natural perfumes are rare. Simple scents, like rose or violet, consist of no one but perhaps a hundred constituents. Scents are used by flowers not only to attract some insects that will fertilize them, but also to repel others they do not want. It is said that the loveliest perfumes are found among the orchids that attract nocturnal insects. Orchids emit one scent during the day and another after dusk. No wonder one entomologist remarks —

> What an opportunity for the perfume manufacturer looking for something new! But he will have to avoid the orchid that smells of carnation by day and fox by night!

Consecration

The religious use of perfumes is conspicuous in Scripture. Perfume used for worship had to be prepared with the greatest of care under the supervision of the Levites (Exodus 30:34-36; I Chronicles 9:29). Holy anointing oil and sacred perfumes were forbidden for secular use (Exodus 30:36-38; 37:29). The perfumed oil required for anointing purposes was made in accordance with a precise and costly recipe (Exodus 30:23, 24; Isaiah 43:24; Jeremiah 6:20). The liturgical expression, "a sacrifice of a swell smell" is common to the Bible (Exodus 29:18; Leviticus 1:9; Ephesians 5:2, etc.).

Divine instructions respecting the composition of the incense to be offered upon the Golden Altar were specific —

> The Lord said unto Moses, Take unto thee sweet spices, stacte, and onycha, and galbanum; these sweet spices with pure frankincense: of each shall there be a like weight: And thou shalt make it a perfume, a confection after the art of the apothecary, tempered (margin, "salted") together, pure and holy . . . . And as for the perfume which thou shalt make, ye shall not make to yourselves according to the composition thereof: it shall be unto thee holy for the Lord. Whosoever shall make like unto that, to smell thereto, shall even be cut off from his people (Exodus 30:34-38).

Because these sweet spices typified the divine estimate of the excellencies of the Lord Jesus as the Son of Man, whose name is "as ointment poured forth" (Song of Solomon 1:3), extreme care had to be taken in their composition.

1. Their ingredients had to be of a rare and precious kind.
2. They had to be compounded in equal proportions.
3. They had to be mixed together to form one compound.
4. It was forbidden to make any similar composition for personal use.
5. Only the seed of Aaron could offer the incense (Numbers 16:40; II Chronicles 26:16-21).
6. The ingredients had to be beaten small and burned with fire, in order that its sweet-smelling properties might be developed.

While various aromatic substances are referred to in a loose way of sweet-smelling perfumes or spices, it is not easy to identify these particularly sweet and fragrant spices in which the first named — stacte — is the only one mentioned elsewhere in the Hebrew Bible (Job 36:27).

STACTE

The Hebrew word, *nataf*, means "drops," and implies that it was one of those fragrant gums which ooze in drops or tears, from a variety of tropical or subtropical plants, and was used in the freely flowing myrrh found in the holy anointing oil.

ONYCHA

The original meaning of this term is "a lion," and suggests the thought of the uncompromising faithfulness, firmness, and decision of Christ who, as "the Lion of the tribe of Judah" set His face like a flint in the accomplishment of His task. Onycha, (onyx, sweet-smelling snail or shell) came from "the horny or calcareous operculum which closed the opening of the shell of certain molluscs."

GALBANUM

This ingredient entering into the composition of the holy incense was a yellowish gum-resin of penetrating odor, which came from a Persian plant. The root of the word signifies "milk," or "fat." The "fat which covered the inwards," was God's portion of the sacrifices, and typifies the internal preciousness of Christ.

PURE FRANKINCENSE

Here we have another precious gum-resin obtained by an incision into the trunk of the Boswellia tree of Southern Arabia and drawing it off. From here it was imported into Israel (Isaiah 60: 6; Jeremiah 6:20). The land of Sheba was also notable for its incense. The Hebrew for "frankincense" means *white*. The richness and abundance of its perfume suggested the English word which implies "frank or liberal incense." This term is emblematic of the purity, piety and acceptability of Him who was holy, harmless, undefiled and separate from sinners.

Perfume and incense are the same. There is but one word in the original. The graces and virtues composing the character of Christ are exquisitely tempered together. His qualities are not only equal, but also harmoniously blended. The art of the apothecary in combining his sweet scents brought out the perfume in its exquisite perfection. It is worth noticing how often the apothecary was made to minister to our Lord. The wise men from the East brought Him not only gold, but also frankincense and myrrh. A sinful woman expressing her great love for Him, poured on His feet precious ointment out of an alabaster box. Mary of Bethany poured very costly ointment upon His head. Joseph of Arimathaea covered the dead body of Jesus with a large quantity of costly perfume. His very name, Christ, means, "anointed." The offering of Himself upon the cross was a sacrifice of a sweet-smelling savor, acceptable to God. Unction is the Latin word for "anointing" and is used of the Holy Spirit. Those anointed with Him become like "a watered garden, full of fragrance rare." When Jesus was anointed by Mary we read, "the house was filled with the odor of the ointment" (John 12:3). All who are Christ-possessed and Spirit-filled create an atmosphere charged with heavenly perfume.

Medicine

The oils compounded by the apothecaries not only possessed aromatic qualities. They also contained healing virtue. The disciples sent forth by Jesus anointed the sick with oil and they were healed. James also speaks of anointing the sick with oil in the name of the Lord. The Laodiceans were instructed to buy of the Lord, "eye-salve to anoint thine eyes, that thou mayest see" (Revelation 3:18). (See Isaiah 1:6; Mark 6:13; Luke 10: 34; James 5:14). Doubtless, this healing oil came largely from crushed olives — the olive tree symbolizing national and individual well-being, prosperity, joy and vigor (Deuteronomy 33:24; Psalm 45:7; 128:3; 133:1; Isaiah 61:3).

The Archer

Taken together, the twelve references to archers denote that they were owners and shooters of bows and arrows (Genesis 21:20; 49:23; Judges 5:11; I Samuel 31:3; I Chronicles 8: 40; 10:3; II Chronicles 35:23; Job 16: 13; Isaiah 21:17; 22:3; Jeremiah 51:3). Ishmael is the first in the Bible to be named an archer. "He grew and became an archer." Although he is actually named as the first archer, Nimrod was "a mighty hunter" and Esau "a cunning hunter" (Genesis 10:9; 25:27); and it can be safely assumed that the only weapons they used in hunting animals for food were bows and arrows — perhaps the very first weapons man invented. Isaac told Esau to take his weapons, "thy quiver and thy bow . . . and take me some venison" (Genesis 27:3). Many Canaanite nations had men who were celebrated as archers (I Samuel 31:3; I Chronicles 8:40; Isaiah 22:6).

Egyptian, Assyrian, Persian, Greek and Jewish bas-reliefs, describing the dress of archers and varying modes of bows, arrows and quivers, prove that those were the most frequently used weapons both for the securing of food and for warfare from earliest times down to the times of Indians and Saxons. In Scotland, The Royal Company of Archers form the Queen's bodyguard when Her Majesty goes north. In many countries there has been a great revival of archery as a form of sport. Over 650 years ago the greatest archers in the world were the English, who fought with bows and arrows in France and in The Wars of the Roses. In uncivilized countries, the bow and arrow still form the chief weapon in warfare and for hunting purposes. How terribly destructive are modern weapons of war alongside the simple weapons of old! Had bullets and bombs been known in Bible days the human race would have been destroyed long, long ago. As an archer's equipment consists of three articles, let us consider them in order —

Bow

Usually this principal weapon, so frequently mentioned in the Bible, was made of tough, elastic, rounded pieces of wood often strengthened with tendons, from five to five feet and a half in length, either almost straight and tapering to a point at both ends, or curving inward in the middle when unstrung. "The string was fixed upon a projecting piece of horn, or inserted in a groove or notch of the wood at the extremity. In stringing it the lower point was fixed on the ground, and the knee being pressed against the inner side, the string was passed into the notch. Their mode of drawing it was either with the forefinger and thumb, or the two forefingers, and, like the old English archers, they carried the arrow to the ear, the shaft passing nearly in a line with the eye."

As for bowstrings, the Egyptians made theirs of hide, string or ox or camel gut. The early Greeks made their strings of twisted leather. Scythian and Parthian bows were in the form of a Roman C. Grecian bows were composed of two circular pieces, often made of horn, united in the middle. Wilkinson in his volume on Ancient Egypt says that the bow, when not used, was kept in a case, intended to protect it against the sun or dampness, and to preserve its elasticity. It was always attached to the war-chariots; and across it lay another large case containing an abundant stock of arrows (Habakkuk 3:9). Hebrew bows were sometimes made of metal (II Samuel 22:35) and were strung treading them. Bending the bow literally means to tread it (I Chronicles 5:18; Psalm 7:12). "Bows of brass" (II Samuel 22:35; Job 20:24; Psalm 18:34), appears to be a poetical expression. The Tribe of Benjamin was famous for its bowmen, so David called his lament over the death of Saul and his sons, "The Song of the Bow" (II Samuel 1:18 ASV), because of the mention of Jonathan's bow. The bow was often used figuratively (Job 20:24; 29:20; Psalms 7:12; 18:34; 78: 57, etc.). Homer wrote of the great bow of Ulysses, the hero of Troy, which no one but himself could bend. Then, Switzerland is proud of William Tell, who was able to skilfully direct his arrows as he handled his bow.

Arrows

Archaeological excavations have unearthed a great quantity of arrows of all shapes and made out of widely different materials. Discoveries show that ancient arrows varied from twenty-two to thirty-four inches in length;

some were made of wood or bone, others of reed. They were frequently tipped with a metal head, and winged with three feathers, as arrows are to-day. Other arrows were made of hard wood and, tapered to a point, were inserted into the reed. At times a piece of flint supplied its place. In Biblical times arrow heads may have been made of bronze. Arrows have been discovered with their heads pierced with holes into which was tow soaked in oil and which was ignited at the moment of use. Sometimes the arrows had poisoned tips (Job 6:4). The practice of tipping arrows with some combustible material may have been in Paul's mind when he wrote of "fiery darts" (Ephesians 6:16; See Psalm 7:12). Arrows were kept in a quiver carried on the back or slung over the left shoulder. In war, they were fixed to the side of a chariot.

The Bible contains many references to the figurative use of arrows. For instance, we have —

"The arrows of the Almighty" (Deuteronomy 32:42; Job 6:4). A strong arm must bend the bow and shoot the arrow. God is the efficient cause of many afflictions permitted for our good.

"They bend their bows to shoot their arrows" (Psalms 64:3; 120:4). Bitter and reproachful words cause many a wound, just as evil or mischievous purposes do (Psalm 58:7).

"Thine arrows are sharp" (Psalm 45:5). The truths of God are sharp and piercing, and go to the very heart (Psalm 38:2; Hebrews 4:12).

"His arrows go forth like lightning" (Zechariah 9:14). There is no need to fear, however, the sorrow or punishment the Lord sends (Psalm 9:5). A loving hand directs every arrow. "A good archer," says the proverb, "is not known by his arrow but by his aim."

God's aim in trials is ever our sanctification. William Blake in *Jerusalem* wrote —

For a tear is an intellectual thing;
And a sigh is the sword of an angel king,
And the bitter groan of a martyr's woe
Is an arrow from the Almighty's bow.

Quiver

An archer was usually furnished with a capacious quiver, about four inches in diameter, and large enough to contain a plentiful supply of arrows. The quiver was carried on the shoulder. It was slung, nearly horizontally under the arm, or over the back, and closed with a cover which, like the quiver, was highly decorated. Among the symbolic applications of the quiver (Job 39:23; Isaiah 49:2; Jeremiah 5:16; Lamentations 3:13), none is so beautiful as that of the Psalmist who describes the home as the quiver, the father as the archer, and the children as arrows (Psalm 127:5).

O happy is the man that hath
His quiver fill'd with those;
They unashamed in the gate
shall speak unto their foes.

How blessed we are if we have been made as polished shafts and are in Gods' quiver ready for Him to use! An archer is at ease when he knows that his quiver is full of arrows. It is ever thus with the divine Archer.

The Architect

Sir Christopher Wren, the famous architect who planned St. Paul's Cathedral, London, writing on architecture said that it has "its political uses. Public buildings being the ornament of a country, it establishes a nation, draws people and commerce, makes the people love their native country. . . . Architecture aims at eternity; and therefore is the only thing incapable of modes and fashions in its principles."

Early Palestinian, Phoenician, Egyptian, Grecian and Roman style of architecture testify to the amazing skill of ancient architects. Many modern architects have copied from their art. Biblical references to palaces, temples, houses, fortifications and tombs, as well as imposing structures which excavations have brought to light but which are not mentioned in the Bible, all point to a superb architectural ability. Wren's sentiment about "public buildings being the ornament of a country," is certainly evident in the ornate buildings Herod prided himself on which he erected throughout the country and which carried his name.

When Solomon built his glorious palace, with the Temple dominating the palace buildings, he was surely aiming at eternity as Wren expresses it. Alas, however, only a few of its ruins remain although Solomon's royal structures made his name synonymous with magnificence. The temple of Rameses II at Adu Sinbel is a striking illustration of the architect's skill to give a building marvelous durability. Several archaeologists have pointed out that Israel never developed a native style of architecture and therefore was not famous for its architects. Content to follow alien models, Israel's buildings, in one way or another, were subject to foreign influence. Often plundered by surrounding nations, taken captive and uprooted from their country, would largely explain the absence of an architecture native to Israel and her own hand.

When David planned a palace in his new capital, he turned to the Phoenicians, who were clever architects and builders in stone. Thus, plans, workmen, and materials were Phoenician (II Samuel 5:11). While Solomon was gifted above all men with wisdom, he likewise turned to Phoenician architects and builders for the building of his more ambitious palace and Temple (I Kings 5:7, 9). The same dependence upon foreign architectural aid may also apply to the building projects undertaken by Hezekiah, Josiah and Jehoiakim (I Kings 16:32; 22:39; II Kings 20:20; 22:5; II Chronicles 32:27; Jeremiah 36:22). Any modern work on archaeology, such as Unger's volumes, proves serviceable to those desiring a fuller study of ancient architects and their work.

That God is preeminent as an architect is gathered from the description found of Him in the Book of the Hebrews where the writer tells us that Abraham "looked for a city . . . whose builder and maker is God" (Hebrews 11:10). The word used for builder is *technites,* an artificer, one who does a thing by rules of art. The margin translates the word as architect, "which gives the necessary contrast between this and the next noun in the verse." *The Amplified New Testament* expresses the verse thus —

> For he was waiting expectantly *and* confidently, looking forward to the city which has fixed *and* firm foundations, whose Architect *and* Builder is God.

The divine skill in planning is seen in the universe of which God is the great Architect. When Wren completed his masterpiece of St. Paul's Cathedral, he wrote this inscription and placed it over one of the interior arches — "If you want to see my monument, look around you." This famous shrine, which has stood the test of time and of war, witnesses to the unique architectural ability of Wren. In a much truer sense, God can say, "If you want a monument of My skill and power look around you." How true it is that "He that built all things is God" (Hebrews 3:4). When this wonderful, visible world is dissolved, and we find ourselves in the invisible realm, the New Jerusalem, how over-awed we shall be as we gaze upon and enter into, all that God's skill and power have planned and provided.

The Armorbearer

Among the armorbearers mentioned in the Bible, those of Saul and Jonathan are the most prominent (Judges 9:54; I Samuel 14:7, 17; 16:21; 31:4-6; II Samuel 23:37; I Chronicles 10:4, 5; 11:39). The armorbearer was a person who carried arms, armor and shields for captains or kings. From the above references we gather that young servants were used for this purpose, and that they supported their masters in battle and helped kill the enemies they had wounded. Such was their loyalty that they were willing to die with their masters (I Samuel 31: 4, 5). Arms and armor mentioned in the Bible, which bearers would carry, are of a defensive nature such as helmet — sword — greaves — shoes — shield, and offensive, such as sword — bow and arrows — sling — spear — javelin — club — ax.

A shield-bearer was usually provided with a sword, which he held ready drawn for the defense of his master and himself. A king was also attended in war by such a person, who was usually a person of rank. Even in peace one of the king's eunuchs carried a circular shield for royal use. The office of armorbearer was the equivalent of the squire of medieval knighthood who carried the shield. How privileged we are as soldiers of our heavenly King to function as His armorbearers!

Only an armour-bearer, firmly I stand.
Waiting to follow at the King's command;
Marching, if *Onward* shall the order be,
Standing by my Captain, serving faithfully.

Only an armour-bearer, now in the field,
Guarding a shining helmet, sword and shield;
Waiting to hear the thrilling battle-cry,
Ready to answer, "Master, here am I."

Only an armour-bearer, yet now I share
Glory immortal, and a bright crown to wear:
If in the battle to my trust I'm true,
Mine shall be the honors in the Grand Review.

Hear ye the battle cry "Forward!" the call:
See, see the faltering ones, backward they fall.
Surely my Captain may depend on me,
Though but an armour-bearer I may be.

The Artificer

The word employed to denote this profession means an "engraver" or "carver" of utensils in wood or metal, or of images (Judges 18:18; I Kings 6:32; I Chronicles 29:5; II Chronicles 34:11; Isaiah 3:3). It is akin to the term craftsman, that is, one who carves, engraves (Deuteronomy 27: 15; II Kings 24:14; Nehemiah 11:35; Acts 19:24, 38; Revelation 18:22). Tubal-cain is spoken of as "an instructor of every artificer" (Genesis 4:22). How gifted of God he must have been! Ellicott writes of him as "the first sharpener or hammerer of every instrument of copper and iron." Tubal-cain probably means coppersmith.

While "brass" is referred to in the KJV the same was an alloy unknown to the ancients. "Copper," found in a comparatively pure state upon the surface of the earth, was the first metal made use of by man. Comparatively soft, it was easily beaten to an edge. With the progress of civilization men learned the art of mixing with copper an alloy of tin, thereby producing a far harder substance, "bronze." Ezekiel speaks of Tubal bringing copper to the market of Tyre (27:13). In Persian, Tubal means "copper."

Lamech, the father of Tubal-cain, composed a poem which had in it many of the elements of Semetic poetry; yet was destitute of God and therefore was art abused. Some writers suppose that Lamech composed his virulent, violent and vicious poem to celebrate the manufacture of a sword by his son, Tubal-cain, the worker in brass and iron. If this was so, then it is an example of "The consecration of poetry to the glorification of Titanic insolence." Read in this light, Lamech's unspiritual song seems to indicate that men must beware of him now that his son has fashioned a weapon for him. In the infancy of humanity the ever-increasing race had an artificer but no altar.

Attention has been drawn to the fact that the word artificer itself is akin to "artisan" or "craftsman," the Greek term being *technites,* from which we have "technique" and similar derivations. The tragedy is that although the wisdom Tubal-cain displayed in the fashioning of metal articles came from God, there was no recognition of God on his part or of the dedication of his discovered art to God. If, in any unique way, we have been endowed with wisdom and ability to do something never before attempted or accomplished, may we always realize that what we were able to accomplish was made possible by the divine Artificer, who fashioned the universe and created man with a marvellous mind.

"What hast thou that thou didst not receive?" (I Corinthians 4:7).

The Artist

While the Bible has no mention of those who worked with paints and brushes, paintings and etchings on tablets and bas-reliefs from ancient times reveal how proficient men were in such an art. To paint with vermilion indicates a skilful use of the brush (Jeremiah 22:14; Ezekiel 23:14). All other references to painting are related to women ornamenting their faces (II Kings 9:30; Ezekiel 23:40). There are three references to pictures.

"Destroy all their pictures" (Numbers 33:52).

"Pictures of silver" (Proverbs 25:11).

"All pleasant pictures" (Isaiah 2:16).

It would seem as if the above "pictures" refer to works of art in ivory or stone, seeing the word picture denotes imagery or engraved figures. "A stone of imagery" (Leviticus 26:1) was a stone formed into an idol. By "pictures of silver" we are to understand figures, or baskets, or dishes of ornamental work.

It is clearly evident that the ancient Egyptians knew a good deal about the art of painting. Tombs have been discovered covered with frescoes or fancy sketches giving portraits of Egyptian life with extraordinary accuracy and detail. Shishak and his captives are illustrated on a sculptural wall at Karnack like a picture book. Mural paintings on tombs and on pottery unearthed in different parts also testify to the ability of ancient peoples to use paint and brushes to indicate scenes, people, plants, trees and animals in striking colors still vivid after centuries. In Israel, because the fine arts became the vehicle of idolatry, God condemned all representation of the objects of heaven or earth (Exodus 20:4; Deuteronomy 5:8).

It is with reservation that we accept Thackeray's sentiment — "I have seen no men in life loving their profession so much as painters." All noble professions have those who are devoted to their particular calling. Skillful artists, however, manifest great patience, care and concentration, and capture our admiration with their life-like presentation. The fabulous sums spent on masterpieces which, when painted a century or so ago, were sold for a paltry figure reveal the present-day interest in this form of the fine arts. But the artist has not yet appeared who is able to copy the great Creator-Artist in one of His matchless sunrises or sunsets; or to mix his colors as God has done in the fascinating variety found in nature. Where is the Rembrandt clever enough to match the sky-blue of the heavens declaring the glory of God?

The Astrologer

At the outset it must be made clear that we distinguish between the astrologer and the astronomer. The latter, as our next cameo indicates, represents a most profitable and fascinating art. Astronomy is the legitimate science of the heavenly bodies — their magnitudes, motions and constitution. Astrology, however, is a science, falsely so-called. This supposed art of the influence of the stars on human and terrestrial affairs, or the foretelling of events by the positions of the stars is a false system of ascertaining the divine will and is a form of idolatry. The only infallible medium for human life is the Word of God.

Monthly prognosticators were those who every new moon professed by observations of it to foretell the future in respect of auspicious and inauspicious days (Isaiah 47:13). Used nine times in the Bible, astrologer implies one who is an enchanter, magician, one who views or divides the heavens.

From earliest days, the stars were believed to have an influence on the fortunes of men (Judges 5:20; Job 38:33). Astrology flourished luxuriously in Babylonia, being held in high esteem by Assyrian and Babylonian professional astrologers who, as early as the sixteenth century B.C. constructed an astrological chart similar to the horoscopes found in secular newspapers and magazines today. Other Gentile nations also countenanced astrology (Daniel 1:20; 2:2, 10). Babylonian astrology, with its announcement of coming events and notification of favorable and unfavorable days, indicated and preserved on clay tablets, is mentioned by Isaiah (47:13).

While not practiced by Israel in early times, astrology came to be recognized by the apostate Jews (Isaiah 47:14, etc.) Jeremiah warned the people against this "way of the nations." Daniel was made chief of the ten wise men who included astrologers. Some translators render "The Magi" or Wise Men, as astrologers. Edersheim says that the wise men who came to the infant child (Matthew 2:1-12) appear to have been astrologers who were met by God in their darkness and led to the Saviour.

Thomson in his *Land and the Book* suggests that many of the ancient forms of divination were closely related. "An astrologer would not only draw his astrolabic figures and diagrams, but observe times, compound magical drugs, recite incantations, write charms and so on, through all the labyrinths of the black art." Apocalyptic prophets declare that strange events in the heavenly bodies are to precede the great and terrible day of the Lord (Joel 2:30, 31; 3:14, 15, etc.).

Today, astrologists abound, and are fattening themselves on the credulity

of the curious by pretending to foretell things to come. It is amazing how
many deluded people there are who
daily consult a horoscope, or who resort to astrologers for guidance about
problems and decisions. What a la-
mentable waste of money! What rub-
bish it is to assert that our natural
birthday is related to a particular
star, and that from the position of
that star information can be gathered
as to what we can expect to happen!
As Christians, we condemn such a
form of idolatry for our destiny is not
wrapped up in the stars but in the
God who created and controls them.
God manifests His will, not through
the intermediary of the stars, but by
His Spirit through His Word. Divine
judgment still rests upon those pro-
fessors of art dealing in "lucky" and
"unlucky" days, specific omens and the
prognostication of future occurrences
by the observation of the planets. *My
soul come not nigh their dwelling!*

The Astronomer

Dr. Edward Young of the seventeenth century wrote of the planet-
studded skies —

'Tis Nature's system of divinity,
And every student of the *night* inspires,
'Tis *elder* scriptures, writ by God's own
hand:
Scripture authentic! uncorrupt by man . . .
Eternity is written in the skies . . . .
Devotion! daughter of astronomy!
An *undevout* astronomer is mad!

Shakespeare speaks of astronomers
as —

These earthly godfathers of heaven's lights,
That give a name to every fixed star.

It is probably true that there are no
atheists among astronomers. Endeav-
oring to penetrate the secrets of the
star-spangled skies they are forced
to confess with the psalmist that —

The heavens declare the glory
of God
And the firmament showeth His
handiwork.

That the wise men who came from
the East to Bethlehem were students
of both the Scriptures and the stars
and learned to connect them is evident from the record that these Magi
saw *His star* and came to worship
Him who was prophesied as the Star
out of Jacob (Numbers 24:17; Matthew 2:2). Among the numberless
stars, the Magi singled out and followed the movement of "His star."
Frequently the Bible dwells upon the
host of heaven that cannot be numbered. "The stars of the sky in multi-
tude" (Genesis 15:5; Deuteronomy 1:
10; 10:22; Nehemiah 9:13; Jeremiah
33:22; Hebrews 11:12). Astronomers
tell us that all the stars visible to the
naked eye from all points of the earth
number around five or six thousand.
Stars seen by the unaided eye are
called lucid to distinguish them from
telescopic stars — millions of which
can be seen only with the aid of modern powerful telescopes. The marvel
is that in spite of the magnitudes of
stars there are not two of them exactly
alike (I Corinthians 15:41).

The Babylonians were keen students of the planets in the celestial
sphere. The Israelites, however, paid
little attention to astronomy because
they felt that the heavenly orbits surpassed human search and were to be
reverenced as the display of God:
glory in rather than investigate (Job
38:33; Psalm 19:1). The stars served
as signs to mark the seasons, the days,
and the years (Genesis 1:14). Then
the Bible declares that the multitudinous stars compose part of the great
army of the skies under the order of
God their Head — their Creator. He
knows them all by name, and gave
each its particular function (Genesis

1:14, 16; 15:5; 22:17; II Kings 20:9-11;
I Chronicles 27:23; Nehemiah 9:6, 23;
Psalms 8:3; 136:9; 147:4; 148:3; Isaiah
24:21; 40:26).

The Israelites were acquainted with
various constellations like Orion Plei-
ades, Bear (Job 9:9; 37:9; 38:33). In
ancient times, stars were thought of
as living beings, able to applaud the
magnificence of creation, or powerful
enough to aid heroes in battle (Judges
5:20; Job 38:7; See I Corinthians 15:
40). The worship of stars, so common
among Gentile nations, was severely
condemned by the law and the prophets (Deuteronomy 4:19; 17:3; II Kings
17:16; 21:5; 23:4, 5; Jeremiah 8:2; 19:
13; Zephaniah 1:5; Acts 7:42). The
stars are often used poetically and
prophetically in the Bible (Genesis
37:9; Daniel 12:3; II Peter 1:19; Jude
13; Revelation 1:6; 2:28; 12:1; 22:16).

In contrast to the ignoble and de-
ceptive profession of astrologers, the
quest of astronomers is legitimate, fascinating, educative and scientific. Astrology would have us believe that
our fate is in the stars, with "luck"
as our Lord. Astronomy directs our
gaze beyond the stars to the God who
created and controls them, and who,
in like manner, causes all things to
work together for good in the lives
of those who truly love Him (Romans
8:28). Astrology, as a science is false,
deluding people into believing that
the motions of the stars determine
life's days. Astronomy is a noble art,
and results in the worship of the Creator in whose hands alone the events
of our life are hid. Meditating upon
the magnitude of the divinely ordained heavens and the stars how insignificant proud man seems to be
(Psalm 8).

The Athlete

The many metaphors, borrowed
from contests between athletes and
between animals, chariot races and
other competitions in the social life of
the Greeks and the Romans, prove
how Paul was enabled by the Holy
Spirit to make a spiritual application
of the sporting events of his time
(I Corinthians 9:24; Philippians 3:12;
I Timothy 6:12; II Timothy 2:5; 4:7;
Hebrews 12:1, etc.). The word athlete can be found in *athleo,* meaning
to engage in a contest, to contest in
public games, and is the word Paul
uses in the phrase "contend in the
games" (II Timothy 2:5 ASV). Strive
is a similar word meaning "to contend" (Luke 13:24; I Corinthians 9:25
ASV), but carries the further significance of agonizing, as an athlete
straining to obtain a prize. *Athlelos*
denotes a combat, a contest or fight
between athletes, and is used in connection with "affliction" (Hebrews 10:
32).

While the actual terms athletics,
games, and sports do not appear in
the Bible, there is yet frequent references to the many activities signified
by them. It may be profitable, therefore, to summarize those sports which
the public was invited either to witness or engage in. The ancient world
practiced pastimes affording recreation and amusement to spectators as
they watched the agility, energetic
action and prowess of athletes.

Although athletics did not occupy a
prominent place in Jewish life, there
were those public games connected
with military sports for which purpose
Jewish youths were instructed in the
use of bow and sling (Judges 20:16;
I Samuel 20:20, 30-35; I Chronicles
12:2). Music and dancing were prominent among the Jews (See II Samuel
2:14; 6:21). Among the Romans there
were gladiatorial fights with savage
beasts. The Greeks had their Olympic,
Isthmian and Nemean Games. The
Apocrypha speaks of a replica of a

Grecian gymnasium set up for the training of the Jewish youth (II Maccabees 4:9-12). Josephus has several references to the games of wrestling, chariot-racing, the contest of wild beasts with each other and with criminals. As a sport, Nero flung the early Christians to the lions. The church historian, Neander, says that, "The games and theatrical exhibitions of the heathen were regarded by the early Christians with a strong disapprobation as they were by the Jews generally, and for better reasons." The persecutions of early believers by their enemies, their danger to person and life from this source, are illustrated in three passages by the cruel games in which at Rome, Ephesus and elsewhere, men were brought forward in the arena to contend with wild beasts or gladiators (I Corinthians 4:9; 15:32; Hebrews 10:32).

Among the sports the Greeks and Romans loved and practiced were running, boxing, jumping, wrestling, dart and discus throwing, and chariot-racing. As pious Jews shunned open spaces for sports, Paul, after his conversion, would not frequent heathen places of athletic competition. Those to whom he ministered, however, were familiar with all kinds of games, hence his constant use of the vocabulary of the athlete. The apostle illustrates the Christian as a boxer, wrestler, runner, gladiator fighting wild beasts. The prize of a wreath of pine or palm leaves, afforded the apostle with illustrations of the goal awaiting the Christian. He also uses, with great effect, the necessity of superb fitness on the part of an athlete, and also strict attention to rules governing a race (Acts 20:24; I Corinthians 9:24-27; 15:32; Philippians 3:13, 14; I Thessalonians 2:19; I Timothy 4:7, 8; II Timothy 2:5; See I Peter 5:4). Among ancient sports men-

tioned in the Bible, we distinguish the following —

Ball-Playing

There is at least one reference to this form of amusement (Isaiah 22:18). Both Jews and Gentiles engaged in various ball games, the development of which are popular today.

Discus-Throwing

In the British Museum, there is a magnificent marble statue of a discobolus, or disc or quoit-thrower. Discs or quoits were round and made of stone, metal or wood, with a hole in the center for a leathern strap to swing it by. Jerusalem had a gymnasium in which throwing the discus was practiced. Perhaps Zechariah alludes to the sport of flinging heavy stones long distances (12:3). References to disc throwing can be found in the Apocrypha (I Maccabees 1:15; II Maccabees 4:9-15). Strong, muscled athletes still engage in this ancient pastime.

Dart-Throwing

What was known as "darting" was performed in different ways — "sometimes with a javelin or dart, or other instrument of a large size, which they threw either with the hand or by the help of a thong tied round the middle of it; sometimes with an arrow shot from a bow or cast out of a sling." Among Goliath's equipment was a bronze javelin, Saul also used his javelin to try to kill David. What we presently know as a game of "darts," is a pleasurable form of an old-time sport.

Wrestling

Quoting from *Grecian Antiquities*, Fairburn says that wrestling was, originally, a trial of strength, in which the stronger of the two was sure to prevail. Later on, Theseus developed it into an art by which men of skill were enabled to throw others far superior to them in bodily strength. The wrestler had to throw his adversary either by swinging him around, or tripping him up, and then to keep him down. The joints and limbs were prepared for the struggle by being well-rubbed with oil. The victory was given to him who gave his adversary three falls.

The word Paul uses for wrestling is akin to *palto* meaning to sway or vibrate, and symbolizes the spiritual conflict with satanic forces engaged in by believers (Ephesians 6:12). Modern wrestling is a more complicated spectacular and financially profitable form of the original Grecian sport. Present-day wrestling, although conspicuous on the part of some wrestlers for acquiring skill, is, in the main, a mere show with pre-arranged holds and falls to satisfy the worldling, out for a thrill.

Boxing

Paul has a brief reference to "boxing." To the Corinthians he wrote, "So fight I, not as one that beateth the air" (I Corinthians 9:26). As a spiritual boxer, Paul did not spend his strongest blows on the air. Dealing with antagonistic powers, he never aimed wildly or missed his blows. Under God, every blow told against the adversary.

When first introduced, boxing was practiced with the hands naked and unguarded, but in course of time the hands were surrounded with thongs of leather, called "cestus," which at first were short and reached no higher than the wrist. Later, the Greeks extended the cestus to the elbow, even

to the shoulder, the first part being filled with metal, adding to the force of the blow. To bear the blows thus inflicted, the body had to be fat, as well as muscular and hardy.

Running

As a noble sport, running goes back to antiquity. The runners mentioned in the Old Testament were remarkable for their swiftness and endurance. Runners like the fifty who ran before Absalom's chariot, had to be swifter than horses. As royal messengers, runners ran speedily to execute their monarch's sentences (I Samuel 8:11; 22: 17; II Samuel 15:1; I Kings 1:5; 14: 27; II Kings 10:25; 11:4). Racing on foot was known to the Israelites for Solomon says that "the race is not to the swift" (Ecclesiastes 9:11. See II Samuel 1:23).

Among the Greeks the exercise of running was held in great esteem, being one of the first sports to be practiced by them and deemed necessary to the perfect warrior. David, speaking of Saul and Jonathan's rapid onset on their enemies, describes them as having the swiftness of the eagle (II Samuel 1:23). Homer gave Achilles the character of "the swift-footed." In his endeavor to illustrate the truth he taught, Paul borrowed many a comparison from ancient sports. His most frequent illustration however, is that of the runner. (See Romans 9:16; I Corinthians 9:24-26; 15:32; Galatians 2:2; 5:7; Philippians 2:16; 3:14; II Timothy 4:7; Hebrews 12:1, 2). In his allusion to the runner in a race with his determination to win the prize, Paul visualized the race-track with a number of the swiftest men running, and the prize going to the runner who saved all his strength for the final lap. With telling effect, we are urged so to run as to obtain a reward — "the prize of the high calling in Christ Jesus."

Observing all the rules, are we running lawfully with nerve and muscle strained, and pressing on with utmost speed is our eye on the goal? Fairbairn observes that —

> There was a period when the runner in the games was *an* uncrowned victor. It was after he had ceased to run, and while the judges deliberated on his claims, ere the crown was placed in his hands. He was at rest, all his labour over; he was calm for he was assured of victory; but he was also expectant till the sign of victory was actually given to him, the sentence passed, his name proclaimed, his crown was given to him.

It is thus that the believer finishing his course, awaits his rewards from the hands of "the righteous Judge." At death, the spiritual runner is at rest. Striving is over and he awaits the final scene when at the day of Christ's appearing, he is crowned (II Timothy 4:8). The crowns which victors of old won soon lost their freshness and faded, but our rewards are uncorruptible and unfading (I Corinthians 9: 25). Athletes can only win their laurels as they practice long, earnest, self-denial — a feature Paul applies to those who would be judged worthy of a prize (I Corinthians 9:23 - 27).

The Author

We usually identify the above term with a person who writes books or articles. An author, however, is also a maker of anything, a creator, an originator. Its Latin form is *auctor*, a person who increases something, or increases the supply of things. In French, author means to increase, produce and is related to *augus*, a word representing a fortune teller's promised

increase. J. T. Shipley in *Origins of Words* tells us that in ancient times, before starting an important project, it was customary to inaugurate it by consulting an *augus;* which inauguration was limited to the important public event of a new regime.

Author occurs twice in the Bible (Hebrews 5:9; 12:2). The reference in I Corinthians 14:33 is omitted in the ASV. "God is not of confusion, but of peace." Two different Greek terms are used to translate what the author meant when he identified author with Christ in his Hebrew letter.

1. "Christ became the author of eternal salvation" (5:9). Here *aitios* denotes that which causes something, hence author, signifying that Christ, exalted and glorified as our High Priest, on the ground of His finished work on earth, has become the personal mediating cause (see ASV margin) of eternal salvation. He is not the merely formal cause of our salvation. He is the concrete and active cause of it. He has not merely caused or effected salvation. He is, as His name "Jesus" implies, our salvation itself (Luke 2:30; 3:6). The next idea of author as "leader" is not lost sight of. Christ being first possessed of salvation became the Author of it for others.

2. "Jesus the author and finisher of faith" (12:2). Here author signifies chief, leader, captain, then author. The Greek word *archegos* is translated "Prince" in Acts 3:15 when the margin has author, just as the ASV gives "captain" in Hebrews 2:10. This second word primarily denotes who takes a lead in, or provides the first occasion of anything. Christ as the Prince of Life, did not receive life from another. "The Prince or Author of life must be He who has life from Himself." Christ is not only the originator of faith, but is also the pioneer

in the life of faith. He is first in the company of the faithful (Hebrews 2: 17; 3:2, 5, 6). So we look to Him as the perfect pattern of faith. "Faith has not only Christ for its Object, but Christ for its supreme example. In His own Person, He brought faith as a perfect end."

The usual sense of the word author is applicable to God as we think of the divine revelation the Bible not only contains, but *is*. The Bible has only one Author, although some 40 writers from different walks of life set down all the divine Author meant the world to know. An ancient Latin epigram reads, "He was the author, our hand finished it." The divine Spirit is the Author of Holy Writ, and holy men of old wrote as they were borne along by the Spirit of wisdom and revelation. The hands of men recorded what the Spirit dictated. What John saw, he wrote in a book. Among the sayings of Sophocles (495-405 B.C.) is the one, "To its author everything is dear." As the Author of the Book, the Spirit holds everything dear — and so should we, its readers! Then it must not be forgotten that in a very definite way, Christ, who dominates the Book, became Himself the Book, to be known and read of all men (John 1:1, 14; I John 1:1).

The Babbler

Shipley, in his *Dictionary of Word Origins* says that babble suggests a mocking imitation of those that talk on and on with little to say: ba . . ba . . plus the intensive or frequentative ending — le, as in trickle, startle, etc. But the word was influenced by Babel, the tower of confusion which the Jews sought to erect as an entrance to heaven. Solomon's references to babbling (Proverbs 23:29; Ecclesiastes 10:11) indicate the confused, incoherent chatter of a drunkard. Webster's definition of a babbler is to prate like a baby; to make a continuous murmering like a brook babbling over rocks; idle, senseless talk. A writer of the eighteenth century gave us the lines —

O for a living man to lead!
That will not babble when we bleed.

Southey wrote of "The arts Babblative and Scribblative."

The Greek word for babbler means a seed-picker and describes a person who picks up a precarious living, like a crow. Bishop Chase says that "the language of such a person was, and is, plentiful and — on occasion — low." Ellicott comments —

The word "babbler" was primarily applied to a small bird of the finch tribe. The idle gossip of the *agora* picking up news, and, eager to retail it, the chattering parasites of feasts, were likened by the quick wit of Athenian humorists to such a bird as it hopped and chirped. So Zeno himself called one of his disciples, who had more words than wisdom. The philosophers, in their scorn of the stranger who was ready to discuss great questions with any whom he met, applied it to Paul (Acts 17:18).

It had been suggested that the Athenians applied the word to Paul, not on account of his speech, but his looks. In this case the American term "carpet-bagger" would give it sense. The slang term "carpet-bagger" originally describes a Northerner who went to the South after the Civil War, to make money by taking advantage of unsettled conditions, or political corruption, or one who carried his qualifications for citizenship with him in a carpet bag.

Of the term used of Paul, W. E. Vine says of babbler — "primarily an adjective, it came to be used as a noun signifying a bird picking up seeds. Then it seems to have been used of a man accustomed to hang about streets and markets, picking up scraps which fall from loads: hence a parasite, who lives at the expense of others, a hanger on. Metaphorically, it became used of a man who picks up scraps of information and retails them secondhand, a plagiarist, or one of those who make a show, in unscientific style, of knowledge obtained from misunderstanding lectures. But Paul was certainly no plagiarist. What he declared was direct information from the Throne of God (Galatians 1:13-15)."

Twice over Paul warns believers to "shun profane and vain babblings" (I Timothy 6:20; II Timothy 2:16). Useless, profitless theological controversy and discussion was scorned by the apostle seeing that it tended to augment dissension and hatred, and unduly exalt mere words and phrases. The word shun is a strong one, and signifies literally "to make a circuit so as to avoid" (Titus 3:9 "avoid"). Dean Alford says of this withdrawing oneself from empty babblings, "The meaning seems to come from a number of persons falling back from an object of fear or loathing, and standing at a distance round about." Those who would rightly divide the Word of Truth must never be guilty of babbling. Alas, preachers with no convictions, and no positive message to proclaim, are often guilty of babbling! God has given us a simple, intelligent, soul-converting Gospel to declare. May grace be ours to echo it forth clearly and convincingly as heaven-sent heralds!

The Baker

Every time we repeat the Lord's Prayer and reach the petition, "Give us this day our daily bread," we should prayerfully remember those whose occupation it is to bake our daily bread. What would you say is the most celebrated baker in the Bible? Is it not the One whom Peter and John, after a night's fruitless work, saw waiting for them on the shore? Wet, cold, disappointed and hungry, reaching the shore, "they saw a fire of coals and fish laid thereon and bread." It must have been Jesus who baked that bread, and prepared that breakfast, for His disciples who were to go forth to "feed his sheep." We serve a Master who is thoughtful about our bodies, as well as concerned about our souls.

How privileged Elijah was to have an angel as a baker! After a long flight from Jezebel, the prophet fell asleep and later was roused by an angel with the call, "Arise and eat!" Opening his eyes, Elijah looked and "behold, there was a cake baken on the coals" (I Kings 19:6). Is this not a further illustration of how considerate God is of His needy servants?

Another baker we read of in the Bible is the chief baker of the King of Egypt who prepared all manner of bakemeats for Pharaoh (Genesis 40:1-22; 41:10).

What a dreadful message Joseph had to deliver to Pharaoh's chief baker, yet he spared no detail of it. "The three baskets are three days: yet within three days shall Pharaoh lift up thy head from off thee, and hang thee on a tree; and the birds shall eat thy flesh from off thee." It was a gruesome doom to pronounce to an outstanding baker, but Joseph did not flinch in breaking the sad news to his fellow prisoner. The variety of pastries this doomed baker produced can be literally expressed as "food, the work of the baker" (Genesis 40:17). Professional bakers who possibly were grouped together, had a street named after them in Jerusalem (Jeremiah 37: 21). No doubt this street — the only street in old Jerusalem of which we know the name — was the one in which the royal bakehouses were situated. These Jerusalem bakers were ordered to supply Jeremiah in his prison with "a loaf of bread out of the baker's street until all the bread in the city was spent."

Before breadmaking became a trade each Jewish family made the bread it needed, a task which, as a rule, fell to the women of the household (Genesis 18:6; Leviticus 26:26; I Samuel 8:13). In private — at home — bakers were women: public bakers like those in the king's courts were usually men (Genesis 40:1; I Samuel 8:13). Eager to entertain the strangers who came to visit him, Abraham hurried to Sara's tent, and said, "Make ready quickly three measures of fine meal . . . and make cakes upon the hearth" (Genesis 18:6). It is suggested that in a house where there were daughters the eldest did the baking, which might explain why Leah was tender-eyed; inflammation being caused by the heat of the oven.

That bread had a prominent place in the daily food of the Jews is evident from the frequent references to it in the Old Testament (Genesis 3:19). Bread, made chiefly from wheat and barley, was used for food in general (Judges 7:13; John 6:13). In times of famine, other ingredients were added (Ezekiel 4:9). Unleavened bread was made very thin, and was broken, not cut (Lamentations 4:4; Matthew 14: 19; 15:36; 26:26). The importance of bread, as the basic food, in the diet of a Jew, explains why it is symbolized in the Bible. As a highly regarded food, bread was not given to animals. "To eat bread" was equivalent to "have a meal." In Isaiah's time to cut bread was to kill it (Isaiah 58:

7). When an Arab of today sees a European cutting bread with a knife, he asks, "Is the bread being killed?"

The greatest honor accorded the baker's ocupation was when Jesus chose bread as a symbol of His own presence and provision in the church, and to represent His body broken for us on the cross (John 6:35; Acts 2:42; I Corinthians 10:16, etc.). Tradition gives the baker a bad name — "pull devil, pull baker," which is supposed to have originated in the old puppet-shows, in which a baker was consigned to the flames by the devil. But one of Scotland's greatest sons was Sir James Y. Simpson, the discoverer of chloroform, the son of the village baker of Bathgate.

Hosea, watching the baker at his task, gathered a fitting illustration of his people. Because the baker failed to notice when his soft cake was ready to be turned, it was burned on the one side and raw on the other. "Ephraim is a cake not turned" (Hosea 7:8) — overdone on the one side; underdone on the other.

In this day of mass production and automation, the original methods of baking bread seem somewhat crude. At times, the baker would prepare his bakemeats on wood or coals (I Kings 19:6; Isaiah 44:19; John 21:9, 13). A flat dough cake, something like a pancake would be placed between two layers of hot ash. This "cake baken on the coals" became unleavened, and was eaten immediately (Genesis 18: 6).

Another method was to bake bread in a clay, bell-shaped oven which was partially buried in the ground, or built into a wall (Exodus 8:3; Leviticus 2: 4; 26:26; Psalm 21:9; Hosea 7:4; Matthew 6:30). Two sorts of ovens were used — portable and fixed. These ovens could be heated by fuel consisting of stubble, grass and dry twigs

(I Kings 17:12; Malachi 4:1; Matthew 6:30). The baking-pan (Leviticus 2: 5; I Chronicles 9:31; 23:29; Ezekiel 4: 3) was either an iron griddle or flat stone both of which were used (I Kings 19:6, ASV margin). When the stone or plate was thoroughly heated the embers would be raked off and the cake laid on and covered with embers, or glowing ashes.

Paul has a practical note about paying for what he ate. "Neither did we eat any man's bread for nought" (II Thessalonians 3:8). Bakers, like other tradesmen — and tradeswomen, like dressmakers — work hard and long, and should not be kept waiting for payment of their account. "Pay that thou owest." A Christian, above all others, should be prompt in payment for goods or services rendered. "Owe no man anything but love."

The Banker

That the services of bankers were indispensable in the first century of Christianity, is evident from the mention of them in the gospels, where we read of "money-changers"; "changers of money"; "exchangers" (Matthew 21:12; 25:27; Mark 11:15; John 2:14, 15). In most cases the ASV gives us "bankers" for "changers." The Greek word for banker is also used for money-changer. *The Amplified Bible* reads —

> Then you should have invested my money with the bankers, and at my coming I could have received what was my own with interest (Matthew 25:27).

> Then why did you not put my money in a bank, so that on my return I might have collected it with interest? (Luke 19:23).

The duty of these Jewish money-changers was to change large denom-inations of foreign money, principally Roman, into the smaller giving silver for gold, copper for silver. The most important department of the early banking system was the exchange of foreign coinage into the half-shekels required for yearly payment into the Temple treasury. It was for the convenience of the Jews of the dispersion that these "changers" were permitted to set up their tables in the outer court of the Temple. E. W. Vine observes —

> In the court of Gentiles, in the Temple precincts, were the seats of those who sold and selected and approved animals for sacrifice and other things. The magnitude of this traffic had introduced the bankers' or brokers' business (Matthew 21:12; John 2:14).

The wealthier members of the profession, like present-day bankers, received money on deposit for purposes of investment in which interest was paid. Under the Mosaic Law, Jews were forbidden to take interest on money from one another (Exodus 22: 25; Leviticus 25:35-38; Deuteronomy 23:19). Coins are mentioned for the first time in the Bible in Ezra 2:69. By New Testament times conditions, owing to the development of Greek, Roman and local currencies, had greatly changed and trading capital was required for business concerns. Thus, our Lord commended the investment of money, yielding a fair and proper interest (Matthew 25:27; Luke 19:23). In the ancient world, rates of interest were very high. The love of usury, or high interest, was the cause of a noisy argument which ended with Christ driving the exchangers from the Temple (Matthew 21:12).

Albert E. Bailey, in *Daily Life in Bible Times* says that —

> It would seem that the Jewish genius for government and international busi-

ness which has characterized the race for two thousand years, received its most promising start during the Babylonian exile. It was a wonderful revelation and an intriguing opportunity to be transplanted from the edge to the very centre of empire.

It is a common fact that in our day of highly developed finance Jews are prominent as bankers, financiers and commercial tycoons.

As now, so in the early days of banking, changers had to be on their guard against counterfeit money. An unwritten saying of our Lord to His disciples reads, "Be ye expert money-changers," or "Be good bankers," meaning, be skillful in distinguishing true doctrine for false. May grace be ours so to trade with our God-given talents that full interest will accrue to Him to whom all we are, and have, belongs!

During the great depression in America, scores of bankers failed, and thousands of investors were left penniless. Banks failed because they were not able to pay out all the money invested. Issued notes became worthless. But God never fails. He is our "never-failing Treasury." He is always able to redeem every promise He has made. All His promises are sure.

The Barber

Hairdressing and shaving have become a skillful and lucrative occupation. The very word barber has gone out of fashion. The barber now is advertised as a hairdresser, hair stylist, tonsorial artist. Here are two expressive proverbs —

"A barber learns to shave by shaving fools."
"No barber shaves so close but another finds work."

Formerly barbers also practiced surgery and dentistry and were called barber-surgeons. While "razors" and "shaving" frequently occur in Scripture, the word barber occurs only once — "Take thee a barber's razor" (Ezekiel 5:1).

The LXX and the Vulgate use the name barber for the Philistine who shaved Samson's head while he slept.

The shaving of a priest's head and beard with a razor, or sharp-cutting instrument symbolized a most desolating judgment predicted by the prophet. Wilson in his *Travels*, describes the barbers in ancient Bible lands he visited.

> The barber wears a girdle drawn around the waist, to which a strap is appended to give his razor a proper point . . . It may be observed that the razor is not drawn towards the face, according to our English custom, but moved forward. The dexterous manner in which the razor is used in the East may be considered as a commentary upon an expression used by one of the prophets.

A few barber shops are still distinguished by a pole painted in spiral fashion with red and white stripes — a sign that goes back to the barber-surgeon days. The red represented "blood-letting" and the white, the "bandaging."

The Bible razor, sometimes used in a symbolic sense (Psalm 52:2; Isaiah 7:20; Ezekiel 5:1) was some form of a flint or bronze knife such as was used in the rite of circumcision (Exodus 4:25; Joshua 5:2). In those far-off days, the men knew nothing of the steel or safety or electric shavers modern civilization has produced. To be "on the razor's edge" means at the critical moment. In his *Bible Manners and Customs* A. Van Deursen reminds us that —

> In ancient times the barber practiced his trade in the open air, in the shade

of a tree. He bound the hair up at the top of the scalp and cut the hair short near the temples and shaved it off. The customer meanwhile sat on a three-legged stool with a soap-dish. in front of him. For shaving and hair-cutting the barber used a "barbers' razor" — "to pass upon the head and upon the beard" (Ezekiel 5:1) — despite its very strange shape.

That some form of razor was in use in Israel from ancient times is evident from the fact that the leper was commanded to shave off all the hair of his head (Leviticus 14:9). Joseph shaved his face to conform to Egyptian custom, before going to Pharaoh (Genesis 41:14). Some of the savages of Polynesia still shave with pieces of flint, while others shave with pieces of shells or sharks' teeth ground to a fine edge. Hebrews wore long beards. It was only during the days of mourning that Egyptians went unshaven. The law forbade Hebrews to round the corners of their heads or mar the corner of their beards (Leviticus 19: 27; Jeremiah 9:26 margin, 48:37). It was a grievous insult, or badge of shame to cut or pluck the Nazarite's hair of head or cheek (II Samuel 10: 4; I Chronicles 19:4; Isaiah 50:6; Jeremiah 48:37). Long hair was also a token of the dedication of strength to God (Numbers 6:5; Judges 13:5; 16: 17). The mother of Samuel was instructed to keep a razor from his head for her child was to be a Nazarite from the womb. By Paul's time, it was not deemed proper but effeminate for a man to have long hair (I Corinthians 11:14). Hair represents what is least valuable — innumerable to man but all numbered by God's providence for His children (Matthew 10: 30).

The Beggar

While the old proverb says, "A beggar can never be bankrupt" — his oc-cupation, even though it may be a self-chosen one, is by no means enviable. How humiliating it must be if a person, through no fault of his own, is forced to beg! It is interesting to discover that while the Bible has a good deal to say about poverty, it names very few actual beggars. Although Blind Bartimaeus, and another blind man, were forced to beg for a living (Mark 10:46; Luke 18:35; John 9:8), Lazarus is the only person named as a beggar in Scripture (Luke 16:20, 22). Hannah, in her prophetic prayer, spoke about the Lord having power to raise the poor out of the dust, and to lift up the beggar from the dunghill (I Samuel 2:8). Paul incorporates the same word when he wrote about the weak and beggarly elements of this world (Galatians 4: 9).

When Jesus said, "Blessed be ye poor" (Luke 6:20), the word He used for poor is the same one He employed when He spoke of Lazarus as a beggar (Luke 16:20). Often the account of The Rich Man and Lazarus is referred to as a "parable." Actually, it is not a parable because of the use of a personal name — a name known to mean, "God is the helper," and symbolizing the outward wretchedness of this Lazarus, distinguished from the Lazarus Jesus raised from the dead (John 11), who had no other help but God. Ellicott suggests that Jesus may have described Lazarus the beggar as a warning to Lazarus of Bethany, who was certainly rich, and sometimes identified as the rich young ruler.

Dealing with the subject of poverty, the Bible leaves us in no doubt as to its reasons and relief. In the early days of Israel, when the people were conspicuous as clans and families flourished, as well as the conditions of life and agriculture, poverty was not keenly felt, nor was it permanent. In principle, there should have been no poor people in Israel (Deuteronomy 15:4). Begging was a practice only known after the captivity. The Apocrypha says, "It is better to die than beg" (See Luke 16:21). As city life and commerce developed, poverty appeared and pauperism began its ravages (Deuteronomy 24:10-21; 26: 13-15). By New Testament times begging was common (Mark 10:46; Luke 16:20, 21; 18:35; John 9:8; Acts 3:2), but Paul stoutly discouraged it in the case of those who were able to work. Honest labor for one's living was encouraged by precept and practice (Ephesians 4:28; I Thessalonians 4:11; II Thessalonians 3:7-12). The fact of genuine poverty was recognized both by Moses and our Lord (Deuteronomy 15:11; Matthew 26:11; Mark 14: 7; John 12:8). David declared that he had never seen God's children begging bread (Psalm 37:25).

Among the Bible reasons for poverty, the following are cited —

1. Individual Folly. Failing to recognize God, men deserve to beg. Poverty came as a divine punishment upon the wicked, as the experience of the Prodigal proved (Luke 15:16, see Psalm 109:10; Proverbs 13:7; 20:4).

2. Bad seasons, involving failure of crops, loss of property. Famines and pestilences (II Kings 8:1-7; Nehemiah 5:8; Joel 1).

3. Wars, with their inevitable raids and invasions. The avarice of men in land-grabbing, taking advantage of adverse circumstances, greed and heartless oppression by the rich (II Samuel 12:1-6; Isaiah 5:8).

4. Over-taxation and forced labor conditions — corruption and perversion of justice, such as the prophets denounced (Isaiah 1:23; 3:15; Jeremiah 22:15; Amos 4:1; 6:1; Micah 2: 1).

5. Extortionate usury — the opportunity for which was provided by the necessity for meeting high taxation and losses accruing from bad harvests (Nehemiah 5:1-8; James 2:1-16). Under the Mosaic Law usury was forbidden. Pledged raiment was to be returned before sundown (Exodus 22: 25-27; Deuteronomy 24:10-13).

In the matter of relief, all classes of the poor are mentioned — widows, orphans, sojourners, or resident strangers possessing no landed rights. Levites are also mentioned as an impoverished class (Deuteronomy 12:12-19; 18). These classes of the poor were objects of solicitude and consideration under the ancient Law (Leviticus 5: 7-11; 19:9-15). A humane spirit had to be shown toward the less fortunate.

1. The poor were entitled to a share in tithes from land, and income derived from produce such as corn and grapes (Deuteronomy 14:28).

2. The poor had the right to glean the corners of the field. The olive trees had not to be beaten the second time; the widow, fatherless and the stranger could gather the leavings; the forgotten sheaf was to be left for them (Leviticus 19:9, 10; Deuteronomy 24:15, 19, 21; Ruth 2:2).

3. The poor were provided for at the approach of Jubilee. Benefits were assured by the celebration of the Sabbatical Year. Those with more than enough were enjoined to be generous toward those less fortunate than themselves (Exodus 23:11; Leviticus 25: 39-42, 47-54).

4. The poor were to receive wages at the end of a day's work. In this way they would be delivered from the shame of begging (Leviticus 19:13; Deuteronomy 24:14, 15).

5. The poor were helped by almsgiving — which was reckoned to be a sign of piety (Job 29:12; Psalm 112: 9; Daniel 4:27). Alms were freely

given in money or in kind from motives of love and pity for the poor, and out of gratitude to the Giver of all (Deuteronomy 15:1; Matthew 6:1-4; Mark 9:41; Acts 4:32-34; Romans 12:13; 15:26; Galatians 2:10). The provision of a poor fund was an aspect of practical Christianity in the early church (I Corinthians 16:1; II Corinthians 9:1). God gives us means for this end (Ephesians 4:28).

The Bible teaches us that there is an honorable poverty — "I know thy poverty but thou art rich" (Revelation 2:9). "In the face of the often corrupting influence of riches, there is a poverty which gives honor to the Israelite who is ready to suffer it worthily, and which is a source of piety and virtue," says W. Corswant (Proverbs 19:1, 22; 28:6; Luke 21:3). In the Psalms and Beatitudes the terms "poor" and "lowly" are synonymous with "piety" and "humility." Corswant also reminds us that it was to these poor, "a veritable *élite* of the nation, morally speaking, that the Gospel was to be preached and by whom it would be accepted" (Isaiah 61:1; Matthew 11:5; Luke 4:18; 7:22). The glory of the Gospel is that the One who died and rose again to make such a Gospel possible was rich yet for our sakes became poor that we through His voluntary poverty might become eternally rich (II Corinthians 8:9).

The Benefactor

Our Lord is the only One in the Bible citing the solitary reference to this particular occupation.

"They that exercise authority . . . are called benefactors" (Luke 22:25). The term, however, meaning, as it does, a well-doer, appears in "partakers of the benefit" (I Timothy 6:2) — "benefit" meaning, well-doing or good work. Originally, *euergetes,* was a title of

honor borne by two of the Greek kings of Egypt before Christ's time, Ptolemy III and Ptolemy VII. This is why the ASV properly spells the word with a capital "Benefactors." Ellicott translates Paul's exhortation to slaves in respect to their masters thus —

> But rather serve them, because believing and beloved are they who are partakers of their good service (I Timothy 6:2, 5).

The thought that good masters profit by the true faithful service of their slaves should always be before the mind of a Christian slave as he serves a Christian master. Vine gives "benefit" as "good deed" and says the same word is translated "good works" (Acts 4:9). Benefactor expresses the agent (Luke 22:25); and benefit, once rendered as "grace" (II Corinthians 1:15), stresses the character of the benefit, as the effect of a gracious disposition of the benefactor.

If a benefactor is one who confers benefits, then God is the greatest Benefactor of all time. As the God of our salvation He "daily loadeth us with benefits" (Psalm 68:19). The proverb has it, "Benefits please like flowers, while they are fresh." There is never anything stale about the provision of our heavenly Benefactor. Alas, we are apt to forget His constant benefactions, hence the call of the Psalmist never to forget His varied benefits (Psalm 103:2)! Cicero once remarked — "He is beneficent who acts kindly not for his own sake, but for another's." The beneficence of God is matchless, for unworthy as we are He always showers His favors upon us for the sake of His own beloved Son (Ephesians 4:32).

> Count your blessings,
>   Name them one by one,
> And it will surprise you
>   What the Lord hath done.

The Bondman

As civilization developed and nations sprang into being, lust for power and possessions resulted in wars (James 5:1, 2), and with wars came subjugation and slavery. In the ancient world, hired service was hardly known. With conquest, the most common form of service was that of slavery which became tyrannous and oppressive (Exodus 6:5; Ezra 9:8, 9). We recognize, of course, that the Old Testament word for service was not restricted to bondservice, such as slaves rendered but was applied to higher relations. Eliezer, a rich man's steward (Genesis 15:2; 24:2), and the king's prime minister (Daniel 9:17), are spoken of as God's "servants." A bondman was one bound with bonds, or a slave. But "bonds" are not only used of oppression, calamity and punishment (Psalms 18:5, 6; 116:3). They are also used metaphorically of a covenant, obedience and obligation Godward. God is spoken of as laying bonds upon Ezekiel, meaning that he was obligated to a constant perseverance in his prophecy (3:25; 4:8; 20:37). Then Eastern politeness demanded that one should term oneself a slave of the superior labored for or addressed (Genesis 32:18; 43:28; Numbers 32:25; Ruth 3:9; I Samuel 25:41).

In dealing with the matter of slavery in Bible times, it is necessary to distinguish the slaves mentioned, and the laws regulating their treatment.

1. *A Gentile Slave*

By "Gentile" we mean all slaves, apart from Hebrews, who were of foreign extraction and, who were in the main, war captives or children of captives (Numbers 31:6, 7, 9; Deuteronomy 20:14; Ezekiel 27:13). Such would be among the number of acquired persons Abraham brought with him out of Haran. This would also include the male and the female slaves Pharaoh gave the patriarch, his 318 household slaves, and the male and female slaves King Abimelech gave him (Genesis 12:15; 13:2; 14:14; 20:14, 16). Property in goods and foreign slaves were handed down from father to son (Genesis 14:14; 17:12; 25:5). In the time of Moses, slavery was in existence. Joseph was sold as a slave, and in Egypt, under Pharaoh, the Israelites were reduced to the status of slaves. Under the Mosaic Law, however, slavery was "regulated by laws mitigating its evils and restricting its duration." The following features are apparent —

1. The regular price of a slave of foreign extraction was thirty shekels of silver (about $10.00 or more than £3). At times the price was forty shekels (Exodus 21:32; Leviticus 27:3, 4; Zechariah 11:12, 13; Matthew 26:15; See Hosea 3:2). Once purchased, the slave became the absolute property of his master, who could resell him, give him away, or hand him on to his heir as an inheritance.

2. Foreign slaves were usually badly treated, being frequently ranked with cattle (Genesis 12:16; 24:35; 30:43; Exodus 20:17). Although denied the laws of justice accorded to free men, slaves were not allowed to be killed. If sufficiently maimed as the result of severe punishment, the slave had a right to immediate emancipation (Exodus 21:20; 21:21, 26, 27).

3. While Paul urged Onesimus, the runaway slave, to return to his master, Philemon, Old Testament fugitive slaves could not be returned to their original owners (Deuteronomy 23:15). W. Corswand says —

The slave profited by a sort of right of asylum, for it was felt that he had not fled without serious cause, but this legal disposition was perhaps only valid for refugees from abroad (Genesis 11:6; I Samuel 25:10; I Kings 2:39, 40).

4. Slaves were granted religious privileges such as the day of rest (Exodus 20:10, 23). They were encouraged to become proselytes of the Jewish faith (Exodus 12:44), and once circumcised, could take part in worship and religious festivals (Genesis 17:12, 13, 23, 27; Exodus 12:43, 44; Deuteronomy 12:12, 18; 16:10; 29:10; 31:12). Other advantages foreign, yet intelligent, well-beloved slaves enjoyed were these —

They were invested with all the confidences of their masters (Genesis 24:2; Matthew 24:45, 46).

Those born in the house were consulted on various matters by their owners (Judges 19:11; I Samuel 9: 5-10; 25:14-17).

They were entrusted with important responsibilities (Genesis 24:2).

They were held in high esteem, many of them coming to own slaves themselves (Genesis 9:25; I Samuel 9:22; II Samuel 9:10).

They married their master's daughter, and profited from legacies (Genesis 15:2; I Chronicles 2:35; Proverbs 17:2).

In Israelite legislation, Hebrews were bidden to remember in their treatment of slaves that they themselves had been captives in Egypt (Deuteronomy 5:15; 15:15; 16:22; 24: 18, 22). Although slaves were never very numerous in Palestine (Nehemiah 7:67), those who were there had to be treated kindly, as human beings. They were not to be slandered before their masters (Proverbs 30:10). The Apocrypha likewise enforces humane treatment of slaves (Ecclesiasticus 33: 24-29). But the lot of foreign slaves

was usually far more cruel than kind. It was frequently the custom of the Assyrians, for example, to remove whole populations of a conquered country to some distant part of their dominion. Bas-reliefs depict women in carts, with their meager possessions, accompanied by their children. Sometimes they are depicted as tearing their hair, covering their heads with dust, and bewailing the captivity.

Some sculptures represent a king seated on a throne, receiving the chief captives brought bound in his presence who were made to prostrate themselves before the king as he placed his feet on their necks (Joshua 10:24). Thus the enemies were made his "footstool" (Psalm 110:1). The severity with which foreign prisoners were treated is dealt with by Dr. A. Van Deursen in his *Illustrated Dictionary of Bible Manners and Customs* —

> Captured prisoners were taken to the capital where they were compelled to pull the royal triumphant chariot. . . . Rebels were punished very severely: hands and feet, noses and ears were cut off, their eyes were put out, and their tongues were torn from their mouths. Ordinary death penalty was by decapitation (II Kings 10:8) or hoisting on poles, whereby the unfortunate victims were tied with their stomachs or throats on the point of a stake so that their own weight pulled them downwards. Shalmaneser III left young lads and girls to burn in a town he had set ablaze. Sometimes prisoners were flayed and their skins were hung taut on the city wall. The inhabitants of every city who had escaped the massacre were taken away captive into slavery (Nahum 3:10). Prisoners were ganged for forced labour.

The cruel custom of captives led before the king by a rope fastened to rings passed through the lip and nose is referred to by the sacred historian (II Kings 19:28). Often in this way they were fastened to kennels at the gate of the city, to be abused and ill-treated by passers-by.

2. *Female Slaves.*

Captive women were not usually chained. The rough soldiers escorting them, however, amused themselves by "discovering their skirts and to see the shame of nakedness" (Nahum 3:5). Corswant observes that "the position of female slaves, whether foreign or Israelite, was always a special one because of the fact that she very often became the concubine of the man who had bought her, or of his sons." Among the laws regulating the treatment of a female slave we note —

1. A woman slave could become the wife of her master's son (Exodus 21:9).

2. If a concubine, she was not freed after six years even if she was an Israelite (Exodus 21:7).

3. The Law took her under its protection (Exodus 21:7-11).

4. She could be bought back by her family (Exodus 21:8).

5. If a concubine were replaced by another she was to be freed if not suitably cared for (Exodus 21:10, 11).

6. If a non-concubine, the female Israelite slave could claim emancipation after six years service (Deuteronomy 15:12, 17).

7. If the slave belonged to her master's wife, she could not become the concubine of her master without the wife's consent (Genesis 16:12; 30:3, 9).

8. A foreign female slave could not be re-sold if her owner had had conjugal relations with her, particularly if she were a mother (Deuteronomy 21:14).

9. A captive woman was allowed to mourn her parents (Deuteronomy 21:13).

3. *Hebrew Slaves.*

Among the Hebrews, or Jews, bond-service was of a mild and equitable character. On the whole, the position of Israelite slaves was easier than that of foreign slaves because of their protection by the Law. Hebrew masters were compelled to treat their hired servants not as slaves with rigor and cruelty, but with courteous consideration as brethren.

1. They had to be liberally remunerated at the close of their service (Leviticus 25:39, 41; Deuteronomy 15:12-18).

2. Israelites must not reduce to bondage Israelites taken in war (II Chronicles 28:8-15).

3. No innocent Israelite could be enslaved against his will (Exodus 21:16; Deuteronomy 24:2).

4. No Israelite slave could be forced to continue in service after six years. In the course of the seventh year, the Jubilee Year, he could claim his freedom and recover his possessions (Exodus 21:1-4). If, however, the slave loved his master, or desired to stay in servitude because of the fear of want, or other reasons, then his master solemnly pierced or bored his ear with an awl — the ear symbolizing willing obedience, as the phrase "give ear" implies —thereby being stamped with the indelible seal of life-slavery (Exodus 21:5, 6; Leviticus 25:10; Deuteronomy 15:17). What a fitting type this is of Christ's devotion to His Father! "Mine ears hast thou opened" (Psalm 40:6-8; Philippians 2:7; Hebrews 10:5). The word "opened" means digged or bored, and is suggestive in the light of the piercing of the ear of the devoted slave. Bishop Handley Moule applied this act to believers in the lines —

My Master lead me to Thy door,
And pierce this willing ear of mine;
And pierced ears shall hear the tone
That tells me Thou and I are One.

5. Sometimes a person was taken a slave in payment of debt. Constrained by penury, a man would sell himself, or his family. When obligations could not be met, the creditor took away the debtor's mortgaged land (Exodus 21:2; Deuteronomy 15:12; II Kings 4: 1-7; Isaiah 5:8; Amos 2:6, 7; Micah 2:1, 2). When taxes increased poverty, there came enslavement for debt (II Kings 16:7-9; 18:14-16; Isaiah 3:14, 15). Thieves, unable to repay what they had stolen had to pay with their person (Exodus 22:3).

6. Stealing for the purpose of slavery was looked upon as a capital crime, both among Jews and Gentiles (Exodus 21:16; Deuteronomy 24:7). Under the Mosaic Law, human life was jealously guarded and liberty deemed to be sacred.

That our Lord and His apostles were familiar with slavery as practiced by Rome is evident from the numerous references to slaves in the New Testament. In many of His parables, Christ made use of Greek words meaning "slave" (Matthew 10:24, 25; 20:27; 24:45-47; Luke 12:35-48; 17:7; John 8:35). *Doulos* means to bind as a slave and was the lowest term in the scale of servitude, coming to mean "one who gave himself up to the will of another" (Romans 6:17, 20; I Corinthians 7:15, 23). Paul, often in real fetters, loved to think of himself as "a bondslave of Jesus Christ" (Romans 1:1; I Corinthians 7:22), and the term, in this connection, was destitute of the idea of a cruel bondage or subjugation represented by forced slavery. Paul was formerly a slave of Satan, but having been bought by Christ he became His willing slave, bound for-

ever to his new Master, who, Himself, is the perfect example of a bondman (Philippians 2:7).

What do we know of this spiritual slavery? Can we sing from the heart with George Matheson? —

Make me a captive, Lord,
And then I shall be free;
Force me to render up my sword,
And I shall conquerer be.

Our Lord once said — "Ye shall know the truth, and the truth shall make you free" (John 8:32, 36).

The poet has reminded us that —
He is the freeman, whom the truth sets free,
And all are slaves beside.

A final word is necessary on the fact that while the Bible records slavery, it nowhere condones it. While Jesus and the apostles "never attacked it directly, its condemnation was implicit in their liberating message." They planted the seeds of love, of a universal brotherhood in Christ Jesus and communion of all in His redemption, which silently and surely undermines slavery — evident in the declaration of Abraham Lincoln, the great slave emancipator. In sending back Onesimus to Philemon, Paul never condoned slavery as a compulsory system. Onesimus went back of his own free will to his master, and returned as a brother in Christ (Philemon). Paul exhorted slaves not to be unduly impatient to cast off even slavery by unlawful means (I Corinthians 7:21-24; See I Peter 2:13-18), or to flee from it as Onesimus, but bide God's time for deliverance and judgment upon their cruel captors.

The Botanist

While the word "botany" is not in the Bible, all that it represents is clearly apparent. A botanist is one who studies the science of plants, flowering and otherwise, and perhaps King Solomon was the greatest botanist of Bible times seeing that among his varied accomplishments — "He spake of trees, from the cedar tree that is in Lebanon even unto the hyssop that springeth out of the well" (I Kings 4:33).

Hyssop is a shrub with a profusion of stems, with flowers fashioned into a blue, or pink, or white crown. One of the smallest plants, it is here contrasted with the mighty cedar, and was associated with different ceremonial usuges (Exodus 12:22; Leviticus 14:6; Numbers 19:6; Psalm 51:7; John 19:29; Hebrews 9:19). It was Solomon who gave us the most beautiful description of Spring ever written. "Winter is past . . . The flowers appear on the earth" (Song of Solomon 2:11-13). He likewise depicts the Bridegroom — symbolic of our Lord — in this way — "His cheeks are as a bed of spices, as sweet flowers: his lips like lilies, dropping sweet-smelling myrrh" (Song of Solomon 5:13).

God must love flowers, seeing He has filled the earth with so many of them. An old proverb reminds us that "every flower reveals a present God."

Since the completion of our English Bible, the knowledge of botany, especially Eastern botany, has largely increased. Varied and many though the plants and flowers of the Bible are, the range is more vast. The Bible rose, for example, was probably the fragrant and beautiful narcissus, found throughout Syria. Today, the variety of beautiful roses is enormous. Artificial hybrids are obtained among plants by cross-pollinating the flowers of different species. Then "grafting" has added considerably to our volume of flowers. A branch of another plant is inserted into a stem of a wild plant as, for example, in the development of a never-ending variety of beautiful roses from the stock of the wild rose. For a table of all the plants mentioned in the Bible, along with the force of their imagery, the reader is referred to the excellent coverage Angus gives us in his comprehensive *Bible Hand-Book*. The lily, for example, which Solomon mentions (Song of Solomon 2:2, 16; 4:5) was likely the "lotus" or winter-lily of the Nile, the roots, stalks and seeds of which were eaten, both fresh and dried. "The lily of the field" Jesus referred to (Matthew 6:28) was the lovely scarlet martagon lily, a stately turban-like flower. Hastings' *Dictionary of the Bible* says that this "lily" may have been "a comprehensive term for the brilliant and many colored anemones, the irises, the gladioli etc., which lend enchantment to the hillside in March and April." Fausset has a rich comment on our Lord's exhortation to consider the lilies —

Wondrous is God's chemistry who out of black mould and invisible vapor builds up that column of chrysolite, and crowns it with its flaming capital. How strange is God's husbandry! Instead of taking the lily into a conservatory, He leaves it out among the thorns. The same soil from which one nature can only extract the harsh astringent sloe with its cruel spines yields to another flexile leaves and balmy blossoms. So the life of faith is not lived in the convent or in the sanctuary *alone,* but out of doors in the unsympathizing world in the midst of secular men. From the same soil and the same atmosphere from which others derive repulsive attributes, the believer can absorb grace and give forth excellence. The same bounties of Providence make Nabal more churlish, make Joseph more generous, tender and forgiving: the same sunshine which elicits the balm of the lily matures in the blackthorn its verjuice: the same shower which makes thistles rank fills the lily cup with nectar, and clothes it in raiment eclipsing Solomon.

The Bible speaks of various flowers in a collective sense, or of a particular flower, both with a literal and figurative sense, as a symbol of the brevity of life, glory or beauty. Flowers, an attractive and magnificent feature of Palestine, come early in spring, but fade all too soon, and are thus figurative of the evanescence of human life and the fading of the treasures and pleasures of this life (Exodus 25:31; 37:17; Numbers 17:8; I Kings 6:18, 29, 32, 35; Job 14:2; 15:33; Psalms 90:5, 6; 103:15; Isaiah 5:24; 18:5; 28:1; 40:6-8; Nahum 1:4; James 1:10, 11; I Peter 1:24). Believers are spoken of as "trees of righteousness, the planting of the Lord" (Isaiah 61:3). "The ordinances of the Church cause them to grow in grace, and in conformity to Christ, and meetness for heaven. Their verdure, beautiful and fragrant, is magnificent in the summer of prosperity, and in the winter of adversity" (Psalm 1:1-3).

The Builder

That the Bible has a good deal to say about builders and buildings is evident from the fact that build, and its cognates, occurs over 400 times. We can understand why building is referred to as "The Oldest Trade in the World." God, as the first Builder, implanted within man, His architectural masterpiece, the instinct and ability to build — and what magnificent structures he has reared in the course of the world's history! Coming from the hand of his perfect Creator, man lives to create, and many of the world's greatest builders trusted "the Mind that builds for aye," as Wordsworth put it. What master-craftsmen those ancient builders were! Their masterpieces of creativity have been copied but never surpassed. Over two and a half millennia ago, when insignificant Greece challenged and conquered Persian tyranny, the Athenians built their marvelous and renowned Parthenon.

As for the Persians themselves, the palace of Darius was without equal in its architecture and sculpture. The towering pillars of what was once the great audience chamber of Xerxes can still be seen rising majestically at Persepolis like "tent poles for the blue silk sky." We go back still further to Egyptian monuments like the Sphinx and the pyramids, still baffling to modern builders because of their immensity, accuracy and durability. Height, and the semblance of power, rather than design, was the purpose of the Pharaohs as they built these massive structures. Then it is to be regretted that the completion of the Aswan Dam means the perpetual submerging of many magnificent monuments like the great statue of Rameses II flanking the entrance to his high temple at Abu Simber, beneath the Nile. Longfellow's lines in *The Builders* seem to express all we feel as we gaze upon remaining evidences of the ancient art of building —

In the older days of Art
　Builders wrought with greatest care
Each minute an unseen part
　For the Gods see everywhere.

Remembering, however, our purpose to outline Bible occupations, let us try to summarize Bible builders and buildings. It is clear that builders worked from a prepared plan or model (Exodus 25:9; I Chronicles 28:11; Psalm 118:22); that there were masons (II Samuel 5:11; I Chronicles 14:1); plasterers (Leviticus 14:42; Daniel 5:5; Matthew 23:27; Acts 23:3); carpenters (I Chronicles 22:15; Matthew 13:55; Mark 6:3). Even in ancient times, locks and keys were added to buildings (Judges 3:23, 25; Isaiah 22:22; Matthew 16:19; Luke 11:52; Revelation 1:18; 3:7; 9:1). Among the specimens of the builder's art mention can be made of —

1. *Cities and Walls*

Cities, with their walls and gates, occupy a prominent place in Scripture. In early times, everyone who needed to build would be a builder. Thus, when in Nehemiah's day, the wall of Jerusalem was being rebuilt, the builders comprised all classes; priests, rulers, merchants, goldsmiths and even women. Before Israel's captivity, Joshua made the city of Ai an heap (Joshua 8:28) and Jeremiah prophesied that the city of Jerusalem is to be rebuilt on her own heap (Jeremiah 30:18). Archaeologists have unearthed ruins of many ancient cities like the ancient Kiriath-sepher, or "The City of Books" (Judges 1:12). Excavations reveal how many of these cities were well-conceived and built, principally of a composition of sand and rubble with facings of heavy stone blocks. Usually there was only one gate, reinforced with iron, in the wall of smaller cities (Isaiah 45:2; Luke 7:12). Above the gate was a lookout for the watchman (II Samuel 18:33). The gate was situated near a well because of the vital importance of water to a city (I Samuel 9:12). Around larger cities double walls were built, the outer wall was sometimes known as a "bulwark" (Isaiah 26:1). At a corner of the inner wall a strong tower or fortress, the last point of defense, was erected (Judges 9:49, 51).

Another city of renown, the ruins of which have been discovered by archaeologists is that of Megiddo, existent at the time of the first kings (I Kings 4:12). This great city was one of the chariot cities, and was known as "the city of the horsemen" (I Kings 9:17-19; II Chronicles 8:6). It was here that Solomon maintained his famous stables. Of "the large house" or palace at Megiddo (I Kings 3:1; 7:12), authorities say that "its superb architectural style compared with Solomon's Temple at Jerusalem on the one hand, and with the Hittites' on the other, and that its execution and design, like the city itself, was manifestly the work of acccomplished craftsmen."

2. *Towers and Fortresses*

The first real builders, as we understand them, are mentioned as having lived after the Flood. The earliest building of which we have any detailed description is the Tower of Babel, the builders of which said — "Go to, let us make brick, and burn them throughly." "And let us build . . . a tower, whose top may reach unto heaven" (Genesis 11:3, 4). It was to be built so high as to be seen from afar and function as a rallying point. Some archaeologists believe that remains of the Tower still exist, after thousands of years, on the right bank of the river Euphrates, where there is a ruin 153 feet above the ground having the appearance of a huge spiral staircase, and having two sides each of more than 600 feet long.

The use of bricks for buildings testifies to the vast alluvial plain, formed by the deposits of the river Nile. Stones, brought from a distance meant great expense, so builders availed themselves of bricks as the best substitute for buildings (Exodus 1:11-14; 5:7-12; Job 4:19; Isaiah 9:10; 65:3). Among other fortified towers was the one at Samaria built on a hill at "the head of the fat valleys" (Isaiah 28:1), and conveniently suited and situated for defense. There were other fortresses at Shechem and at Taanach. Because of the protection these well-built towers afforded it was natural for the Israelite to think of God as an impregnable Fortress (I Samuel 2:2; Psalms 18:2; 31:3; Jeremiah 16:19, etc.).

3. Houses

The Bible says that "every house is builded by some man" (Hebrews 3:4). The houses of Eastern nations differed, and still differ, from our own in many respects. "They were generally low, flat-roofed, with few external windows, and arranged in a quadrangular form, with a courtyard in the center. These characteristics are the results mainly of the difference of climate, but in part also of a difference in state of society. The excessive heat of the East, the primitive manners of the inhabitants, and the insecurity which unfortunately prevailed in some parts, naturally lead to different architectural arrangements." The builders, for the most part, used bricks (Genesis 11:3; Nahum 3:14). Sometimes only mud was used, the metaphorical use of which was employed by Job and Paul (Job 4:19; II Corinthians 5:1-4; See Ezekiel 13:10, 11). Albert E. Bailey in *Daily Life in Bible Times* gives us a vivid description of the prosperous merchant's house Abraham lived in before leaving Ur of the Chaldees (Genesis 12:16; 13:2, 5-7) which among other features had a chapel on the ground floor in which an altar was built on a raised platform under which the family dead were buried (Deuteronomy 26:14; I Samuel 28:13; Psalm 106:28; Isaiah 8:19; Amos 6:10). Isaiah, an aristocrat, probably related to royalty, lived in a house above the average (Isaiah 9:10). The majority of houses inside a city wall, however, were small, four-walled, in single-story buildings made of soft-baked bricks on a foundation of stone or rocks. The framework of the doorway was composed of two stone sideposts and upper doorpost which constituted the threshold (Exodus 12:7; I Kings 14:17). One window was considered enough (Joshua 2:18). As the houses were the same height and adjoined each other, access from one to the other was easy (Matthew 24:17). W. Corswant says that "the houses of Palestine in archaic times seem to have had sometimes a circular plan — therefore these constructions must be thought of as being like the little domed houses of Upper Syria — but they were much more often almost rectangular." The first New Testament reference to house-building is found in the descriptive simile our Lord used when speaking of the necessity of having a good foundation (Matthew 7:24).

One of the most remarkable creations in the world is Petra, "the rose-red city half as old as time," lying deep in the arid mountains of southern Jordan. Founded about the fourth century B.C. by the Nabateans, the houses and tombs carved out of solid rock reveal what unique builders those Arabians were. Today, it takes an expert climber to scale the cliffs in order to reach these one-time rock dwellings. Can it be, as one prophetic teacher suggests, that Petra will afford a hiding place to persecuted Jews during "The Great Tribulation"?

4. Temples

It would be easy to fill pages with records of building achievements in the realm of temple worship, both Christian and heathen. Archaeological excavations in Palestine have exposed ruins of temples at Gerizim, Beth-shan and Lachish. Ruins of heathen, Babylonian, Egyptian and Grecian temples are for all to see. The Bible mentions temples at Ophrah and Shechem (Judges 8:27; 9:47; See 17:5).

With the purpose in mind of centralizing worship at Jerusalem, David planned for the abolition of the temporary Tabernacle with its curtains, for a more permanent building of stone — a plan God praised but did not permit David to execute because he had shed blood abundantly (II Samuel 7:1, 2; I Kings 8:3, 5, 18; I Chronicles 22:8, 9; 28:2-10). David, however, prepared all the necessary materials for the Temple, the exact design of which the Lord gave to David, and which, in turn, he gave to Solomon (I Chronicles 28:11-19).

SOLOMON'S TEMPLE

Succeeding his father as king of Israel, Solomon set about the erection of the temple David envisaged and prepared for, and which retained the general proportions of the Tabernacle doubled (I Kings 6:2; II Chronicles 3:3). Solomon renewed with the king of Tyre the contract for all necessary timber for the Temple (I Kings 5:2-11). This magnificent structure, when completed, was dedicated with prayer and bountiful thank-offerings (I Kings 8; II Chronicles 5-11). Fulfilling a prophecy, the temple became a symbol of God's resting place with Israel, and thus was itself both a prophecy and a type (II Samuel 7:6, 10, 13) — a type of Israel and of the church, and is a prophecy of God's abiding presence (Jeremiah 7).

The word temple itself is a translation of two words; and means either the whole consecrated precinct, or the portion appropriated as the local abode of God's presence. In the first sense — including the outer or unroofed court — markets were held and the rabbis met their pupils there (Matthew 21:12). It is to the second aspect our Lord refers when He said, "Destroy this temple," that is, the indwelling of the divine nature in His Person. This is the term applied to the church as the temple of God (I Corinthians 3:16; 6:19).

Solomon's temple retained its original splendor only thirty-four years. After the care of several kings of Judah, it became an object of envy and was pillaged by Shishak, king of Egypt, who carried away its great treasures. After undergoing several profanations, the temple was finally plundered during the first siege of Jerusalem, and burned by the Chaldeans under Nebuchadnezzar in 584 B.C. (II Kings 24:13; 25:13-15; II Chronicles 36:17-20).

ZERUBBABEL'S TEMPLE

While we do not have much information, it is certain that this temple lacked the glory of the first (Ezekiel 3:12). Returning from Exile, the Israelites, encouraged by the prophet Zechariah, set about the building of another temple. Then governor Zerubbabel gave his support to the cause which explains why his name was given to the temple. Antiochus Epiphanes profaned this temple by erecting an image of Jupiter on the altar of burnt offering in 163 B.C. It remained in this polluted and dishonored condition for three years, when Judas Maccabaeus purified and repaired it in 160 B.C. (I Maccabees 1:21, 45, 47; 4:28; II Maccabees 6:2).

HEROD'S TEMPLE

Essentially, the continuation of Zerubbabel's temple (Haggai 2:9), its repairing or rebuilding, was undertaken by Herod the Great, about sixteen years after Christ's birth, 20 B.C. This temple filled the Israelites with enthusiastic admiration, of which we have a few echoes in the gospels (Mark 13:1, 2). Herod, who spared no expense in restoring the temple to its original magnitude and splendor, employed 18,000 workers for nine and a half years in its restoration. After the death of Herod, the Jews continued to ornament and enlarge it. At the beginning of our Lord's ministry, the temple was still unfinished, though forty-six years had elapsed since Herod collected his materials and began his work (John 2:20). Under Titus, Jerusalem was destroyed by fire, and in the same month, August, in which the first temple was burned by Nebuchadnezzar, Herod's temple suffered the same fate in 73 A.D. (Matthew 24:1-3). Thus, according to Christ's prophecy thirty-seven years before the event, the Jews' "house was left unto them desolate" (Matthew 23:38). The apostate Emperor Julian tried to rebuild this temple but was thwarted in his efforts. Every year Jews from all over the Holy Land gather at the "Wailing Wall" to observe the anniversary of the destruction of Herod's temple by the Romans, as well as the destruction of Solomon's temple by the Babylonians, which happened to be the same day of the year.

Ezekiel, in one of his visions, describes the reconstruction of Israel's original temple at Jerusalem (Ezekiel 40:48). Much controversy has raged around the question as to whether the prophet gives a symbolical picture of a spiritual temple or an actual temple to be built during our Lord's millennial reign. This we do know, that when He finally surrenders His mediatorial and sacerdotal kingdom to the Father, in heaven, material temples will not be required for "the Lord God Almighty and the Lamb shall be the temple" (Revelation 21:22).

As to the word build itself, the Bible uses it in many ways. For instance —

1. To erect, or build any kind of structure (Deuteronomy 28:30).
2. To strengthen and increase knowledge, faith, love — and the other graces (Acts 20:32).
3. To cement and knit together spiritually: thus believers are united to Christ by faith, and among themselves by love (Ephesians 2:22).
4. To preserve, bless and prosper (Psalm 127:1; Jeremiah 24:6).
5. To settle and establish (I Samuel 2:35).

Then the Bible tells us that God is not only a Builder, but the first one. Out of nothing, He planned and perfected the marvelous universe, fresh wonders of which are being daily discovered. As a builder, God operates in many ways as a study of the following passages prove (I Samuel 2:35; II Samuel 7:27; I Kings 11:38; I Chronicles 17:10; Psalms 28:5; 51:18; 89:4; 102:16; 127:1; Jeremiah 18:9).

The Hebrew of the phrase, "Made he a woman" (Genesis 2:22) reads, "He built up into a woman." Formed out of the side of man, woman is one side of man who, though he may have several sides to his nature and character, yet without women, one integral portion of him is lacking. Ellicott comments, "Eve's formation is described as requiring both time and care on the heavenly Artificer's part. Thus woman is no casual or hasty production of nature, but is the finished result of labor and skill. Finally, she is brought with special honor to the man as the Creator's last and most perfect work."

Abraham had a revelation of God as a builder for "he looked for a city which hath foundations, whose builder and maker is God" (Hebrews 11: 10). John gives us a description of this Holy City to be known as "The New Jerusalem" (Revelation 21). As a roll of citizens is being made up just now, we are thrice blest if our name is inscribed on heaven's birth-register.

Christ, likewise, is a master-builder. "I will build my church" (Matthew 16:18). We are reminded that "He that built all things is God" (Hebrews 3:4), and God in, and through Christ, and by the Spirit is the great Builder of His temple — imperishable because eternal. A true church for eternity is being built in this world upon the foundation of the apostles and prophets, Jesus Christ Himself being the chief cornerstone (Ephesians 2:20). The mystic fabric known as "The Church of the Living God" is "God's building" (I Corinthians 3:9; Ephesians 2:21). At present, those who form "The Temple of God" are being built up in Christ (I Corinthians 3:16; 6:19; II Corinthians 6:16; Colossians 2:7), and are described as "living stones" of such a temple (I Peter 2:4, 5).

Paul compared himself to a "wise masterbuilder" (I Corinthians 3:10). The apostle not only laid the foundation of many a visible church, or body of believers, but he also built several churches, as his matchless epistles to them prove. The Greek significance of "wise masterbuilder" is not merely that Paul was an architect or builder but a "masterbuilder." Thayer in his Greek Lexicon defines the term as "the superintendent on the erection of the buildings" (See I Corinthians 7:14; II Corinthians 11:28). All who labor for the salvation of souls are likewise builders. Emerson has the couplet —

> He builded better than he knew;
> The conscious stone to beauty grew.

Many a spiritual builder, toiling away unnoticed and often discouraged, is building better than they realize. They build for eternity, and only then will discover the value of their work. If, as a fellow-builder with Christ, you feel your labor is in vain remember those of old who said — "The God of heaven, he will prosper us; therefore we his servants will arise and build" (Nehemiah 2:20).

Three prominent characteristics of a good builder are skill, strength and action, all of which God possesses to perfection, and has manifested in all He has built, and is building. As under-builders, God can make possible for each of us, skill to contrive — strength to provide — action to complete.

The Butler

Another ancient Bible occupation prominent both in practice and literature in modern times is that of the butler. As the Hebrew word for "butler" is the same as for "cupbearer," of old the butler was a cupbearer. The terms imply "to give to drink," and a butler or cupbearer was an important man, an officer of high rank, responsible for serving drinks to his king. The office was one of honor and profit among the Persians, and is often found depicted on Egyptian and Assyrian monuments. The butler would fill the king's cup with wine, then pour some into the palm of his own hand and taste it to ascertain if there was any poison in it, before offering the cup to the king. The French for "butler" is *bouteillier,* a bottle-bearer or cupbearer.

Although in Bible times the butler or cupbearer was a manservant having charge of the king's wines and liquors, in more modern times the butler is usually a head servant who has charge of under-servants, waits on the table and supervises, etc. It is interesting to note that Rab-shakeh, one of the generals commanding the forces of Sennacherib, the Assyrian, was an official name, meaning "chief cupbearer," and corresponds to "the chief of the butlers" in the court of Pharaoh, king of Egypt, at a much later period (Genesis 40; 41; II Kings 18:17).

1. *Pharaoh's Butler*

The first mention of this officer of considerable importance is found in the history of Joseph who owed his liberation from prison, and opportunity to attain greatness in Egypt to the interposition of Pharaoh's chief butler or cupbearer (Genesis 40; 41:9). As the *chief* butler, Joseph's one-time fellow prisoner occupied a prominent position in the court. Why Pharaoh cast him into prison we are not told. Perhaps the king suspected him of dropping poison into the cup, or it may be that a jealous fellow-servant carried a story to Pharaoh. What we do know about this chief butler is that however dignified, prominent and conscientious he may have been as a servant, he had one serious flaw in his character. Although Joseph foretold his deliverance from prison and made a pathetic appeal to him, he forgot all about him — a fault resulting in two more years in prison for Joseph.

Yet, in the end at a crucial moment, the chief butler, back in the full confidence of the king, remembered Joseph and became the means of his release and of his ultimate advancement to ruler over all the land of Egypt. At the right hour, the chief butler for Pharaoh's relief, and out of gratitude to Joseph, spoke a good word in the king's ear, and thus became an instrument in the hand of God, a link in a great providence.

2. *Artaxerxes' Butler*

From Nehemiah himself we learn that he held a similar post in the Persian court, to that of Rab-shakeh in the Assyrian court, and to that of "the chief butler" in the Egyptian court. Nehemiah, who, in his memoirs bear-

ing his name, is revealed as "a gifted and accomplished man of action, well versed in the ways of the world, and well equipped to meet difficult situations," and a man whose "religious zeal contributed to form a personality of striking force and power" has the distinction of being the only named butler in Scripture.

The intimate relationship that existed between Artaxerxes Longimanus and Nehemiah testifies to the confidential relations between them, and of Nehemiah's thoroughly trustworthy character. The high esteem in which he was held led the king, who was solicitous for Nehemiah's welfare, to look into the cause of his sad, distressed countenance (Nehemiah 2:2). If selfishness marred the otherwise good demeanor of Pharaoh's butler, Nehemiah the cupbearer is conspicuous for his unselfishness. Born in Babylon it is probable that he had never seen Jerusalem, and as a true patriot he felt God would have him go to the land of his fathers to assist in the rebuilding of the war-ravaged city. The matter weighed heavily upon his mind and he could not hide his sorrow. Since Nehemiah was usually a smart, and cheerful servant, the king inquired as to what was troubling him. Nehemiah opened his heart to the king and begged for leave of absence. Appointed as governor of Jerusalem, the butler became a great religious and political reformer, who gave a fresh start to the people of God recently released from captivity. Once his task was accomplished, Nehemiah wrote about it and returned to his butlership. Success and honor did not turn his head.

3. *Solomon's Butlers*

One of the things impressing the queen of Sheba when she came all the way to Jerusalem to see the greatness of Solomon's reign, were the king's stately butlers or cupbearers, adding, as they did, to the grandeur of Solomon's court (I Kings 10:5; II Chronicles 9:4).

Bishop Butler, of the seventeenth century, whose *Analogy* is unrivaled, and who called attention to the presence of conscience in every person, and explained the purpose of conscience in a way not hitherto attempted, confessed to his chaplain as he came to die —

"Though I have tried to avoid sin and to please God . . . I am afraid to die."

"My lord," said his chaplain, "you forget that Jesus Christ is a Saviour."

"But," said Bishop Butler, "how am I to know that Christ is a Saviour for *me?*"

"My Lord," replied the chaplain, "it is written, *Him that cometh to me* I will in no wise cast out."

"True," said Butler. "I have read that Scripture a thousand times, but I never felt its full value till this moment — stop there, for now I die happy."

This is the only way for the Butlers, and for all others with different names to live and die happy.

We feel that we must close this section on the butler by recounting the record of a Christian butler who lived in France some 300 years ago, and whose name was Nicolas Herman but who became renowned as "Brother Lawrence." The secret of his Christian life was the practice of the presence of God. As a gentleman's butler and servant, Lawrence felt he was too awkward and clumsy and entered a monastery where he expected his faults to be corrected. When given kitchen work he disliked, he was disappointed. Another duty was to buy wine for the monastery but having no

aptitude for business and being somewhat lame, this task was also unwelcome. But like Nehemiah the butler, Brother Lawrence sent up short prayers to God and confessed that he felt more united to God in his outward and distasteful employments than when he left them for devotion in retirement.

Practicing the presence of God has been forcefully emphasized in the lines on *Christian Living* by Edgar Tramp —

A man I know has made an altar of his factory bench.
And one has turned the counter in his store
Into a place of sacrifice and holy ministry.
Another still has changed his office desk
Into a pulpit desk, from which to speak and write,
Transforming commonplace affairs into the business of the King.
A Martha in our midst has made her kitchen table a communion table.

The most commonplace duties gather a halo of glory about them when accomplished for the love of God, and in the consciousness that His fatherly eye is upon us.

The Buyer

In the realm of commerce today, a buyer is an important and well-paid person. He must have an innate feeling about the selling value of certain goods, and know where and how to buy to the best advantage of tradesman and customer alike. An old proverb has it — Buyers want a hundred eyes; sellers none." We also read that, "The cheaper buyer takes home bad meat." Did Solomon have such a buyer in mind when he wrote? — "It is nought, it is nought, saith the buyer: but when he is gone his way, then he boasteth" (Proverbs 20:14). Does this mean that the buyer cries down the goods he wants to purchase? Nought, here, means "bad or worthless." He may boast that he has outdone the seller, and got the goods below their value to discover afterwards that "there are more foolish buyers than foolish sellers."

While the word buyer occurs only three times in the Bible (Proverbs 20: 14; Isaiah 24:2; Ezekiel 7:12), an examination of the verses in which "buying" and "selling" are mentioned reveals the range of commodities dealt with in both material and spiritual, and also the practical exhortation James has for all buyers and sellers (4:13). The term "buy" implies the purchase of any commodity (Genesis 49:30; Ruth 4:5; II Samuel 24:21). A glance at commerce in the Bible shows that among the many products of Canaan, both saleable and exportable, were oil, wine, wheat, barley, oak timber, honey, fruits and spices, balsam, sand, wool and leather (Genesis 43:11; II Samuel 1:24; II Chronicles 2:10; Ezekiel 23; 26:2; 27:6, 17, etc.).

Other countries, like the mysterious Ophir and Tarshish, traded in silver and gold. Yarn came from Egypt (Proverbs 7:16, ASV). A list of some 118 articles coming from foreign countries into Palestine was drawn up soon after Solomon's time; and with the increase of imports and exports, buying and selling became recognized professions.

There are at least two references to buying and selling used spiritually in the Bible. First of all, to buy means to obtain something from God by waiting upon Him in His appointed way — "Buy and eat" (Isaiah 55:1), which implies, "You have no money, come therefore and buy on My terms — though salvation is infinitely valuable, I will charge you nothing for it

— it is perfectly free." When Solomon exhorts us to "Buy the truth, and sell it not" (Proverbs 23:23), he seems to say, "Spare no cost for truth's sake, neither depart from it for any gain; be a merchant in buying it; but never be tempted by evanescent things of earth to surrender it — for it is the richest, the most precious jewel you possess."

The Calker

How chagrined I was to discover that although, through the last fifty years or more, I have read the Bible through scores of times, yet I never knew that such an occupation as a calker was mentioned in "the impregnable rock of Holy Scripture," as Mr. W. E. Gladstone called the Bible! It was while gathering material for this present volume that I came across a chapter on calkers in Dinsdale Young's book on *The Sanctity of Daily Life*. A master of memorable words, Ezekiel the dramatic prophet is the one who used this strange, maritime word, twice over, in a most powerful way (27:9, 27). The term is modern as well as ancient — like everything else in God's Word.

Webster defines a calker in a threefold way —

1. One who drives tarred oakum, or cotton twist or wicking, into the seams between the planks of a ship or boat to prevent leaking.
2. To tighten a joint formed by overlapping plates by driving the edge of one plate into the surface of the other.
3. To stop up the crevices of, as of windows.

A calk itself is explained as being a piece of tempered metal projecting downward on the shoe of a horse to prevent slipping — also a similar device worn on the sole of a shoe for the same purpose.

Doubtless in Ezekiel's day calkers were carpenters who built and filled up the joints of a ship, hence, the marginal rendering of the word, "stoppers of chinks." The Hebrew word for calkers means "strengtheners," which is most suggestive. One of the Hebrew words used in the Old Testament for "repair" is the same Ezekiel uses for "calkers." Is it not blessed to know that God Himself is the divine Calker? Isaiah speaks of Him as "The repairer of the breach" (58:12). How many breaches there are for Him to repair in so many of our homes, and in other relationships of life! What power is His to fill in the seams of a life to prevent it from sinking.

It is the other significance of calkers, however, that intrigues one, namely, "strengtheners." In Ezekiel 27 Ezekiel is found powerfully and prophetically depicting the fall of the proud and affluent Tyre, which the prophet compares to a gallant and imposing ship with wise men as its "calkers." Surely such a ship with the ample endowments indicated by Ezekiel would have a prosperous voyage and end up honorably! The tragedy is that the ship was destined to destruction with its ruin complete even to falling "into the heart of the seas" with even its calkers forever obliterated. What a picture of the doom of Tyre, and how such an ancient prophecy has been ancient history for centuries!

If ship and boats, even the grandest and best equipped of them, or others not so costly and magnificent, need "calkers" or "strengtheners," have not humans, whether high or low, constant need of calking? Are you a spiritual calker? Is this not the necessary ministry Isaiah had in mind when he wrote? —

They helped every one his neighbour; and every one said to his brother, Be of good courage (margin, Be strong).

So the carpenter encouraged the goldsmith (41:6-8).

Dinsdale Young says that "the goodliest vessels, as they sail life's ocean, have times when they cry out for 'calkers.' Ordinary quiet folk can often be 'calkers' to such as are in many ways superior to them. My brother, you need not be a genius to be a 'calker,' and a graciously effective one.' To those who are laden with trials, discouraged by the way, or who have yielded to temptation, we can be the means of undergirding them with strength. Prayer for others can work miracles.

It will be noticed that the "ancients" or "elders" were "calkers" to Tyre, and while the gathered experience of age can help others from becoming shipwrecks, all of us whether old or young, can join the army of strengtheners. Ezekiel also says that "wise men" were "calkers," and it is commendable when wisdom is not wasted on selfish ends but used for the encouragement and uplift of others. Although Tyre had "calkers" to help her, she yet ignominiously perished, teaching us that human agencies, beneficial though they may be, are not sufficient in themselves. God Himself must be our refuge and our strength. As the divine Calker, He never fails (Psalm 46:1).

The Captain

Used frequently in the Bible, this military term is represented in the Old Testament by thirteen different Hebrew words, and means a "prince," "officer," "chief," "ruler," as well as a military commander. Ezekiel often employed the term as the secular head of the Messianic kingdom. The New Testament has three or four Greek words for captain.

1. It was the Greek word for the Persian vizier, for the Roman military

tribune, the commander of a Roman cohort made up of about 1,000 soldiers, constituting the garrison of Jerusalem (John 18:12; Acts 21:31-37; 22: 28; See Mark 6:21; Revelation 6:15; 19:18).

2. Another word is *strategos,* from which we have "strategy," a term made up of two words *stratos* — an army, and *ago* — to rule. Originally representing the commander of an army, captain came to denote a civil commander, a governor, the high magistrate, or any other civil officer in chief command (Acts 16:20, 22, 35, 36, 38). It is used of the chief captain of the temple, a Levite, having command of the Levites who kept order in the temple and guarded it by night (Luke 22:4, 52; Acts 4:1; 5:24, 26; See Jeremiah 20:1).

3. Still another Greek word for captain means author, leader, initiator and is used thus of our Lord as the One who initiated our salvation (Hebrews 2:10, See Joshua 5:14, 15). As the "Author" or "Captain" (Hebrews 12:2), Christ is the One who took the lead in, and provided the first occasion of our faith. (See Acts 3:15.)

How condescending it is on the part of our great God to offer Himself as our Captain. "God himself is with us for our captain" (II Chronicles 13:12). Because of His almightiness, He is well able to order and prosper the battle for His good soldiers. In his elaborate exposition on "Christ, the Captain," old Benjamin Keach has this observation, and application of the occupation of a captain —

A Captain doth not only come off a conqueror, but improves his conquests and victories to many degrees of advantage.
1. To the discouragement of adversaries.
2. In spoiling their forts and strength.
3. In the erecting of trophies.

4. In disposing the prey, to gratify and reward his. soldiers with him in the war.

Then Keach goes on to apply the simile to Christ —

Jesus at His first coming did weaken the kingdom of Satan, spoiled principalities, set up trophies of His victory, made a shew of them openly, led captivity in triumph, and will complete the work of His second coming (Ephesians 4:9; Colossians 2:15). Then He will take the old dragon and bind him for a thousand years (Revelation 20:2, 10). Delivering up the Kingdom to the Father (I Corinthians 15: 24, 28), Christ will retain the honorable title of the Captain of our salvation for ever, even for ever.

The Carpenter

This word, describing a most important occupation, is actually a contraction of *cart*penter, literally one who makes carts. Most of the workers in wood mentioned in the Bible, were foreigners, thus the new cart carying the Ark of the Lord sent back from the country of the Philistines was made there (Genesis 45:19; Numbers 7:3, 7, 8; I Samuel 6:7, 10, 14). The woodwork for Solomon's temple came from the capable hands of the carpenters from Tyre (II Samuel 5:11; I Kings 5:18; I Chronicles 14:1; 22:15). It was probably after the Exile that the Israelites adopted the trade (II Kings 24:14, 16; Jeremiah 24:1). The first time carpenters are mentioned in the Bible is in connection with the repair of the Temple during the reign of King Josiah (II Kings 22:5, 6; II Chronicles 24:12). Out of the thirteen references to carpenters in Scripture only four references specifically state that they were artificers in wood (II Samuel 5:11; II Kings 12:11; I Chronicles 14:1; Isaiah 44:13). The other references (Ezra 3:7; Isaiah 41:7;

Jeremiah 24:1; 29:2; Zechariah 1:20), denote any kind of a craftsman, but especially a "worker in timber" (I Chronicles 22:15). Says Hastings —

> Elsewhere in the Old Testament carpenter (also Matthew 13:55; Mark 6:3) probably surpassed in variety those of any other craftsman, for they comprised not only those of the modern carpenter and cabinet-maker, but also of the ploughwright, woodcarver and other specialized arts and crafts of today.

Archaeological discoveries and bas-reliefs and murals describe some of the tools used by workers in wood in Bible days. Various axes and hatchets are mentioned (Deuteronomy 19:5; Psalm 74:6; Jeremiah 10:3). Then we have the necessary hammer, or wooden mallet in those days (Judges 4:21), the saw (Isaiah 10:15), the measuring line or "rule" (Isaiah 44:13); the sharp metal pencil or "stylus" for outlining the work; planes or more likely chisels and compasses (Isaiah 44:13).

While carpenters are not mentioned, they must have been active in Noah's time, seeing that the Ark, meant to float rather than sail, is the first wooden construction we read about in the Bible. "Noah was a preacher of righteousness, and the building of the Ark was his sermon. . . . Every plank Noah laid, every pin Noah and his sons fastened, called out to men, 'Judgment is coming.'" In spite of any opposition or ridicule encountered, Noah went on building, preparing "an ark for the saving of his house." When the wooden house was finished, God said, "Come thou, and all thy house, into the ark." Then God shut the door. If other carpenters, apart from Noah and his three sons, assisted in the creation of the Ark, it is terrible to realize that they perished in the waters of judgment. Helping to construct the means of salvation they failed to take advantage of a God-planned avenue of escape from the deluge. Is it not sadly possible to be associated with Christian work, yet in spite of a Christian profession and activity, die in sin and be lost forever because of failure to enter the ark of salvation?

Isaiah gives us an amusing description of a carpenter of wooden articles (Chapter 48). The prophet ridicules the ideal of an idol being able to do anything good or bad. A carpenter takes a piece of oak or pine — wood that will not soon rot — and with his tools fashions an object like a human being or beast. Chips and shavings are gathered from the floor to make a fire to cook and to warm his hands, and the carpenter's product is set up in a temple or house of worship. People bow before the idol of wood and praying to it say, "Deliver me, for thou art my god!" Isaiah shows that the strangest use to make of timber, skill and time is to expend them in the making of a god. The product of the carpenters which the prophet pours contempt upon, is no more ridiculous than the idols men fashion with their own hands today and worship.

One of the mysteries of grace is the fact that Jesus in His humiliation became a carpenter who, in His day, was a village joiner. He was not only a house carpenter but also a wright making most of the field implements such as plows, yokes, goads and saddles. The people of Palestine made use of the services of woodcutters, carpenter-joiners, cabinetmakers, and wood-carvers, and Joseph of Nazareth, our Lord's foster father was proficient in these arts. While Jesus Himself never spoke of the trade of His youth, His references to woodworking and to stone-working testify to His personal knowledge of these trades (Matthew

7:13, 24; 16:18; 21:33; Luke 14:28; 20:17; John 2:20). Is He not referred to as a carpenter Himself? (Matthew 13:55; Mark 6:3).

In His boyhood days, Jesus would note how all sorts of people would come to Joseph's humble workshop to order new wares or to have old things mended. How intently He would watch Joseph as he took a plank, planed and fashioned it into a utensil or farm implement! Can we not imagine how Joseph would teach Jesus how to use the saw, chisel and hammer, and how to drive nails?

Like any other Jewish lad of His time, Jesus would leave school at the age of fifteen and, according to custom, being the oldest in the family, would follow the trade of the home. As Joseph was a carpenter, quite naturally Jesus went to the bench and wrought at the same trade making doors and window shutters, laying beams and floors of houses and fashioning yokes for the oxen and plows for the farmers. The villagers would bring their broken things for Him to mend, which was most fitting, seeing He had come to mend a broken world. His fifteen years in the carpenter's shop provided Jesus with a deep insight and also with forceful illustrations for His oral ministry.

Some of you may know that poem by G. A. Studdert Kennedy, an Army chaplain in the First World War, who, because of his protest of the distribution of cigarettes among the soldiers in the trenches, became known as "Woodbine Willie." His poem, with the title, *It's Hard to be a Carpenter*, goes —

> I wonder what He charged for chairs
> At Nazareth.
> And did men try to beat Him down,
> And boast about it in the town,
> "I bought it cheap for half a crown
> From that mad carpenter?"

> And did they promise and not pay,
> Put it off to another day,
> Oh, did they break His heart that way,
> My Lord, the Carpenter?

Such an expressive poem proves forcefully that Jesus had to face the difficulties and testings of a normal working life. Although, when He was thirty, He gave up His practical work to become a preacher and teacher, He must have felt that His years at the bench were important years in His development. Further, if the Son of God spent most of His life on earth working with His hands, we can see how feasible it is to be a Christian *and* a working man — or woman. (See under Introduction — *The Choice of a Trade*).

The Greeks thought of manual labor as being beneath them, and somewhat degrading. But Paul wrote to the Greek Church, "Let it be your ambition to keep calm and look after your own business, and to work with your own hands, as we ordered you" (I Thessalonians 4:11, NEB).

When He came to die, carrying His own heavy cross would remind Him of the beams He used to carry at Nazareth. Accustomed to wood and nails He had them as He died. Strange, is it not, that the wood, made up as a cross, spoke of His occupation. Then others fixed two pieces of wood into the cross and drove the nails through His hands and feet, and, after His death, with the end of a hammer two other men drew out the nails with great skill and gentleness, while they held His limp body. How appealing is the picture of Holman Hunt of the workshop at Nazareth. Joseph is dead and Jesus is the carpenter. Mary enters and, for a moment, her eye catches sight of a shadow cast upon the wall. It is the shadow of two arms stretched out against a rack of tools which takes the form of a cross. Jesus, tired at His work, has let go the saw, that He may utter His evening prayer and in doing so He stretches out His weary arms. It is the shadow of the cross.

Observe the expressive lines of George Macdonald —

O Lord, at Joseph's humble bench
Thy hands did handle saw and plane,
Thy hammer nails did drive and clench,
Avoiding knot and humouring grain.

Lord, might I be but as a saw,
A plane, a chisel, in thy hand! —
No, Lord! I take it back in awe,
Such prayer for me is far too grand.

I pray, O Master, let me lie,
As on thy bench the favoured wood;
Thy saw, thy plane, thy chisel ply,
And work me into something good.

No, No; ambition, holy-high,
Urges for more than both to pray;
Come in, O gracious Force, I cry —
O workman, share my shed of clay.

That I, at bench, or desk, or oar,
With knife or needle, voice or pen,
As thou in Nazareth of yore,
Shall do the Father's will again.

Thus fashioning a workman rare,
O Master, this shall be Thy fee:
Home to Thy Father Thou shalt bear
Another child made like to Thee.

The Centurion

During the existence of the Roman Empire, the centurion represented an influential position in the Roman army. From the word "century" (an hundred), a centurion was an officer in command of a hundred men, and it was a rank corresponding, more or less, to that of a captain in modern armies. It was exclusively a New Testament occupation, although there were commanders of hundreds in the Israelite army (Numbers 31:14; I Samuel 22:7; II Samuel 18:1; I Chronicles 13:1; 26:26; 27:1; 28:1; 29:6; II Chronicles 1:2; 23:1, 9; 25:5). The centurions mentioned, both named and unnamed, were all sympathetic officers. The sacred writers, with propriety, present them in a favorable light.

Frequently mentioned in gospel history, centurions, whose ordinary duties consisted of drilling a hundred soldiers, inspecting their arms, food and clothing, and commanding them in the camp and in the field, were sometimes posted on detached service as seen in the case of the conduct of Paul to Rome. Both Cornelius and Julius, the only two named centurions, appear to have been taken from the legion in which there were sixty centurions, for discharge of special duties. Evidently there were several centurions stationed at Jerusalem under the chief captain (Acts 21:31). From a carving on an ancient tomb, a centurion is presented wearing a helmet and a more ornate harness of better quality. By courage and loyalty a centurion could work his way up from the ranks of ordinary soldiers and be commissioned as an officer by the general of the Roman army. Good conduct was the outstanding qualification for promotion.

The more conspicuous New Testament centurions can be developed into a most profitable meditation. For instance we have —

The centurion outstanding for his faith (Matthew 8:5-13; Luke 7:2-10).

This Roman officer, recognizing that Jesus was far superior to himself called Him, "Lord." The language he used of himself denotes his position and power. Sending a request to Jesus for the recovery of his dying servant, he expressed the faith that if Jesus but gave a word at a distance the desired effect would assuredly follow, as it did. Commending the centurion for his faith, Jesus said, "As thou hast

believed, so be it done unto thee."
For a full treatment of the miracle
performed, the reader is directed to
All the Miracles of the Bible.

*The centurion who confessed Christ's
Deity* (Matthew 27:54; Mark 15:39,
44, 45; Luke 23:47).

What a remarkable testimony Christ
received from this Gentile! How striking was the homage he paid to the
crucified One at Golgotha! Whether
the centurion understood the full import of his declaration or not, is difficult to determine. Without doubt, he
knew that Jesus was totally different
from all other prisoners he had dealt
with.

"Truly, this was the Son of God"
(Matthew and Mark). "When
the centurion saw what was done
he glorified God, saying, Certainly this was a righteous man"
(Luke).

This centurion's confession of Christ's
deity is the more impressive seeing
that Jesus had been condemned by
the Jewish leaders for claiming to
be "the Son of God." Thus, as Fairburn puts it, "It was ordered that an
intelligent heathen confessed the very
faith which the Jewish rulers repudiated and by so doing became a sign
of the transference of the kingdom
from Jewish to Gentile hands."

*The centurion who became a bap-
tized Christian* (Acts 10.)

This Roman, a Gentile by birth, is
presented as a devout man, and one
who feared God with all his house,
before he became a confessed Christian. It seems most likely he knew all
that transpired at Calvary, and of
what his fellow-centurions had said
about Jesus Christ at His death. Pious
and charitable, truthful and straight-
forward, he was open to conviction,
and became the willing recipient of
the Gospel. Of these three centurions

we have dealt with, Fairbairn comments that —

All the three, indeed might be regarded as signs of a like description,
for as the faith in each one of them
was remarkable, so there is in the
application made of it a distinct point-
ing, in one form and another, to the
gathering of the heathen into the fold
of Christ.

Among other centurions in apostolic
times, we have the one whom Paul
questioned as to his rights as a Roman
citizen (Acts 22:25, 26); and Julius,
the only other centurion to be named
in the New Testament (Acts 27:1, 6,
11; 28:16). It was this kind of officer
who entreated Paul most courteously
and saved his life when threatened by
the soldiers. Then we have his gracious care of Paul during the voyage
to Rome, and of his oversight of the
apostle until he delivered his charge
over to the Roman authorities. While
at first he was not willing to accept
Paul's advice during the stormy voyage (Acts 27:11), we can imagine
how, ultimately, he came, not only to
admire Paul for his faith (27:24, 25),
but as the result of the miracles at
Melita (28:1-10), to recognize the
reality of Christianity. What a thrilling story he must have told to his
fellow-centurions when he returned
from his special assignment!

The Chamberlain

The importance of this position, and
the fact that it was one of considerable influence, is gathered from the
desire of the people of Tyre and Sidon
when they sought the favor of Herod
Agrippa through the mediation of
Blastus, the king's chamberlain (Acts
12:20). Blastus did not have charge
of the treasure chamber, but the king's
bedchamber, and was the equivalent
to a chief valet, responsible for the

king's wardrobe and other personal matters. It was a position involving honor and intimacy. It was this aspect Thomas Hood, of the 18th century, had in mind when in adapting the office, he wrote —

> Guilt was my grim chamberlain,
> That lighted me to bed.

In the Old Testament a chamberlain was akin to a eunuch, that is, an officer oriental monarchs placed in watchful charge of their harems (Esther 1:10, 12, 15, etc. II Kings 23:11). At times, the term is equivalent to a "cupbearer" or "steward." In modern parlance a "chamberlain" is a treasurer or receiver of public money and is known as the city chamberlain. In Europe, the occupation denotes one of the high officers of a court. In London, the Lord Chamberlain has charge of the royal palace. He sends out the sovereign's invitations, telling them how to dress in coming to the palace. The New Testament usage of the term implies a manager of a household, or a city treasurer responsible for keeping accounts of the city's revenues. Erastus, we read, was "the treasurer of the city" (Romans 16:23). If the Erastus Paul mentions as being at Corinth (II Timothy 4:20), is the same person it would seem as if he had resigned his position as treasurer in order to become a traveling evangelist and assistant to Paul, proclaiming the treasures of grace. Here we have another illustration of an occupational name becoming a surname, for among English-speaking peoples Chamberlain is a fairly common name.

The Chancellor

The only chancellor mentioned in the Bible is Rehum who three times over is identified with his profession (Ezra 4:8, 9, 17). In the Apocrypha "chancellor" is rendered "story-writer" (I Esdras 2:17). Sayce translates the term as "postmaster." Among the Assyrians the office represented someone who was "master, or lord, of intelligence." In his Concordance, Young interprets the word as meaning, "Master of taste, counsel, reason." Martin Luther speaks of the magistrate who restored peace at Ephesus at the time of the riot against Paul as "chancellor" (Acts 19:35). With us today a chancellor represents various offices —

1. The chief minister of state in certain European countries.
2. The chief secretary of an embassy.
3. An official secretary of a nobleman, prince or king.
4. The chief judge in England — the Lord Chamberlain.
5. The head of a university.
6. A member of the British cabinet in charge of public income and expenditure as the highest finance minister of the government — the Chancellor of the Exchequer.

Ben Jonson, of the 16th century, in his tribute to Lord Bacon, wrote —

> England's high Chancellor, the destined heir,
> In his soft cradle, to his father's chair,
> Whose even thread the Fates spin round and full
> Out of their choicest and their whitest wool.

It is said that the office of chancellor was introduced into England by Edward the Confessor, and under the Norman kings, the chancellor was made official secretary of all important legal documents.

The Chapman

Occurring only once in Scripture (II Chronicles 9:14) a chapman was a traveling merchant in ancient times.

In the ERV of I Kings 10:15 "chapman" is given in the place of "merchant-man." The ASV has "trader" in both references. Chapman is still used in some areas for a traveling merchant. Originally chap was a man, properly a merchant, and a chapman a merchantman. Hence the saying, "If you want to buy, I'm your chap." A chap-book, a small, inexpensive book containing stories or ballads, was so called because it was sold by chapmen. The Hebrew significance of the word implies "those who go about" as merchants.

The Charmer

The four references to this ancient occupation make interesting reading (Deuteronomy 18:11; Psalm 58:5; Isaiah 19:3; Jeremiah 8:17). The word itself means to charm, juggle, fascinate, and opens up a study of charms, magic and sorcery, which old-time charmers trafficked in. For a further treatment of all that is related to the practice of occult arts by these magicians or enchanters, the reader is referred to the material found under *The Sorcerer*. At this point, we simply draw attention to the charming of snakes practiced long ago (Ecclesiastes 10:11; Jeremiah 8:17).

The Cheesemaker

How ancient, yet modern, is the Bible! In these days when almost all nationalities produce a variety of cheeses, and cheese-making has become a trade of some importance it may surprise you to know that such an art goes back to the time of Job (10:10). David's brothers, and David himself, had to have their cheeses (I Samuel 17:18; II Samuel 17:29). The milk of large and small animals was a staple article of food, and was usually kept in skins. The cheese made di-

rectly from the sweet milk resembled our cottage cheese (Deuteronomy 32:14; Judges 4:19; Proverbs 27:27; 30:33). Fairburn remarks that "the want alone of any fixed term for cheese, and the rareness of the allusions that appear to be made to the subject in Scripture, are clear signs of the very inferior place which it had as an article of food among the ancient Hebrews." Oddly enough there are twenty references to butter or cheese in the New Testament. The Tyropoeon valley in Jerusalem received its name, The Valley of the Cheesemakers, from the industry carried on there and probably was where they all lived.

The Clerk

The Greek word used for clerk is *grammateus* from which we have "grammar," and as used by Luke, the historian, means a writer, or scribe (Acts 19:35). The scribes of the Old Testament frequently mentioned along with "the recorder," seem to have attended to the royal correspondence. (See further under *The Scribe*.) In Roman times, the town clerk — an office of dignity and responsibility — was a public accountant or secretary, chosen by the people, chiefly to register the names of the conquerors and their rewards, publicly in the theater. Decrees were first approved by the senate and then sent to the assembly, which formally passed them. At Ephesus, the town clerk feared that he would have to account to the Roman governor for the irregularly constituted assembly. "The Roman administration viewed any irregular or unruly assembly as a grave and even capital offense, as tending to strengthen among the people the consciousness of their power and the desire to exercise it." Hence, the town-clerk's alarm, and his effort to appease the mob gathered by Demetrius the silversmith against the gospel preachers (Acts 19:35-41). Fausset says that "his speech is a model of judiciousness and perfectly carried his point. Such excitement, he reasons, is undignified in Ephesians, seeing that their devotion to Diana of Ephesus is "beyond question" (See Proverbs 15: 22). With us, a town clerk is an important elected official who keeps the records of a town.

The Comforter

A look at a Bible concordance surprises one how much there is about comforters and comfort in "the comfort of the Scriptures" (Romans 15:4). When Jesus said that He would not leave His own comfortless, or orphans, (the word comfortless is *orphanos* from which we have "orphan") He meant it, and supplied them with a divine Comforter and comfort in abundance. "The term signifies bereft of a father, parents, guardian, teacher, guide and indicates what must be the permanent ministry of the Holy Spirit to the disciples of Jesus, in comforting their hearts." In harmony with these parting words Jesus had called the chosen twelve "little children" (John 13:33), without Him they would be "orphans" — comfortless, desolate. The coming of the Holy Spirit would make Christ and the Father forever real to them, an abiding spiritual presence.

Let us first consider the heart-warming word comforter used twelve times in the Bible (thirteen with the same, original word, advocate of I John 2: 1). The word Jesus used for comforter means "one called alongside to help" and is similarly used by the apostles (John 14:16, 26; 15:26; 16:7; See II Corinthians 1:4; Ephesians 6: 22; Colossians 4:8; I Thessalonians 4: 18). As used of the Holy Spirit, Com-

forter suggests that He is One both willing and capable of giving aid. The term denotes an advocate in court, one who intercedes, a teacher, an assistant. In the widest sense our Lord promised to send His disciples another helper like Himself. There are two Greek terms for our English word another — "*allos*" another of the same sort and "heteros" another of a different sort. It was the first word Jesus used when He said "another Comforter" — another like Myself. Vine reminds us that "comforter" or "consoler" corresponds to the name Menahem given by the Hebrews to the Messiah.

Alas, there were those who failed to find a comforter to console them (Psalm 69:20; Ecclesiastes 4:1; Lamentations 1:9)! Job found his friends to be "miserable comforters" (16:2). The margin gives "troublesome" for "miserable." Instead of helping to assuage Job's grief they only added to it by their persistent charge that he deserved all his afflictions.

The term "comfort" and "comfortably" represent inward joy, strength, consolation, support, assistance, (Genesis 5:29; II Samuel 10:3; Job 6:10; 10:20), as well as encouragement with alleviation of grief. To "speak comfortably" means to speak to the heart with a degree of tenderness, and is an Hebrew expression for "wooing" (Ruth 2:13). It was thus that Joseph spoke to his brethren winning them from fear to confidence (Genesis 50: 21). David was urged to win back the hearts of the people in like manner (II Samuel 19:7; See II Chronicles 30: 22; 32:6; Zechariah 1:13; John 11:19, 31; I Thessalonians 5:14). While we use "comfort," "console" and "solace" as interchangeable terms, there may be a shade of difference between them.

Comfort. This homely, intimate

term implies the imparting of cheer, hope and strength as well. Fort means "strength." There is also in this oft-used word the addition of the lessening of pain.

Console. Webster says that this word "emphasizes the alleviation of grief or the mitigation of the sense of loss rather than distinct relief."

Solace. Consolation in trouble, or the lifting of the spirit bringing relief from loneliness, sadness, as well as from grief or pain, is here implied. How true it is that the multitudinous comforts of God delight the soul (Psalm 94:19)! If, for any reason, these comforts have been lost, the promise is that they can be restored (Isaiah 57:18). Is it not encouraging to know that we have God (Isaiah 66:13; Romans 14:4; II Corinthians 1: 4), Christ (Matthew 9:22; John 14: 16, 18), the Holy Spirit (John 14:16, 26; 15:26; 16:9; Acts 9:31), the Scriptures (Isaiah 40:2; Romans 15:4) and the Saints of God (II Corinthians 7: 6, 13; I Thessalonians 4:18) as our comforters to cheer and assist us amid the sorrows and trials of our earthly pilgrimage?

Shakespeare has the line in *King Henry VIII* — "Now I am past all comforts here, but prayer." Yet what a great source of comfort prayer is. To carry all our sins and grief to the divine Comforter is a sure source of relief. May we always remember that the Holy Spirit is our present Author of abiding comfort — the Scriptures, the established grounds and means of it — godly friends the instruments and helpers of it (Job 10:21; Psalm 119: 49, 50; II Corinthians 1:5-7; 7:6, 7). Comforted of God, are you exercising this God-like ministry?

The Commander

While this occupation is mentioned only once in the Bible there are hun-

dreds of references to commands and commandments, etc. "Behold, I have given him . . . a leader and commander to the people" (Isaiah 55:4). Here, the term means "one who commands, gives precepts, and sets up." While the verse refers primarily to the historic David (Psalm 78:70, 71), they were realized fully in Christ who came as "the faithful and true witness" (John 18:37; Romans 1:5; 3:14), and the "captain" or "leader" of our salvation (Hebrews 2:10). The Latin philosopher, Cicero, wrote, "It is necessary that he who commands well, should have at some time obeyed." Jesus is the perfect Commander, and commands well because He delighted to obey His Father, even unto the death of the cross. Byron speaks of those who have power to sway others "with that commanding art." Is not this art our heavenly Commander's in an abundant measure? As the Creator of all, He has the right to command all, even nature itself (Isaiah 5:6; 45: 12; Romans 4:7). For ourselves, His commands are not grievous, and what He commands, He supplies for His commands are His enabling.

To command implies at least two things:

1. To charge by authority (Deuteronomy 11:22).
2. To cause a thing to be done (Isaiah 5:6; 13:3).

Is it not blessed to know that God commands the blessing of life, or the strength of His people, when by His will and power He furnishes it (Psalm 68:28; 133:3)? "Give what Thou commandest then command what Thou wilt."

The Confectionary

While this particular occupational word occurs only once in the Bible and should be placed under the section dealing with Female Occupations, seeing that women are mentioned as confectionaries (I Samuel 8:13), we include it here because it was likewise a male occupation (Exodus 30:35). Fuller reference to this art can be found under THE APOTHECARY. The ASV renders "confectionaries" as "perfumers," and "confection" as "perfume," the latter word meaning "something put together or compounded." When the King James Version was being translated a confectionary meant a person who compounded drugs, medicines and perfumes, but not sweetmeats as common today. With us a confectioner is a tradesman who handles an ever-growing variety of sweets and candies. The French for "confection" is *confiscrie,* implying "to candy," thus the fancy confectionary proprietor calls himself a *confiseur.*

The confection was a preparation of sweet spices. The fourfold ingredients were as stated (Exodus 30:34-36), and were used in incense and perfume to be offered to God in the sanctuary. It is from this perfume that David draws his analogy, "Let my prayer be set before thee as incense" (Psalm 141:2); and which is also typical of Christ who offered Himself upon the cross for a sacrifice of a sweet-smelling savor. All who are His are likewise as a sweet-smelling savor (II Corinthians 2:15; Ephesians 5:2).

The Cook

Evidently both males and females were cooks in early Bible times (I Samuel 8:13; 9:23, 24) — the males slaughtering, as well as cooking animal food. Samuel's cook was commanded to serve Saul with a choice portion of meat. Cooks of both sexes existed at kings' courts, for when the Israelites were impatient to be given a king, Samuel said of them when he did appear that he would take their

daughters to be cooks. Egyptian monuments and bas-reliefs sometimes depict kitchen scenes, in particular the royal kitchens of Rameses III(See I Kings 4:22, 23).

As to the articles of food in use among the Israelites and surrounding nations, the reader is referred to the summary found in any well-known Bible encyclopedia. Food, it would seem, was divisible into two main classes —

1. *Vegetable Foods.* Going back to primitive habits, there is reason to believe that in general, men were vegetarians rather than flesh eaters (Genesis 2:16; 3:2, 6). Divine permission to eat animal flesh was first given to Noah after the Flood (Genesis 1:29 with 9:3). Chief place among foodstuffs which cooks used were wheat, barley, fine flour, meal and millet. Then there were edible "herbs" in general — "things that are sown" (Genesis 25:29, 34; Numbers 11:5; Isaiah 61:11; Ezekiel 4:9). Then there was the food of trees — "plant all manner of trees for food" (Leviticus 19:23; Job 15:33) — such as olives, figs, grapes, dates, mulberries, nuts, etc.

2. *Animal Foods.* Originally, people were confined by law to the cooking and eating of animals and birds regarded as "clean" (Leviticus 11:2, 3; Deuteronomy 14:4-20; II Samuel 12:4). Goats, sheep, gazelles, hart, fish and various birds were prized. Doubtless professional cooks were not numerous, as they are today. As we have already seen, bakers were numerous enough to give their name to a street, or bazaar, where they baked and sold bread to the public. The majority of people, being poor, cooked their own food. We cannot subscribe to the proverb that "God sends meat; the devil sends cooks." Douglas William Jerrold, of the 18th century, wrote, "The greatest animal in creation, the

animal who cooks." Many of us bless God for a devoted wife who is a good cook.

The Coppersmith

While the Bible mentions only one who followed this occupation, namely, "Alexander the coppersmith" (II Timothy 4:14), the numerous references to workers in copper or brass (Genesis 4:22; Ezra 8:27), testify to an extensive use of this metal. Because in the Hebrew, copper bears the same name as bronze, the latter being an alloy of copper and tin, wherever brass is mentioned copper is meant, seeing bronze is not a natural metal (Deuteronomy 8:9; Job 28:2; Ezekiel 22:18). Excavations have yielded remains of copper tools, vases, mirrors, implements of all kinds containing little or no tin. The discovery that the mingling of copper with other minerals gave a harder, more durable metal, quickly spread, and was widely used. The word copper itself is derived from an old name belonging to the island of Cyprus, the metal being known to the ancient as Cyprian brass, probably because that island was one of the chief sources for this metal. Tyre is mentioned as having copper mines (Ezekiel 27:13).

That the Israelites knew how to dig out and smelt metals is clearly evident from different Scriptures (Deuteronomy 4:20; 8:9; Ezekiel 22:18). Their mirrors were of polished copper (Exodus 38:8, margin) and their bows were made of the same metal (Psalm 18:34; Hebrew), as were their helmets (I Samuel 17:38). They must have had some secret of rendering copper harder than ours is. It was hard, well-tempered and capable of taking a fine polish and therefore was of high value. Bronze is less subject to tarnish and takes on a finer polish. Brass, with its component element of zinc, was not known to the ancients.

Alexander the coppersmith, or artificer in bronze, belied the name he bore. Alexander means "the helper of men," but he was the hinderer of Paul (I Timothy 1:20) and did the apostle much evil. Excommunicated from the church, Alexander withstood Paul and made shipwreck of faith and of good conscience, and even blasphemed with Hymenaeus. The excommunication often brought with it temporal judgment, as sickness, to bring the excommunicated to repentance. But there is no evidence that the coppersmith, delivered to Satan, ever repented (I Corinthians 5:5; II Corinthians 12:7; II Timothy 4:15, 17).

The Cosmetologist

Although the actual word "cosmetics" is not in the Bible, its root is in the term *cosmos* meaning arrangement, beauty, or world. "God that made the world and all things" (Acts 17:24). Great is His beauty, and everything from Him bears the imprint of His loveliness. The cosmetologist is one who practices the art of beautifying the skin with salves, cosmetics and other contrivances which beauticians use. In the section dealing with THE APOTHECARY, reference is made to perfumes and scents. Here we are dealing solely with the use of cosmetics by women millenniums ago. Although women, almost the world over, are spending colossal sums of money on all kinds of make-up accessories making cosmetics, thereby, one of our chief and more profitable industries, their efforts to begin where nature left off, are by no means new. Many writers, like Corswant and Bailey, who bring us interesting information about aspects of Eastern life in Bible times, draw attention to objects like toilet accessories, ointment pots, small make-up instruments, and cosmetic scoops of wood and ivory found in women's tombs.

Quite recently the daily press carried a report from Jerusalem of a cosmetics factory of 2,500 years ago discovered in a hill near En-gedi, an Israel settlement on the western shores of the Dead Sea. Professor Benjamin Magar, the Hebrew University archaeologist who led the expedition in this area, said that large barrels, jars of design never found here before, and small gracefully shaped perfume jars support the idea that at least some of the buildings unearthed were used for the manufacture of balsam — one of the most precious perfumes of the ancient world. An alabaster ointment vessel imported from Egypt and Syro-Phoenician pottery was found. This we do know, that in Nehemiah's time Jerusalem had a corporation of perfumers who possessed a technique which was already ancient, or imported their goods from abroad (Exodus 30:25; Nehemiah 3:8).

Since Jezebel's day, and probably long before, women have resorted to cosmetics in order to enhance their beauty. A. E. Bailey in *Daily Life in Bible Times* says that from the representations of people we find on monuments, reliefs, seals and plaques, and also from the testimony of graves we can know in certain particulars how women adorned themselves. Describing Sarah, for example, A. E. Bailey after enumerating what the wife of Abraham looked like, goes on to speak of her make-up in this informative way —

Her compact consisted of a couple of scallop shells from the Persian Gulf — one to hold the cosmetics and one for a cover. Her colors, whether paint or powder we do not know, could be green and black anyway, and in ad-

dition a little white, red, yellow and blue for extra touches as occasion required. Just when she applied the colors we do not know. At her girdle she carried a small conical copper box with leather cover that held her toilet-kit, tweezers, ear-pick, stiletto, and a round-ended paint stick. More than likely at home she kept a bronze razor, and used cuttlefish bone as a depilatory. When she was ready for parade she must have been a beauty. Though she may have discarded a good deal of this town make-up when her husband became a nomad, she kept it by her for occasion. According to the story in Genesis 12:12-16, where she went back to civilization for a time in Egypt, even Pharaoh could not resist her.

For Christian women today, the use or nonuse of cosmetics is a matter to be settled personally, and in the light of apostolic teaching that those who are the Lord's should be more concerned about the possession of a lovely character rather than the creation of artificial beauty (I Timothy 2:9; I Peter 3:3). If only some women we know spent as much time on their knees as they do before a mirror, what attractive saints they would be. The most enviable form of beauty is not applied but acquired by faith. It is the never-failing "beauty of the Lord" (Psalms 27:4; 45:11).

The Counsellor

Often referred to in Scripture, this occupation is described in many ways — as a lawyer or judge (Daniel 3:2, 3), as one who gives counsel (II Samuel 15:12), as a man of counsel (Psalm 119:24), as a viceroy (Daniel 3:27; 6:7), as well as a counsellor (Isaiah 40:13; Mark 15:43). Because a council is an assembly of counsellors, or persons in consultation (Acts 25:12) there is not much to choose between a counsellor or councillor. Perhaps the latter was more of an official adviser than the former. Among the most notable of Bible counsellors is the wealthy Joseph of Arimathaea, who placed his grave at the disposal of Jesus (Matthew 27:57; Mark 15: 43). A counsellor, it would seem, was a confidential adviser (Romans 11: 34), one who gave counsel, or dispensed justice (Daniel 3:2, 3). In these modern times a counsellor is one whose profession is to give advice in law, and manages causes for clients in court.

The Lord is known as a Counsellor, and His promises are the expression of His immutable counsel. The promises are quoted in proof of His immutabilty (Hebrews 6:17, 18). The Trinity deliberately planned the whole part of our salvation; and, as each within the blessed Trinity are possessed of infinite wisdom and knowledge, they can direct and admonish us in all things (Isaiah 46:10; Acts 4: 28). Because the Lord is wonderful in counsel (Isaiah 28:29), He is able to counsel us aright (Psalm 16:7) through His testimonies as our counsellor (Psalm 119:24).

I've found a Friend, oh, such a Friend!
So kind, and true, and tender,
So wise a Counsellor and Guide,
So mighty a Defender!

The Craftsman

Already, when dealing with THE ARTIFICER we have seen that in some cases both craftsman and artificer are from the same word *technites*, from which we have technique or art (Acts 19:24; 19:38; Revelation 18:22). Craft, however, is used in a bad sense, as well as a good one. For instance, when Jesus' enemies tried to take Him by craft (Mark 14:1), the word here means guile, deceit, a bait (See also Job 5:13; Luke 20:23; I Corinthians

4:2; Ephesians 4:14). When Paul wrote "being crafty, I caught you" (II Corinthians 12:16), he implied that he tried in every way to win the Corinthians. But usually the word stands for a particular art or trade (Deuteronomy 27:15; II Kings 24:14, 16; Hosea 13:2; Acts 19:25). Nehemiah refers to Lod and Ono, as being the valley of craftsmen (11:35).

The volume in your hands is an attempt to classify the various and varied crafts which are directly or indirectly mentioned in the Bible. A fuller knowledge of the arts and crafts of ancient times has come to us from Assyrian, Babylonian and Egyptian written and illuminating records. Examples of ancient handcraft, buried and preserved through centuries, have also been discovered to add confirmation to Biblical records. Extensive explorations in Egypt have given to the world many priceless relics of superb craftsmanship, some of them dating from the very dawn of civilization. Many secrets perished with those old-time craftsmen. Many modern artists, for example, would like to know how some of those early painters mixed such abiding colors. Craftsmen of long ago seemed to have had so much pride and pleasure in their work. Even today the Arab has many phrases of encouragement for a man at his work, such as, "Peace be to your hands," "May God give you strength." In these days of automation and mass production, much of the skill of craftmanship has vanished. Whatever task we represent, whether secular or spiritual, may we be workmen that needeth not to be ashamed, as Paul expresses it (II Timothy 2:15, 16).

The Cupbearer

Under THE BUTLER we pointed out that cupbearer and butler are equivalent terms. Therefore, all we are drawing attention to in the repetition of this occupation is to speak of the cup that was used. The Hebrew for "thou shalt deliver Pharaoh's cup into his hand" is "I placed the cup upon Pharaoh's palm" (Genesis 40:13), the word for "palm" being the same as used of the *hollow* of Jacob's thigh (Genesis 32:25). As used by Joseph in the interpretation of the butler's dream it means the hollow produced by bending the fingers inward. The Hebrews always spoke of placing the cup in a person's hands (Psalm 75:8; Jeremiah 51:7; Ezekiel 23:31). "Joseph, though probably speaking in the Egyptian language, nevertheless used the Hebrew idiom, saying, 'Thou wilt give Pharaoh's cup into his hand,'" comments Ellicott. "It is the Egyptian cupbearer, who, using the idiom of his own country, speaks of placing the cup upon Pharaoh's palm, the reason being that Egyptian cups had no handles or stems, but were flat bowls or saucers, held in the very way the cupbearer describes."

The Daysman

This expressive occupational term is elsewhere translated as reprove, rebuke, chasten, convince, reason, decide, plead and chasten, "Neither is there any daysman betwixt us, that might lay his hand upon us both" (Job 9:33).

The word "daysman" as used by Job implies a judge, intercessor, referee, arbitrator. The margin of the KJV and ASV gives, "one that argues," "an umpire." The combination days — man arose from the use of the word "day" in a technical sense, to signify a day for dispensing justice, a day of trial. Originally, it was dais — man, a man who sits on a dais; a sort of lit de justice. Hence Peirs Ploughman —

And at the day of doom
At the height of Deys sit.

The same word "daysman," or judge, is connected with the Scripture phrases, "the day of the Lord"; "the day shall declare it" (I Corinthians 3:13). Paul speaks of 'man's judgment" or "man's day" (I Corinthians 4:3). Tyndale translates Exodus 21: 22, "he shall paye as the dayesmen appoynte him." The oldest instance of the term given in 1489 reads, "Sir, the dayesmen cannot agree us."

"It was the Eastern custom for a Judge," says A. W. Evans, "to lay his hands upon the heads of two parties in disagreement, thus emphasizing his adjudicatory capacity and his desire to render an unbiased verdict. Job might consider a human judge as capable of acting as an umpire upon his own claims, but no man was worthy to question the purposes of Jehovah, or *metaphorically* to 'lay his hands upon' Him." In Christ we have a Mediator on a level with God, and also on a level with ourselves, the God-Man, Jesus, who brings God and man together. Through the blood of His cross we were reconciled to God. Did not Christ Himself say that "no man cometh unto the Father but by Me" (John 14:6)? "One Mediator . . . between God and men" (I Timothy 2:5; See Job 19:25-27).

The Deliverer

For the ten references to a deliverer, some five different words are used to describe his activities. He saves (Judges 3:9, 15); snatches away (Judges 18:28); lets escape (II Samuel 22:2; Psalms 18:2; 40:17; 70:5; 144:2); looses (Acts 7:35); rescues (Romans 11:26). That the Bible has a great deal to say about deliverance of all kinds is evident from the hundreds of times the word is employed.

While there were human deliverers raised up by God and endowed with skill and power to emancipate His people (Judges 3:9, 15; Acts 7:35), in the majority of cases He Himself is presented as the Deliverer (II Samuel 22:2; Psalms 18:2; 40:17; 70:5; 144:2; Romans 11:26). For many instances of His power to deliver run your eye over the passages in the concordance where He acted in this manner.

The English word for deliver is used in two general senses, namely "to set free," and "to give up or over." The various Hebrew and Greek words for "deliver," recur more than 600 times in Scripture. The most frequent translation means to "set free," "to draw out," "to let or cause to escape" (Genesis 32:11; Psalms 25:20; 143:9; Isaiah 46:2; Matthew 6:13, etc.). Another frequent word is *nathan* meaning "to give over, up," "to give" (Genesis 32:16; 40:13; Hosea 11:8; Matthew 5:25; 11:27, etc.). Other original words for "deliver" imply "to bring forth" (Genesis 25:24; Exodus 1:19, etc.), "to restore" (Genesis 37:22; Deuteronomy 24:13).

Old Testament deliverers, like Moses, Joshua, Gideon, and others, were national deliverers of Israel from physical bondage and distress, and were types of Him who is the God of deliverances (Psalms 32:7; 68:19, 20 ASV), and of the Lord Jesus Christ who came preaching deliverance to the captives (Luke 4:18). Deliverer is one of the titles by which the victorious Captain of our salvition is designated (Romans 11:26; I Thessalonians 1:10; Hebrews 2:14, 15). Among the many aspects of His power as the Deliverer, He can emancipate us from the devil and all his wiles and works (Psalm 18:17, 19; Luke 1:74, 75; Colossians 1:13; II Timothy 4:17, 18), from the fear of death, coming wrath

and hell (Psalm 86:13; Hebrews 2:14, 15; I Thessalonians 1:10), from trials, trouble and transgression (Psalms 34:6, 19; 39:8; 81:7; 91:15).

Our obligation is to claim by faith the full release which the mighty Deliverer has for each of us. We must call upon Him, and trust His promise, and when delivered bless and glorify His name (Psalms 50:15; 72:11; 91:15; 106:43; Jeremiah 1:18, 19; 39:18; Daniel 3:28).

He comes, the prisoners to release,
In Satan's bondage held;
The gates of brass before Him burst,
The iron fetters yield.

The Destroyer

While there is a connection between the previous occupation considered, and the one before us, for often deliverers are destroyers, yet we separate the two because many destroyers revel in their destruction. As destroy, and its cognates occur over 700 times in the Bible, we need to know who our destroyers are, what they are out to destroy, and how we can be delivered from the paths of any destroyer (Psalm 17:4). Here, again, we have a variety of original terms of one specific word. For instance, the word the Psalmist used for destroyer means, a "burglar" or "one who breaks in or forth." The devil is the satanic burglar out to rob us of God and of eternal peace but a Greater than the devil can keep us from his paths (Psalm 17:4). Although he is a cruel destroyer, let us never forget that Satan is a defeated one, and is subservient to the will of God.

Often the word used of destroyer signifies a supernatural agent of destruction, or destroying angel, executing divine judgment (Exodus 12:23; Job 33:22; Hebrews 11:28, ASV. See II Samuel 24:16, 17; Isaiah 37:36; I

Corinthians 10:10). "Stroy" or "strew," meant "to scatter things" around, to which "strewn" is closely related. To construe implies "to put two and two together." To construct something is to put things together, and to destruct is to reverse the process — destroy what is builded. Destruction as used of the wicked (John 3:16; Hebrews 11:28), does not mean annihilation, extinction or cessation of being, but ruin or loss of well-being hereafter (Matthew 10:28; Luke 13:3, 5). If a sinner lingers and dies in his sin he is so ruined as to be unfit to serve the purpose for which God intended. There are cases where destroy is translated by words meaning, "to render idle, unemployed, inactive, inoperative." They are put, not out of existence, but out of business, "made without effect" (Romans 6:6; I Corinthians 6:13; Galatians 5:4), "brought to nought" (I Corinthians 1:28). In a right, just sense God is a Destroyer of all the works of the wicked one. He puts them out of action, just as He will put the devil himself out of action when he is cast into eternal fire (Revelation 20:10). Cowper in *The Task* writes of a king —

> As dreadful as the Manickean god,
> Adored through fear, strong only
> to destroy.

But the King of kings is strong not only to destroy. True, He is the enemy of all evil, and metes out destruction upon everything persistently antagonistic to His holy nature. As the God of love, however, His heart yearns to deliver all who are under the dreadful power of him who is the god of this world.

The Divider

A divider, or a judge, is one who divides into equal parts, as heirs to an inheritance should do (Luke 12:

13). The word divide is capable of several meanings, "to mark off by boundaries or limits, to separate" (Matthew 12:25); "to take asunder, to distribute into parts" (Luke 15:12; I Corinthians 12:11), "to discriminate, to be at variance with oneself, to be divided in one's mind" (James 2:4, ASV), "to cut straight or to handle aright" (II Timothy 2:15). What is intended here is not dividing Scripture from Scripture, but teaching Scripture accurately. God is renowned as a divider in creation, history, redemption and judgment (Genesis 1:4-18; Deuteronomy 4:19; Psalm 60:6; Isaiah 51:15; 53:12; Daniel 5:28). The Bible likewise is a great divider (Hebrews 4:12). It was Goethe who wrote —

> Divide and rule, a capital motto!
> Unite and lead, a better one!

"Divide and rule" is not always a capital motto. Dictators and the devil are actuated by such a hellish motto. Alexander Pope was nearer the truth when he penned the lines —

> Each would the sweets of sovereign
> rule devour,
> While discord waits upon divided
> power.

"Unite and lead" is a more pleasing motto we have.

The Diviner

The majority of Bible diviners are presented in a bad light. Correct divination does not come, even as Horace affirmed, from Apollo —

> Whatever I state either will come to
> pass or will not,
> Truly the great Apollo has given me
> the art of divination.

Coleridge was more correct when he said that, "On a divine law divination rests." Diviners, and their divination, bring us to the subject of sorcery as practiced in Bible times. There is a sense in which prophecy resembles divination in that the Spirit-inspired were able to peer into the future and predict coming events. Old Testament prophets were not only *forth*-tellers, echoing forth a God-given message for their own times, but also *fore*tellers with prophecies related to times beyond their own. As Fairburn expresses it —

> Divination differs from prophecy, in that the one is a human device, while the other is a divine gift; the one an unwarranted prying into the future by means of magical arts, superstitious incantations, or natural signs, arbitrarily interpreted; the other a partially disclosed insight into the future, by the supernatural and of Him who sees the end from the beginning . . . . In Scripture language the diviners were *false* prophets and divination was allied to witchcraft and idolatry (Deuteronomy 18:10, 18; Joshua 13: 22; Jeremiah 27:9).

The divination of true prophets was divine, that is, of God. It is interesting to observe that the word most commonly used for divination, which means, "to divide, to apportion lots" is used of false prophets and soothsayers (Deuteronomy 18:10, 18, etc.); of necromancers, who professed to evoke the dead (I Samuel 28:8); of heathen augurs and enchanters (I Samuel 6:2; II Kings 17:17; Zechariah 10:2); of making prognostications by means of arrows, inspection of entrails, etc. (Ezekiel 21:21); of arts and incantations (Genesis 44:15; Numbers 23:23; 24:1). Charmers, enchanters, witches and wizards, were the media of divination. God enacted stringent laws against divination, and repudiated all forms of it. Diviners were deceivers, and all who acted upon their divinations were dupes of fraud and deception (Leviticus 19:26, 31; 20:6, 27; Deuteronomy 18:10-12). We also have the vehement declarations

of the prophets in connection with the practices of divination (I Samuel 15: 23; Isaiah 8:19; Jeremiah 14:14; 29:8, etc.).

As to the numerous methods of divination practiced by the Egyptians, Babylonians, Canaanites and Syrians, and from which the Israelites had difficulty in freeing themselves (I Samuel 28; Hosea 4:12), the following are mentioned more fully by Corswant in his dictionary.

The examination of the liver of sacrificial victims; the condition of this organ permitted all sorts of infinitely precious oracles to be derived from it (Ezekiel 21:21).

Consultation by means of a cup, from patterns produced by fragments of precious and brilliant substances thrown into a goblet of water, or the shape taken by one or more drops of oil poured on water in a metal bowl (Genesis 44:5, 15).

Divination by arrows bearing a name or signs — the first drawn from the quiver indicating direction, or town to be attacked first (Ezekiel 21: 21; Hosea 4:12).

Observation of the flight of birds was common to the Greeks and Romans. There is a probable allusion to the observation and interpretation of the course of clouds and serpents by Moses (Leviticus 19:26; See II Kings 21:6).

Dreams were reckoned to be interpretative of God's will. Cultivating the art of interpreting dreams, played an important part in ancient times (Genesis 40; 41; Jeremiah 23:27; 29: 8).

Evoking the spirits of the dead, and, by ventriloquism, imitating the voice of a dead friend, was often practiced by soothsayers as we shall see when we come to THE NECROMANCER (Deuteronomy 18:11; I Samuel 28; II Kings 21:6; Isaiah 8:19; 29:4).

Astrology, as we saw when dealing with THE ASTROLOGER, was practiced by many peoples, particularly the Mesopotamian as the best means of discovering the mysteries of life and the future (Daniel 2:27; 4:7; 5:7, 11).

The practice of incantations and sacred delirium, provoked by heady vapors or the use of spirits and narcotics was likewise common (Isaiah 47:12; Jeremiah 27:9; Nahum 3:4). Different forms of soothsaying were countenanced by certain kings and flourished unchecked until Josiah's reform abolished them (I Samuel 28; II Kings 9:22; 21:6; 23:24). In New Testament times there were magicians and exorcists who practiced divination, but who were made to cease their evil art under the mighty power of God (Acts 8:9; 13:6-8; 16:16; 19:13; See Revelation 19:10). For the child of God the infallible Scriptures are the only media of revelation as to the future.

The Doctor

Generally, we think of the medical doctor when we use this term. If a loved one is ill we hasten to call the doctor. In the Bible, however, those known as doctors were teachers of the Mosaic Law, were mostly Jewish rabbis, and in great repute among the Jews. Doctor means to lead, to teach, and that which is taught is doctrine (Luke 2:46; 5:17; Acts 5:34 — doctor of the law — I Timothy 1:7). Lord Bacon called Paul, "The Doctor of the Gentiles."

In early Latin, doctor meant, "learned" and was used by medieval universities as the title for their degrees, and is still employed in this way. Thus an M. D. is a "Doctor of Medicine," and Ph. D, a "Doctor of Philosophy," and so on. Such a title also describes honorary degrees, as well as earned ones. For instance, a D. D. is a "Doctor of Divinity." It is to be regretted that honorary degrees have been cheapened by the appearance of disreputable degree mills, providing all kinds of degrees, as worthless as the parchment describes them.

For the exposition of the medical aspect of the term "doctor," the reader is referred to the study under the section of THE PHYSICIAN, in which Bible physicians and their methods of healing are dealt with.

The Dyer

While dyers are not mentioned in the Bible dyeing is, and as the latter is not possible without the former, there must have been such an occupation in antiquity. Dyeing is one of the oldest of the crafts. Clothing, hangings and veils, bright with colors greatly loved by the Israelites, Egyptians and other Eastern peoples prove the production of colored material by expert hands. Several archaeologists believe, not without reason, that traces of dyers' workshops exist in some Palestinian ruins. That the art of dyeing was known and practiced as early as the time of the Exodus is evident from the fact that one of the coverings of the tabernacle was "rams' skins dyed red" (Exodus 25:5; Judges 5:30, ASV). Ezekiel also speaks of "dyed attire." From ancient monuments and remains found in Egyptian tombs there is ample proof of the perfection of dyeing in the time of Moses. Pliny mentions that the production of colors was known to the ancient Egyptians.

An interesting fact is that Tola and Pual (Judges 10:1, "Tola the son of Pual"), are colors, as well as clan names. Tola means "the scarlet dye" and Pual was the name of another dyestuff known as "madder" which was used for producing "Turkey red" on cotton and for dyeing dull reds on wools for rug making. It was the custom near Damascus for a father to plant a new *madder* field for each son that was born, which later became his inheritance.

It is thought that the Jews acquired from the Phoenicians the secret of dyeing — a trade in which they excelled — and later held the monopoly in this trade in some districts. A Jewish guild of purple dyers is mentioned on the tombstone in Hieropolis. A Jewish stronghold in Asia Minor, Akhissar by name, was famous as a dyeing city. In the twelfth century the Jews were dyers and glass workers at Tyre. From the Mishna, it is clear that in New Testament times, dyers were a numerous and flourishing body in Jerusalem, and employed both animal and vegetable dyes.

In his fascinating volume, *Archaeology and the New Testament*, Dr. Merrill F. Unger writes that —

> On Greek inscriptions are met woolworkers, linenmakers, tailors, tanners, potters, bakers and even slave-dealers . . . Another was the guild of dyers, who made a specially famous purple ("Turkish red") from the madder root of the region, rather than from the shell-fish as the Phoenicians did. Lydia of Thyatira seems to have represented her guild at Philippi (Acts 16:14), where she sold her dyes and dye stuffs.

Doubtless ancient methods of dyeing appear somewhat crude alongside our modern ways of coloring different materials. To dye rams' skins red, the skin would be tanned in sumac, then laid out on a table and a solution of dye rubbed on. After the dye is dry, the skin is rubbed with oil and finally polished. Bedouin shoes made up of this colored material are attractive. Wool was usually dyed before or after being spun (Exodus 35:25). Because of the simple method of dyeing, dyers usually colored their hands and their arms to the elbow with a rich indigo or turkey red, a feature Shakespeare in his *Sonnets* uses with effect —

> My nature is subdued,
> To what it works in, like the dyer's hand;
> Pity me then and wish I were renewed.

As to the colors dyers worked with, the same are used with considerable latitude in the Bible in which colors are often referred to in different terms marking certain shades, or which vary according to the objects described. Then the symbolism of many of these colors adds richness to the Bible's color vocabulary.

White

The prevailing color of the Palestinian sheep being white (Song of Solomon 4:2; 6:5), and likewise the color of the snow (Psalms 51:7; 68:14; Isaiah 1:18), white is identified with linen, clothes and wool (Esther 1:6; 8:15; Ecclesiastes 9:8; Mark 9:3). Symbolic of innocence, purity, joy, nobility and elegance (Esther 8:15; Isaiah 1:18; Ecclesiastes 9:8), white is used to describe the throne of God, Christ, angels, saints, agents of God (Psalm 51:7; Zechariah 1:8; 6:3; Matthew 17:2; Mark 9:3; 16:5; Luke 9:29; Revelation 6:2; 19:14).

Yellow

The word rendered greenish was probably a greenish yellow, since it is also used of "yellow gold" (Leviticus 13:49; 14:37; Psalm 68:13). This attractive color, although rare in the Bible is suggested by dove's feathers which may have been golden or tawny yellow glints. Jeremiah speaks of faces changing color and becoming pale yellow (30:6). See also the yellowish stain of leprosy (Leviticus 13:49; 14:37), and the yellowish color of the plague horse (Revelation 6:8).

Black

Darker colors, like black and brown, merge into each other, and are not clearly distinguishable. Jacob's small cattle "ring-straked, speckled" (Genesis 30:39), showed white mixed with black or brown in the case of the sheep, and black mixed with white in the case of the goats. Laban's black sheep were probably dark brown (Genesis 30:32, ASV). Black also signifies dark-complexioned (Song of Solomon 1:5; Hebrew). The symbol of vexation, death and judgment (Jeremiah 8:21; 14:2; Zechariah 6:2, 6; Revelation 6:5), black was the color of tents, hair, horses, ink and the torrent blackened by melting ice (Song of Solomon 1:5; 5:11; Job 3:6; Zechariah 6:2, 6; Revelation 6:5).

Red

The word for red is likewise used of the reddish-brown color of the red heifer and of the chestnut horse (Numbers 19:2; Zechariah 1:8). Note the precise color distinction between red and its companion sorrel (bay, Zechariah 6:3, 7). Red, the color of blood, of the sky, of the eyes, of wine (II Kings 3:22; Proverbs 23:31; Song of Solomon 5:10; Isaiah 63:2, 3; Nahum 2:3; Matthew 16:2) — where red means "the color of fire," is symbolically used of the apocalyptic horses and of the dragon (Zechariah 1:8; 6:2, 3; Revelation 6:4; 12:3). Interesting, is it not, that red is the color denoting godless Communism?

Green

Green, we are told, is not a color adjective (Esther 1:6, ASV margin), but a noun signifying green plants and herbs (Genesis 1:30; Mark 6:39). As we have already noted, a kindred word rendered greenish (Leviticus 13:49; 14:37), is probably a greenish yellow (Psalm 68:13). The color of the grass, gardens, leaves, wood, unripe fruit (Genesis 1:30; 9:3; Exodus 10:15; Deuteronomy 12:2; II Kings 16:4; 19:26; Job 39:8; Psalm 37:2; Mark 6:39; Revelation 8:7), green is expressive of vigor and prosperity (Job 15:32; Psalm 92:14; Jeremiah 11:16, 17; Daniel 4:4; Hosea 14:8). In nature green is everywhere and so restful to man, and nourishing to animal life.

Blue

The difficulty in deciding the exact color expressed as blue is found in the fact that purple and blue are two shades of purple, the red tone predominating in the former, and the blue tone in the latter. Since blue predominates in our modern purple, it would be well to drop the cumbrous terms red-purple or purple-red, and blue-purple and purple-blue, in favor of the simpler names of purple and violet, as in the margin of Esther 1:6; 8:15. Both shades were obtained by the use, as a dye, of a colorless fluid secreted by a gland of a shellfish which was found in great quantities on the Phoenician coast. Priestly, royal, and costly garments were conspicuous for the sky color of blue (Exodus 25:4; 27:16; 28:31, 37; Numbers 15:38; Esther 8:15; Jeremiah 10:9; Ezekiel 23:6; 27:7).

Purple

The original word for purple denoted the purplefish and then came to describe the purple dye extracted by the Tyrians for the shell fish murex purpura. Tyre became the chief manufacturing center of the purple cloth for which Phoenicia was famous throughout the ancient world (Ezekiel 27:7, 16). This color, a deep red, tinged with violet, found secreted in the gland of shellfish caught off the coasts of Africa, Asia Minor and Phoenicia (Acts 16:14), was of great value and thus became the characteristic color of royalty, power and fortune (Exodus 25:4; 26:1, 31, 36; 35:25; Judges 8:26; Esther 1:6; 8:15; Song of Solomon 7:5; Proverbs 31:22; Ezekiel 27:7; Jeremiah 10:9; Daniel 5:7, 16, 29; Revelation 17:4; 18:12). Worn by kings, the Jews derisively robed Jesus, "the King of the Jews" in purple (Mark 15:17; John 19:2).

Crimson

Both crimson and scarlet are shades of the same color, and were both from the same insect, termed in Hebrew, "the scarlet worm." The Phoenicians, who were past masters of the art of making and using this coloring matter, obtained it by crushing a tiny cochineal insect or its dried eggs. From ancient times down until 1850, this was still used for wool and silk. As the word crimson is from a term meaning, "a little worm," it is profitable to note that Jesus, in prophecy, speaks of Himself as a "worm" (Psalm 22:6). At Calvary, Jesus was crushed resulting in His crimson blood being able to make the black heart of the sinner whiter than the snow (Isaiah 1:8). Scarlet-colored garments were regarded as a mark of distinction and prosperity, and symbolize purity, slaughter and apostasy (Genesis 38: 28, 29; Exodus 25:4; 26:1; II Samuel 1:24; Proverbs 31:21; Matthew 27:28; Revelation 17:3 - 6; 18:12 - 16).

Vermilion, mentioned as a pigment (Jeremiah 22:14; Ezekiel 23:14), was associated with crimson. Israel used minium, a colored matter of mineral origin, probably lead oxide, and a fine, vivid red for frescoes and mosaics. Gray occurs only in the expression "gray hair," while grisled, literally "gray" apparently means black with white spots (Genesis 31:10; Zechariah 6:3, 6).

The four liturgical or ecclesiastical colors, as listed in the priests' code (Exodus 25) were blue, purple, scarlet and white. Fine linen thread, spun from yarn, was dyed in the first three colors. Natural white thread was used in weaving the rich material for the various hangings of the tabernacle, and for certain parts of the priests' dress (Exodus 35:25).

Joseph's "coat of many colors" — a fine ankle-length tunic with sleeves (Genesis 37:31 - 33) — was a garment made up of pieces of cloth of different colors. Joseph's Coat, is the name of two American ornamental plants with variegated foliage. During the American Civil War cloth was so scarce that rugs and carpets were cut up and made into overcoats. Men who wore such coats were called Josephs in allusion to Joseph's coat of many colors.

It was the dyers' art of blending colors that inspired Alexander Pope to pen the lines —

All manners take a tincture from our own,
Or come discolored through our passions shown.
Or fancy's beam enlarges, multiplies,
Contrasts, inverts, and gives ten thousand dyes.

As a lad, I was greatly intrigued by a slogan outside a dyers' establishment which I often passed. It read —

We dye to live
We live to dye.

The Embalmer

Although there are only four references to embalming (Genesis 50:2, 3, 26), it was an art practiced by the physicians, and one, the secrets of which have been almost lost. Today, physicians attend only to the living —

unless a post-mortem, an examination to find out the cause of death, is ordered. But Egyptian physicians could do what modern physicians cannot do, namely, embalm bodies so that they did not decay.

That ancient embalming was a remarkable trade, or art, is proven by the fact that in some of our museums there are mummies with discernible features. If Jacob's tomb is discovered, who knows, we may yet know how he looked. This we do know, professional embalmers cared for the body of the patriarch (Genesis 50:1, 2). In Egyptian vaults, great numbers of mummies have been found after a lapse of two or three thousand years. A specifically Egyptian method of treating dead bodies, embalming is mentioned in the Bible only in the cases of Jacob and Joseph. Our Lord's body was wrapped by Nicodemus in "a mixture of myrrh and aloes, about an hundred pounds weight . . . . as the manner of the Jews is to bury" (John 19:39, 40). This, however, was quite distinct from embalming. It was prophesied that His body should not see corruption (Psalm 16:10), thus He needed no embalming to preserve His body from decay seeing He was to rise again on the third day after His death.

Burial is first mentioned in connection with the death of Sarah (Genesis 23:4). Abraham paid Ephron the Hittite four hundred shekels of silver for the cave of Machpelah for a family burial place. While burial came to be the Hebrew law and custom, we do not know for certain whether the Hebrews originally cremated their dead. Tacitus, the Roman historian, mentions that the Jews buried instead of burned their dead in accord with the almost universal practice of the time. If the Jews, before they became Jews, cremated their dead, it is possible that Abraham, who had lived in Egypt, borrowed the burial custom from the Egyptians, and after the Egyptian manner embalmed their dead. Thus both Jacob and Joseph were embalmed. Even after the destruction of Jerusalem and the Temple by the Romans in A.D. 70 under Titus, many Jews scattered throughout the Roman Empire embalmed their dead and brought them back to Judea for burial.

Embalming and burial were practiced by the Egyptians because they thought the soul could not survive the dissolution of the body. Doubtless belief in the resurrection of the body did much toward instituting the Hebrew practice of embalming and burying some of their dead, instead of burning them as virtually all ancient peoples around the Mediterranean did. Generally, however, the Israelites paid great attention to the care of corpses without actually embalming them. Here, for example, is how W. Corswant summarizes the usual practice of burial —

Immediately after death, the deceased's eyes were closed with a kiss and his toilet performed. In ancient times the dead man was clothed in his usual attire, for, in the realm of the dead, the king was recognized by his diadem, the warrior by his sword, the prophet by his cloak; but according to the New Testament, we know that in Roman times — and the natives of Palestine still today observe the same customs — the corpse, having been washed and scented with aromatic substances, was wrapped in a linen cloth, a napkin was placed on his head and his feet and hands were bound round with little bands. This sort of embalming was very different from that practiced by the Egyptians, but certain people devoted considerable sums to the purchase of funeral spices.

As to the process of embalming as practiced by the Egyptians, Herodotus, the ancient historian, gives us a detailed account of the long and costly method involved in this art in which the Egyptians excelled. The time for embalming was forty days, then followed seventy days of mourning (Genesis 50:1, 2, 25, 26), while the cost of embalming was a "silver talent" or around 750 dollars (250 pounds). Prices varied according to the ability of relatives to pay. The brain and the intestines were removed from the corpse, and then the preservation of it was made possible by saltpeter, myrrh, aloes and other substances, which were either wrapped around it by means of bandages, or were placed in its cavities by incisions made in the corpse. The embalmed body was then placed in a coffin on the lid of which were painted features of the deceased. Sometimes these coffins were placed upright against the wall, a perpetual *mento mori* to the survivors. Generally, however, embalmed bodies were buried in a rock or subterraneous vault in the ground. After the lapse of centuries many preserved mummies have been discovered therein. Doubtless, the Egyptian method of burying in the sand impregnated with salts and natron, which preserved the body, first suggested the process of embalming, creating thereby, a distinct class of embalmers who became famous throughout the then known world.

The embalming of the body of Jacob must have cost Joseph a great sum of money. Grief, however, that grows out of love is apt to be extravagant. Before Christ died a woman who was a sinner broke her alabaster box of precious ointment, and poured its contents upon the Master's feet. "Against the day of my burying hath she kept this" (John 12:7). The woman lavished what she could ill afford

on Jesus while He was yet alive. She did not keep all the violets for the grave, or kind words for the adornment of a tombstone. Is there not a lesson in all this for our hearts?

The Enchanter

The dictionary describes an enchanter as one who lays others under a spell by charms or sorcery, or who delights or fascinates in a high degree. An enchantress is either a woman of bewitching charms or a sorceress. Old Testament enchanters were suave and subtle, charming and crafty, persuasive yet pernicious in their influence. Enchanter is probably a Babylonian word, meaning, "one who used conjurations." Much that we have written under THE DIVINER is applicable here for although enchanters represent their own particular mode of divination, they are one with sorcerers, wizards, magicians and soothsayers, practicing the necromatic art in numberless forms. Nine varieties of the occult arts are referred to in one single passage (Deuteronomy 18:10, 11; Jeremiah 27:9).

Enchantment is an Old Testament term used to describe the employment of various charms, and all kinds of magic arts as the following passages prove (Exodus 7:10-22; 8:7, 18; Leviticus 19:26, 31; Numbers 23:23; 24:1; II Kings 17:17; 21:6; Ecclesiastes 10:11; Isaiah 2:6; 47:9, 12; 57:3, etc.). The Bible alone refers to these arts, either supposedly or pretentiously supernatural, as being common to all Oriental races. They were practiced in Chaldea (Daniel 5:11), Babylon (Ezekiel 21:21), Assyria (II Kings 17:17), Egypt (Exodus 7:11), Canaan (Leviticus 18:3, 21; 19:26, 31), Asia (Ephesus, Acts 19:13, 19), Greece (Acts 16:16), Arabia (Isaiah 2:6). The Mosaic Law strictly forbade the countenance of secret arts, which constituted a peculiar temptation to Israel to apostatize (Deuteronomy 18:9-12). Enchanters, whose incantations were by lustral fires, fumigations, fascinations and illicit charms, were forbidden by God seeing they were a constant incentive to idolatry, clouded the mind with superstition, and were closely allied to deception (Matthew 24:24). To all such the godly Jew had to say, "Dear delusion, sweet enchantment, hence!"

The original terms used for the word, enchantment, indicate its manifold operations and subtlety. Dwelling on these various terms Dwight M. Pratt says that the first word means "to wrap up," "muffle," "cover," hence "clandestine," "secret." This hidden element enabled the magicians to impose on the credulity of Pharaoh in imitating or reproducing the miracles of Moses and Aaron. "They . . . did in like manner with their enchantments" (Exodus 7:11, 22). But they were utterly unable to perform a genuine miracle. (Exodus 8:18).

Another word implying "to hiss," "whisper," refers to the mutterings of sorcerers in their incantations. The Latin word for enchant — *In-canto* means to sing over or against someone. The Hebrew term *nahash* (Deuteronomy 18:10; II Kings 21:6, etc.) also means "serpent," and conveys the idea of cunning and subtlety employed by the enchanters. Divination by serpents was the form of prognostication sought by Balaam (Numbers 24:1). God's people, however, were immune against such enchantment (Numbers 23:23). Shalmaneser forced this forbidden art upon the captive Israelites (II Kings 17:17). Elijah protested against this heathen practice introduced during the apostasy under Ahab (I Kings 21:20).

A further word means "to whisper," "mutter" and indicates the imitation of the hiss of serpents. The offensive practice of serpent-charming is referred to by Solomon (Ecclesiastes 10:11). See "the voice of charmers (ASV margin enchanters), charming never so wisely" (Psalm 58:4, 5; Isaiah 3:3). The art of charming serpents, known as Ophiomancy, is still practiced in the East.

Then we have another word meaning "to bind with spells," "fascinate," "charm," descriptive of a species of magic practiced by binding knots — a method indicated by the monuments of the East. This particular word is also used of the charming of serpents (Deuteronomy 18:11; Psalm 58:5). Isaiah makes clear the moral mischief and uselessness of all forms of enchantment (Isaiah 47:9, 12).

We also find another word implying "to cover," "to cloud," hence "to use covert arts," and suggests a form of divination associated with idolatry. Auguries were gathered from the clouds (Isaiah 2:6; Micah 5:12). This practice of augury, or uttering oracles in a state of divine frenzy, was forbidden by Moses (Leviticus 19:26; Deuteronomy 18:10, 14). Forms of magical art are mentioned in the New Testament where we have jugglers (II Timothy 3:8, 13), seducers (Revelation 2:20), magicians and soothsayers (Acts 8:9; 13:6, 8; 16:16; 19:13).

The excellent summary Dr. Pratt gives in his contribution to the subject of enchantment in *The International Standard Bible Encyclopedia* is worthy of repetition —

> All these forms of enchantment claimed access through supernatural insight, or aid, to the will of the gods and the secrets of the spirit world. In turning away faith and expectation from the living God, they struck a deadly blow at the heart of true re-

ligion. From the enchanters of the ancient Orient to the medicine-men of today, all exponents of the "black art" exercise a cruel tyranny over the benighted people, and multitudes of innocent victims perish in body and soul under their subtle impostures. In no respect is the exalted nature of the Hebrew and Christian faiths more clearly seen than in their power to emancipate the human mind and spirit from the mental and moral darkness, the superstition and fear, and the benighting effect of these occult and deadly arts.

The Engraver

Conspicuous in this most skillful art is God who carved the Law upon the two stones, or tables (II Corinthians 3:7), and Moses who, upon two stones, engraved the names of the children of Israel (Exodus 28:11). The New Testament word for graven is associated with the Greek term from which we have "character" (Hebrews 1:3, margin), and is frequently used in the last book of the Bible (Revelation 13: 16, 17, etc.). Engravers, working upon various hard objects like wood, ivory, metal or stone, left in what they carved the witness of their skills. Bezaleel's Spirit inspired workmanship was in gold, silver, brass (Exodus 35:3; 38:23), stone and wood (Exodus 31: 1-5).

"Carving" and "engraving" are used interchangeably in the Bible. The first reference to engraved objects is the signet, or seal, of Judah (Genesis 38: 18). Seal engraving, and engraving devices, the Israelites learned in Egypt; engraving existed in Mesopotamia from about 2,000 B.C. Assyrian and Egyptian cylinders bear the engraving of various seals. "From the earliest times it has been the custom in the Orient for men of affairs to carry constantly with them their signets," says James A. Patch. "The seal

was set in a ring, or, as was the case with Judah, and as the Arabs do today, it was worn on a cord suspended about the neck. One of the present day sights in a Syrian city street is the engraver of signets, seated at a low bench ready to cut on one of his blank seals the buyer's name or sign."

In addition to the strict engraving of the two onyx stones having six each of the 12 tribes' names (Exodus 28: 9-21) we have the prophet Zechariah's reference, "One stone . . . I will engrave (literally, *open the opening)* thereof" (3:9). Actually this implies as Fausset suggests, "I (God) will prepare for Him (Messiah) an exquisitely wrought body, a suitable temple for the Godhead (John 2:21)." The engraving of the stone is suggestive of the wounds, languor and passion of Christ, who is figured by that stone. He is the "stone cut out of the mountain without hands" (Daniel 2:45). "Mine ears hast Thou opened" (graven) by "a body hast thou prepared me" (Psalm 40:6; Hebrews 10: 5). His wounds are eternally graven upon His hands and feet. Paul had a body engraven with the marks of the Lord Jesus (Galatians 6:17).

Among the foreign nations, the Jews were associated with engraving. In particular stonecutting had reached a high degree of perfection, as some of the Egyptian temple-figures reveal. Even today men marvel at the workmanship of the Sphinx and the Pyramids. The hardest substance presented no difficulties to those ancient engravers. The prohibition imposed upon the Israelites, "Thou shalt not make unto thee any graven image" (Exodus 20:4), explains why engraving or sculpturing remained undeveloped among them, as it has to this day among the Moslems. The magnificent temple, however, with all its elaborate sculpturing and cherubim carved in its wooden fittings, indicate the employment of Jewish, as well as foreign, craftmanship (I Kings 6:23).

What a privilege is to be ours when His name is engraven in our foreheads! (Revelation 22:4). It means that we shall be the perfect reflection of Christ Himself (John 13:16; I John 3:2). Publicly and openly the mark will signify that we belong to Him. As the name represents the person, so His saints are to bear Christ's moral likeness and become who and what He is.

The Eunuch

Primarily, and literally, the eunuch was an emasculated man, or one naturally incapacitated for the purpose of marriage, and who, therefore, was appointed to guard harems found in all the royal palaces of Egypt, Babylon, Persia and Ethiopia (Daniel 1:3, 7; Esther 1:10-15; 2:3, 14; Acts 8:27). *Eunuch* actually means, "one who guards the bed." The eunuchs, being emasculated and deprived of their virility, were safe with the charge of wives, concubines and the female apartments of the palace. In the Persian court eunuchs were "keepers of the women," through whom the king gave commands to the women, and kept men at a distance (Esther 1:10, 12, 15, 16; 2:3, 8, 14). Daniel and his companions were possibly mutilated so as to become eunuchs of the Babylonian king (II Kings 20:17, 18; Daniel 1:3-7). Prisoners of war were often made eunuchs. Then we have the Assyrian Rabsaris, or chief eunuch (II Kings 18:17). Even the kings of Israel and Judah had foreign eunuchs (II Kings 9:32; Jeremiah 38:7), as guardians of the harem (Jeremiah 41: 16); and, for military and other important positions (I Samuel 8:15; I Kings 22:9; II Kings 8:6; 23:11; 25:1).

The Ethiopian, although a eunuch, was a great man, who rode in a chariot and had many attendants. As chamberlain to the queen of Ethiopia, he had charge of all her treasures (Acts 8:27-39). A *eunuchi* sometimes implied the high office of "chamberlain," without the accustomed emasculation. So the Ethiopian and a few eunuchs of the Old Testament may have been un-mutilated men (I Chronicles 28:1). Potiphar, for example, is spoken of as a "eunuch," or as the Hebrew implies, an "officer," but he was a married man with a child too, if Asenath was the daughter of Joseph's master, as some think (Genesis 39:1; 41:45). Sometimes eunuch is synonymous with cup-bearer.

Although eunuchs became important persons, acquiring position and power, their acquisition did not remove the sense of degradation and loss (II Kings 20:18; Isaiah 39:7). The barbarous practice of self-mutilation and the mutilation of others, prevalent throughout the Orient, carried with it serious religious disabilities.

The practice was abominable to the Jews as a people (Leviticus 22:23-25; Deuteronomy 23:1). Eunuchs were regarded as dry and useless wood (Isaiah 56:3).

The Law excluded eunuchs from public worship for two reasons. First, because self-mutilation was often performed in honor of a heathen god. Second, because a maimed creature of any kind was deemed unfit for God's service (Leviticus 21:21; 22: 24). Later, however, this ban was removed (Isaiah 56:4, 5).

Our Lord used "eunuchs" in a figurative sense (Matthew 19:12). "Were made eunuchs" may have been an allusion to those in the courts of Herod who were born continent from natural infirmity, or emasculated as "eunuchs of men." But Jesus employed "eunuch" as a term with reference to power, whether possessed as a natural disposition, or acquired as a property of grace, of maintaining an attitude of indifference toward the solicitations of fleshy desire. There has always been those noble souls "who have made themselves eunuchs for the kingdom of heaven's sake." They have abstained from marriage, and the use of carnal pleasures, so that free from the cares of the world, they could devote themselves more exclusively to the service of God. Geo. B. Eager, in his exposition of the subject before us says that —

> It is possible for men to attain as complete control of the strong instinct of sexual passion as if they were physically sexless, and the resultant victory is of infinitely more value than the negative, unmoral condition produced by self-emasculation. These "make themselves eunuchs" with a high and holy purpose, "for the kingdom of Heaven's sake"; and the interests created by that purpose are so absorbing that neither time nor opportunity is afforded to the "fleshly lusts, which war against the soul" (I Peter 2:11). They voluntarily forego marriage, even, undertake virtual "eunuchism" because they are completely immersed in and engrossed by "the kingdom of Heaven" (John 17:4; I Corinthians 7:29, 33; 9:5).

In the three classes of eunuchs, Jesus spoke of (Matthew 19:12), He permits, but does not command or recommend, celibacy as superior in sanctity to wedlock. Jesus recognized that marriage is the norm of man's condition, and that the union thereby effected, transcends every other natural bond, even that of filial affection (Matthew 19:5, 6). "He that is able to receive it, let him receive it." He used the term eunuch figuratively to describe those who naturally or arti-

ficially, or by self-restraint became divested of sexual passion (I Corinthians 7:26, 32, 34). Origen, one of the early fathers, misunderstood the figurative language of Jesus, and his own comment on Matthew 19:12 shows that he afterwards regretted having taken it literally, and acting upon it. It has been pointed out how significant it is that Jesus expressed no condemnation of the horrible practice of emasculation. "It was in keeping with His far-reaching plan of instilling principles rather than dealing in denunciation (John 3:17; 8:11). It was by His positive teaching concerning purity that we are shown the lines along which we must move to reach the goal. There is a more excellent way of achieving mastery of sexual passions." Paul, for instance, is a shining example of how to bring the body into subjection to a Spirit-controlled mind.

The Exchanger

The word Jesus used for exchangers in His parable of the talents means "one who sits at a table to change money" (Matthew 25:27). They were "changers of money" or "bankers" as the ASV expresses it (Mark 11:15; John 2:14). The table or stand of a moneychanger was where he exchanged foreign money for a fee, or dealt with loans and deposits (Luke 19:23; John 2:15). A full discussion of this occupation can be found under THE BANKER.

The Executioner

What a grim and undesirable occupation this term represents! It is from its Greek form that we have the English word speculator, which originally meant a look out officer, as a scout. It was an office requiring vigilance. Under the Roman emperors those represented thus were members of the bodyguard, messengers, watchers and executioners. The executioner responsible for the beheading of John the Baptist was a soldier of the guard of Herod Antipas (Mark 6:27, ASV). The office of executioner was a recognized one in all ancient nations. To "execute" usually implies to execute judgment, or vengeance (Exodus 12:12; Psalm 149:7; Jeremiah 21:12; John 5:27; Romans 13:4; Jude 15). Potiphar, whose official residence was also the public park, executed the king's sentence (Genesis 37:36 margin; 40: 3). See also Nebuzaradan and Arioch (Jeremiah 39:9; Daniel 2:14). George Stimpson in his most informative volume *A Book About the Bible* has an interesting paragraph dealing with the old-time custom of executing criminals on a Friday —

> The custom of executing criminals on Friday, which in Europe dates back at least to the Middle Ages, is supposed by some authorities to have arisen from the fact that Jesus was executed by crucifixion on Friday, the sixth day of the week according to the old Jewish calendar. In America, Friday used to be the favorite day for the execution of persons condemned for capital punishment. No adequate explanation has ever been offered as to why the sixth day of the week should be preferred as the day for execution. It is generally assumed, with some reason, that the ill luck associated with Friday by superstitious people arose from the connection of that day with the crucifixion of Jesus, . . . Friday was popularly known as hangman's day. . . . Curiously enough, the ancient Scandinavians, as well as the Hindus, regarded Friday as the luckiest day of the week.

The Exorcist

While we have only one reference to exorcist in the Bible (Acts 19:13-16), there are frequent manifestations of exorcism by Christ and His apostles. Exorcist means, "one who adjures out demons." Vine says that, "The practice of exorcism was carried on by strolling Jews, who used their power in the recitation of particular names." Spells, such as the name of Solomon, magic charms, and incantations were used. 'The profane use of Jesus' name as a mere spell was punished by a demon turning on the would-be exorcist; these 'vagabond Jews' were pretenders. Jesus Himself implied that some Jews actually cast out demons, probably by demoniacal help, others in the name of Jesus, without saving faith in Him" (Matthew 7:22; 12:27; Mark 9:38).

Exorcism, in the strict etymological sense, is not used in the Bible. Exorcists was used in such a way as to discredit professional casting out of demons, impostors deluding people by witchcraft or diabolical agency. Corswant points out that exorcism was honored by the Pharisees and that many Scribes and doctors of law were skilled in it, going from place to place practicing their art (Matthew 12:27; Luke 9:49; 11:19). In common with the Gentiles, the Jews attributed physical and mental illnesses to the presence and performance of evil spirits in the body of those who were their victims. As expulsion of demons was the only cure, exorcists, resorting to professional magical formulae, devoted themselves to their task.

That Christ Himself, and His immediate disciples had power in all its proper vigor to chase out demons from human bodies, is evident from the exorcism we read of in the gospels and The Acts (Mark 1:34; 3:11; Luke 6:18). He had no need to resort to any incantation or magic. With all authority as the Son of God, and in the name and power of God, and the assistance of the demon-possessed themselves, He relieved those who were oppressed of the devil (Acts 10: 38). When charged by the Pharisees that He cast out demons by Beelzebub the prince of demons, Jesus implied that such a power depended on special acts of prayer and fasting. Jesus used no spell, but uttering the all-commanding word of expulsion, the evil spirits rendered His authoritative command unquestioning obedience (Matthew 8:16; Luke 8:29).

Altogether there are seven cures of people possessed with demons reported in the gospels, the cases presenting a varying amount of detail which is profitable to study —

1. The demoniac at Capernaum (Mark 1:21-23; Luke 4:33)
2. A man born blind and dumb (Matthew 12:22; Luke 11:14)
3. The Gergesene demoniac (Matthew 8:28; 15:22; Luke 8:26)
4. The unknown blind man (Matthew 9:32, 33)
5. The daughter of the Syro-Phoenician woman (Mark 7:25)
6. The distressed, epileptic child (Matthew 17:14-21; Mark 9:14-29; Luke 9:38)
7. The woman with a spirit of infirmity (Luke 13:11).

Confidently, Jesus spoke of Himself as acting by "the finger of God" or by "the Spirit of God" — the "finger" being symbolic of the Holy Spirit, just as the "arm" is symbolic of the Lord Himself (Isaiah 53:1) — sometimes His will and command were indicated even without speech (Luke 13:13, 16). Demons knew Him as the Lord, and His mere presence on the scene was sufficient to alarm them and to put an end to disastrous possession.

Both before and after the resurrection Christ delegated the power to exorcise to His disciples who were told to remember that the authority was given them. No incantation was recited. The name of Jesus, representing His command was sufficient and was uttered, not as a spell, but appealed to as "the source of all spiritual power," as not only the badge of discipleship, but also the name of the everpresent Lord of spirits and the Saviour of men (Matthew 10:1; 28:19; Mark 3:15; 6:13; 16:17; Luke 9:1; 10: 17; John 14:13; Acts 3:6; 4:10; 5:16; 8: 7; 16:18; 19:12-16; James 5:14). The apostles knew that the proper and effective use of the power to exorcise meant a reliance upon the presence and living power of Christ from whom alone power to do any mighty work comes (John 15:5).

Our gracious Lord and His empowered apostles "dealt with demoniacs as they dealt with all other sufferers from the malign, enslaving and wasting power of sin, with the tenderness of an illimitable sympathy, and the firmness and effectiveness of those to whom were granted in abundance measure the presence and power of God."

Church historians show how by the end of the third century exorcists were made an order in the Christian Church, much to the fostering of superstition, especially in connection with baptism. Josephus, educated though he was, was guilty of the most abject superstition and demoniac activities and expulsion (See *ANT* III. VII. ii. 5). For a study of exorcism in Old Testament times, and also in periods following the third century, the reader is directed to a reliable Bible encyclopaedia, or to a church history work like Fisher's.

The Extortioner

Here is another of the few unworthy occupations of the Bible. An extortioner was a greedy person, guilty of pillage, plunder, robbery, rapaciousness, covetousness. Extortion is the "spoiling" or thieving of what others possess (Ezekiel 22:12). The word can also mean "ravening" (of wolves) (Matthew 7:15; Luke 11:39, ASV). Extort is to twist out of a person, just as distort means to misshape him. Bible extortioners are usually grouped with evil associates (Psalm 109:11; Ezekiel 22:12; Matthew 23:25; Luke 18:11; I Corinthians 5:10, 11; 6:10); and wherever extortion is used there is the idea of snatching away from another what is not lawfully possessed. The gain is greedily gotten. The publicans, or taxgatherers were especially guilty of this sin (Luke 18:11). Paul includes extortion among a category of the grossest sins of humanity (I Corinthians 5:10, 11), and affirms that the door of heaven is closed against those guilty of such a sin (I Corinthians 6:10).

If, then, an extortioner is one who greedily snatches away from another that which does not lawfully belong to him, we certainly have all too many in our so-called affluent society who live by plunder. Contrary, though it may seem, our much vaunted civilization is crawling with greedy thieves. Extortion is hard to stamp out in some labor circles, as America and Britain know only too well. Communism and despotism are likewise notable for snatching away from others by strife, greed and oppression that to which they have no right.

The Fanner

The word Jeremiah uses for fanners is given as "winnowers" or "strangers" in the ASV margin (Jeremiah 51:2). Fan likewise is translated as "winnow" or "fork" in the ASV (Ruth 3:2; Isaiah 30:24; Jeremiah 15:7; Matthew 3:12; Luke 3:17). The *fan* in question was the agricultural instrument shaped like a winnowing fork, which is still used by the Syrian farmer.

Threshing was followed by winnowing, the latter process requiring two tools, namely a shovel and a fan (Isaiah 30:24). The threshed corn was heaped up, a favorable wind being essential for winnowing. The wind was not to be too strong, but a breeze like that which still blows, morning and evening, in the land Ruth winnowed (Ruth 3:2; Jeremiah 4:11). Once the wind was right, the grain was thrown into it, and the heavier grains fell straight down and the straw fell by the side of the threshing floor. This chaff was burned up with fire (Matthew 3:12). A strong wind blew the chaff away (Psalm 1:4). With his shovel, or wooden fork, the fanner repeated the throwing of the corn into the air until it was rid of all foreign matter. When we think of a fan we have in mind something designed for cooling purposes. But the Bible fan was a five- or six-pronged fork or spade, "a winnowing shovel."

The striking feature is that Bible references to "fanning" or "winnowing" are mostly metaphorical, describing the discriminating judgment of God between the godly and the ungodly, together with the destruction of the latter (Isaiah 30:28; Amos 9:1; Luke 3:17). Winnowing, in the literal sense is only found in Ruth (3:2). Elsewhere, it is the symbol of the means by which God purifies His people from moral evil, and inflicts punishment on evildoers. Peter knew what it was to have Satan as the fanner, sifting him. As Jesus prophesied, in the winnowing process Peter lost the chaff of self-confidence, but the wheat of a humble trust remained. In using the figure of the fanner, Christ described how He will separate

His wheat from the chaff in the day of judgment (Luke 3:17).

Old Testament references to God as a fanner, are related to His use of Israel in the subjugation of her enemies, and of their deserved destruction. A great destroying wind wiped out Babylon (Isaiah 41:16; Jeremiah 4:11; 15:7; 51:2). For the uselessness of chaff, both to God and the farmer see Job 21:18; Psalm 1:4; Isaiah 33:11; Jeremiah 23:28. By the word of His power, and by applications and tribulations, God knows how to segregate the pure grain from the useless chaff.

The Farmer

Although this name is not in the Bible the word "farm" is (Matthew 22:5), and a farm presupposes a farmer, or one who cultivates the fields. The same word for "farm," *agros*, from which we have "agriculture" is rendered "field" or "piece of ground." Farms, as we know them, were not common in Palestine in Bible times. In Bible history, the Jewish people are introduced to us at a period when they were largely engaged in agrarian pursuits which is the reason why we have so many references to agricultural occupations.

Husbandry, the Biblical term for "agriculture," or farming, was highly esteemed as an art in which God instructed the husbandman (II Chronicles 26:10; Isaiah 28:26). Fausset reminds us that when the Hebrews became a nation and occupied Canaan that —

> The agriculture learned in Egypt made them a self-subsisting nation, independent of eternal supplies, and so less open to external corrupting influences. Agriculture was the basis of the Mosaic commonwealth; it checked the tendency to the roving habits of nomad tribes, gave each man a stake in the soil by the law of inalienable

inheritances, and made a numerous offspring profitable as to the culture of the land. God claimed the lordship of the soil (Leviticus 25:23), so that each held by a divine tenure, subject to the tithe, a quit rent to the theocratic head land-lord, also subject to the sabbatical year.

Our Lord's frequent allusions to farmers, fields and their products indicate how familiar He was with the agricultural pursuits of His time. Many farming methods then employed still prevail in the East, where change from antiquity is resisted. The three prominent branches of agriculture which the farmer represented were —

1. *The Growing of Grain*

Among the agricultural operations associated with this fruit of the field, and frequently mentioned in the Bible, we have (Matthew 13:3), plowing, sowing, reaping, threshing and winnowing. As to the farmer's implements we have the plough, the yoke, the cart, the sickle, the sieve, the fan, the shovel, the hand-mill or stones.

2. *The Care of Vineyards*

As grapes, olives and figs served an important part in the diet of the Bible, great care was bestowed upon the vineyards — a task well-adapted to the farmer's routine as most of the attention a vineyard required could be given when his other crop demanded no time (Numbers 18:30; Isaiah 5:1-6).

3. *The Raising of Flocks*

The Jewish people reckoned flocks as a necessary part of wealth. They were important as a source of food and raiment. (I Samuel 16:11; Psalm 23; Matthew 18:13; John 10:12). The account of the wealth of both Job and Hezekiah reveals their interest in the above most profitable pursuits.

The fact that no department of human industry has enriched the language of

Scripture, and in consequence the language of the spiritual life in all after ages, with so many appropriate figures of speech, is a striking testimony to the place occupied by agriculture in the life and thought of the Hebrew people.

Metaphors taken from the earth, things growing out of it, and the tillage of it, make an interesting study we have not space to develop in this glimpse of the farmer. The reader, however, can profitably pursue this aspect, noting, with the aid of a concordance other uses, and references to the following agricultural metaphors —

The seed is used to signify the engrafted Word of God (I Peter 1:23).

The ministry of the sun's heat, rain and dew illustrate divine influences in the spiritual germination of the Word as seed (Isaiah 44:3; John 6:63).

Roots, branches, leaves, flowers and fruit likewise carry a spiritual significance (Deuteronomy 29:18; Job 13:25; 15:33; 19:28; Isaiah 5:24; Matthew 3:8; John 15:1-3; Jude 12).

Plants symbolize the church and the believer (Isaiah 5:7; Matthew 15:13).

Trees are often used by way of similitude (Isaiah 11:1; 41:19; Jeremiah 11:19).

Thorns sometimes represent wicked and mischievous men, and the efforts of Satan to buffet us (Numbers 33:55; Hosea 2:6; II Corinthians 12:7).

Olives were used to describe the great dignity God invested His chosen people with (Jeremiah 11:16; Zechariah 4:3, 11, 12; Romans 11:17).

The vineyards, in metaphor and parable, are suggestive of the people of God, and of what He expects from His own (Deuteronomy 28:30, 39; Song of Solomon 8:11, 12; Isaiah 3:14; 5:1).

Wine signifies divine grace, and also wrath (Judges 8:2; Psalm 104:2; Proverbs 9:5; Joel 3:13; Revelation 14:10; 18:6).

Plowing is a fitting symbol of affliction, repentance and diligence (Psalm 129:3; Isaiah 28:24-26; Jeremiah 4:3; Luke 9:62).

Harvests are employed to describe the reward of good works and also evil deeds (Psalm 126:5, 6; Hosea 6:11; John 4:35, 38; Galatians 6:7-9).

Chaff and stubble denote false doctrine and the destruction of the wicked (Amos 9:9; Obadiah 18; Matthew 3:12; Luke 22:31; I Corinthians 3:12).

Grinding of grain, like its winnowing, is also used symbolically (Exodus 11:5; Job 31:10; Isaiah 47:2).

Yokes which the oxen wore are made to illustrate both satanic bondage and full allegiance to Christ (Matthew 11:29; II Corinthians 6:14).

The Feller

The solitary reference (Isaiah 14:8) to a common occupation of the time when wood was so necessary for building, is used in a figurative sense of the devastation the king of Babylon produced by his triumph. Kings boasted that wherever they conquered they cut down forests and left the land bare (II Kings 3:19, 25; Isaiah 37:24). The fir tree, the cedar, and the oak were natural symbols of kingly rule (Isaiah 14:8; Jeremiah 22:6; Ezekiel 17:3; 31:3), but what power have the proud monarchs of earth when the judgments of the Potentate of time are abroad (II Samuel 3:34; II Kings 6:5). Nebuchadnezzar became as a tree great and strong, with height reaching unto heaven, and the sight thereof to the ends of the earth (Daniel 4:10-16), but in one fell swoop the mighty tree was laid low, and another planted in its place (Daniel 4:17, 18). As trees, planted by the

Lord, we are safe and secure from the destructive work of the satanic feller.

The Fisherman

The meditation before us has an honorable significance seeing that many of the first disciples Jesus called were fishermen. Although there are few references in the Bible to those of this occupation, they are nevertheless brought into prominence by the record of those Galilean fishermen, like Peter, "The Big Fisherman," who left their ship and nets to follow Jesus (Matthew 4:18,19; Mark 1:16, 17).

Among the characteristic features of those who lived off the sea, the following, suggested by James A. Patch in his *International Standard Bible Encyclopaedia* sketch, can be noted —

Fishermen in Bible times, as now, formed a distinct class, and lived together as a community. The Fish Gate at Jerusalem implies an adjacent fish-market, with stocks of fish supplied chiefly through Tyrian traders who imported it (II Chronicles 33:14; Nehemiah 3:3; 12:39; 13:16). Because of the distance from the fisheries of Phoenicia and the climate, fish sold at Jerusalem would be salted or dried by the sun. Fish from the Lake of Galilee would be fresher.

Fishermen were strong and tough. The strenuousness of their work ruled out the weak and indolent (Luke 5:2). They were also crude in manner, rough in speech and in their treatment of others (Luke 9:49, 54; John 18:10). Before they were tempered by Christ's influence, fishermen James and John had the nickname "sons of thunder" (Mark 3:17). Further, their exposure to all kinds of weather made them hardy and fearless. They were accustomed to bear with patience the most trying circumstances. Toiling for hours without success, they were al-ways ready to try once more (Luke 5:5; John 21:3).

These traits, and others, made them successful "fishers of men" (Matthew 4:19; Mark 1:17). Their earthly occupation was a parable of their divine vocation. It was so with David the shepherd who became "the Shepherd of Israel" and Paul the tentmaker who was used by God for fashioning men's bodies into tabernacles of the Holy Spirit.

As to the fish caught and traded in, while there are many references to fish in the Bible, no particular kind of fish is distinguished by name. Corswant expresses it —

Fish, as the work of the Creator and subjected to man's domination, are not the object of any classification, except that which, ritually, distinguishes between clean fish provided with fins and scales, and unclean fish which lacked them. And so the Israelites could eat fish properly so-called (Genesis 1:21, 26, 28; 9:2; Leviticus 11:9; Numbers 11:5, 22; Job 12:8; Psalm 8:8; Ezekiel 38:20).

The catfish, being without scales, could not be eaten by the Jews (Deuteronomy 14:9, 10). Some writers suggest that this species was the "bad fish" (Matthew 13:47, 48). Fish of the prescribed kind was a favorite article of diet among the Hebrews (Numbers 11:5). Galilee fish, of which there was abundance and variety, together with bread, formed the customary food of the population (Matthew 7:10; Luke 11:11). See also the miracles (Matthew 14:19; 15:36). The risen Lord and His disciples partook of grilled fish (Luke 24:42; John 21:9). The destruction of their fish was a heavy blow to the Egyptians whose rivers, canals and lakes abounded in fish, and who lived much on it (Exodus 7:18-

21; Numbers 11:5; Psalm 105:29; Isaiah 19:5).

In ancient times the fish was worshiped as the emblem of increase or fertility. The Philistines and Assyrians practiced the worship of Dagon, half-man half-fish. Such idolatry, however, was divinely forbidden (Deuteronomy 4:18). Upon the walls of the Catacombs the early Christians symbolically represented Jesus as a fish, because the five letters of this word in Greek provide the initial letters of the five words, "Jesus Christ, God's Son, Saviour." Figurative use of fish has a place in Scripture. Our Lord likened the kingdom of heaven to a net, cast into the sea, which gathered fish of every kind, good and bad (Matthew 13:47). Captivity is symbolized by fish caught in a net (Psalm 74:13; Jeremiah 16:16; Amos 4:2; Habakkuk 1: 15-17).

For the actual task of fishing spearhooks and lines were used (Job 41:7; Amos 4:2; Matthew 17:27). While various kinds of nets were employed, the dragnet was the chief instrument for catching fish (Habakkuk 1:15), and required the dexterity of the practiced fisherman. The spreading of nets signified the desolation of Tyre and the use by Syrian fishermen today of this ancient site for the spreading and drying of their nets is a striking instance of fulfilled prophecy (Ezekiel 26:5, 14). Fishing is also the illustration used for taking souls in the Gospel net, not to be destroyed but to be saved alive. Peter, the fisherman, knew that when he caught fish in the Lake of Galilee that they were alive, but taken out of their natural element they quickly died. But the souls he was to catch were dead in sin, but came into possession of eternal life as soon as they were landed on the shore of salvation (Ezekiel 47:10; Matthew 4:19; Luke 5:5-10). Fishing likewise

symbolizes the sudden destruction by invading enemies (Ecclesiastes 9:12; Jeremiah 16:16; Ezekiel 29:3-5).

The One who created the sea and all that is in it, delivered some of His mighty messages from a fishing boat (Matthew 13). And He it is who waits to use His own as fishers in the great sea of humanity. For such a blessed task, much patience and skill are required. "He that winneth souls is wise."

The Footman

In modern parlance, a footman is a male servant whose duties are to attend the door of a royal or official carriage, and undertake other duties in the palace or mansion. But in Old Testament days, footmen were swift runners who attended kings and who were highly valued in war (I Samuel 8:11; 22:17; I Kings 14:27, margin). As footsoldiers, they were indispensable (I Samuel 4:10; 15:4). David praised God for his ability to run swiftly (I Samuel 17:28, 48, 51; 20:6; II Samuel 22:30; I Chronicles 12:8; Psalm 18:29). Persons of rank, when riding, were always attended by servants on foot (II Kings 4:24). Sudden changes in worldly positions are indicated by Solomon when he wrote about princes "walking as servants" (Ecclesiastes 10:7). The runners were able to keep up the pace no matter how fast the horses ran. Elijah was a swift runner, able to run before the chariot of Ahab. Runner is sometimes translated "post," and footmen were often used to deliver important messages with haste. Their energy led Job to say, "My days are swifter than a post" (Job 9:25). Persian footmen have been known to run without intermission, 120 miles in fourteen hours, and were thus valuable to the king or general they accompanied into battle, for bringing back official tidings of events (II Samuel 18:19). Asahel, famous for his swiftness of foot, was one of David's thirty heroes (II Samuel 23:24). As a simile, Jeremiah uses the footman to illustrate the fact that the man, wearied in a footrace, should not measure his speed against that of horses (Jeremiah 12:5; See I Kings 18:46).

The Forerunner

Our last cameo dealt with swift runners, who were often forerunners, but we have only one Bible reference to an actual forerunner, or one that runs before, and then it is used of our Lord Jesus Christ (Hebrews 6:20). The original word, *prodromos,* is classical Greek, and implied a scout reconnoitering, or a herald announcing the coming of the king and making ready the way for the royal journey. While the term forerunner is never applied to John the Baptist, he was actually a forerunner seeing he was sent before to the Lord to prepare His way (Isaiah 40:3; Malachi 3:1; Matthew 11:10; Mark 1:2; Luke 7:27). It is in this sense that Christ is our Forerunner for He entered heaven to prepare a place for His people to which He will ultimately bring them (John 14:1-3). He opened the gates of heaven by His atoning blood and priestly intercession (Hebrews 12:2).

The ASV in Hebrews 6:20 reads, "whither as a forerunner Jesus entered for us," and Hastings says that this change from the KJV is important because "to the readers of Hebrews it would be a startling announcement that Jesus had entered the Holy of Holies as a forerunner. Thither the Jewish high priest, one day in a year, went alone (Hebrews 9:7). He was the people's sole representative, but he was not their forerunner, for none might dare to follow him. The keynote of this epistle is that all believers

have access with boldness to the presence of the Most Holy God 'in the blood of Jesus,' they have this boldness because their High Priest has inaugurated for them a fresh and living way (Hebrews 10:19). Already within the veil hope enters with assurances, for Jesus has gone that way that we may follow too. As the Forerunner of His redeemed He has inaugurated their entrance."

The Founder

Strange as it may seem, the first reference to the occupation represented here is associated with idolatry (Judges 17:4). The other four references to the founder (Jeremiah 6:29; 10:9, 14; 51:17), signify one who melts, refines and purifies. We use the word foundry, but those who labor in one are not called founders but molders, which represents a most difficult part of foundry work. Founding implies "pouring" or "casting." Articles made in an iron foundry are made of what is called *cast* iron and are called castings — a word the Bible frequently uses. A founder is also one who founds, or establishes an institution.

Hiram, a widow's son, was a founder who, in the foundry, he set out in the Jordan valley where there was clay to form his molds, cast two large pillars with ornamented top for the entrance to the temple and also cast a "sea," which held 8,000 gallons of water, and which stood up the back of twelve molten oxen (I Kings 7:16, 23). Zarephath means "a foundry." Perhaps the widow's son, with whom Elijah lodged, may have worked in one of the foundries at Zarephath, making images for worship. Those old-time molders of molten metal required, first of all, a pattern, as God gave to Moses for the tabernacle.

Then came the making of the mold, a hard and intricate task. A furnace, however, was necessary to make the iron so fluid that it would run into all the tiny recesses of the mold, otherwise there would not be a perfect cast. Egypt is called the furnace where God melted His people. How full of spiritual instruction are all the aspects of the molder! Are we not thrice blessed when we are willing for the heavenly Molder to shape and mold us as He deems best?

The Fowler

As the peoples of the East were fond of eating small birds, snaring appears to have been a favorite occupation of the Jews, judging by the numerous allusions to the practice in the Old Testament. Bas-reliefs on Egyptian monuments show how this art reached a high degree of perfection in that country, gins and traps of various kinds being used. A fowler, then, is one who, by various means, strives to catch fowls for human consumption. Biblical references to fowlers are of a symbolical nature (Psalms 91: 3; 124:7; Proverbs 6:5; Jeremiah 5:26; Hosea 9:8). These professional bird catchers used different kinds of nets, traps and snares. The gin was a trap consisting of a net and a stick acting as a spring. All of these contrivances supplied Old Testament writers with images to express the arts of the wicked (Psalms 9:15; 25:15; 35:7; 142:3; Isaiah 8:14).

It is somewhat interesting to examine the various methods and equipment fowlers used, and which the Bible generally uses in a figurative sense. There was, for instance, the use of a decoy bird. A young bird would be taken from the nest, and tamed. It would be confined in a hidden cage, and the song of the captive bird would entice others of the same kind to the spot to be killed by arrows of concealed bowmen or the use of the throw-stick so effective when thrown into a flock of birds (Ecclesiastes 9: 12). Ovid, the Latin philosopher may have had this method in mind when he wrote —

> The pipe sounds sweetly whilst the fowler is ensnaring birds; and the villainous poison lies concealed in the sweet honey.

Another method, which Gene Stratton-Porter speaks of, was that of sewing a captured bird's eyelids together and confining it so that its cries would call large numbers of birds through curiosity to the spot of the distressed call. Fowlers were cunning enough to cover up the trap they used, for experience had taught them that birds avoid the snares which show too conspicuously. Birds caught would be used for caged pets, for food, or in the cases of doves, for sacrifice.

At the back of, and inspiring all evil men as they seek to ensnare the unwary is Satan, whom the Bible brands as the diabolical arch-fowler who, with great subtlety and deceit in his snares, or temptations, has brought ruin to mankind. While those who oppress and plunder their neighbors or seek to ensnare them into sin or danger are called fowlers (Psalm 124:7; Jeremiah 5:26), they are but the offspring of their father, the devil, who constantly plans and schemes to destroy God's people, especially their leaders. Does not Paul warn us against the snares or traps of the devil (II Timothy 2: 26)? The word the apostle uses for recover, originally signified to awake from a deep sleep, or from a fit of intoxication. It was an artifice of fowlers to scatter seeds impregnated with drugs, which caused birds to sleep and which allowed the fowler to draw the net over the birds with greater security.

That snares represent loss or destruction is evident from many Scriptures (Exodus 10:7; I Samuel 18:20; Psalm 69:22; Proverbs 12:13; 13:14; 22:5; 29:6; Romans 11:9; I Timothy 3:7; 6:9). The symbolic use of snares forms a profitable meditation. Paul employs the word to describe those allurements of Satan, overtaking one unawares. God warned the Israelites that Canaanitish pleasures would ensnare them, and that trapped, they would be found living like the heathen around (Exodus 34:12; See I Samuel 18:21; Psalms 91:3; 119:110; Proverbs 7:23). The snare of an ephod — monument of victory — being changed into an idol indicates the evil effect of idolatrous worship on the Israelites (Judges 8:27). The witch of Endor thought the servants of Saul were spies waiting to catch her in a trap and thereby have her killed according to the Mosaic Law. She did not know that Saul himself was seeking her aid through his emissaries (I Samuel 28:9). The plans and efforts of evil men to destroy David were caught in their own Satanic devices (Psalm 69:22). Says Ovid, "The fowler has fallen into his own snares." Jeremiah draws a strong comparison between wicked men entrapping their fellows and fowlers catching unsuspected birds by means of a decoy bird (Jeremiah 5: 26). Believers must be watchful unless they are snared in an evil time (Ecclesiastes 9:12). Death hath its snares (Psalm 18:4; Jeremiah 48:43). Amos gives a vivid picture of a trap with tongues and jaws like a common rattrap. It was light, and the bird caught by the foot easily sprang up with it from the ground in its vain attempts to escape (Amos 3:5). In our affluent society we ought to give heed to our Lord's warning as to prosperity being a snare (Luke 21: 34). An ancient writer has said, "He who fears all snares falls into none."

Is it not good of God to offer us the promise and provision of deliverance from all the snares of the fowler of hell? Saul tried hard to trap David, but as a bird sometimes in its struggles slips the hair and escapes from the snare set for it, so David knew that God delivered him from evil plans to destroy him. He escaped as a bird out of the snare of the fowlers (Psalm 124:7). Sometimes snares held fast, sometimes they broke, and when they did, there was joy in the heart of a freed man like the wild exultation in the tiny breast of an escaped bird (Proverbs 6:5). Wherever he goes, the messenger of God is in danger of being trapped, and must therefore be on the alert (Hosea 9:8; See Proverbs 7:23).

The Fuller

In *The Workmen of the Bible*, Donald Davidson asks the questions as to the imagery behind the promise that though our sins be "red like crimson, they shall be as wool" (Isaiah 1:18) —

What was it that first suggested these graphic similes to the mind of the prophet? Had he seen a blood-red sun sinking like a ball of fire behind some snow-clad mountain peak? Or had he, as he meditated in an eastern garden seen in the flowers the contrast which conjured up the thought, on the one hand the flaming, flaunting, riotous crimson of the poppy, and on the other the calm, serene, snow-white purity of the madonna lily? Or may it have been that, as he mingled with the crowds in the busy streets, the gaudy, bright-red finery of some courtesan brought to his prophetic eye a vision of the snow-white robes of the redeemed, whiter than any fuller on earth can whiten them? Did Isaiah find inspiration in watching the mysterious processes of the fuller?

Much that we have said on THE DYER is applicable to THE FULLER, seeing the fuller was usually the dyer. The Bible presents a fuller as one who cleansed and dressed cloth (II Kings 18:17; Isaiah 7:3; 36:2; Malachi 3:2). The work of the fuller was twofold. He dealt with the web fresh from the loom, or with soiled garments that had already been worn which he cleaned by steeping and treading in water mixed with an alkaline substance, or soap, or nitre (Proverbs 25:20; Jeremiah 2:22), and fuller's earth. The new or "undressed cloth" (Matthew 9:16; Mark 2:21, ASV) after being steeped in the similar mixture, would be stamped and felted, then bleached with fumes of sulphur, and finally pressed in the fuller's press. The fuller, like the tanner, whose operations were evil-smelling, carried on his occupation outside the town, near to a body of water for washing purposes. Isaiah speaks of "the fuller's field" (Isaiah 7:3; 36:2), where there was a conduit of an upper pool, and where there would be enough room to spread out the cloth for drying and sunning. *En-rogel* is said to mean, "the spring of the fuller" (Joshua 15:7; 18:16). As part of the fuller's task was that of cleansing and whitening garments for festive and religious occasions, we can appreciate the reference to Christ's garments so white that no fuller on earth could match (Mark 9:3). White garments also describes the spotless righteousness of Christ put on by the saints (Ecclesiastes 9:8; Revelation 3:4, 5, 18; 6:11; 7:9, 14). The art of the fuller, which is of great antiquity, is incribed on some Egyptian monuments replete with vat, and cloth being processed by the hands and feet of the fuller. The Syrian indigo dyer still uses a cleaning process closely allied to that pictured on these monuments.

The Gardener

While there are over fifty references to gardens in the Bible, the term gardener is only used once (John 20:15), where the occupation means "keeper." As it is still a common practice in Palestine to set a watchman over gardens during their productive seasons, the man referred to by John was not one who did manual labor in a garden but a watchman, corresponding to those mentioned in the Old Testament (Job 27:18; II Kings 17:9; 18:8, etc.).

As there are some 300 botanical terms occurring in the Bible, the same are evidence that the Hebrews delighted in orchards and gardens with all their fruit and flowers. Says Fairburn, "It must be remembered that all these terms occur incidentally in their laws, their poetry, their history. Trees and flowers enhanced the enjoyment, or relieved the gloom, of almost every scene in Jewish life. . . . Gardens, and occasionally the shelter of a single tree, were a chosen scene of retirement and devotion; and it was in such cool and fragrant bowers that the rabbis loved to collect their disciples, and deal forth their wisdom."

The history of man begins in a garden (Genesis 2:15) and concludes in a city (Revelation 21:2). In between there is the. sacred hill of Calvary, (Luke 23:33), through which *paradise lost* can become *paradise regained*. God provided the first garden, and a deep love for gardens is seen again and again in the Bible. The Creator fashioned the original garden to bring forth fruits and flowers for His delight, and ours. Under the divine Gardener, Adam labored in the same capacity to dress and keep the garden of Eden (Genesis 2:15). The first occupation then, was that of a working-gardener, Work came before sin. The world's first sinner, however, was a gardener. Rudyard Kipling wrote the lines —

> Oh, Adam was a gardener, and the God
> who made him sees,
> That half a proper gardener's work is
> done upon his knees.
> So when your work is finished, you can
> wash your hands and pray,
> For the Glory of the Garden that it may
> not pass away!
> And the Glory of the Garden it shall
> never pass away.

What kind of a gardener Adam became we are not told. This we do know — that the garden which God "planted" for him was perfect in every way. It was destitute of any obnoxious weeds which only appeared after the first gardener sinned (Genesis 3: 18). Being perfect, the garden of Eden required no immediate atten· tion, but where the necessary tools came from to dress and keep the garden, we are not told. Doubtless God instructed His gardener how to fashion what was required to keep his garden-home in order.

Then is it not somewhat significant that like the first Adam, the second Adam was a gardener too? Dr. Donald Davidson comments:

> It took the second Gardener to make good what the first gardener had spoiled. When Adam was expelled from Eden through the subtlety of the serpent, the prophecy made that day was that He would put His heel upon the serpent's head. And was not the Man who walked in the Garden of Joseph of Arimathaea that resurrection morning the One of whom the law and the prophets had spoken? Well might Mary Magdalene take Him to be the Gardener, the Gardener foretold from the beginning of the world. For the ancient prophecy was now fulfilled, and the work of Redemption was at last complete.

It is impossible to exhaust the thought, so rich in spiritual sugges-tion, "Supposing Him to be the Gardener!" Let the precious truth ever be uppermost in your mind that sin can never creep into the garden of your heart if Jesus is the Gardener. Adam in his garden fell an easy prey to Satan, but you have the assurance that the second Adam has crushed the tempter under foot, and that, therefore, where Jesus is the Gardener, the garden is secure.

As to Bible gardens themselves, the following features can be noted of various enclosures bearing the general name of garden. There were the hanging gardens in Babylon, which were the wonder of the then known world (Deuteronomy 11:10-14). The magnificent gardens surrounding the royal palace of Susa (Esther 1:5; 7:7, 8), were described by Milman as,

> Those airy gardens, which yon palace
> vast
> Spread round, and to the morning airs
> hang forth
> Their golden fruits and dewy opening
> flowers;
> While still the low mist creep in lazy
> folds
> O'er the house-tops beneath.

While no hedges surrounded the original garden, enclosures fenced with a hedge or wall, planted with flowers, shrubs and trees, gradually appeared (Proverbs 24:31; Isaiah 1: 8). As water is essential for the life of a garden, the provision of the rivers in Eden (Genesis 2:10-14) was copied by all gardeners after Adam. For his remarkable gardens, Solomon had a "fountain of gardens" or a fountain sufficient to water many gardens (Song of Solomon 4:15).

Various gardens can be identified. We have, for instance, "the garden of nuts" — a plantation of walnuts, almonds, and other nut-bearing trees (Song of Solomon 6:11). Then there were enclosures dedicated to the cultivation of the vine, olive and pomegranate (Song of Solomon 4:13-15), an "orchard of pomegranates" and "all kinds of fruit" (Ecclesiastes 2:5). Mention is made of "a garden of herbs," like the one the unscrupulous Ahab created and murdered its owner to secure (I Kings 21:3). That there were vegetable gardens is evident from the culinary vegetables the Hebrews lived on like gourds, cucumbers, melons, onions, garlic, etc. From the flower gardens, much loved perfumes came like myrrh, aloes, cassia, saffron and others (Psalm 45:8; Song of Solomon 4:12-15; Isaiah 1:8 "garden of cucumbers").

Gardens were often used as burial places. Manasseh and Amon were buried in Uzza's garden (II Kings 21: 18, 26). Abraham's burial ground was a garden with trees in and around it (Genesis 23:17). The garden of Gethsemane was our Lord's favorite resort for devotion (Matthew 26:36; John 18:1). "It was in a garden of light Adam fell; in a garden of darkness, Gethsemane, the Second Adam overcame the tempter and retrieved us." Christ was crucified and buried in a garden (John 19:41, 42). Cemeteries, alas, became the centers of superstition and image worship, the awful counterpart of the primitive and pure Eden (Isaiah 1:29; 65:3; 66:17).

Gardens are likewise used in a symbolic sense. Israel, now as a desolate, barren wilderness is to blossom as the rose, and her desert become like the garden of the Lord (Isaiah 51:3; Amos 4:9). Moses compared Israel with valleys widely shaded and with well-watered gardens (Numbers 24:6). The garden of Eden became the symbol of a very fertile land (Genesis 13: 10; Isaiah 51:3; Ezekiel 28:13; 31:9, 16, 18; Amos 9:14; Revelation 2:7). The church of Christ is "a garden enclosed." She is a garden because of her fruitfulness. She is God's husbandry (I Corinthians 3:9). She is enclosed or barred because hid to the world she is "hid in Christ" (Colossians 3:3). The world knows her not (I John 3:1).

The believer also is a garden, and a well-watered one because of the indwelling Spirit, the living water (Jeremiah 2:13; 17:8; John 4:13, 14; 7:37-39). As gardening was one of the ordinary occupations of the Jews they knew that a well-watered garden expressed abundant happiness and prosperity (Isaiah 58:11; Jeremiah 17:8; 31:12); and that a waterless garden indicated spiritual, national and individual barrenness and misery (Isaiah 1:30). The believer, as a tree planted by rivers of waters (Psalm 1: 3), brings forth the fruit of the Spirit both in and out of season (Galatians 5:23; See Ecclesiastes 3:1-11; Ezekiel 47:12; Matthew 21:19). May grace be ours so to live "like a watered garden, full of fragrance rare!"

Mary mistook Jesus for a gardener, but when He said, "Mary," she knew it was her Lord. Yet, is He not *the* divine Gardener, the Lord of Life and death, and as such the Gardener of our souls? No gardener likes his garden to be full of weeds. He aims at a weedless garden, full of flowers through the changing seasons. How the divine Gardener seeks to keep the garden of your soul and mine, free from those weeds of sin, preventing the full glory and fragrance of the fruit of the Spirit! Heaven is spoken of as a garden or "the paradise of God," in which there is the tree of life, bearing twelve kinds of fruit, and having leaves for the health of the nations. Surely then, Jesus will continue to be the divine Gardener.

The Goldsmith

We have six references to this most responsible occupation in the Bible, in which a goldsmith means one who refines, purifies, and works with precious gold (Nehemiah 3:8, 31, 32; Isaiah 40:19; 41:7; 46:6). The goldsmiths Nehemiah mentions probably lived together in a separate community (3:8, 31). Those Jeremiah refers to were ashamed of their products (10:14). Among the products of their arts apart from idols was beaten work (Exodus 25:18; 37:7, 17, 23; Numbers 8:4; I Kings 10:16), plating (Exodus 25:11, 24; 26:29, 32; 30:3), wire or thread for embroidery or jewelry (Exodus 39:2). The goldsmith's art was to a certain extent subsidiary to that of the engraver, or carver, for almost all the ornamental pieces of furniture were overlaid with gold, either wholly or in part. The Bible presents an astonishing number of golden objects all of which prove the skillful art of the goldsmith (Judges 8:24; I Samuel 6:4; Psalm 115:4; Isaiah 2:7, etc.). The process of overlaying is referred to by Isaiah (41:7; see I Kings 16:18, 20).

As to metal, the goldsmith worked with gold figures prominently in the Bible. As the chiefest of all minerals it was looked upon as the principal and most precious of treasures (Job 22:24; Zechariah 13:9). The fact that the ark was covered inside and out of pure gold, and that the vessels of the Tabernacle were made of pure gold proves that a certain standard of gold was known to the Israelites as they left Egypt for the wilderness. Gifts of the Pharaohs to the temples of their gods were of pure gold. When the tomb of Tutankhamen, the young Pharaoh who died more than 3,000 years ago, was opened, the golden treasure discovered was an inner coffin of solid gold, so heavy that it took

four men to lift it. The four great shrines of wood were plated with gold and there was a large amount of golden jewelry and ornaments. Gold can be traced back to the earliest times of the human race. God made Havilah a gold-producing country, the gold of which land was good (Genesis 2:11, 12). Ophir, Tarshish and Sheba were also among the main sources of gold (I Kings 9:28; 10:11; Psalm 72:15). As a medium of currency, gold was reckoned by weight, shekels and talents, and was most plentiful during the reign of Solomon (I Kings 10:14, 21). Abraham was rich in gold (Genesis 13:2; 24:35). The first money in gold was used by the Jews in the time of Darius, 406 B.C.

Because of its preciousness, gold is used to symbolize many things. In the gold which the wise men presented to the young child, Jesus, they recognized His deity. When Christ Himself urges us to secure gold tried in the fire, He illustrated the sterling worth of a Christian character. Gold is often used as a symbol of purification (I Peter 1:7; Revelation 3:18). Metaphorically, gold plays a large part either as a term of comparison — thus the Law of God, wisdom or even the esteem of man are far superior to it (Job 28:15; Psalms 19:10; 119:72, 127; Proverbs 3:14; 8:19; 22:1; 25:12). The value of the prayers of God's people is seen in that He places them in golden vessels (Revelation 5:8). In contrast to the false religious empires built up by Satanic power, the city of God is represented as being of "pure gold" (Revelation 21:18-21). Gold signifies the pure doctrine of the Gospel, as silver and precious stones do (I Corinthians 3:12).

Gold and earthly treasures are, by the permission of God, at the will and command of men. No matter how much gold a person possesses, he can be dispossessed of it, or his gold can canker and corrupt (James 5:3). But in Christ and His Word we have golden treasures none can rob us of, and which, because they are incorruptible, never canker or lose any of their virtue and value (I Peter 1:23). Too many make gold their god, and come to prove what a false object of trust and worship it is.

The Governor

The English word for governor carries with it several implications of occupations in the Hebrew and Greek. When used of the Persians and Assyrians the word implies a general, ruler, or prince directly appointed by the king. In several cases governor means "one lifted up," "a prince," "a captain" (I Kings 20:24; 22:26; II Kings 18:24; II Chronicles 1:2; Ezra 5:3; 6:13). With the development of nations and governments, rulers became necessary. Applied to Joseph, governor suggests that he was second after King Pharaoh in the court of the palace (Genesis 41: 40; 42:6; See I Kings 18:3; Daniel 2: 48). Joseph was virtually ruler over Egypt. When used to describe the occupation of Pilate, Felix and Festus (Luke 3:1; Acts 23:26; 26:30), governor originally meant a financial official appointed directly by the emperor to govern his provinces. Usually a person of high social standing such as a governor had full authority, military, judicial and financial as he governed in the emperor's name. The word Peter uses (I Peter 2:14) suggests a prince or leader.

The terms chiefly in use in the New Testament are derived from a word meaning "to drive" or "to lead"; *ethnarch*, for instance, suggests "ruler of a people" (II Corinthians 11:32), and originally implied the ruler of a nation living with laws of its own in a foreign community. The governor of the feast (John 2:8, 9, ASV "ruler") was probably one chosen to control and arrange for the Feast. The word Paul uses for "governors" (Galatians 4:2, ASV "house manager") were the tutors controlling the ward's person, the steward of his property. Vine says that the word denotes "a superior servant responsible for the family housekeeping, the direction of other servants, and the care of children under age."

Among Christ's gifts to His Church are "governments" (I Corinthians 12: 28, ASV "wise counsels"). Here, the word implies the rule and guidance presbyters or bishops provided the church with. These "governors" or church leaders (Acts 20:17), were those men who by "wise counsels did for the community what the steersman or pilot does for the ship." The comparison of a country's control with the steering of a ship is an old one (James 3:4 ASV "steersman").

One of the glorious titles given our Lord is that of governor (Matthew 2: 6), and here means one who leads, or guides, or goes on before, and is the same word used of Joseph in Acts 7: 10. A writer of the seventeenth century wrote, "You can only govern men by serving them. The rule is without exception." Christ is the perfect Governor of men because He was willing to serve them (Luke 22:27). The word Matthew uses for rule can imply to "feed," as a shepherd. Isaiah, describing the millennial glory of Christ, declared that the government of the earth is to rest upon His shoulder, and that of the increase of his princely power and rule there is to be no end (Isaiah 9:6, 7). When He returns to rule there will be no frontiers to His kingdom. The present question is, Do we recognize Him as the Governor of our lives?

On the duties a Christian owes to civil government see Romans 13:1-10; Titus 3:1; I Peter 2:13-17; II Peter 2:10; Jude 8.

The Guide

The most despicable guide in the Bible is Judas, who conducted the enemies of his Master to His capture and ultimate death. No wonder he committed suicide (Acts 1:16). Christ was betrayed by an intimate friend (Psalm 55:13). As a noun, guide means a "leader" (Psalm 48:14; Proverbs 2:17; Micah 7:5), a "captain," "ruler," "judge" (Proverbs 6:7), a "conductor" (Romans 2:19). There are guides who neither lead, nor tell the way. Of such were the Pharisees whom Jesus called "blind guides" (Matthew 23:16, 24). Edmund Burke once wrote, "Great men are the guideposts and landmarks in the State." But the religious leaders of the nation, destitute of true greatness, failed as guideposts in leading the nation back to God. They were "blind leaders of the blind" (Matthew 15:14). They should have been true guides of the blind, and lights to others in darkness (Romans 2:19).

Among the trusty guides mentioned in the greatest and safest of the guidebooks, the Bible, we have the devoted wife and mother exhorted by Paul to "guide the house" (I Timothy 5:14). It is her occupation to be responsible for the management and direction of household affairs. The Holy Spirit is another Guide whose province it is to lead and guide us into all truth (John 16:13). As "the Spirit of Truth," His guidance into every phase of truth is unerring. Philip was an under-guide as he led the Ethiopian into the truth of the Gospel (Acts 8:31).

The believer's great and infallible Guide is God Himself, who offers Himself as our Guide even unto death, and beyond it to everlasting bliss (Psalm 48:14). He it is who guides us continually (Isaiah 49:10), enabling us to guide our affairs with discretion (Psalm 112:5). The Guide of your youth (Proverbs 2:17), He remains at our side through the wilderness of this world (Psalm 78:52; Jeremiah 3:4), guiding us in the way of peace (Luke 1:79), and to fountains of water of life (Revelation 7:17). Samuel Johnson in *The Ramblers* gives us this wonderful conception of God —

From Thee, great God, as spring
    to Thee we tend,
Path, Motive, Guide, Original,
    and End.

How blessed we are to have such a Guide who is able to guide us with His eye — guide us in judgment — guide us on every side — guide us with His counsel (II Chronicles 32:22; Job 31:18; Psalms 25:9; 32:8; 73:24).

Guide me, O Thou great Jehovah,
    Pilgrim through this barren land:
I am weak, but Thou art mighty,
Hold me with Thy powerful hand.
    Bread of heaven,
Feed me till I want no more.

The Harvester

Although the Bible has a lot to say about harvests and harvesting, only twice do we read of the harvester himself — "When the harvestman gathereth the corn" (Isaiah 17:5). "As the handful after the harvestman" (Jeremiah 9:22). The word for harvester is, of course, the same as reaper (Ruth 2:3, 4; Amos 9:14, etc.), who is depicted as longing for cool weather during the reaping season (Proverbs 25:13). The word harvest, used some eighty times, is also the word for reaping (Leviticus 19:9; Matthew 6:26, etc.).

For the Hebrews, who were an agricultural people, harvests were of great importance (Genesis 8:22; 45:6), even as they are for multitudes today who may be near to, or far removed from the actual production of food. Seasons have changed very little since Bible times. The beginning of harvest varied according to natural conditions, but usually took place about the middle of April in the eastern lowlands of Palestine, and in the latter part of the month in the coast plains and later still in the high districts. Barley harvest usually came first and then wheat. From the wheat harvest until the fruit harvest no rain fell (II Samuel 21:10; Proverbs 26:1; Jeremiah 5:24). Harvesting, or reaping lasted about seven weeks.

Three of the seven principal feasts of the Hebrews, correspond to the three harvest seasons (Exodus 23:16; 34:21, 22) —

1. The Feast of the Passover, which was held in April at the time of barley harvest (Ruth 1:22).

2. The Feast of Pentecost, held seven weeks later at the wheat harvest (Exodus 34:22).

3. The Feast of Tabernacles, held around October during the fruit harvest (Leviticus 23:33-44).

Harvests were not only occasions for mutual rejoicing and festivities, but also seasons when the people expressed deep gratitude to God for His goodness. The fruit of the earth reminded the people that the God of Sinai was also the Lord of seed time and harvest — the One responsible for their material welfare as well as their religious life.

Among definite laws regarding harvests were the following —

Gleaning was forbidden (Leviticus 19:9; 23:22; Deuteronomy 24:19). Firstfruits had to be presented to God (Leviticus 23:10, 40). The people could reap no harvest for which they had not labored (Leviticus 25:5).

Harvests are likewise used in a figurative sense by the prophets, Christ and His apostles.

A destroyed harvest often typified divinely permitted devastation or affliction (Job 5:5; Isaiah 16:9; 17:11; Jeremiah 5:17; 50:16).

The time of harvest frequently meant the day of widespread destruction. Jeremiah gives us a picture of a great city God cut down and destroyed because of its iniquity (Jeremiah 51:33, see Hosea 6:11; Joel 3:13).

"The harvest is past" implied that God's appointed time had come and gone. As the farmer gathers what is useful into his barns, and leaves the stubble in the field to rot, so God is to gather His wheat — true believers — into His heavenly barn and abandon the tares — the godless (Jeremiah 8:20). God knows the promising time to cut off the wicked (Isaiah 18:4, 5).

Christ often referred to the harvest of those souls, yearning for deliverance and reaped by consecrated soulwinners (Matthew 9:37, 38; 13:30; Mark 4:29; John 4:35; Galatians 6:7-9). Explaining the parable of the tares, He said "the harvest is the end of the age" (Matthew 13:39), and is equivalent to the dreadful picture John gives of divine judgment and wrath when the wicked and rebellious of the earth are punished (Revelation 14:15).

"Joy in Harvest" is symbolic of great joy (Isaiah 9:3), the joy of the soul-winner when he receives his "crown of rejoicing" (Psalm 126:5, 6; I Thessalonians 2:19, 20). "Harvest of the Nile" (Isaiah 23:3) is likewise a simile of an abundant harvest or reward.

Where are the reapers? Oh, who will come
And share in the glory of the "Harvest Home"?

Oh, who will help us to garner in
The sheaves of good from the fields
of sin?

The Healer

While heal, and its cognates, occur over 150 times in the Bible, as a term applied both to physical and spiritual diseases, healer appears only once and means "one who binds up" (Isaiah 3:7), and applies, not so much to the binding up of wounds as to the girding with clothes of a destitute person.

That God Himself is the Healer of the diseases of body and soul alike is evident from a consideration of the Biblical teaching on "healing." "I am the Lord that healeth thee" (Exodus 15:26). "Who healeth all thy diseases" (Psalm 103:3). "The Sun . . . arise with healing in his wings" (Malachi 4: 2). A fact that must be borne in mind is that all healing is divine. Physicians may be able to prepare the way for healing, surgically and medicinally, but only God can heal. Ambroise Paré, the father of modern surgery, who served under four kings of France, is remembered by his famous saying, "I dress the sick; God heals them." Gifts of healing come only from the Holy Spirit (I Corinthians 12:9, 30). And that He can and does heal, with or without means, is proven by Bible miracles, and by human experience.

In my previous volume on *All the Miracles of the Bible,* attention is given Bible healings, particularly those of Christ and His apostles. Christ's ministry was one of healing as well as that of teaching and saving men (Mark 1:14, 32-34, etc.). When He commissioned both the Twelve and the Seventy they were to heal the sick as well as preach the kingdom of God (Mark 6:7, 13; Luke 10:1, 9). Christ predicted that after His ascen-

sion, His disciples would still have the gift of healing, and the Book of Acts provides us with ample evidence of the exercise of such a gift by those prominent in the early church (Acts 3:7; 5:12-16; 8:7; 19:12; 28:8; James 5:14).

As to the nature of the gift of healing, it will be observed that —

The exercise of the gift was ordinarily conditional on the faith of the one needing the healing (Mark 6:5, 6; 10: 52; Acts 14:9).

There had to be faith not only in God, the Giver of the gift, but in the human agent possessing the gift (Acts 3:4; 5:15; 9:17).

The human agent himself had to be a person of great faith (Matthew 17: 19). The power possessed of inspiring the needy with confidence indicates the addition of a strong, magnetic personality. J. C. Lambert, in his *I.S. B.E.* article says that

The diseases cured appear for the most part to have been not organic but functional; and many of them would now be classed as nervous disorders. The conclusion from these data is that the gifts of healing to which Paul alludes were not miraculous endowments, but natural therapeutic faculties raised to their highest power by Christian faith.

Modern medical science has come to recognize the dependence of the physical upon the spiritual, of "the control of bodily functions by the subconscious self, and the physician's ability by means of suggestion, whether waking or hypnotic, to influence the subconscious soul and set free the healing powers of nature, provides the *physiological* basis." As J. C. Lambert further remarks that faith in God

working through the soul upon the body, is the mightiest of all healing influences, and that one who by his own faith and sympathy and force of personality can stir up faith in others may exercise by God's blessing the power of healing diseases.

As to the permanency of the gift of healing, while church historians tell us that such a gift was claimed and practiced by some of the early fathers, it would seem as if the exercise of this gift along with others, gradually ceased. In recent years, however, largely through the activity of various faith healing movements, some of which are not commendable, healing of bodily ailments and diseases has come to the fore. So-called faith-healers who are hostile to the ordinary practice of medicine, and who are ignorant of the marvels of the subconscious mind to produce the psychical basis of healing, are not to be trusted. With all in his faith in the Spirit's gift of healing, and experience of His power, Paul yet chose Luke the physician as his companion, and likewise urged Timothy to resort to medicinal means of healing for his stomach ailment. To quote J. C. Lambert again —

> Upon the modern church there seems to lie the duty of reaffirming the reality and permanence of the primitive gift of healing, while relating it to the scientific practice of medicine as another power ordained by God, and its natural ally in the task of diffusing the Christian gospel of health.

To conclude, there must be the careful distinction between God's ability and His willingness to heal. That He is able to heal any kind of physical infirmity or disease cannot be doubted. He alone is the Healer. But, while He does not willingly afflict His children, He yet permits sickness, pain or disease to overtake them, as in the case of Paul's "thorn in the flesh." Sufferers may not understand God's purpose in the allowance of physical ailments. Yet, resting in His good and acceptable will, grace is theirs to climb nearer to Him by the path of pain. Full emancipation from all the ills the flesh is heir to is a future benediction (I Corinthians 15:44; Revelation 21:4).

The Herdman

Jabal who was "the father of such as have cattle" (Genesis 4:20), can be looked upon as the first herdman of the Bible. Like Abel before him, Jabal was a shepherd. The difference between a shepherd and a herdman is that the former cared for flocks of sheep, while the latter looked after herds of cattle. Often, of course, the two occupations were combined, as in the case of Jacob's sons (Genesis 46:32-34; 47:1-3). Amos, the first of the prophets to write a book was "one of the herdmen of Tekoa." Abraham, Lot and Isaac had herdmen in their employ (Genesis 13:7, 8; 26:20; I Samuel 21:7). The herdman and his herd came to know one another. Each animal could be given a name, to which it would answer. In the New Testament herd is only used of swine (Matthew 8:30-32; Mark 5:11, 13; Luke 8:32, 33). Amos used the term "cowherd" (7:14).

Sometimes a herdman represents a "sheepmaster," one who tended, fed and sheared sheep. Herdmen were seldom owners of sheep but were hirelings. Mesha, a chief of Moab, was a "sheepspotter" (II Kings 3:4). In ancient times, and in the East today, spotting or marking the wool with different dyes was a method of distinguishing sheep of different flocks. Thus, originally, a herdman was one who painted one or more spots on the backs of animals as a means of identification. Does not the divine Herdman place His own distinguishing mark upon His sheep? "The Lord knoweth them that are his" (II Timothy 2:19).

The Hewer

Under a previous cameo, THE FELLER the reader will find material to add to this section. Hewers and hewing are frequently mentioned in the Bible. Probably forced labor was employed in the manufacture of axes, saws and hammers and the use of them for tree-felling and for the extraction of stones from quarries. The 80,000 hewers Solomon used for the wood and stone work of the temple were practically slaves (I Kings 5:15; II Chronicles 2:10, 18).

The felling and gathering of wood, like drawing water, was deemed a menial task. It was thus that Joshua set the Gibeonites to hewing wood and drawing water as a punishment for their deception. If it had not been for the oath which Joshua had sworn, the Gibeonites would have been killed (Joshua 9:21, 23, 27). The hewers must have been men of massive strength for tree-felling and the hewing of stone out of rocks.

As for the implements the hewers used, smiths or workers in heavy tools of cutting and carving provided the necessary axes (II Kings 6:5; Jeremiah 50:16), saws (II Samuel 12:31), hammers (Isaiah 41:7). Although present methods of tree-felling and stonecutting were known to the ancients, some modern implements are but a development of what they used.

Axes

Among the different axes used, the most frequently mentioned are the felling axes and the carpenter's axe (Deuteronomy 19:5; 20:19; I Kings 6: 5, 7; Psalm 74:5; Isaiah 10:15). The judgment-ministry of John the Baptist and of Christ is symbolized by an axe hewing down fruitless trees (Matthew 3:9, 10; Luke 3:9). The same figure is employed to describe the destruc-

tion of idols and of God's enemies (Deuteronomy 12:3; I Samuel 11:7; 15:33; Isaiah 22:16; Daniel 4:14, 23; Hosea 6:5).

Saws

The use of this implement goes back to antiquity. Stones for the temple were shaped by saws (I Kings 7:9). A stonecutter was one who hewed out and shaped stones. The word is used of Joseph of Arimathaea who had hewn out of rock a sepulchre for himself, but which he gave for the burial of Christ's body (Matthew 27:60; Mark 15:46). Isaiah uses it figuratively of Israel hewn out of a rock (51:1). The prophet also uses the carpenter's saw in a figurative sense (Isaiah 10: 15). Tradition has it that being sawn asunder (Hebrews 11:37) refers to the torture inflicted upon Isaiah by Manasseh.

Jeremiah uses the hewing out of stone cisterns to illustrate the schemes and programs which Israel had conceived for pleasure and profit but which were doomed to failure because God had been omitted from them and because they were contrary to His revealed word and will.

The Horseman

As horses were the only means of transportation by road in Bible times both horses and horsemen figure prominently throughout the Scriptures. Letters were sent by posts, or postmen, on horseback (Esther 8:10). Access from one place to another was by horseback (II Kings 9:18, 19; Esther 6:9, 11). In the main throughout the Old Testament, however, horsemen and horses are associated with warlike operations and the appearance of these war horses and their riders created a great impression. Job supplies us with a remarkable description of the spirited war horse (39:19-25).

Some of the horsemen were known as "chariotriders" — a chariot having two horses and one driver. Horses and chariots were the property of kings and rulers. The horsemen themselves were warriors of stamina, skill and courage.

Horses — the noblest and most useful of animals — are sometimes spoken of as "strong ones" or "swift steeds" (Judges 5:22; Jeremiah 8:16; Micah 1:13, ASV). Although there is no allusion to horses among the animal wealth of Abraham (Genesis 12:16), he must have possessed a number. The first direct reference to horses is found among the property the people gave to Joseph in exchange for grain during Egypt's grievous famine (Genesis 47:17). Israel was warned against keeping horses lest they should glory in their strength and forget God. Trust in horses is put in opposition to trust in God (Deuteronomy 17:16; Psalms 20:7; 33:17; Isaiah 30:16; 31: 1-6). Today as the nations are trusting in their nuclear weapons little mention is being made of the necessity of trusting the Lord God.

The majority of horses came from Egypt (Isaiah 31:1; Ezekiel 17:15), where they were one of the chief sources of commerce. Pharaoh had his horses and horsemen, which in war were associated with iron chariots (Exodus 14:9; Joshua 11:4). Countless numbers were required by the Canaanites (Joshua 17:16, 18). The Philistines were a military people, well-disciplined and armed, with 31,-000 war chariots and 6,000 gallant horsemen at their services (I Samuel 13:5). These lancers, archers and charioteers presented a formidable sight, and gave a nation ascendancy in time of war (Jeremiah 46:4; Nahum 3:2, 3). In Old Testament days the horses were apparently unshod (Isaiah 5:28).

David wrote a warning against trusting in horses and chariots, which was often done in days of war (II Samuel 8:4). Solomon disregarded the ancient law in a great way (Deuteronomy 17:16) in the multiplication of horses and their riders. The record has it that he possessed 40,000 stalls of horses and 12,000 horsemen, as part of the nation's military equipment (I Samuel 8:11; I Kings 4:26; Song of Solomon 1:9). When the Jews returned from Exile they brought 736 horses with them (Nehemiah 7:68).

As the Jews degenerated the horse figured as an object of idolatry. Being deemed sacred to the sun they were kept in the temple (II Kings 23:5; Ezekiel 8:16). War chariots were placed at the entrance of the sacred edifice (II Kings 11:16; 23:11). In Josiah's great reformation these objects of idolatry were removed.

The equipment of horsemen is used to enforce spiritual and moral lessons. Bit and bridle are compared to the tongue (Psalm 32:9; Proverbs 26:3; James 3:3). Horsebells and "precious clothes for chariots" (Ezekiel 27:20; Zechariah 14:20) are also used figuratively. Occasionally "horses" are used as symbols of divine prophecy. The "horse" is mentioned fifteen times in the Book of Revelation, thirteen times in vision form (6:2, 4, 5, 8; 9:7, 9, 17; 14:20; 19:11, 14, 19, 21), and twice otherwise (18:13; 19:18). "Horsemen" numbering "twice ten thousand times ten thousand" are also referred to (9: 16, ASV).

Horses and chariots of fire were associated with the translation of Elijah (II Kings 2:11). The great strength of the horse is symbolic of the greater strength of God (Psalm 20:7; 33:17; 76:6). The various colored horses are symbolic of international and national crises. White is the symbol of triumph, victory, conquest (Zechariah 1:

116   *The Householder — The Hunter*

8; 6:3; Revelation 6:4). Red symbolizes revolution, war, bloodshed (Zechariah 1:8; 6:3, 6; Revelation 6:4; 19: 11-15). Black stands for disease and pestilence (Zechariah 6:6; Revelation 6:5). Pale or green or livid — famine, misery, death (Zechariah 6:3; Revelation 6:8). Jeremiah uses the figure of "horses" when he asks, "What are the petty troubles that fall on one compared with what others suffer, with what might come on himself?" The man wearied in a foot race should not venture, as Elijah had done (I Kings 18:46), to measure his speed against horses.

Surprisingly enough, horses and horsemen are not mentioned either in the gospels or in the epistles. Apart from the Book of Revelation, the only mention of horses in the New Testament is in James 3:3. Horsemen only occur elsewhere in Acts 23:23, 32. The nearest approach to war horses and their riders is in the use of legion (Matthew 26:53; Mark 5:9, 15; Luke 8:30). In the time of Christ, a "legion" represented a complete army of infantry and cavalry of upwards of 5,000 men.

The Householder

Here we have the title of an occupation Jesus seems to have delighted in and which He applied directly to Himself. In the parable of the vineyard, we can readily see that the householder is the Lord Himself (Matthew 20:1-16). In fact, the term is used only by the Lord in relation to Himself (Matthew 13:27, 52; 20:1; 21:33), and means despot, ruler, or the one commanding the household made up of the family unit and all who serve the family. The same Greek word is translated, "master of the house" (Matthew 10:25; Luke 13:25). As the Master, He has absolute owner-

ship and uncontrolled power. He is Lord (Luke 2:29; Acts 4:24; Jude 4, ASV). All authority is His, and He must be followed and obeyed by the church in all matters of faith and worship (Matthew 23:8, 10). "Goodman of the house" (Matthew 20:11; 24:43; Mark 14:14; Luke 12:39), expresses the same thought as "householder" or "master" (See Proverbs 7:19). As the Goodman or Master, of the house, He has every right to a guestchamber. "*My* guestchamber" (Mark 14:14), a form implying discipleship on the part of the owner of the house.

In His choice of the title of householder and the application of it to Himself, our Lord intended His parable (Matthew 13:24-30) to set forth the pattern of patient wisdom. As the Lord He knows that He can defeat the malice of His foes but He always chooses His own time and plan. (For a fuller study of THE HOUSEHOLDER see the author's *All the Parables of the Bible*.) As the church, which the Lord purchased with His own blood, is referred to as a "spiritual house" (I Peter 2:5), He is indeed its Householder, or its Master. The question of paramount importance is, Are we as members of His household subject to His control in all things pertaining to life and service?

The Hunter

Only two Bible characters are actually named as having this occupation. Nimrod was a mighty hunter before the Lord (Genesis 10:9); and Esau was a cunning, or skillful, hunter (Genesis 25:27; 27:30).

When Nimrod, the great figure of Biblical antiquity who owed his prominence to his wickedness, is said to have been a mighty hunter "before the Lord," the same does not mean that in humble dependence upon the Lord he pursued his craft as a hunter.

Josephus translates the passage, "He did evil against the Lord." Before can mean "opposition" (Numbers 16:2). Benjamin Keach says, "More rightly the phrase 'before the Lord,' is to be understood to denote an aggravation of his tyranny, because he did not act obscurely or privately, but openly and in the face of the sun, imposing his government without respect to men or dread of an allseeing Divinity (Genesis 6:11; 13:13). Nimrod is said plainly to be 'mighty' upon the earth, which is by any means to be understood as his rule over men" (I Chronicles 1:10).

Nimrod gloried in his fleshly strength, prostituting it for unholy purpose. As a hunter, he abused his craft violently to oppress and subdue men. Although he attained prowess hunting animals, he himself was more of a wild beast than a human being in that he had greater sport in hunting men. In order to fulfill his ambitious desire, namely, the conquest of his fellowmen, all other considerations became subservient to such an ignoble purpose. If, as some scholars suggest, the name Nimrod implies, "He will revolt," then the name indicated the nature of one who aspired to be the leader of a revolution against divine authority. He was destitute of divine piety and set himself against the divine will. Nimrod's plans, however, were frustrated by the miracle of the confusion of tongues (Genesis 10:5, 18, 25). Thus the wickedness of this mighty hunter was rebuked by God.

In ancient times hunting was regarded as an art of highest importance. Thus Ishmael became an archer and lived on the produce of his bow and arrow (Genesis 21:20); and Esau was skillful in the "chase" (Genesis 25:27). Wild animals and birds were appreciated as food (Leviticus 17:13; Hosea 9:8). When, to the Israelites, hunting was no longer a necessity, they still hunted for the roebuck, the gazelle, the hart and the wild goat (Deuteronomy 12:22; 14:5), as well as for the destruction of wild beasts (Deuteronomy 12:15; I Kings 13:24; Proverbs 28:15). While hunting is not conspicuous in the literature of the Hebrews, the records of other great nations have numerous references to such an occupation. It is worthy of note that, although the Bible does not mention the hunting dog, it was familiar to Josephus.

Those whom God uses to fulfil His purpose are referred to as "hunters" (Jeremiah 16:16). Enemies of the righteous are likewise spoken of in the same way (Job 10:16; Proverbs 6:26; Micah 7:2). The satanic hunter, the devil, always lies in wait to plunder the divine flock. All who are the Lord's are his prey. A hunter is one that pursues, or eagerly follows after his prey. Unwearied in the chase, he is satisfied when he has caught his game. It is thus with the devil, whose game are the godly and ungodly alike. He is never weary *of* such pursuit, nor weary *in* it. Hunters usually hunt for recreation and not out of any hatred for the creatures they hunt. But the devil hunts the souls of men out of that implacable hatred he bears to them, and also the hatred to God who seeks to bless those whom the devil would destroy.

Hunting is also attributed to God, when He inflicts those punishments upon the ungodly they had first inflicted upon the godly. "He shall hunt them" (Psalm 140:5, 10, 11). Here "to hunt" means to chase to a precipice or to overthrow (see Habakkuk 2:17). Various implements were used in hunting — nets, bow and arrow, pitfalls, snares, traps, gins, slings and clubs, many of which are used to expose the desires of the wicked (Job

41:19; Psalms 9:15; 25:15; 35:7; 142:3). To review all the metaphors drawn from hunting, huntsmen, their traps and their victims, the reader is referred to *Bible Metaphors* by Benjamin Keach. It is most profitable to note New Testament references to those who succumb to worldly snares (Luke 11:54; 21:34, 35; Romans 11:9; I Timothy 3:7; 6:12; II Timothy 2:26, etc.).

The Husbandman

The different Hebrew and Greek words used of this occupation denote the husbandman as a plowman, a man or cultivator of the soil, a tiller of the ground (II Chronicles 26:10; Joel 1:11; Zechariah 13:5; Matthew 21:33; John 15:1, etc.). The first man to be named thus was Noah, who after the Flood "began to be an husbandman" (Genesis 9:20), "tiller of the ground" (Genesis 4:2). Husband not only describes a man who has a wife, but one who directs and manages with frugality. So we speak of a person who husbands his resources or strength. A husbandman, then, is one who knows how to till or work the soil to the best advantage. Originally, suggesting "a householder," or "master of the house," husbandman became limited in its meaning to "farmer" or "tiller of the soil." Both the pride over an abundant harvest and the difficulties of the husbandman are recognized in the Bible (Jeremiah 31:24; 51:23; 52:16; James 5:7). In the parable of the householder, the wicked husbandmen were those Jewish leaders who rejected God's claims as the Owner (Matthew 21:33).

Our Lord referred to the Father as the Husbandman, and as such He sows, cultivates, prunes and expects abundant fruit for His own (John 15:1). Developing the metaphor as applied to God, Benjamin Keach says that four things are supposed —

1. That an husbandman must have ground to work upon.
2. A stock to defray the charges and expense requisite to manage it.
3. Skill and knowledge to perform it.
4. Instruments, and whatsoever else is needful for such an undertaking, or employment.

Then Keach elaborates on these aspects as applied to God the Husbandman —

1. God is a rich Husbandman; for all the world is His (Exodus 9:29).
2. He is a great and honorable Husbandman, and all bow before Him.
3. He is a skillful and wise Husbandman. None can teach Him.
4. He is a diligent and careful Husbandman. He is never guilty of neglect.
5. He is a generous and liberal Husbandman. All partake of His bounty.

Husbandry, antedating all other arts (Genesis 2:5), is a kindred term, and is used by Paul as a type of the church of God. "Ye are God's tilled land, or God's field" (I Corinthians 3:9). Here we have the suggestion of the diligent toil of the apostles, both in the ministry of the Gospel and in the care or cultivation of church life. Life in Christ had to produce the fruit of the Spirit hence the apostolic emphasis on the necessity of spiritual fruitfulness in the believer. It is said of King Uzziah that "he loved husbandry" (II Chronicles 26:10), meaning he loved to foster agriculture. Those who labor in the vineyard of the heavenly Husbandman should likewise love husbandry in the spiritual sense. A proverb has it, "Good husbandry is good divinity." Shakespeare speaks of "husbandry in heaven." The church needs more of it on earth.

The Innkeeper

There are five interesting references to inns in the Bible (Genesis 42:27; 43:21; Exodus 4:24; Luke 2:7; 10:34). In ancient times the inn was a lodging place for passing the night. Vine says it was a place where all were received, and denotes a house for the reception of strangers, a *caravanserai,* translated "inn" in the parable of the good samaritan (Luke 10:34), with provision for the shelter of cattle and beasts of burden. "Find in an inn a place of rest." In the days of the Patriarchs, the inn was a resting place where tents might be spread near water and pastures (Exodus 4:24). Some kind of shelter was necessary for caravans, not only for rest while traveling but also for protection from dangers. In modern Palestine, hotels are now found along the popular routes of travel.

We must be careful not to confuse the Eastern inn with inns we are familiar with today. In Bible times the inn was a structure without a landlord, without furniture and without food or provender. The latter could be purchased nearby. The sons of Jacob took all necessities along with them (Genesis 42:27). In some cases inns had a superintendent or host as with the inn our Lord depicted (Luke 10: 34, 35). Generally speaking, however, inns were located in remote places (Jeremiah 9:2; 41:1) — habitation here was likely an "inn."

While the Bible does not say so, tradition tells us that innkeepers were usually untruthful, dishonest, oppressive and infamous; and that the repute of public inns forced the early Christians to prefer the keeping of open homes for travelers, which may account for the repeated commendation of Christian hospitality (Hebrews 13:2; I Peter 4:9; II John 5). Women connected with some of the inns were often of a loose character. "Rahab the harlot" is given as "Rahab the innkeeper" (Joshua 2:1) in the *Targum.*

The most celebrated inn in the Bible is the one connected with Jesus' birth. Arriving late, Joseph and Mary found the guestchamber already occupied and had to resort to the clean animal quarters. Thus Jesus was laid in the safest and most convenient place, preserved from the annoyance and evil associations of a public inn. His first humble bed, then, was a place reserved for cattle. Manger is derived from the verb meaning "to eat" or "a feeding place." It may be necessary to point out that the Bible nowhere states a stable _in connection with Christ's birth. Pictures depicting the wise men worshiping Him in a stable surrounded by cattle is not based upon Scripture. In A.D. 165 Justin wrote — "Having failed to find any lodging in the town, Joseph sought shelter in a neighboring cavern of Bethlehem." Some fifty years later Origen declared that "at Bethlehem is shown the grotto where Christ first saw the light." It is said that the mother of Constantine the Great, identifying the grotto converted it into a chapel, and that later a basilica was erected over it.

Numerous expressive poems and hymns have been written about the inn in which Joseph and Mary failed to find accommodation. Ada Blenkhorn's poem begins with the verse —

No warm, downy pillow His sweet head
  pressed;
No soft, silken garments His fair form
  dressed;
  He lay in a manger,
  This heavenly Stranger,

The precious Lord Jesus, the Wonderful Child.

The Instructor

The Bible has much to say about instructors, divine, pastoral and parental. The instructor, or catechist, in the Old Testament was one who taught others the principles of the divine truth. Matthew Henry says of Abraham that "he not only took care of his children, but that his whole household, including his servants were *catechised*" (Exodus 12:26). Priests and Levites also functioned as instructors (Leviticus 10:11; Deuteronomy 33:10). The school of the prophets was designed to instruct or teach, those young men called to represent God.

In the New Testament, an instructor was one who taught others the principles of the Christian faith. The original of "catechist," meaning, "to instruct," also carries the significance "to answer," "to echo." One writer observes that, "Classically the word was used of the sounding down of rushing water, of the falling of music from a ship in the sea. Then it came to signify the sounding down of words of command or instruction." It was thus that Luke instructed Theophilus in truth divinely received (Luke 1:4). In Christ's commission, the disciples were commanded to go and "teach" or "instruct" (Matthew 28:18-20). Christ Himself was the Great Catechist, or Instructor (Matthew 16:13, etc.). He was more than a Teacher, but as a Teacher He appeared as One having unique knowledge and unusual influence. "Never man spake like this man." God is also magnified throughout Scripture as the infallible and patient Instructor of His own (Deuteronomy 32:10; Psalm 32:8; Isaiah 28:26, etc.). The Pharisees, who were supposed to be teachers of God's ancient Law, were more concerned in their instruction of the people with vain traditions. What anathemas Jesus heaped upon them for prostituting their occupation as professed, religious instructors!

Paul is prominent as a master instructor (Acts 14:21; 19:8, 9; I Corinthians 3:2). What skill and clarity of thought were his as a teacher of divine truth! If "instruct" means "to whet or sharpen," or "nurture" (Romans 2:20; I Corinthians 4:15), then the apostle excelled in whetting the appetites of the saints for the things of God. Of his apt illustration about "ten thousand instructors," Ellicott says —

Paul had a right to address the Corinthians as a father would his children. They may have had since their conversion a host of instructors, but they could have only one father who beget them in Jesus Christ. That father was Paul. "I have begotten you." I, emphatic as opposed to "many." The word rendered instructors originally signified the slave who led the child to school but subsequently had the larger meaning, which we attach to the word pedagogue (Galatians 3:24, 25). This is a contrast implied between the harsh severity of a pedagogue and the loving tenderness of a father.

What is said of Paul is also true of Peter and John, both of whom nurtured, or instructed, believers in the faith (I Peter 2:2; I John 2:13). Correcting, or instructing, is used of family discipline (Hebrews 12:6, 7, 11), as well as of the discipline of a school (Acts 19:9; Romans 2:20; Hebrews 12:9). The word Paul used for "instruction" in Philippians 4:12 means to initiate into the mysteries of the faith, as the ASV indicates. "I learned the secret." Dr. H. H. Meyer remarks that, "Of the pedagogic experience, wisdom and learning of ancient sages, the Book of Proverbs forms the Biblical respository" (See Proverbs 1:4, 5, 8; 17:10; 22:6; 23:13, 14). Sound Biblical instruction by Spirit-taught teachers is sorely needed in church and home life today.

The Interpreter

There is, of course, a close association between this occupation, and that of THE INSTRUCTOR we have just considered. A true interpreter is one who instructs or expounds as he interprets. Although there are only four references to the interpreter in the Bible, there are over sixty cognates of the term with a wide variety of uses, the majority of which are found in the Book of Daniel. Two words are used by Moses for interpreter. The first one means "to treat as a scorner or foreigner" (Genesis 42:23). The other Hebrew word means "to interpret or explain" (Genesis 40:8). The Greek word Paul uses for interpreter (I Corinthians 14:28), means "one who interprets or explains fully" and implies a person with ability to explain the words of a different language — a thorough and competent interpreter.

In ancient times when dreams were regarded as manifestations of divine intervention in human affairs, it was essential to have those who were qualified to explain such mysterious revelations. Thus, in the court of the Pharaohs there were those who were known as interpreters of dreams, or sacred scribes — wise men (Genesis 41:8, ASV margin). In Joseph's day there were official interpreters whose occupation it was to translate foreign languages into the Egyptian tongue for the court (Genesis 42:23). Ambassadors at foreign courts had to be able to act as interpreters (II Chronicles 32:31; Ezra 4:7). In Daniel's time there was a similar body of wise or learned men at the Babylonian court for the same purpose (Daniel 2:

2; 4:6). These interpreters were often promoted to high position in the court of their heathen masters: Joseph (Genesis 40:8, 44), Daniel (Daniel 1:3-5, 11-16; 2:1; 4). It is interesting to observe that Joseph acted as an interpreter of dreams at the beginning of the covenant people's history, and that Daniel functioned in the same way toward the close of their history. Daniel's interpretation of the mystic handwriting on the wall brought him added promotion which continued into the reigns of Darius and Cyrus. To Daniel was granted supernatural spiritual insight enabling him to interpret the significance of successive monarchies right down the ages until the coming of Christ to earth to usher in His dominion.

Of Elihu's reference to the intercessory or ambassadorial ministry of angels in interpreting to man what God requires of him in the way of conduct, as well as explaining the mystery of His dealings with men (Job 33:23). Ellicott has this suggestive comment —

> This angel, who is one among a thousand, and discharges the function of an interpreter, is a remarkable anticipation of the existence of that function with God which is discharged by the Advocate with the Father (Romans 8:34; Hebrews 7:25; I John 2:1). It is impossible for us who believe that all Scripture is given by inspiration of God not to see in this an indication of what God intended afterwards to teach us concerning the intercession and mediation of the Son and the intercession of the Holy Spirit on behalf of man (Romans 8:26; See John 14:16).

Many of the prophets are also described as interpreters, or ambassadors, explaining to Israel the message of God as they were able to receive it (II Kings 18:26; II Chronicles 32:31,

ASV, Isaiah 43:27). What all God-called interpreters had to bear in mind was the principle that no truth divinely given was of "private interpretation" (II Peter 1:20). They were forbidden putting their own construction, or meaning, upon the "God-breathed" Words (II Timothy 3:16). Too many expositors are like those about whom Christopher Pitt of the seventeenth century wrote in *The Art of Preaching*

> Talks much, and says just nothing for an hour.
> Truth and the text he labours to display,
> Till both are quite interpreted away.

Says C. H. Schodde, "The moment the Bible student has in his own mind what was in the mind of the author or authors of Bible books when these were written, he has interpreted the thought of the Scriptures." Interpretation not only included the gifts of expounding dreams, and of translating one language into another, but also that of exposition, or showing the sense and import of any truth. On the part of the true interpreter there had to be deep spirituality of life in order for him to give the interpretation of any matter from the divine standpoint. It was John Morley who wrote, "A greater interpreter of life ought not himself to need interpretation." Of such was Jesus, the divine Interpreter who interpreted or expounded to His disciples on the Emmaus Road the truths in Old Testament Scriptures concerning Himself (Luke 24:27).

Among the special spiritual gifts bestowed upon some believers in the early church was that of speaking with tongues, which necessitated another gift, namely that of the power of interpreting or explaining ecstatic utterances (I Corinthians 12:12-30; 14:5-28). A person who spoke in tongues might possess the gift of interpreting his strange message for the benefit of the assembly, or, on the other hand, he might not. "In the latter event his duty was to keep silence, unless an interpreter were at hand to make his message intelligible to the other assembled worshipers (I Corinthians 12:10, 30; 14:26)."

The hymnist has taught us to sing that when the heart is perplexed by the seeming mysteries of life, "God is His own Interpreter, and He will make it plain." Doubtless you are familiar with the person John Bunyan describes as Interpreter, "a very grave person, who bore his great commission in his look." He could be easily identified by these features —

> His eyes were lifted up toward Heaven . . .
> The best of Books was in his hands . . .
> The law of truth was written upon his lips . . .
> The world was behind his back . . .
> He stood as if he pleaded with men . . .
> A crown of gold did hang about his head.

Charles Lamb in *Essays of Elia* speaks of one who "When he goes about with you to show you the halls and colleges, you think you have with you the Interpreter at the House Beautiful."

The Inventor

Inventions imply inventors, and the seven-fold reference in Scripture to different kinds of inventions forces us to think of the occupation before us. Only once does inventor appear, namely when Paul uses the word in the plural form of those who pervert their gift, "Inventors of evil things" (Romans 1:30). Here, the term means "one who finds out something." The corrupt minds of these inventors contrive or scheme out things others never thought of. Among the articles in *The Common Book of Prayer* we have this one — "A fond thing vainly invented and grounded upon no warranty of Scripture." Such are the evil inventions the godless conceive.

We owe our advanced civilization, with all its amenities, to noble-minded inventors whose manifold inventions have benefited mankind. Often necessity drove them to their beneficial inventions. A Greek saying reminds us that, "There is nothing more inventive than suffering." To which we can add the French proverb that, "Fear is a great inventor." One man's invention is improved on by another inventive mind. "Invention breeds invention," wrote Emerson.

Taking the Biblical references to inventions we have the engines invented by cunning or skillful men used by King Uzziah in the defense of Jerusalem (II Chronicles 26:15). These engines, called "balista" by the Romans, could eject stones weighing 300 pounds a quarter of a mile. This is the first notice that occurs in world history of the use of machines for throwing projectiles. Pliny expressly says that these engines of destruction originated in Syria. Today scientists have invented the most terrifying missiles well able to destroy the world. The best brains seem to be bent on inventing more dreadful man-destroying bombs than any yet produced.

Divine judgment overtook those inventions alien to the divine will. "Thou tookest vengeance of their inventions or works" (Psalm 99:8). Retribution can be expected for the works and ways of men who are not of God, but only gratify the sinful desires of those who engage in them. We have a similar thought in Psalm 106:29 — "They provoked him to anger with their inventions: and the plague brake in upon them" — and also in verse 39, "Thus were they defiled with their own works, and went awhoring with their own inventions." The people conformed to the lifeless idols they had invented, and thus became spiritual adulterers (Psalm 73:27).

Solomon's reference to the knowledge enabling him to find out "witty inventions" (Proverbs 8:12), implies the desire to discover well-thought-out plans or devices. "Witty" means wise, discreet, intelligent (Proverbs 1:4, where "discretion" can be translated "thoughtfulness" — a word used in a bad sense in "wicked devices" 12:2). Solomon also gave us this expressive fact: "God hath made man upright; but they have sought out many inventions" (Ecclesiastes 7:29). Too often the inventions have been adverse to the uprightness man was created with. His inventions were — and are — devised and contrived to gratify ends God never intended. Interpreting the above verse in the light of the context it would seem that among man's inventions was the breaking of God's primeval marriage, joining one man to one woman (Matthew 19:4-6). In the gross polygamy Solomon invented, he experienced the bitter fruits of disobedience.

Amos wrote of those who invented instruments of music, like David (6:5). Those the prophet described fancied they could equal David in his remarkable musical skill (I Chronicles 23:5; Nehemiah 12:36). "They defended their luxurious passion for music by his example; forgetting that he pursued this study when at peace and free from danger, and that for the praise of God; but they pursue for their own self-gratification, and that when God is angry and ruin is imminent." From Jubal the first inventor "of all such as handle the harp and organ" (Genesis 4:21), men have designed instruments producing music sublime and uplifting.

The Jailor

Before considering all that is implied by this unenviable occupation, a word is necessary about the term itself, whether it is jailer, jailor or gaolor. Joseph T. Shipley in his *Dictionary of Word Origins* says that "gaol" is from the Old French *cageoler* which is derived from "cajole" meaning to chatter like a bird in a cage — a chattering to entice wild birds to be caught. From the thirteenth century spelling "gaiole" we have the English "jail."

In Bible times "imprisonment" was more of a preventative measure to be sure of the culprit's whereabouts (Leviticus 24:12; Numbers 15:34). Prisons among the Egyptians and Assyrians were totally different from their punitive confinement of today. In the day of Christ, prisons followed Greek and Roman models, which meted out a more positive and repressive treatment. Josephus the Jewish historian says that the prison in which John the Baptist was beheaded was the Castle of Machaerus (Matthew 5:25; 14:3, 10, See Mark 6:17; Luke 12:58; 22:33; 23:9). Prisons in which Peter and John were put by Jewish authorities were known as "the common prison" or "public ward" (Acts 4:3; 5:18; 8:3). As for Paul, he experienced the mild form of restraint and the severity of "the inner prison," and also the horrors of the Mamertine dungeon (Acts 16:23; 28:30; II Corinthians 6:5, See Hebrews 11:36; Revelation 2:20). Prisons of our day are vastly different from those of centuries ago when prisoners were cast into damp and dark dungeons, and with chains rusting on their limbs sat huddled together on rotting straw. We have become more humane in the treatment of prisoners.

The Bible has a great deal to say about prisons and jailors or keepers of prisons. Some of the saintliest men in Scripture found themselves in prison: Joseph spent several years in prison during his sojourn in Egypt, and for part of the time was an assistant jailor (Genesis 39:20, 23; 40:3, 5). Joseph's prison was known as "The Round House" signifying a round-like tower used as a prison. Joseph had already found a disused cistern to be a convenient place of detention (Genesis 37:24). The same word for "prison" is also given as "dungeon" or "dungeon house" (Exodus 12:29; Jeremiah 20:2; 32:2; 33:1; 37:16; 38:6; Zechariah 9:11). Four different places are mentioned as places of detention (Jeremiah 37:15, 16). Often imprisonment was rigorous and cruel. There was, for instance, the prison house of the Philistines in which Samson was blinded and then bound with fetters of brass (Judges 16:21-25; See I Kings 22:27; II Chronicles 16:10; Psalm 107:10). Jeremiah speaks of a prison as "a house of bonds" (37:15). One form of irksome punishment was that of being placed in stocks (Jeremiah 20:2; 29:26), compelling the prisoner to sit in a crooked position (II Chronicles 16:10).

Some of the Bible characters who endured imprisonment experienced remarkable happenings. Peter, sleeping between two soldiers (Bible jailors were usually soldiers), bound to each of them by a chain, had a strange warder visit his cell. It was the angel of the Lord who had come to free him. Paul, too, was under a good many jailors at Philippi, Jerusalem, Caesarea and Rome. But "in prisons oft," the apostle was still an ambassador for Christ, although in bonds. At Philippi, Paul and Silas as prisoners triumphed over their adversity and sang praises to God at the midnight hour, and as General Wm. Booth expressed it, "God was so pleased with those prayers and praises that He said, Amen! with a mighty earthquake." The jailor was about to commit suicide supposing all his prisoners had escaped. It was the rule that if the prisoner escaped then the jailor had to suffer the same punishment destined for the prisoner. But through the display of God's power in the material world, the jailor and all his household were saved. How differently that jailor treated his prisoners after he accepted Christ as Saviour! "He washed their stripes" — stripes he had inflicted.

Typically, a prison can represent souls held in bondage by sin, doubts or fears (Psalm 142:7; Isaiah 42:7; Matthew 12:29; John 8:32, 36). But a full emancipation is offered to all prisoners through Him who was kept a prisoner until He died to set the sin-bound free (Isaiah 53:8; 61:1; Zechariah 9:12; I Peter 3:19). He alone can break the power of cancelled sin, and set the prisoner free.

The Judge

Something of the tremendous impact of divine justice is felt in multitudinous references to judgment. Over 700 times in Scripture judge, judgment, and their cognates are mentioned. As the Judge of all the earth, God has laid down the principles of both divine and human judgments. The Hebrew word for judge originally meant to "pronounce the oracle." When Moses, who was the nation's judge after Israel left Egypt, sat "to judge the people," he actually gave divine decisions on all matters presented by the people (Exodus 18:13-20). Then the term took on a wider application (18:25, 26). Thus, at the outset, a judge was a priest who pronounced divine oracles. But with the process, the functions of a judge were exercised by an outstanding leader chosen from among the elders on account of his wisdom or superior skill in warfare, and to all intents and purposes became a king (Judges 8:22). One of the main duties of a king was to judge (II Samuel 15: 1-6; I Kings 3:9; II Kings 15:5). "Judge" and "king" are used synonymously (Hosea 7:7; Amos 2:3). Authority was based on custom.

Moral qualifications, as well as valor, were necessary on the part of those set apart to judge. The prophets often denounced the corruption of the purity of justice by bribery and false witness (Proverbs 6:19; 12:17; 18:5; Isaiah 1:23; 5:23; 10:1; Amos 5:12; 6:2; Micah 3:11; 7:3). Kings, acting as judges, sometimes pronounced unjust sentences (I Samuel 22:6-19; I Kings 22:26; II Kings 21:16; Jeremiah 36: 26). Ahab was an evil king who influenced local courts to do his will (I Kings 22:1-13). Scripture is clear, however, regarding the character of a judge. "The sacro-sanctity of Judges is marked by their bearing the designation 'gods' as exercising some of God's delegated power (Psalm 82:1, 6; Exodus 21:6 where the Hebrew for 'gods' is 'judges'), God being the source of all justice."

Moses, the judge, made it clear that judges must be "able men, such as fear God, men of truth, hating covetousness" (Exodus 18:21). Fees for judgment were not allowed, but were regarded as bribery (I Samuel 12:3). A judge had not to wrest or pervert judgment, respect persons, or take a gift — a practice common among Eastern judges (Leviticus 19:15; Deuteronomy 16:19). He was likewise instructed "not to be afraid of the face of man, for the judgment is God's" (Deuteronomy 1:17; II Chronicles 19: 6, 7). His first duty was to exercise absolute justice, indifferent to popular opinion, showing the same partiality to rich or poor, to Jew or foreigner (Exodus 23:2, 3).

The seat of judgment was an open space before the gate of the city, the place of public resort (Exodus 18:13; Ruth 4:1, 12; Psalm 69:12; Proverbs 8:15). It was here that each party presented his case to the judge, with the accused appearing in court clad in mourning, and the accuser standing on the right hand of the accused (Deuteronomy 1:16; 25:1; Psalm 109: 6; Zechariah 3:1, 3). The only evidence allowed by the court had to be given by, at least, two witnesses (Deuteronomy 17:6; 19:5, See Matthew 18:16; II Corinthians 13:1; I Timothy 5:19). If the prescribed law was not quite definite, recourse was had to the divine oracle (Leviticus 24:12; Numbers 15:34). After a full hearing of a case, sentence was pronounced and the judgment carried out.

The Book of Judges is thus named because just as the designation the Books of Kings contains the exploits of the various kings of Israel and Judah, so Judges implies that it is a book containing a series of narratives of judges, or champions, or chieftains, who in turn, because of their devotion, prowess and wisdom were used by God to deliver His people and to administer justice. "Without assuming the state of royal authority, they acted for the time as vice-regents of Jehovah, the invisible King." Once the monarchy was instituted the king tried all cases at the palace gate (I Kings 7:7; Proverbs 20:8).

As a noun, judge is used of God, "a Judge who is God of all." He who is the Judge of His is at the same time their God (Hebrews 10:30; 12:23; James 4:12, ASV). Nothing is more frequently attributed to God in Scripture than the title of Judge, and as such He is the supreme Lord of the whole earth (Genesis 18:25; Psalms 58:11;

82:1). Christ is also presented as a Judge (Acts 10:42; II Timothy 4:8; James 5:9), as well as those who try and decide a case (Matthew 5:25; Luke 12:14, 58; 18:2, 6).

As a verb, judge means to weigh evidence and pronounce judgment, or to condemn and give sentence (Acts 15:19; 16:4; I Corinthians 6:1). Paul urges the saints to exercise a discerning judgment of all things as to their true value, remembering at all times the judgment seat of Christ, before which they themselves must appear (Romans 14:10; I Corinthians 2:14; 3:12-15; II Corinthians 5:10).

The Keeper

This general term is applied to a good many occupations in the Bible. Generally the keeper was one who observed, guarded, or preserved, and is used for the first time of Abel who is described as, "a keeper of sheep" (Genesis 4:2; I Samuel 17:20, 22). Then we have "keepers" of vineyards (Song of Solomon 1:6; 8:11) — "keepers" of prisons (Genesis 39:21; Acts 5:23; 16:27, etc.) — "keepers" of women (Esther 2:3) — "keepers" of the watch, of walls, of doors, of gates (II Kings 11:5; 22:14; 23:4; I Chronicles 9:19; Song of Solomon 5:7). "Keepers of the field" (Jeremiah 4:17) is an allusion to the open, exposed Arabian plantations necessitating guards who were placed at certain distances around the field.

The "keepers" who were overwhelmed at the appearance of the risen Christ were "the keeping men" of the guards of the garden (Matthew 28:4). Cain asked if he was his brother's keeper (Genesis 4:9). Achish made David "keeper" of his head, or commander of his bodyguard (I Samuel 28:2). Young mothers are exhorted to be "keepers at home" (Titus 2:5).

Solomon used the term, metaphorically, of the decay of bodily powers — "The keepers of the house shall tremble" (Ecclesiastes 12:3). "Keepers" here refer to the hands and arms which become paralytic or affected through the feebleness of old age.

Down the years the designation of "keeper" has been applied to various other occupations. It was commonly used of certain offices in early royal court circles. There were the keeper of the purse — keeper of the royal wardrobe, a position Harhas held in King Josiah's reign (II Kings 22:14) — lord keeper of the great seal, whose office since 1757, has been merged in that of the Lord Chancellor. Thomas Gray (1716-1771) wrote —

> My grave Lord Keeper led the brawls,
> The seals and maces danced before him.

"Keepers" was the name given in 1843 to a staff of men employed by Irish landlords to watch the crops and prevent their being smuggled during the night. Asaph was "the keeper of the king's forest" (Nehemiah 2:8).

The word used for keepers by Matthew (28:4), meaning to watch over, preserve, keep, is likewise used of the keeping power of God and of Christ in relation to those saved by grace. All the saints are not only saved, but secure (John 17:11, 12, 15; I Thessalonians 5:23). John speaks of Christ as their Keeper (I John 5:18; Jude 1). Psalm 121 is the "Psalm of the Keeper" — "the Lord is thy keeper" (121:5). For "preserve" in this psalm read "keep." The persistent repetition of this word is one of the chief beauties of the psalm. As our Keeper, He never sleeps — keeps Israel — keeps all from evil — keeps the soul — keeps our going out and our coming in, now and forevermore. Run your finger over all the references relating to being kept, and you will be comforted to know that divine guardianship covers every phase of life here below. Having such an almighty Keeper constantly about us, we should never have a fear nor a care.

The King

A study of Biblical royalty reveals a mixed bag of kings and queens. King Josiah was as godly as King Jeroboam was ungodly. For a full presentation of the triumphs and tragedies of royalty in past ages, the reader may permit me to refer to a previous volume of mine entitled *All the Kings and Queens of the Bible*, in which I endeavor to classify the monarchs who reigned in ancient times, and their influence upon the countries they ruled over. Much that should be written under this notable occupation of THE KING will be found in the above volume, such as The Divine Right and Heredity of Kings — The Responsibilities of Kingship — The Range of Sovereignty — The Royal Incomes — Symbols of Royalty. To quote from my *Preface* —

> In Holy Writ you can read of thrones, palaces, empires and dominions; and of royal pageantry as gorgeous and glittering as any of more modern times. In this great Book of royalty you have the rise and fall of mighty dynasties and kingdoms and all the subtle intrigues of court life. . . . What stories, noble and notorious, revolve around those monarchs! Many of them were mighty as they reigned, but came down to dishonored graves.

The appellation — king — is applied

1. To God, as the Supreme Ruler and Governor of the world (Psalm 44:4; 47:7).
2. To Christ, as the King or Head

of His church (Psalm 2:6; 45:1; Ephesians 1:22).

3. To all true Christians who are heirs of the kingdom of glory, and are enabled to war against, and to conquer Satan, sin and all spiritual foes (Revelation 1:6).
4. To the devil himself (Revelation 9:11).
5. To death, king of terrors (Job 18:14).
6. To sovereign princes, or chief rulers (Proverbs 8:15).

From the devotional aspect, reference can be made to a most helpful book by Frances Ridley Havergal entitled, *My King*, in which she has given us precious daily thoughts for all who are the King's children. Some of these thoughts are herewith abbreviated, and adapted.

The Source of Kingship is God Himself. "By the king's reign." "He hath made thee king over them." The leading provisions of the covenant made with the people God loved were a lamb for atonement and a king for government. The kingship of Christ sprang from the everlasting love of God for His people; "God will provide himself a lamb" — "I have provided me a king." God says in His majestic sovereignty, "I have set my king"; and we say, in lowly and loving loyalty, "Thou art my king."

The Promise of the king — "I will be thy king" — testifies to God's knowledge of human need. Our heart, like that of the world, suffers hopeless anarchy without a ruler. How lawless and desolate men are who confess, "We have no king." Would that multitudes of kingless hearts could be heard crying, "Give us a king"! How soon their wail would end if only the divine promise could be appropriated, "I will be thy King" (Isaiah 57:10, 18; Hosea 13:16; Micah 4:9). This other King, one Jesus is able to subdue all

things unto Himself (Acts 17:7; Philippians 3:21). Are we not thrice blest when out of a loyal and loving heart we can confess, "Thou art my King"? The oath of an earthly sovereign may be broken, but the King of our lives "keepeth his promise forever."

The Indwelling of the King is another comforting truth. Earthly rulers may visit their own people, or those of another country, but the pageantry of their visit is soon over like a dream. Our King, however, dwells within each of His subjects. "Is not the king in her?" He is the abiding One (Luke 24:29; John 14:23; II Corinthians 6:16). We also have the joyful privilege of going forth with the King and following Him, withersoever He goeth. "The King said, Wherefore wentest thou not with me?" Now we fight under His banner, but ultimately we are to sit with Him on His throne (II Timothy 2:12; Revelation 3:21).

The Kingship of the King is another glorious aspect of all we have in Christ who came as "the King near of kin to us." He became our bone and flesh (II Samuel 5:1. See Deuteronomy 18:15). He was made like unto His brethren (Deuteronomy 17:13; Hebrews 2:17). If the King is indeed near of kin to us, the royal likeness will be recognizable (Psalm 14:13). "Each one resembled the children of a king." If He is our King, then He desires our beauty — which is but a reflection of His own (Psalms 45:11; 90:7; 149:4).

The Sceptre of the King is the symbol first of kingly right and authority, and next of righteousness and peace. His is the golden sceptre held out to us, "the right sceptre," the sign of sovereign mercy (Psalms 45:6; 85:10; Amos 1:5. See Esther 5:2; Hebrews 4:16; 10:22). When we recognize His sway, we rejoice His heart (I Chronicles 29:9). Resting on His word — His kingly Word of power — we learn the secret of a tranquil mind (I Samuel 14:17, margin). In believing any word of the King, there is rest (Mark 9:23; I Thessalonians 2:13).

The Business of the King requires haste (I Samuel 21:8). As our King, He has every right to command us to make haste (II Chronicles 35:21). As we think of the multitudes still without Christ, we must go to them in the spirit of holy haste. Thus hasting, we shall rise from privilege to privilege, and go from strength to strength (Psalm 84:7; John 9:4). As His subjects, we must be ready to do whatsoever He may appoint (II Samuel 15:15; I Chronicles 26:20).

The Light of the King's Countenance is Life, said King Solomon (Proverbs 16:15). The King's countenance with all it implies of cleansing, salvation, peace, joy and beauty is prominent in Scripture (Numbers 6: 26; Psalms 4:6; 21:6; 43:5; 44:3; 89:15; Acts 2:28).

The Omniscience of the King can be gathered from the fact that no matter is hid from Him (II Samuel 18:13). Such an attribute striking terror to the King's enemies, spells comfort of His friends. All things are naked and opened unto His eyes (I Kings 10:3; Hebrews 4:13). Amid the perplexities and mysteries of life we cannot understand the King's purpose, but our unerring King knows what is best for His servants (John 5:20). As our Righteousness (Jeremiah 2:5; 3:6), He cannot act contrary to His own character.

Working with the King. Plants and hedges are about the last place we would expect a king to work (I Chronicles 4:23). But it does not matter where our lot is cast, or how lowly our task, there we can dwell with our heavenly King and accomplish His purpose. Are we not laborers together

with Him (Haggai 2:4; Mark 16:20)? If we are faithful in this divine fellowship of labor, then the King will recompense us with a reward (II Samuel 19:3, 6; Matthew 25:34; John 17:24).

Seeing the King in His beauty. When, as the King, our Lord appears to gather His own around Him we shall see Him in all His beauty (Isaiah 33:17). We shall see His face with joy (Job 33:26).

> From glory unto glory! Our faith
> hath seen the King;
> We own His matchless beauty, as
> adoringly we sing.

But as we linger amid the shadows, awaiting the coming King, we have the privilege of eating at His table, as His sons. Having received the qualifying position of adoption we have the right to eat in His banqueting house. When we gather around His table we eat and drink of Him who is Himself our heavenly food (John 6: 51, 55; See I Kings 4:27). May grace be ours to let our Lord the King speak unto us! Approaching the throne of grace, we speak unto the King (II Samuel 14:15; Psalm 62:8). Is it not far better to be silent and let "my Lord the King speak" (Isaiah 52:6; Habakkuk 2:1)?

The Laborer

If you ask someone his occupation and he replies, "Well, I am *only* a laborer," he implies two things, namely that he is not a skilled craftsman, and that because his task is menial, his pay check is smaller than a workman who has a trade. The laborers in the parable were hired by the day, and paid their low wage at the end of the day (Matthew 20:1-8). In industry today we have all kinds of laborers, but while laborers are in the majority, we must rid ourselves of the idea that laboring is an occupation of little value. Commerce and industry would stand still if it were not for the hard work of laborers who are by far the largest class of workers in any country.

A railway line was once called a "navvy" because canals came before railways, and the laborers who dug the canals were called "navigators," and then, for short, "navvies." When we stop to think of it most of the necessary things of life — as well as the most disagreeable — are done by laborers. Laboring, then, is a responsible, as well as a respectable, occupation. A president of the United States of America was once asked: "What is your Coat-of-Arms?" His reply was, "A pair of shirt sleeves." Solomon reminds us that the laborer has one great compensation — his sleep is sweet, whether he has much to eat or spend or otherwise. Laborers, working hard at a pick and shovel do not require sleeping pills, as the rich often require (Ecclesiastes 5:12).

Most of the Bible laborers were more or less slaves, like the Israelites in Egypt and those Christians Paul wrote of as servants, or slaves, under a yoke. In the widest sense today, a laborer is any one who works. The fourth commandment covers us all when it says, "Six days shalt thou labour."

Solomon asks what profit hath a man of all his labor (Ecclesiastes 1:3; 3:9). While some forms of labor may be profitless, the toil of multitudes have produced some of the wonders of the world. John Webster of the sixteenth century wrote of —

Laboring men
Count the clock oftenest.

While industry today may be suffering from too many clockwatchers, workers with a conscience give a good day's work for a good day's pay.

In the New Testament laborer is used in various ways. It covers a field-laborer or husbandman; a workman in a general sense (Matthew 9:37, 38; 10:10; 20:1, 2, 8; Luke 10:7; Acts 19:25; I Timothy 5:18). Paul uses the term to describe false apostles and evil teachers (II Corinthians 11:13; Philippians 3:2; see Luke 13:27), "workers of iniquity" or evil laborers. Our Lord compared His faithful servants who watch and work for souls to "laborers" of whom there are all too few (Matthew 9:37, 38). Spiritual laborers are worthy of their meat (Luke 10:7), and whom the Master calls and uses, He graciously provides for. Are we not laborers together with Him (I Corinthians 3:9)? With Him — does this not imply that God Himself is also a Laborer? If we are in the yoke with Him, are we pulling our weight? Paul could say that he labored more abundantly than others (I Corinthians 15:10). Of Epaphras, Paul says that he was "always labouring fervently" for the saints in his prayers, and the word he here uses for "labor" means to agonize, strive, wrestle. Is this intensity in intercession ours as we pray for saints and sinners alike? In the fields, white unto harvest, there are fellow-laborers, acting together with us in the Gospel as an operating power (I Corinthians 3:9, ASV "God's fellow-workers," who belong to and serve God. See Philippians 2:25; 4:3; Philemon 1; III John 8, ASV).

Let me labour for the Master,
From the dawn to setting sun.

The Lampdresser

The only person in the Bible to be named as a lampdresser is Aaron, who not only had the duty of lighting the lamps of the Tabernacle, but who also dressed them (Exodus 30:7, 8; Numbers 8:3). In my early days we had no gas, no electricity. Oil lamps and candles were the only means of night illumination. What a trial a smoking lamp was, with ill-trimmed wick, a source of worry and irritation.

The lamps Aaron dressed were not the practical form of oil lamp with sharply tapering spout which were possibly kept alight all night in Israelite homes (Job 18:6; Proverbs 31:18), but the candlestick, or rather candelabrum, which was a work of art of pure gold, having three pairs of branches springing from the shaft and rising straight from the base with shaft and six branches terminating at the same height. At each of these points were "bowls like unto almonds" to hold the olive oil and wicks. There was a number of small implements belonging to this seven-branched lamp such as "tongs" and "snuff-dishes" (Exodus 25:6, 37; 35:8; 40:24).

It is somewhat significant to notice that for the humble daily and necessary duty of dressing the lamps Aaron received divine instructions. God, who ordained the lighting of the lamps which were to be rich in typical meaning, also ordained the duties regarding their dressing which had to be done in quietness and secrecy. There had to be no spectators for this menial duty in the regular routine of the day. In the seclusion of the empty tabernacle, for none but the eye of God to see, the lamps had to be dressed. Does this not teach us that the lowliest duty can be encircled with spiritual fragrance, that when God and drudgery are brought together, the latter becomes a task angels will fain undertake?

The Lapidary

From *lapis,* meaning, "a stone," we have "lapidary" meaning a craftsman who cuts, polishes and engraves precious stones or gems. Such an occupation was common among the peoples of Bible lands, who were able to subject to their skill, not only stones, but wood, stone, ivory, clay, bronze, gold, silver and glass. Bezaleel was spirit-empowered to undertake all manner of workmanship which would include the preparation of the precious stones used on priestly garments (Exodus 31:3). A comprehensive article on the precious stones in Scripture can be found in the *Zondervan Pictorial Bible Dictionary*. Among the beautiful, priceless stones we have the agate (Isaiah 54:12; Ezekiel 27:16), which was probably an oriental ruby; the amethyst (Revelation 21:20) which the ancient Greeks believed had the power of driving away drunkenness; the beryl, a gem of yellow gold lustre (Exodus 28:20; 39:13, etc.); the carbuncle, from "carbo," a glowing coal (Exodus 28:17; Ezekiel 28:13); an emerald, which includes several brilliant red stones (Exodus 28:18; Ezekiel 28:13); a diamond, used for cameos and seals (Exodus 28:18; Ezekiel 28:13); a jasper, an opaque gem of various tints (Exodus 28:20; Revelation 4:3; 21:11, 18, 19); a ligure, or lyacinth, or jacinth, a transparent gem found in Ceylon and India (Exodus 28:19; Revelation 9:17; 21:20); onyx, generally transparent, and a pale green color (Exodus 25:7; Ezekiel 28:13); sapphire, a transparent, very hard gem, generally sky blue; hence its application to the floor of God's throne in heaven (Exodus 24:10; Ezekiel 1:26; Revelation 21:19); sardius, a flesh-colored gem, found largely at Sardis, in Lydia (Exodus 28:17; Revelation 4:3; 21:20); topaz, a yellow gem, with a red, gray, or green tinge, and found in South Arabia (Exodus 28:17; Job 28:19; Ezekiel 28:13; Revelation 21:20). The reader is referred to THE ENGRAVER for fuller information on such a craft.

An inspiring thought is that God is the greatest Lapidary of all time. Not only did He create, and deposit, in the earth all the brilliant gems men and women love to possess, but He is cutting and polishing a most marvelous collection of His own jewels — or His own precious, peculiar property, as the word Malachi uses implies (3:17). These goodly pearls cost His beloved Son His ruby blood. They may not be polished after the similitude of a palace yet (Psalm 144:12), but when He comes to make them up they will reflect His beauty (II Thessalonians 1:10), and be made to inhabit a city the foundations of which are garnished with all manner of precious stones (Revelation 21:19).

The Lawgiver — The Lawyer

A distinction must be drawn between a lawgiver and a lawyer, even though the former includes the latter occupation. Usually, those who prescribe laws are well-trained lawyers who are qualified to frame and expound necessary laws.

In the Old Testament the term "lawgiver" is found six times, and is from a root meaning "to cut" or "engrave," and is the same word used by Isaiah as "graveth" and "graven" (22:16; 49:16). Then the term came to signify the enactment of a law which was afterward engraved on the public archives. The original for "lawgiver" implies a tribal or kingly ruler, the person wielding the symbol of authority, the prescriber of laws (Deuteronomy 33:21; Isaiah 33:22. See Numbers 21:18); and also, the ruler's or commander's staff, which is parallel to scepter (Genesis 49:10; Psalms 60:7; 108:8). "Judah is my sceptre" — the scepter expressing the lawgiver's authority. While Moses is preeminent as a lawgiver under God, he is never given this title.

In the New Testament, lawgiver is used of God, the sole Lawgiver, the supreme Source of all law, with power to rule and judge, save and destroy (James 4:12). "To criticize the Law is to presume to take His place, with the presumption of enacting a better law." Passages where kindred Greek words are used refer to the Law of Israel (Romans 9:4; Hebrews 7:11).

Coming to THE LAWYER we find that the term belongs more to the religious sphere than the legal. Bible lawyers occupied themselves with the study of the oral and written law of Israel, and were practically identical with the Scribes (See study on THE SCRIBE). Used eight times in the New Testament (Matthew 22:35; Luke 2:46, ASV; 7:30; 10:25; 11:45, 46, 52; 14:3; Titus 3:13) "lawyer" implies one versed in the law and who is able to teach or expound it. Although Zenas is named as a lawyer, "there is no evidence that he was one skilled in Roman jurisprudence," says Vine. "Therefore the term may be regarded in the usual N. T. sense as applying to one skilled in the Mosaic Law."

The article in Hastings' *Bible Dictionary* grouping together the kindred terms "lawyer," "scribe," "doctor" says that —

A comparison of Luke 5:17 with Luke 5:22 and Mark 2:6 and Matthew 9:3 shows that the three terms were used synonymously, and did not denote three distinct classes. The scribes were originally simply men of letters, students of Scripture, and the name first given to them contains in itself no reference to the law; in course of time, however, they devoted themselves mainly, though by no means exclusively, to the study of the law. They became jurists rather than theologians, and received names which of themselves called attention to that fact. Some would doubtless devote themselves more to one branch of activity than to another; but a "lawyer" might also be a "doctor," and the case of Gamaliel shows that a "doctor" might also be a member of the Sanhedrin (Acts 5:34).

Although the works of jurists covered the study and interpretation of the Law — the instruction of Hebrew youths in the Law — decisions regarding questions of the Law, these Bible lawyers who, more or less, gave their service gratuitously, spent much time handling all sorts of problems relating to the bill of divorce, mentioned seven times in the Bible (Deuteronomy 24: 1, 3; Isaiah 50:1; Jeremiah 3:8; Matthew 5:31; 19:7; Mark 10:4), which was intended more as a deterrent than a legalization (Deuteronomy 24:2-6; Matthew 19:8; Mark 10:5). These lawyers spent much of their time debating what kind of writing material should be used when drawing up the bill — how it should be worded — whether or not it would be legally binding. This is the reason for their insistence on certain standard formulae.

Our Lord's condemnation of the lawyers of His time was justified. "Woe unto you also, ye lawyers!" (Luke 11:45-54). The professed interpreters of the Law claimed that they had a monopoly of the power to interpret, yet did not exercise the power. They prostituted their calling in that they utilized their time discoursing with wearisome minuteness fantastic legends and traditions, instead of leading the people into a reverential study of the divine oracles. As guides they were guilty of perversions in that they substituted the traditions of men for the commandments of God. Further, professing to be helpers, they neither helped nor sympathized with the troubles of those who sought their assistance (See Romans 2:17-23).

Originally, Israel had no book of written law. Custom was the rule as expressions like, "Such a thing is not done in Israel," and "It is a folly in Israel" (Genesis 31:32; 38:24) indicate. The time came, however, when it was not left for "every man to do what was right in his own eyes." Beneficial customs had to be codified and so divine oracles became the Law (Exodus 18:16; Deuteronomy 12-26), which Law, the lawyers condemned by Jesus had failed to instruct the people in. They stood self-convicted of incompetency as religious teachers and reserved the "woes" pronounced upon them by the One who came as the embodiment of God's ancient Law.

The Leader

The word Isaiah uses for leader (9: 16) "The leaders of this people cause them to err," means "one who causes a person to be happy." The word is used by Solomon, "Happy is every one that retaineth" (Proverbs 3:18). The margin has it, "They that call themselves blessed," but they caused the people to err, and as Ellicott comments, "There was no class so contemptible and base as that of spiritual guides whose policy was that of a time-serving selfishness." Another word for leader is "one who goes before" and is used of Jehoiada, the leader of the Aaronites (I Chronicles 12:27), and of army leaders and captains (I Chronicles 13:1; II Chronicles 32:21). The word of those who "lead captive silly women laden with sins led away with many lusts" (II Timothy 3:6) means to seduce. When Christ called the Pharisees "blind leaders of the blind" (Matthew 15: 14), He used the Greek word meaning "a leader of the way" (Acts 1:16) or a "guide" as the KJV expresses it, and which they are so named in Matthew 23:16, 24. (See Romans 2:19). Failing to lead the people the right way, those false religious leaders earned the scorn of the perfect Leader who, Himself, is "The Way" (John 14:6).

Isaiah identified our Lord as a God-given Leader and Commander. "Behold, I have given him for a witness to the people, a leader and commander to the people" (55:4). While, directly, there may be an historic reference here to David (Psalm 78:70, 71), yet the gift was only fully realized in Him who was "the faithful and true witness" (John 18:37; Revelation 1:5; 3:14), and the "captain" or "leader" of our salvation (Hebrews 2:10). What a Prince among leaders Jesus has been — and is! "Ten thousand times ten thousand, and thousands of thousands" were charmed to confess His voice divine, and followed Him faithfully until the end of life's pilgrimage. To multitudes came the highest honor of martyrdom in the cause of their Saviour-Leader, whose infallible leadership myriads of present-day saints obediently recognize. Both the present and the future need have no fear for those who can sing out of a heart of love for such a perfect Guide —

> He leadeth me, he leadeth me,
> By His own hand He leadeth me:
> His faithful follower I would be,
> For by His hand He leadeth me.

The Lender

Much that can be found under THE EXCHANGER is relevant here for moneychangers doubtless trafficked in moneylending. It is interesting to notice that the word Solomon and Isaiah used for lenders (Proverbs 22: 7; Isaiah 24:2)means "to cause to be bound." The prophet was indignant at the growing tendency of Israel —

already on the way to becoming a nation of moneylenders — to indulge in luxury which led to debt, and to the avarice which traded on the debtor's possessions. How many there are who find it hard to shake off the shackles of a moneylender! Benjamin Franklin once said: "If you would know the value of money go and try to borrow some; for he that goes a-borrowing goes a-sorrowing." The "exchangers" our Lord was familiar with were brokers, or bankers (Matthew 25:27, ASV).

With us, moneylending is purely of a commercial nature and is woven into the very texture of our economic life. Governments, as well as individuals often become dependent upon those who have money to loan on interest. In the Old Testament, the charitable tone of legislation on the subject of loans, indicates that in the early days of Israel, moneylending was not to be developed commercially. Under the Mosaic Law borrowing and lending were recognized but were strictly regulated (Deuteronomy 15: 1-6; 23:19, 20; 24:10, 11; 28:12, 44).

1. Interest on loans made to the poor was prohibited. Because of the goodness of God to Israel, the poor had to be treated generously. Loans were not granted to enable a man to start or extend his business, but only to meet the pressure of poverty. To the borrower, a loan was a misfortune, to the lender a form of charity (Exodus 22:25; Leviticus 25:35-38; Deuteronomy 28:12, 44). Interest could be charged on a loan to a foreigner, but profit out of a brother's distress was forbidden (Deuteronomy 23:19).

2. In spite of early laws against lending on interest, or usury, loans on interest became common (Isaiah 24: 2; Jeremiah 15:10), and was an evil that had to be corrected (II Kings 4: 1-7; Isaiah 50:1; Matthew 18:23).

Nehemiah himself, who had been a creditor and taken usury, had to rectify matters relating to mortgaged lands and interest (Nehemiah 5; 10).

3. While loans played a large part in Israel's social life, lending to the poor without charged interest was regarded as a mark of piety (Psalms 15: 5; 37:21, 26; 112:5; Proverbs 19:17; 28:8). At times, relations between debtor and creditor were far from pleasant (Jeremiah 15:10).

4. Although Christ assumed loans to be a normal factor in social life, He yet taught His followers to lend, even to enemies, without reasonable hope of any return. So to do, was Godlike (Matthew 25:27; Luke 6:24, 25; 16:5, 19:23). "Christ did not discuss lending for commercial purposes, and so does not necessarily forbid it." Debt is sometimes used as a synonym for sin (Matthew 6:12; 18:23; Luke 7: 41; Colossians 2:14).

The Lieutenant

With us, a lieutenant in the army is a commissioned officer just below a captain. The Biblical connotation of the term, however, is somewhat different. When Darius I, King of Persia (512-486 B.C.) came to power, he divided his vast empire into a large number of provinces over which he placed viceroys, chosen from members of noble Persian families. These satraps, as they were called (Ezra 8:36; Esther 3:12; 8:9; 9:3), were the lieutenants or princes (Daniel 3:2, 3, 27; 6:1). A satrap, as a protector of the realm, had the responsibility of the civil and administrative matters of the province; and held the position of a vassal king. If ostentatiously rich, he could be a tyrannical person. His power, however, was regulated by the presence of a royal scribe, whose duty it was to report to the "great king" on the administration of the province.

The Magician

There is a world of difference between Bible magicians and those we are familiar with today. All of us are fascinated with the present-day magician skilled in the art of pretension, and so startling in performance. How intrigued we are as he clutches things out of the air, and makes persons and objects supposedly disappear! As to sawing a lady in half — what a trick that is! With magicians of Scripture it was otherwise. They claimed to produce effects by the assistance of supernatural beings or by a mastery of secret forces in nature; and were classed with sorcery and witchcraft.

While magicians, as such, are only named in the Old Testament (Genesis 41:8, 24; Exodus 7:22; Daniel 2:10, 27, etc.), the sorcerers of Paul's time were the equivalent of the foregoing. The word Luke uses for "sorcery" is *magos* from which we have "magi" and "magicians" (Acts 8:9, 11; 13:6, 8). The nations surrounding Israel knew and practiced all kinds of divination. There was a regular order among the Egyptians devoted to magic and astrology. Jannes and Jambres, mentioned by Paul, are supposed to have been two chiefs of Pharaoh's magicians (II Timothy 3:8, 9). Rah-mag is called "chief of the magicians" (Jeremiah 39:3). Albert Bailey says —

Magicians were to be found on every corner; in fact, magic underlay the entire thinking of the Egyptians, permeated all their life, found embodiment in all Egyptian art, and bridged the chasm of death to operate in the underworld. The court of every Pharaoh had a battery of magicians, and what they could do was marvelous! Stories of their exploits are found in a XVII Dynasty papyrus now in Berlin. In one of them a magician cut off a goose's head, placed it at one side of a courtyard and the body at the other; then to a recital of his hocus-pocus the two parts hopped rhythmically towards each other, joined properly, and the goose went off cackling.

The people of God were forbidden recourse to any kind of charlatanry. All forms of magic, augury, and necromancy were prohibited although some forms of magic were "tinged and alloyed with religion." That many of "The Magi," called "wise men," were noble men and skilled in devising, through signs, the will of heaven, is evident from the fact that Daniel, "chief of the Magi," foretold the coming of Christ's kingdom (2:44; 9:25); and that the wise men from the East were divinely directed to Christ's birthplace. Philo says of *the Magi*, from which we have "magician," that they were sacred scribes "who gave themselves to the study of nature and contemplation of the Divine perfections, worthy of being counsellors of kings." Such a type was different from Pharaoh's magicians who practiced tricks and dealt in occult powers (Exodus 7:11, 12; 8:7, 18, 19); and Balaam's enchantments (Numbers 23:23; 24:1); and the magical arts of Simon Magus (Magus from "magos," the magician), and also Elymas (Acts 8:9, 10; 13:6-12). Under THE ENCHANTER, further material will be found on this most interesting aspect of Bible study.

The Magistrate

In the early days of Israel, the magisterial office was limited to hereditary chiefs, but Moses made the judicial office elective. In his time "the heads of families" were fifty-nine in number, and these, together with the twelve princes of the tribes, composed the Sanhedrin or council of seventy-one. Some of the scribes were entrusted with the business of keeping the genealogies and in this capacity were also regarded as magistrates. But the term took on a wider application as the original words for magistrate reveal. For instance, the office was —

Equivalent to that of a Judge (Ezra 7:25; Luke 12:58; Acts 16:20) (Compare material under THE JUDGE).

Represented one able to restrain. With authority there was power (Judges 18:7).

Exercised by the high priest (Acts 23:5), by the ruler of the synagogue (Matthew 9:18, 23; Luke 8:41).

Applied to the first and foremost ruler (Luke 12:11, 58), and as such had to be obeyed (Titus 3:1).

Leader of a host. One word used for magistrate is *strategos*, from which we have "strategy." This term is used of a Roman "praetor" or magistrate of the Roman colony at Philippi (Acts 16:20-38). The praetors were attended by lictors or "sergeants" who executed their orders.

Employed by those who were chief in power, and with standing and authority to appear in the Sanhedrin (Luke 14:1; John 3:1; Acts 3:11; 4:36; Romans 13:2).

From the doublet in Latin, *magister*, meaning "greater" becomes "magistrate," and in Old French "maistre" is "master." Christ is designated "Prince of the kings of the earth" (Revelation 1:5). The same word for "prince" here is used of Moses, the judge and leader of Israel (Acts 7:25, 27); *Archon*, another Greek word for "magistrate" is used to designate Satan, the prince or chief of fallen angels (Matthew 12:24; Ephesians 2:2). It is also a collective term describing those clothed with high power of civil authority from the emperor down (Romans 13:1-3; Titus 3:1). Vine says of *archon* that it depicts one "acting in capacity of one who received complaints, and possessing higher authority than the judge, to whom the magistrate remits the case." Cicero has this distinction: "The magistrates are the ministers of the laws, the judges the interpreters of the laws." The same philosopher reminded us that, "The magistrate is a speaking law, but the law is a silent magistrate." It is to be hoped that all in magisterial office today have proved the proverb to be that, "The magistrate and the office discover the man."

The Maker

In many interesting ways God is depicted as *the Maker*. As the Maker of man, He is purer than His product (Job 4:17). He is often resisted, frustrated by the work of His hands (Isaiah 45:9; Hosea 8:14). As the Maker of all, He is sometimes reproached and rejected by all (Job 35:10; Proverbs 14:31; 17:5; 22:2; Isaiah 51:13). As a Maker, He is loving (Isaiah 54:5), and righteous (Job 36:3), and worthy of worship (Psalm 95:6; Isaiah 45:11). Taken together, all the references to God as the Maker, magnify His creative acts (Job 4:17; 32:22; 35:10; 36:3; Psalm 95:6; Proverbs 14:31; 17:5; 22:2; Isaiah 1:31; 17:7; 22:11; 45:9, 11, 16; 51:13; 54:5; Jeremiah 33:2; Hosea 8:14; Habakkuk 2:18; Hebrews 11:10).

Hebrew words used for maker imply the ability to fashion, frame, construct, constitute, to grave, to form as a potter does his clay, to accomplish, to put into execution. This designation of the Almighty is akin to that of the Creator (Ecclesiastes 12:1; Isaiah 40:28; 43:15; Romans 1:25; I Peter 4:19). "Made," "maker," are used of Creation itself (Genesis 1:7, 16, 31; Matthew 19:4). "The sea is his, he *made* it" (Psalm 95:5) — of man, made in the divine image (Genesis 5:1). Coleridge speaks of one, "He was his Maker's image undefaced" — of the Ark (Genesis 6:14) — of the Tabernacle (Exodus 25:8) — of idols (Judges 18:3; Isaiah 2:8) — of the one new man, the church (Ephesians 2:15) — of the eternal city (Hebrews 11:10), which is the archtype of the earthly one which God chose for His earthly people. Vine says of the word used for maker that it signified "one who works for the people, and came to denote, in general usage a builder or maker" (Hebrews 11:10). The first word *technites*, denotes an architect, designer; the second, *demiourgos*, the actual framer. Thus the universe, the church, the heavenly city, "the Lord God made them all." How all His works praise Him!

The Manservant

Material under THE BONDSMAN and THE LABORER can be consulted at this point. It may be that menservants usually coupled with maidservants, or female slaves, were not the free, voluntary attendants which laborers were. In the main, menservants were employed to undertake menial tasks such as the caring for cattle. It is curious to note that male and female servants are sandwiched in between "asses" and "asses" as if treated in the same category. The "she asses" (Genesis 12:16) along with the "camels" were especially valuable as the monarch's choicest gifts (See Genesis 24:35; Exodus 20:10, 17; Deuteronomy 5:14; Nehemiah 7:67; Jeremiah 34:9; Luke 12:45, etc.).

The Mason

Both in ancient and modern times, masons represent hewers of stone, makers of hedges, walls and buildings. A marginal reference says that "masons" were "hewers of the stone of the wall" (II Samuel 5:11). They cut and dressed stone for building purposes. A glance at the Bible references to masons indicates the various processes and instructions associated with such a necessary occupation (Exodus 20:25; II Samuel 5:11; I Kings 5:17; 6:7; 7:9; II Kings 12:12; 22:6; I Chronicles 14:1; 22:2, 15; II Chronicles 24:12; Ezra 3:7; Isaiah 5:2; 22:16; Ezekiel 40:3; Amos 5:11). Among the tools employed by these workers in stone we have the saw, the plumbline, the measuring reed, the level, the hammer. There were those known as "stone-squarers" (I Kings 5:18), from the Phoenician city of Gebal who were skilled in this branch of industry. As the Jews had little skill in architecture, they relied upon the Phoenicians for craftsmen to quarry and prepare stones for David's palace and for Solomon's Temple (II Samuel 5:11). Tradition has it that the man with the withered hand was a mason, and implored Jesus to heal him in order that he might be able to work again at his trade, and so be saved from the shame of begging his bread. His physical disability made his case more than ordinarily pathetic, therefore, and Jesus restored the power of the man's right hand (Luke 6:6).

A proverb has it, "He is not a mason who refuses a stone." Temples and buildings, like the pyramids, still in a condition of good preservation after centuries of exposure testify to the skill of ancient masons to fashion the very best out of their material. "It is clear that the important buildings and works referred to in the Old Testament were constructed with the care of the wall-builders, and the ruins of fortifications or dwellings in the grand manner of an earlier age bear witness today to the ingenuity of the men who built them."

The Master

Several meanings are associated with this term occurring over 190 times in Scripture. Various Hebrew and Greek words are used to express the significance of the one English word, master. The masters described, differ in quality, some being as kind as others are cruel. Benjamin Warfield, in his monumental work *The Lord of Glory*, says,

> The simplest honorific titles are represented as those most frequently employed in addressing Him — Rabbi, with its Greek renderings, "Teacher" and "Master," and its Greek representative "Lord."

In his expository *Dictionary of New Testament Words,* Vine distinguishes seven different Greek terms for master, and because of all He is in Himself, and of His use of these, Jesus affirmed His right to all they signify.

Didarkatos

Frequently rendered "master" in the gospels as a title of address to Christ, this word means a teacher. Christ spoke of Himself as "the Teacher" (Matthew 8:19; 23:8; Mark 4:38; John 13:13, 14). Others used it of Him recognizing in Him a Teacher above all teachers. "He taught them as one having authority, and not as the scribes" (Matthew 7:29). As the Teacher come from God, He is Source and Channel of truth, and is able by His Spirit to lead and guide us into all truth (Matthew 17:24; Mark 5:35; Luke 8:49; John 11:28, etc.). Christ addressed Nicodemus as "the teacher in Israel" (John 3:10 asv), but alongside of the divine Teacher, he was but a learner.

This particular word is also associated with —

1. All preachers of the Word (Ecclesiastes 12:11).
2. Those who instruct scholars (Luke 6:46).
3. Those who rule over servants (Ephesians 6:5).
4. Those who ambitiously affect vain applause, or covet precedency and superiority above others (Matthew 23:10; James 3: 1).

Kurios

This expressive appellation meaning "lord" denotes one who possesses authority and exercises power (Matthew 6:24; Mark 13:35; Luke 16:13; Acts 16:16, 19; Romans 14:4, asv; Ephesians 6:5, 9,. etc.). This particular Greek word has a wide range of application — as a term of respect toward a superior — as a master or owner of slaves or property. Warfield reminds us that this ordinary Greek honorific of especially high connotation is the prevailing form of address in Luke. To have Christ as Lord means to acknowledge His heavenly authority and involves submission to His will and word. Too often it is insincerely used of Him (Luke 6:46). Peter recognized Jesus as Lord or his "Superior Officer" (Luke 5:5, 8). As used sincerely by His disciples, the title "Lord" meant their recognition of His Messianic dignity. When those early Christians called Jesus, "Lord," they implied that He was the true divine Lord in opposition to an earthly potentate, like the one on the imperial throne of Rome who claimed lordship over men. May grace be ours to sanctify Him as Lord in our life!

Despotes

As this word indicates, master can mean one who has supreme authority, absolute ownership and uncontrolled power, and is addressed both to God and to Christ (Acts 4:24; II Peter 2: 1; Jude 4; See I Timothy 6:1, 2; II Timothy 2:21; Titus 2:9; I Peter 2:18). It may seem somewhat incongruous to employ a term used of a master of slaves who exercises over them such autocratic authority to illustrate the Lordship of Christ. Yet to Jude — a bondslave of Christ — his one and only Master was a Despot of the right kind (Jude 4, 17, 21, 25). As a love-slave, the apostle loved to think of the Master as his "despotic Master and Lord." Who, because of all He accomplished for man's emancipation from sin, has every right to control every phase of life in those redeemed by His precious blood. Has He our unquestioning obedience?

Rabbi

Here we have an Aramaic word, meaning, "my Master" — which was a title of respectful address to Jewish leaders (Luke 3:12) and was a common form of address to Christ (Matthew 26:25, 49; Mark 9:5; 10:51). This title expresses the relation of the disciple to the teacher and applied to Christ extols Him as the chief Lawgiver and Teacher, who alone is to be followed in matters of faith and worship (Luke 6:40). Garfield observes that, "It remains true that *Teacher* as a form of address is characteristic in Luke, of non-followers of our Lord." Nicodemus greeted Jesus respectfully as *Rabbi* (John 3:2). But he was only *a* teacher. Christ came as *the* Teacher, and as the culmination of the revelation of God is alone able to unfold to us the complete truth of God. The intensified form of "rabbi"

— *Rabboni* is used twice in the gospels (Mark 10:51; John 20:16).

Epistates

This Greek term used of master denotes a chief, a commander, overseer, and when addressed to Christ, is a recognition of His supreme authority, rather than His instruction (Luke 5: 5; 8:24, 45; 9:33, 49. See LXX II Kings 25:19; II Chronicles 31:12; Jeremiah 36:26; 52:25). This strong term, used only by Luke, acknowledges Christ as our absolute Leader who demands, and must have, the unquestioning and unhesitating obedience of His followers.

Kathegetes

Matthew uses a word for "Master" which has a higher implication than the one denoting that Christ is "Teacher." It is the above, meaning, Guide (10:24, 25; 23:8, 10), or "one that goes before." Wonderful, is it not, to have Jesus not only as our Governor, or Ruler, but also as our Guide, who is able to lead us into all truth, and also to direct our steps in the journey of life. We do not know the way, but we know the Guide and if our hand is in His, then all will be well.

Kabernetes

This arrestive term used of master, means the pilot or steersman of a ship, or a governor or guide, and appears in steering, pilotage (I Corinthians 12: 28 "governments"). We have this word as "master" (Acts 27:11) and as "shipmaster" (Revelation 18:17. See LXX Proverbs 23:24; Ezekiel 27:8, 27, 28). As our Master, Christ is likewise the Steersman on the voyage of our life. "Jesus, Saviour, Pilot me."

A corresponding appellative, capable of the highest implication when applied to Christ, is His favorite fig-urative expression of "housemaster" which sets forth "His relation to His disciples, whether in didactic or parabolic statement." In one of His parables, God is likened unto the housemaster (Mark 13:35; Luke 14:21, See THE HOUSEHOLDER). Garfield reminds us that "the simple honorifics 'Master' and 'Lord' rise in Matthew's hands to their highest value; 'Master' becomes transformed into the more absolute 'Master of the house,' with His despotic power governing all things in accordance with His will, and disposing of the destinies of men in supreme sovereignty." All the designations applied to Jesus suggest "a unitary conception of His person of the highest exaltation."

As His church in the spiritual house, Jesus is the Master of the same. It is to be wondered whether all the household of faith recognize Him as *Master*. Can you subscribe to what saintly George Herbert wrote after vowing to serve Jesus as *My Master and Governor?* —

How sweetly doth "My Master" sound!
  My Master!
As ambergris leaves a rich scent
  Unto the taster;
So do these words a sweet content,
An oriental fragrancy, "My Master."

The Masterbuilder

Scripture introduces us to the sheepmaster, the taskmaster, the shipmaster — here we have the building master, a term Paul alone uses of himself as the builder of the church, and of churches (I Corinthians 3:10). The word itself is from the realm of building and means "chief architect," and has a wider application than our "architect." Paul not only planned but performed. Further, the apostle was not indulging in self-laudation when he spoke of himself as a "masterbuilder." He was careful to indicate that all he had accomplished at Corinth was what God had given him grace to do (I Corinthians 3:10 with Romans 1:5; 12:3).

The Mediator

Applied some six times in the New Testament, principally to Christ, this term means "the one in between," "a go-between" or "the middle man" (Galatians 3:19, 20; I Timothy 2:5; Hebrews 8:6; 9:15; 12:24). This glorious, evangelical word is used in two ways in the New Testament. Vine reminds us —

1. A mediator is one who mediates between two parties with a view to producing peace (I Timothy 2:5).
2. A mediator is one who acts as a guarantee so as to secure something which otherwise could not be obtained. Thus, in Hebrews 8:6; 9:15; 12:24 Christ is the Surety of "the better covenant," "the new covenant," guaranteeing its terms for His people.

While the word mediator does not appear in the Old Testament, the truth it expresses is illustrated. The necessity and nature of mediation, covering God's approach to man, or man to God, not directly but through the interposition of another, has a prominent place in the Bible. An instance of one party coming between two parties to remove their differences is found in the "daysman," "arbitrator," "umpire" who "lays his hands upon both" the litigants, in token of his power to adjudicate between them and then reconcile them (Job 9:32, 33). Christ is fully qualified to act as our Daysman (see cameo on THE DAYSMAN). He is the One "who gives us a day" to judge and decide a controversy — lays His hands on both the contending parties (I Kings 3:16) and effects a reconciliation. The need of such a Daysman is felt by every awakened conscience.

Moses was often a mediator between Jehovah and the Jews, and in this respect was a remarkable type of Christ (Exodus 20:18-21; Deuteronomy 5:4, 5; Galatians 3:19; Hebrews 8:5, 6). Other mediating prophets between the Lord and the nation of Israel are Samuel, Nathan and others. How they could plead with God on behalf of men! (I Samuel 9:9; Jeremiah 14:19-22; Amos 7:2, 5, etc.). But it is in Moses that "we have for the first time a recognized national representative who acted both as God's spokesman to the people, and the people's spokesman before God" (Exodus 19:8; 33:11). Because of the different aspects of mediation which must be distinguished, attention is drawn to the exhaustive article on this theme in *The International Standard Bible Encyclopedia.*

Our Lord Jesus Christ has all the properties of the perfect Mediator. He, it was, who undertook to come between God and the sinner, with a view to reconciliation (Romans 5:10; Ephesians 2:16; I Timothy 2:5). He, Himself, declared Himself to be the sole Representative in mediatorial grace toward a world of sinners lost and ruined by the Fall. "No man cometh unto the Father, *but by me*" (John 14:6). How this excludes any approach to God through the mediation of angels, saints, images, and the Virgin Mary, all of which have no countenance from Scripture. Christ alone by His satisfaction to God and intercession with Him, and by His powerful and gracious influence on sinful men, is able to bring God and the sinner together into a covenant state of agreement (Hebrews 8:6; 12: 24).

Paul says that a "mediator is not a mediator of one" (Galatians 3:20), meaning, of one party. He is a person who interposes between two parties at variance, for the purpose of reconciling them. This is what Christ accomplished through the cross. God and sinners, whether Jews or Gentiles, are brought together and made one. To "atone" means to be "at one" with God (Ephesians 2:18; I John 2:2). The sense of sin may cause a sinner to hide from God (Genesis 3:10), and the holy character of God prevents Him communing with a sinner as such (Habakkuk 1:13), but Jesus comes between and the believing sinner has access to God through Him. Sin made a great breach between God and man, and the need of a Mediator implies a difference between two parties. By His death, Christ dealt with this difference, and now all who are estranged from God can be at peace with Him. Whatever estrangement there is between God and man, necessitating the ministry of a Mediator, it began, and continues on man's side. God has never offended man and has therefore no need of reconciliation toward Him. But man the transgressor has deep need of reconciliation with God.

Further, Christ is the Mediator of sinful men only, not of angels. The unfallen angelic host have no need of mediation and the doomed angelic host are beyond His mediation. The breach here will never be healed. Then to function as the perfect Mediator, Christ had to be God, to act for Him, and man, to enter into the interests of the human race. In the Person of Christ we have God and man, the God-man, "Emmanuel, God with us" (II Corinthians 5:17, 19; I Timothy 3:16). Paul insisted upon the humanity of Jesus, "One Mediator, who is between God and man,

himself man, Christ Jesus" (Philippians 2:7, 8; I Timothy 3:16). As the Mediator, Christ not only had the great transaction of making peace committed to Him. He was also invested with full power and authority to produce such a peace, and possesses all the divine attributes to bestow it. It is because He made a perfect sacrifice for sin as the Son of God, and the Son of man that He is unique as a peerless Mediator.

As the Mediator between God and men, Jesus must of necessity have something to offer in behalf of the offender, before reconciliation could be effected. Think of the stupendous task involved in such mediation! The broken law had to be magnified (Isaiah 42:21). The curse had to be removed (Galatians 3:10). Guilt had to be expiated (Isaiah 53:10). Enmity and estrangement had to be destroyed (Ephesians 2:16). Man might have asked, Who is sufficient for these things? Who has the qualifications for such a tremendous task? Man, himself, was not able to redeem himself, nor act as a mediator for his fellows (Psalm 49:7). But the Child born of Mary, who was at the same time the mighty God, by His finished work at Calvary died as the Just for the unjust to bring us unto God (I Peter 3:18). He, then, is our way of access with confidence to God (Hebrews 10:19-22), and the One by whom God makes His covenant of peace sure to us (II Corinthians 1:20-22). Possessed of the nature and attributes of both deity and humanity, Christ comprehended the claims of God and the needs of man. As the Sinless One, He was able to offer Himself as an expiatory sacrifice on behalf of men.

In heaven, Jesus continues His mediatorial ministry as the Advocate and the Great High Priest, interceding for His true church (John 17; Hebrews 7:

25). At the right hand of the majesty on high we have the consummation of the Old Testament mediation of a sacrificing priesthood, and a mediatorial office that will only cease when its purpose of reconciling all things to God is accomplished (Zechariah 14:9). Till then, Christ —

Pursues in Heaven, High mighty plan,
The Saviour, and the Friend of man.

The Merchant

Merchantman is now an English word used only of a trading vessel, as distinguished from a navy ship, "a man of war." Vessels, however, received this name because originally they belonged to merchantmen, and were used by them to carry goods. In Bible times there were merchants which Isaiah and Ezekiel speak of as merchant princes whose ships came from almost as far as Britain. *Emporos*, from which we have "emporium," a place of trade — which is one of the words used for merchant (Matthew 13:45; Revelation 18:3, 11, 15, 23), denoted a person on a journey, a passenger on a ship, rather than a merchant. Bible merchants were traders and, in the main, heathens. The Canaanites excelled in commercial pursuits, so much so that the "Canaanite" and "merchant" were convertible terms (Isaiah 11:1-12; Hosea 12:7 margin; Zephaniah 1:11). Nehemiah tells of heathen merchants from Tyre who came to Jerusalem with fish and other kinds of commerce and sold them to the people on the Sabbath.

As nations developed, international trade with its interchange of commodities and services became common in Bible lands, with itinerant merchants or tradesmen, trading in oil, wheat and barley, wine, timber, wool, leather, fruits and spices, gold and precious stones (Genesis 37:28; 43:11; I Kings 10:15; Isaiah 19:9; Matthew 13:45, etc.). We have a record of good commerce during the reign of King Jehoshaphat (I Kings 22:49, 50). Palestine occupied an extremely important position as a regular trade route. The Sea of Galilee because of its great fish industry became the center of a large trading business to all parts of the then known world. These merchants, or middlemen, had close contact with surrounding nations by sea and land. As traveling tradesmen they passed from country to country, both buying and selling. Often transactions were in the form of a barter, one article being exchanged for another (I Kings 4:26; 10:15-29). Merchants, as well as kings, employed professional scribes to record transactions (I Samuel 8:17; Isaiah 33:18; Jeremiah 36:26).

There are a few allusions to trading in the Mosaic Law. Legislation prohibited merchants using or giving false weights (Deuteronomy 25:13). Albert E. Bailey says that in Israel, "Honesty became a byword. Excavators have found under the counters of the merchants two sets of weights; a heavy set to use when buying, a light one when selling" (Hosea 12:7). Both Amos 9:4-8) and Micah (6:10) condemn the use of deceitful measures. There are also references to the "market" and "marketplace." In ancient times there were no shops as we know them today. One word used for "merchant" is *emporos*, from which we have "emporium," a place of trade. Of old, merchants used open bazaars for the buying and selling of all merchandise (Ezekiel 7:12; 27:13, 17; Matthew 11:16; Mark 7:4; Acts 16:17).

Tragic, is it not, that the first article of merchandise referred to in the Bible is a human being. Jacob's sons sold their brother Joseph to a company of traveling Ishmaelite merchants, the price received for him being about three pounds, or almost nine dollars about as much as Judas received for selling Jesus. Over 190 years ago there appeared in an English newspaper this advertisement — "*For sale, a negro boy, sound, healthy, and of mild disposition.*"

As an honorable occupation, the merchant is one of the symbols Jesus used of Himself. Merchants today offer bargains but where is there such a bargain as the heavenly Merchant offers when he cries, "Come buy . . . *without money*" (Isaiah 55:1)? Then does He not urge us to buy of Him gold, raiment and medicine (Revelation 3:18-20)? As the skilled Merchant, Jesus had some costly pearls in His possession, but for "the pearl of great price" — His church, He gave all that He had. For her, He spilt His blood upon the cross (Matthew 13:45, 46). In the strictest sense Jesus is not "the pearl of greatest price," as the hymnist expresses it. No one, and nothing, could ever purchase Him for He is God's unspeakable gift. But with His church it is different for "with His own blood He bought her." Do we, as His, recognize our responsibility as under-merchants to traffic with the redeeming Gospel He made possible?

The Meteorologist

In our scientific age, weather forecasting has become an art, and for travel and other purposes we eagerly await reports from a meteorological center. Space satellites are enabling us to judge, more accurately, the trend of atmospheric conditions. Through TV, radio or newspaper daily reports all of us have become weather conscious.

Weather forecasting is getting to be big business in the United States. The government still has by far the greatest forecasting facilities from coast to coast, but private firms are on the increase.

The commercial weather prophets count among their clients ice-cream, soup and raincoat manufacturers, who have to plan production schedules on the weather.

Many of the private weather bureaus are small operations which cannot hope to compete with the United States Weather Bureau's network of stations. The freely available data provided by the government are often used by private firms as the basis for their own forecasts.

But the one thing that these private organizations can provide is a carefully tailored service to meet the specific needs of their clients, who are usually located in one relatively small area.

There are four direct references to "weather" in the Bible (Job 37:22; Proverbs 25:20; Matthew 16:2, 3). Let us take the phrase in Elihu's discourse, "Fair weather cometh out of the north." As it was not the custom to talk about the weather in the East, there is no word in Hebrew to correspond to our English term. In "a magnificent piece of poetry" (Job 36, 37), it is evident that in such an early age of man's history there was a knowledge of science which modern science cannot gainsay. How eloquent this portion is of God's power in nature! As to atmospheric disturbances and their influence on the weather, note the following aspects in Job 36, 37 —

God draws up the water from the ocean and distills it in rain and mist upon the earth for man's benefit. He also displays the lightning, and covers the heavens with the depths of the sea (36:30, ASV, margin).

No one can understand the disposition of the clouds and their relation to electricity. He holds in His hand the lightning flash and commands it where to strike (36:30, 32, ASV, margin). The distant reverberation of the thunder terrifies the heart (37:1). Thunderstorms are sent by God for human correction, or for the enrichment of the soil (37:13).

It is a scientific fact that rain is a form of electric action — that none can explain the nature of lightning, the balancing of the clouds — why the south wind is warm, or the sky like a molten mirror (37:2, 7, 15-18).

God, as the Creator, causeth His wind to blow from the north, thus dismissing the storm and restoring fair weather. The ASV has rendered the literal meaning most beautiful, "Out of the north there comes a golden splendor" (37:22).

Solomon, whose unique wisdom covered a knowledge of weather conditions, wrote that "a north wind driveth away rain" (Proverbs 25:23). He knew that a north wind clears the air, and links this on to a backbiting tongue producing an angry countenance.

The classic passage on the weather, however, is in our Lord's reply to the Pharisees who sought a sign from Him but were refused and also rebuked by His reply (Matthew 16:1-3; Mark 8: 11). "Jesus answered them and said, When it is evening, ye say, It will be fair weather: for the sky is red. And in the morning, It will be foul weather today: for the sky is red and lowering — sullen or gloomy. Hypocrites! ye can discern the face of the sky; but can ye not discern the signs of the times?" Jesus condemns them for having natural foresight but being destitute of spiritual foresight. Weatherwise as to the coming storm and sunshine, the Pharisees were blind to the signs of the spiritual sky with their tokens of the coming sunshine of truth, or the coming storm of the foul weather of God's judgments.

The Moneychanger

What has been written under THE BANKER and THE EXCHANGER is applicable here, where the moneychanger (Matthew 21:12; Mark 11:15) implies the changer of small coins. In our Lord's time, the Jewish priests developed a most lucrative business changing Roman money into Jewish currency earning, thereby, Christ's condemnation of turning God's house into a den of thieves.

The Musician

The many references to musicians, singers, musical instruments and songs indicate that "the happy God" meant His people to be joyful and to praise Him with everything having breath (Psalm 148-150). The numerous references to all aspects of music indicate how the Hebrews in ancient times were devoted to the study and practice of music. Apart from poetry, music seems to be the only other art cultivated by ancient Israel. The heat of the climate precluded the Orientals from the enjoyment of athletic exercises, and also indisposed them to public entertainment. That music was cultivated in Western Asia at a very early period is evident from the fact that the invention of "the harp and organ" — representatives of all stringed and wind instruments — is ascribed to Jubal (Genesis 4:21). Jabal, his brother, is referred to as the ancestor of shepherds, and everywhere, and at all times, shepherds have been fond of music, with the pipe and flute as their constant companion. The Greeks have a legend that it was Pan, god of the shepherds, who invented the flute.

David, the skillful harpist is a classic illustration of the association of music with life in the fields.

The Bible does not say very much about musicians themselves. Those serving the temple rendered voluntary service, but there developed a class of hired, professional musicians who attended great occasions, banquets, marriages and funerals. Our Lord referred to the latter when calling attention to children in a marketplace playing at weddings and funerals. He spoke of those who were piped to but did not dance, who were sorrowed over but did not mourn (Matthew 11: 17, ASV). From His knowledge of life at that time, Jesus illustrated what actually happened at Eastern funerals (Matthew 9:23), when professional mourners were engaged to make a tumult with instruments and voices, and weep and wail (Mark 5:38).

Some fifty-five of the Psalms bear the caption *To the Chief Musician*. Dedicated to the recognized precentor or choir leader of the temple, the superscription can imply one or two things, namely, that he was author of these particular psalms, or that they formed an official collection, entrusted to the preeminent choir master for public worship in the temple. Chosen by David, the three chief musicians were Asaph, Heman and Jeduthun (I Chronicles 15:16-19), who were also known by the official title "the King's seers" (I Chronicles 25:5; II Chronicles 35:15).

Asaph, the reputed author of Psalms 50, 73-83, is first spoken of when the ark was taken to Jerusalem (I Chronicles 15:16-19). It was Asaph who led with cymbals the music performed in the tent, housing the Ark (I Chronicles 16:4-37). Heman and Jeduthun discharged the same office at Gibeon (I Chronicles 16:41, 42). The four sons of Asaph conducted under their father sections of the great chorus. The families of Heman and Jeduthun also furnished choir leaders for temple services (II Chronicles 5:12). These musical sons "formed a guild, and played a prominent part at each revival of the national religion."

Jeduthun, a Levite, and chief singer and instructor, was first known as Ethan (I Chronicles 9:16; 16:38, 41, 42; 25:1, 3, 6; II Chronicles 5:12; 35: 15; Nehemiah 11:17). Psalms 39, 62, 77 are dedicated to him. As he was one of David's choir leaders, perhaps he introduced a method of conducting a service of song which became associated with his name.

Heman. This musician and seer, the Levite son of Joel and grandson of Samuel (I Chronicles 6:33), must not be confused with the noted wise man of the same name (I Kings 4:31). Heman, one of the leaders of the temple singing (I Chronicles 15:17), had fourteen sons and three daughters who assisted their father in the chorus. A musician of spiritual power, Heman is spoken of as "the king's seer in the matters of God" (I Chronicles 25:5; II Chronicles 35:15).

Some of the titles of the psalms carry a musical connection. Thirtle, in his study of these titles suggests that they were anciently appended to the preceding psalms. Neginoth (Psalms 4, 6, 54, 55, 61, 67, 76) means "with stringed instruments." Maybe these particular psalms were the only ones accompanied with stringed instruments. Nehiloth (Psalm 5) implies a "wind instrument," possibly a flute, although Scofield says that the title means "inheritance," and indicates the character of the Psalm. The righteous are the Lord's inheritance. Gitteth (Psalms 8, 81, 84) is supposed to refer to an instrument invented in Gath or to a tune composed there. Scofield, however, says the word means "winepress" and speaks of harvest in respect to judgment, which Psalm 7, to which the title should be appended, actually is. Higgarjon implies "a solemn sound," probably a musical note equivalent to largo (See Psalm 19:14). A word is given as meditation, and 92:3 as a "solemn sound." These musical titles of some of the psalms prove that a good deal of thought was given to the musical accompaniment in David's time, and that these expressions were meant to guide the musicians.

The Musical Instruments

Musical instruments go far back in human history and were originally designed to assist man in his praise to God, as the last Psalm (150) indicates —

Praise Him with the trumpet's sound;
  His praise with psaltery advance:
With timbrel, harp, string'd instruments
  And organs, in the dance.
Praise Him on cymbals loud: His praise
  On cymbals sounding high.
Let each thing breathing praise the Lord.
  Praise to the Lord give ye.

Uncertainty exists as to the exact number of musical instruments mentioned in the Bible, as well as the precise nature of the instruments in question. This we do know, that the music performed on all such instruments was of a joyful nature, and accompanied real music (I Samuel 10:5; Amos 6:5). Bible instruments fall into three categories, namely, stringed, wind, striking or percussion.

THE HARP

Among the stringed instruments "the harp" is the first to be mentioned in the Bible (Genesis 4:21), and was invented by Jubal. Originally, the harp was a humble instrument made up of two pieces of wood fixed together at right angles with a few strings made of animal gut running between them which were plucked by the finger. The wood used for the harp and other instruments was more than likely that of the fir, or cypress tree (I Kings 10:12). Egyptian and Assyro-Babylonian monuments depict the sounding board of a harp decorated with mosaic or inlaid ivory work and a ram's-head ornament at the end, with a figure in front engaged in beating time with his hands. Harps were of various sizes, and made up of a varying number of strings. Albert E. Bailey informs us that —

> Isaiah himself had a harp, one of the large ones that stood on the floor and had forty-seven strings. Half a dozen of the young men had smaller ones (Isaiah 23:16), some with three or four strings, arranged above a sounding board out of which two horns grew, as on a Greek lyre: some had a triangular sounding board across which six or eight strings were stretched as in a modern zither.

Some harps were made up of eleven strings, and usually played with the fingers (I Samuel 16:16). According to Josephus, the Jewish historian, "the harp had twelve strings in contrast to the lyre made up of ten strings and played with a plectrum." The most common form was made up of ten strings with the ten fingers manipulating the harp (Psalms 33:2; 57:8; 81:2; 92:3; 144:9; Isaiah 5:12; Amos 5:23; 6:4-6), and not being very large would be played while walking (I Samuel 10:5; II Samuel 6:5).

King David was a skillful player on the harp. John heard in heaven "the voice of harpers harping with their harps" (Revelation 14:2). What music there is in the words John uses! Many of us are not at all musical, but in heaven we are to have a "golden harp, strung and tuned for endless years," as the poet Cowper expresses it. Just what "the harps of God" are like we are not told. This, however, we do know, that no one will be able to play them whose own nature has not first been tuned to the will of God. Only the redeemed will be able to sing the new song to the accompaniment of the harpers.

Music was employed to cast out evil spirits (I Samuel 18:10), to soothe the temper, or excite the inspiration of a prophet (II Kings 3:15).

THE LYRE

Referred to by many scholars as *cithara,* the lyre was a stringed instrument resembling the harp, and which, because it was portable and comparatively light, could also be played while walking (Genesis 31:27; Isaiah 23:16), and which was only used in hours of rejoicing because of its clear sound (Genesis 31:27; Job 21:12; 30:31; Psalm 137:2). The captive Jews refused to play and sing in a foreign land (Psalm 137:3, 4). "One of the temple orchestra instruments, its tone is described as sweet, tender, soft and lyrical" (Psalm 81:2; Isaiah 24:8). Evidently the lyre was a popular instrument among the cultured classes of Israel. Like the harp, the lyre was made of almug wood (I Kings 10:12), but lacked the resonant body of the harp and was more like the modern guitar than the harp. In form it consisted of "a rectilinear-shaped box from which rose two arms, connected above by a cross bar; the strings ran down from the ladder to the soundbox, to which, or to a bridge on which, they were attached." It was struck with a plectrum or small piece of ivory or metal used to strike, or pluck the strings.

THE ORGAN

Along with the harp, the organ is mentioned as being the first instrument invented by man (Genesis 4:21). Jubal's ancient organ, while the beginning of the huge booming organs played in cathedrals, was a very simple affair. Distinguished from the harp, the organ, as a wind instrument, was likely composed of several unequal pipes, closed at the bottom, which, when blown into at the top, gave a shrill and lively sound (Psalm 150:4). One authority writes of it as being "most probably the bagpipe — an instrument of the highest antiquity and of very general use in the East." Lee G. Olson in the *Zondervan Pictorial Bible Dictionary* says that the organ the psalmist mentions was perhaps an advanced form of the one Jubal made and was "constructed of a skin-covered box with ten holes and each of them able to produce 'ten kinds of songs,' so that the whole organ was able to produce 100 'kinds of songs.' It was used solely as a signal instrument to call the priests and the Levites to their duties. Its tone was very strong." How appealing, inspiring and reverential is the music pealing forth from our magnificent organs of today! What marvelous playing great successors of Jubal, like Mozart, Handel, Beethoven and Mendelssohn were capable of! For church worship, nothing is comparable to an organ played by sanctified, as well as skillful, hands.

THE PSALTERY

This stringed instrument accompanying the voice is linked to an instrument of ten strings (Psalm 33:22, "sing with the psaltery and an instrument of ten strings"). Josephus speaks of it as having twelve strings, and says that the original word for psaltery means a "leather bottle," and that the psaltery was so named because of its shape (I Samuel 10:5; Psalm 92:3; 108:2). The modern psaltery is a flat instrument, of a triangular form, and strung from side to side with wire. Although the Bible psaltery resembled the harp in its general shape, it yet differed from it seeing the body or belly, or sound box, was placed at the top instead of the bottom of the instrument. The early fathers with their fondness for symbolism saw in the "ten strings" a symbol of the "ten commandments" and in the four sides of the instrument, the four gospels. *Psalterian* from which we have "psaltery" was not always restricted to a particular instrument, but sometimes covered a wide range of stringed instruments.

THE SACKBUT

In David's time the sackbut was among the musical instruments used at the court of the king of Babylon. From mural pictures it appears to have been the favorite of dissolute women. Of Oriental origin and popular among the Greeks and Romans, the sackbut was another form of the harp, triangular in shape, having four strings, shrill, and high toned (Daniel 3:5, 7, 10). It was not as the English term implies, a wind instrument.

Coming to wind instruments there are at least four we can mention.

THE DULCIMER

This instrument of the highest antiquity and of general use in the East is identified as the "organ" Jubal invented (Genesis 4:21), which was totally different from the organ of today. The old spinet resembled its tone. Tradition identifies the dulcimer with the bagpipe and is thus described by Servius. Nero is said to have had the ambition to be known as a piper. It was similar to the symphonia of the Greeks. This instrument is not mentioned among those used in the temple. Some writers identify it as the

shepherd's pipe or flute (Job 21:12; 30:31; Daniel 3:5, 15).

THE FLUTE

It is not easy to determine precisely what kind of flutes, or pipes, are meant by the different Old Testament names they bear. Bas-reliefs depict them as a straight pipe, with or without a reed, and with one or two parallel tubes — one for the melody, the other for the accompaniment. Resembling the oboe or clarinet, sound was produced by blowing through or across a hole, or holes. Reeds were made of cane or bone, or ivory. It was played on its own or to the accompaniment of other instruments. It was in demand at weddings, feasts and funerals (I Samuel 10:5; I Kings 1:40; Job 21:12; Isaiah 30:29; Jeremiah 48:36; Matthew 9:23; 11:17). The Greeks regarded Asia Minor as the birthplace of the flute, and it is quite possible that the Jews brought it with them from their Assyrian home. The flute is still made of reed, and of bronze.

THE HORN

Originally, the horn was a ram's horn, or cow's horn without a mouthpiece, and is the only temple instrument still being used today in synagogues. It was employed chiefly as a signal instrument both in religious and secular ceremonies. This primitive trumpet, powerful and raucous in tone, giving either a short or long note, was used in ancient times exclusively for war-like purposes. It sounded a call "to arms" (Judges 6:34; I Samuel 13:3; II Samuel 20:1) — warned of the enemy's approach (Jeremiah 4:5; 6:1; Amos 3:6) — was heard throughout the battle (Amos 2:2) — sounded the recall (II Samuel 2:28). As to the religious use of the horn, these occasions can be noted —

1. The horn was blown at the proclamation of the Law (Exodus 19:13)
2. At the Year of Jubilee (Leviticus 25:9)
3. It heralded the approach of the ark (II Samuel 6:15)
4. Its blast heralded a new king (II Samuel 15:10)
5. Prophetically, it was associated with divine judgment, and Israel's deliverance from captivity (Isaiah 18:3, etc.)

The modern cornet is a development of the ancient horn — *khatzozerah,* a metal trumpet, is sometimes translated "cornet."

THE TRUMPETS

While somewhat similar to the horn, the trumpet differed from it in that it was not curved as the horn, but made in varying sizes of a straight silver or bronze tube, without valves, terminating in a bell-like ending and producing a clear sound. Josephus says of the silver trumpet that "in length it was not quite a yard. It was composed of a narrow tube somewhat thicker than a flute, widened slightly at the mouth to catch the breath, and ended in the form of a bell, like the common trumpets." The modern bugle is a development of the Bible trumpet.

The trumpet was an instrument of national importance, being used more for ceremonial purposes than orchestral playing. Trumpets serve to summon the people to the door of the Tabernacle for instructions regarding the breaking of camp and the call to proceed. Trumpets were blown by the priests (Numbers 10:8), and not by the Levites who were the recognized musicians of the Temple. Two silver trumpets were the minimum for service and 120 the maximum (II Chronicles 5:12). For their use on religious occasions see Exodus 19:13; Leviticus 25:9; II Samuel 15:10. The Feast of Trumpets prepared for the Day of Atonement on the tenth day (Joel 2:15). This Feast reminded the people of their covenant, and put God in remembrance of His promises (Numbers 10:9; Isaiah 43:26). The sound of a trumpet imaged God's voice and word (Isaiah 58:1; Hosea 8:1; Zephaniah 1:16; Revelation 1:10; 4:1). Paul's reference to the trumpet giving an uncertain sound (I Corinthians 14:8), implies that foreign tongues spoken in an assembly would be as useless to the Corinthians as the military trumpet to the army, if it did not give distinct notes expressive of command. The trumpets of God which will gather the elect, and sound the imperious call to judgment dominate the New Testament (Matthew 24:31; Revelation 8:2-9. See Isaiah 27:13; Joel 2:1). Paul associates the trumpet with the rapture of the saints (I Corinthians 15:52; I Thessalonians 4:16). The trumpet shall sound and the dead shall be raised and the living changed and the church complete summoned to meet the Lord in the air.

Among the percussion, or sounding instruments, the principal one was evidently

THE TIMBREL

Akin to the old English tabor, the timbrel, which goes back into remote antiquity was similar to the tamborine. It was a hoop-shaped band of thin wood ten or 11 inches in diameter and 2 inches in depth, over which was tightly stretched a piece of skin. Five holes were cut in the band in which thin metal disks or bells were hung loosely so that when struck by the hand they jingled (Job 21:12; Isaiah 24:8; Jeremiah 31:4). The expression of women "tabering upon their breasts" (Nahum 2:7) means beating their breasts in sorrow just as they would beat a tamborine. The order of procession followed as the singers went first, "damsels with timbrels" in the middle, "players on stringed instruments" following after (Psalm 68:25). The timbrel was usually played by women (Exodus 15:20; Judges 11:34; I Samuel 18:6). Although not listed among the musical instruments employed in the first and second temples, the timbrel is yet listed in the Psalms (68:25; 81:2; 149:3; 150:4). As a rhythm indicator it was used for religious observances, dances and joyous occasions. Often the timbrel is associated with other instruments (Genesis 31:27; I Samuel 10:5; Isaiah 5:12; 30:32). Egyptian and Assyrian monuments depict performers beating a small barrel-like drum fixed at their waist. The term drum does not appear in the Bible.

The tabret, which was more like a "mandolin" is figured to be the equivalent of the "timbrel." Ezekiel has the phrase, "The workmanship of the tabrets . . . was prepared in thee in the day that thou wast created" (28:13), which means, "no sooner wast thou created, like Adam, thou wast surrounded with tabrets, the emblem of Eden-like joys."

THE SISTRUM

Only once is this percussion instrument mentioned in Scripture (II Samuel 6:5). The KJV gives us "cornets," the ASV "castanets," and the margin "sistra." The sistra or castanet was much loved by the Egyptians and is often depicted on their monuments (Psalm 150:5). It was made up of "two thin, longish plates, bent together at the top so as to form an oval frame, and supplied with a handle at the lower end. One or more bars were fixed across the frame, and rings or disks loosely strung on these made a jingling noise when the instrument was shaken."

THE CYMBAL

Made of silver or brass, this only permanent percussion instrument in the temple orchestra was well-known in the ancient world, and was certainly popular in Egypt. In Israel the cymbal was confined to religious uses being employed in ensembles (I Chronicles 15:16; II Chronicles 5:12; Ezra 3:10; Nehemiah 12:27; Psalm 150:5), and in processions (II Samuel 6:5). Usually about five inches in diameter, the cymbal had a handle fixed in the center and was little different from those used today. The two types referred to by the psalmist, "loud cymbals" and "high sounding cymbals" were slightly different in that the former were larger than the latter and were played with both hands. High sounding cymbals, being much smaller, were played by one hand. Asaph, David's chief singer, was also a cymbal player (I Chronicles 16:5). Those who have knowledge and eloquence and yet lack true love to God and men are compared by Paul to a tinkling cymbal (I Corinthians 13:1). Cymbal is from a root meaning to tingle or tinkle.

THE BELLS

Around the bottom of the high priest's robes was an embellishment with pomegranates made of double-stranded yarn alternating with bells of gold. (Exodus 28:33-35; 39:25). These small bells of jingles were used in worship by primitive tribes as well as in Israel. The Persian royal robe had an attachment of small bells. Women are represented as wearing "tinkling ornaments" probably small bells about the ankles to attract attention (Isaiah 3:16, 18, 20). Bells symbolize the sounding forth of the Word (Romans 10:18). Bells were attached to the bridles and belts of warhorses in order to train them to the noise and tumult of battle (Zechariah 14:20).

THE TRIANGLE

The margin for "instruments of music" (I Samuel 18:6) gives us the Hebrew rendering, "three stringed instruments," and was likely a percussion instrument corresponding to the triangle used today in orchestras and bands. The triangle is said to have been a Syrian invention. The phrase above has been variously translated as "triangular harps," "three-stringed lutes" and "three-stringed fiddles."

What must not be forgotten is the fact that the oldest and finest instrument is the living voice, and that for centuries instrumental music by itself — of which Haydn is said to have been the father — was unknown. As instruments were invented they were used only to accompany the singer. With the wonderful development of instrumental music we now have orchestras and bands, unaccompanied by human voices. W. Corswant observes that —

> The most important form of music was the song, and that the essential purpose of instrumental music was to underline the thought and to make the sung word more easily understood. . . . Music was selfsufficient and became the means of expression alongside the spoken word.

In intelligent worship the Word has precedence over ornamental accompaniments (I Corinthians 14:15); and music must not drown but be subordinate to the words and sense (Amos 8:3). The New Testament has little to say about music and musicians. It would seem as if the early Christians used their voices in praising God. Good singing is not dependent upon a man-made instrument expressing a great variety of moods and feelings (Psalms 29:12; 77:1; 95:1; 149:6).

The Book of Psalms can be looked upon as the praise-book of God's ancient people (Psalm 102). There were, of course, other songs (Exodus 15; Song of Solomon), but the whole history of Israel is permeated with the constant, spontaneous praise to her God for His greatness and goodness. The great Hallel Psalms (113-118; 136), were doubtless the ones Jesus and His disciples sang as they left the Upper Room for the garden. That praise was an integral part of the temple ritual is evident from the mighty choirs that were formed. Whether the people responded to the priests in antiphonal fashion, or whether there were two choirs has been questioned. This is evident, that there were 4,000 who praised the Lord (I Chronicles 23:5). Out of the 30,000 David chose for temple service, 4,000 were selected for musical service (I Chronicles 15:16). Later on, when under Solomon the temple was built, "two hundred fourscore and eight" were instructed in the songs of the Lord (I Chronicles 25:6, 7; II Chronicles 5:12-14; 7:6). Solomon formed the choir into a distinct body, supplied with furnished homes and salary (Ezekiel 40:44). The choir numbered 2,000 singers and was divided into two choirs. In the second temple, the orchestra and the choir personnel were greatly reduced, with five years of musical training being requisite to membership in the choir. The oft-repeated, exclusively Old Testament word "Selah" is supposed to indicate a pause in the singing, when the singers would meditate upon the august truths they were singing about — an action worthy of emulation in our congregational singing today.

The term minstrel is used in a twofold way. First of all, it implies a stringed instrument itself (II Kings 3: 15); and secondly, the player of the instrument (Matthew 9:23). The term is now used almost exclusively of the player himself. The late Sir Harry Lauder, the famous Scotch singer spoke of himself as "God's Minstrel."

The Necromancer

Used once in the Bible, this occupational name is related to Spiritualism or Spiritism, and means one who inquires of the dead (Deuteronomy 18: 11), for the purpose of securing information and guidance of the living. A necromancer then was an evoker of spirits of the dead — one who pretended to awake the dead to reveal the secrets of the invisible world and of futurity (Ezekiel 12:22-25). Necromancy is said to have originated in the East. The Greeks affirm that it was invented by Orpheus. Such a black art was prohibited by the law of Moses, which exposed its devotees to severe punishment (Leviticus 20: 27; Deuteronomy 18:10, 11). Yet the practice of it continued. With the official establishment of Christianity by Constantine, necromancy was strictly forbidden. Today, its practice is widespread in the diabolical cult of Spiritualism. The prophet's phrase about "consulting the teraphim" (Ezekiel 21: 21), may have been a form of Spiritualism if, as is probable, the teraphim were ancestral images, raised by superstition to the rank of household gods. How these were consulted we do not know, but as "an illustration of the use of the image of a dead person, we may remember that a modern medium will often ask for a portrait of a deceased relative for the alleged purpose of entering into communication with the departed spirit." Isaiah suggests the association of medium-ship and spiritism with the ventriloquial whispers and mutterings which are supposed to be characteristic of the utterances of the dead (Isaiah 8: 19). Saul's interview with the witch at Endor provides us with an instance of necromancy (I Samuel 28:7-25). This portion presents the difficulty of what God had heretofore condemned, now countenancing. The only feasible explanation appears to be that God availed Himself of the pretended skill of the witch in order to effect His own purpose. The reader is asked to compare further material under THE WITCH.

The Officer

W. Corswant, in his *Dictionary of Bible Times,* lists some seventeen principal officials mentioned in Scripture, as well as a number of subordinate officials. There are some eight to ten different Hebrew and Greek words used to denote various officers, domestic, civil and military. For instance:

1. One set up over others (I Kings 4:7).
2. A eunuch, in charge of a harem, and also of court routine business (Genesis 37:36).
3. A scribe, writer, or clerk (Exodus 5:6; Deuteronomy 20:9).
4. A police officer, or bailiff, or exactor of a fine imposed by a magistrate (Luke 12:58).
5. One who is an assistant or under-ruler (Matthew 5:25).

The word office is applied to the priest (Exodus 28:1; Luke 1:8, 9), the midwife (Exodus 1:16), the deacon (I Timothy 3:10), the bishop (Acts 1:20; I Timothy 3:1). The threefold office of prophet, priest and king is ascribed to Jesus. When He referred to "the officer" (Luke 12:58), He alluded to one who was always in court to execute its sentence as soon as it was

delivered — to the bailiff of the Sanhedrin (Matthew 26:58; Acts 5:22,
26). It was this summary method of
doing justice He had in mind when
He said that He would return quickly
and reward every man as he deserved
(Revelation 22:12). One of the words
translated "officer" is also given as "attendant" (Luke 4:20, ASV; Acts 13:5,
ASV). The hymn has it, "Each in his
office wait."

The Orator

Herod and Tertullus are named as
orators (Acts 12:21; 24:1). It is interesting to notice that the word used
in Herod's case is from the root from
which we have "demagogue," while
the word used of Tertullus is from a
Greek term from which we have "rhetoric" — the theory and practice of eloquence. The training of Tertullus was
not legal but rhetorical, who, as a professional speaker, knew how to make
a skillful presentation of a case in
court (See Isaiah 3:3), as he did in
pleading against Paul before Felix
(Acts 24:1-9) in Latin, the language
of the Roman courts. Men of this class
were ready to plead or defend any
cause, and, possessing a good deal of
glib eloquence, with a due admixture
of flattery, were in constant demand.
Quintilian, the Latin philosopher, said
that there are three qualities which an
orator ought to display, namely,

> He should instruct,
> He should move,
> He should delight.

When Isaiah speaks of "the eloquent
orator" (3:3), the margin expresses
the phrase as "the skillful enchanter,"
the one who is skillful in whisperings
or magic for the word employed is
derived from the verb for "charmed
serpents," or incantation (Psalm 58:
5). Shakespeare in *Julius Caesar*
has Mark Antony say —

> I come not, friends, to steal away your
>   hearts:
> I am no orator, as Brutus is;
> But, as you know me all, a plain, blunt
>   man,
> That loves my friends.

Although orators are few and far between, those of us who are "plain,"
and who love God and the souls of
men, can bear eloquent witness to the
saving grace of Christ. Always ready
and willing to speak a good word for
Him is to possess heaven's oratory.

The Organist

As organs (Genesis 4:21; Job 21:12;
30:31; Psalm 150:4), imply those well-
able to manipulate them, there must
have been skillful organists in Bible
times, even though their instruments
were not as complicated and magnificent as present-day organs. Reference
is made to material under THE MUSI-
CIAN. Alexander Pope has the couplet

> While in more lengthened notes and
>   slow,
> The deep, majestic, solemn organs
>   blow.

Mozart, we are told, composed music
at five years of age. It is said that
when he was six he saw a large organ
for the first time in a monastery on the
banks of the Danube. After gazing at
it for awhile, he said to his father,
"Please explain to me those pedals,
and let me play." An attendant pushed
aside the stool, and the child-prodigy,
standing upon the pedals began to
play in such a way that the monks at
supper stopped to listen, and then
hastened in astonishment to their
chapel. Seeing no player, they thought
it must be a miracle till one of the
monks went up the stairs and found
the boy, absorbed, moving his small
yet skillful hands along the keys and
producing wonderful harmonies.

The Ornithologist

While this actual term, meaning, a student and lover of birds, is not used in the Bible, ornithology is woven into the texture of the Word of God. For the guidance of the reader the most appealing handbook on Bible ornithology is Alice Parmelee's remarkable volume on *All the Birds of the Bible,* published by Harper and Brothers, New York. With over 300 Bible references and sixty-four pages of pictures all dealing with the feathered creation, this study is one we can heartily recommend. Alice Parmelee shows how many of these lively creatures, which St. Francis of Assisi called his "little brothers and sisters," flit through the Scriptures and were sometimes an integral part of many events. The authoress quotes two outstanding American ornithologists, Dr. Robert Cushman Murphy and Dr. Dean Amadon, who paid high tribute to Bible bird watchers in the statement, "To judge from the Old Testament, the inheritors of the Land of Canaan were extraordinarily good naturalists."

There are almost 400 birds of remarkable variety and quantity in Palestine yet the Bible only mentions about fifty of these birds in forty-five books of the Bible from Genesis to Revelation. The majority are referred to in the lists of clean and unclean birds and animals (Leviticus 11:2-23; Deuteronomy 14:20). In addition to his other outstanding qualifications Solomon spoke with wisdom about animals and birds (I Kings 4:33). Then what a lover of birds Christ was — and no wonder, seeing He helped to fill the world with these "extraordinarily vital scraps of feathered energy, defiant of gravity, undaunted by arctic cold, tropical heat, or all the immensities of space" (Matthew 6:26; 8:20; Luke 9:58; 12:24, etc.).

Among the birds specifically mentioned we have —

The Bittern — a heron-like bird of marshy environment and mournful call (Isaiah 14:23; 34:11; Zephaniah 2:14).

The Chicken — the common domesticated barnyard fowl our Lord knew of (I Kings 4:22, 23; Matthew 23:27) (See symbolic use of the cock — the male species Matthew 26:74; Mark 13:35).

The Cormorant — swimmer and diver among the birds (Leviticus 11:17; Deuteronomy 14:17; Isaiah 34:11; Zephaniah 2:14).

The Crane — the long-necked, long-legged wading bird with a loud croak (Isaiah 38:14; Jeremiah 8:7).

The Cuckoo — an unclean bird which the RSV translates "seagull" (Leviticus 11:16; Deuteronomy 14:15).

The Dove — symbol of love, peace, purity and sorrow (Genesis 8:8-12; 15:9; Psalm 68:13; Song of Solomon 2:14; Isaiah 38:14; 59:11; Matthew 3:16; 10:16; 21:12. See Turtledove).

Among the birds turtledoves or pigeons could be offered in sacrifice, and sacrificed according to special instructions (Leviticus 1:14-17; 5:8; 15:14, 29; Numbers 6:10).

The Eagle — the large, hawk-like bird with powerful beak, talons and wings (Exodus 19:4; Leviticus 11:13, 18; Deuteronomy 28:49; 32:11; Psalm 103:5; Isaiah 40:31, etc.).

The Falcon — species of hawk with long pointed wings and long tail (Leviticus 11:14).

The Glede — another species of vulture or hawk, judged unclean (Deuteronomy 14:13).

The Hawk—fast-flying, sharp-tongued,

curved-back predator similar to the eagle and considered unclean (Leviticus 11:13, 16; Deuteronomy 14:15; Job 39:26, 27).

The Heron — long-legged, marsh-inhabiting, wading bird also unclean. (Leviticus 11:19; Deuteronomy 14:18).

The Ospray, now osprey — a fish-eating hawk, able to hold slippery fish (Leviticus 11:13; Deuteronomy 14:12).

The Ossifrage — or bearded vulture, called "gier eagle" (Leviticus 11: 13, ASV).

The Ostrich — largest and fastest running bird (Job 39:13-18; 30:29; Lamentations 4:3).

The Owl — another unclean bird (Leviticus 11:16, 17. See Psalm 102: 6; Isaiah 34:15; Screech Owl, Isaiah 34:13, 14).

The Partridge — related to chicken. It was swift and sneaky, and a game bird. (I Samuel 26:20; Jeremiah 17:11).

The Peacock — renowned for beautiful plumage (Job 39:13).

The Pelican — unclean because of its eating habits (Leviticus 11:18; Psalm 102:6; Isaiah 34:11).

The Pigeon — species of common rock dove (Genesis 15:9; Luke 2:24).

The Quail — ground-dweller, food-scratcher, good for food (Exodus 16:13; Numbers 11:31; Psalm 105:40).

The Raven — an omnivorous eater, similar to the large crow (Genesis 8:7; I Kings 17:4; Job 38:41; Isaiah 34:11).

The Sparrow — a prolific, small, seed-eating bird (Psalms 84:3; 102:7; Matthew 10:31, etc.).

The Stork — a marsh bird, long-legged, heron-like with strong wings (Psalm 104:17; Jeremiah 8:7; Zechariah 5:9).

The Swallow — noted for its swiftness and piercing repeated call (Isaiah 38:14).

The Turtledove — wild pigeon of migratory habits, and similar to mourning dove (Genesis 15:9; Luke 2:24).

The Vulture — hawk-like bird that feeds on carrion (Job 28:7; Isaiah 34:15).

Many of the habits and habitat of birds are alluded to in Scripture — their flight, their shelters, their food, their song, and, in some cases, their rapacity (Genesis 15:11; 40:17, 19; I Samuel 17:44; II Samuel 21:10; Psalm 79:2; 104:12; Proverbs 26:2; 27:8; Ecclesiastes 10:20; 12:4; Song of Solomon 2:12; Isaiah 31:5; Ezekiel 17:23; Daniel 4:12, 14; Hosea 9:11; Matthew 13:4; Mark 4:4; Luke 8:5). The instinctive observance of seasons of migration as birds return every spring from their winter quarters, is made to illustrate a tacit reproof of God's people not returning to Him once His judicial wrath was past, and the spring of His gracious favor had come (Jeremiah 8:7). Parent birds hovering over their young symbolize God's solicitous and affectionate care for His people (Isaiah 31:5). Birds are wise, but the God who created them possesses greater wisdom (Job 35:11). Men are worth far more than the birds (Luke 12:24). Regarded as the emblem of superhuman intelligence the bird is used, proverbially, as the carrier of news (Ecclesiastes 10:20). Facts would reach the king's ear in a marvelous way, as if a bird had carried them.

If this brief cameo begets a desire for a fuller knowledge of Bible birds may you experience with Alice Parmelee, "a new insight into Scripture, a fresh perspective on art, and many deeper friendships both with ancient

Bible people and with bird watchers today." As a reader of her most delightful book, I share her "pleasures, satisfactions and enlightenment."

The Overseer

Here we have a term expressing an occupation exercised both in the secular and spiritual realms. In the Old Testament "overseer" is used exclusively of those occupying a secular position. The word implies one who inspects or overlooks — a foreman or inspector (Genesis 39:4, 5; II Chronicles 2:18; 34:12, 13, 17) — an officer (Genesis 41:34) — a ruler (I Chronicles 26:32) — an administrator (Proverbs 6:7). Excavation work on one of the two temples found at Beth-shan uncovered an Egyptian inscription upon one of them reading that the temple had been founded by "an overlord of soldiers, commandant of the archers of the lord of the two countries, royal scribe and grand overseer under Ramses." Isaiah has the phrase "thine exactors (overseers) righteousness" (60:17).

Coming to the New Testament, overseer is strictly confined to those engaged in spiritual work, and describes those who are called of God to rule the flock (Romans 12:8), or to preserve or care for it (Acts 26:17; I Peter 5:2). The terms bishop, elder, overseer appear to be interchangeable. A bishop was not so much a defined official but one who had general oversight and as such was blameless in character (Titus 1:5, 7). "Bishops and deacons" (Philippians 1:1) imply "such as oversee and such as serve." Bishop indicates the character of the work undertaken, and elder, the age, gravity, spiritual maturity and understanding of the one holding such an office. In his address to the church elders at Ephesus, Paul warned them to feed the church over which they had been made overseers or bishops. Writing to Timothy, the apostle further remarks that such overseership is a "good work" (I Timothy 3:1, 2). The word he used for "overseers" can be expressed as "watchers" on account of the solemn work assigned them (Acts 20:28; I Thessalonians 5:12, 13; Hebrews 13:7, 17 etc.). Christ as the Bishop of our souls always watches over us, and cares for us (I Peter 2: 2, 5).

Oversight signifies complete charge of a task (II Kings 12:11; 22:5, 9) — to be entrusted with (Nehemiah 13: 4) — to look carefully over and thoroughly inspect (Hebrews 12:15, ASV; I Peter 5:2).

The Peacemaker

In classical Greek a peacemaker was an ambassador sent to arrange peace between his own country and another. Peacemakers, was a nickname given to a Bedfordshire regiment because no battles were indicated on its colors. The adjective Jesus used when He said, "Blessed are the peacemakers" (Matthew 5:9) signifies one who makes peace. The term is also given as "peaceworkers," and represents those who not only make peace between those who are at variance, but working peace as that which is the will of God for men. Speaking peaceably (Jeremiah 9:8), those who sow peace, make it (James 3:18, ASV margin). Ellicott observes that "rightly does this beatitude follow on that of 'the pure in heart,' for it is the absence of all baseness and impurity that gives the power to make peace." Christ came to provide peace on earth (Luke 2:14), a provision that will not be fully realized until He returns as the Prince of Peace (Isaiah 9:6, 7; 11:6-9; Micah 4:3). As the Son of God and the Son of man, He made peace between God and man, between Jew and Gentile, at the price of His outpoured blood (Ephesians 2:16; Colossians 1: 20). Because God is love, therefore through Christ the great Peacemaker, all who, according to their capacity, share in peacemaking bear the family likeness. As sharers in divine sonship, they are recognized as "the sons of God." Richard Glover remarks that we can experience the blessedness of peacemakers by

1. Doing nothing to break peace;
2. Doing nothing to increase existing variance;
3. Doing all in our power to heal strife.

May grace be ours to re-echo the prayer of Eliza Scudder —

Grant us Thy peace, that like a deepening river
    Swells ever outward to the sea of praise.
O Thou of peace the only Lord and Giver,
    Grant us Thy peace, O Saviour all our days.

The Philosopher

As used by Luke, philosophers were lovers of wisdom (Acts 17:18), which, in the original, is the same word Paul uses for philosophy (Colossians 2:8). Philologus, a believer in Rome to whom Paul sent a salutation, means "a lover of words." The most celebrated philosopher and teacher among the Jews in the apostle's time was Gamaliel, to whom Paul owed a great deal (Acts 5:34; 22:3). At the outset let it be affirmed that both Old and New Testament writers are in complete accord with the true spirit and purpose of philosophy, as the pursuit of truth and the purpose and endeavor to express more fully and clearly the nature of divine revelation to man. Though

foolishness to the philosophical Greek, Christ crucified was "the wisdom of God" (I Corinthians 1:2). In Greek usage a philosopher was one who had "zeal for, or skill in, any art or science."

When Paul wrote of "philosophy" it was in a derogatory sense and referred to unsound and pernicious teaching (Colossians 2:8). With genuine philosophy the apostle had every sympathy. What he deprecated were the philosophies of the Epicureans and the Stoics whose superficiality is revealed in that they "spent their time in nothing else, but either to tell or to hear, some new thing" (Acts 17:18, 21). The Gnostics which Paul encountered, were among the ancient philosophers who, in spite of their professed wisdom, knew not God (I Corinthians 1:18 - 2:6; 3:18-21). Their philosophies were "subtle dialectics and profitless speculation . . . combined with a mystic cosmogony and angelology." Warnings against these self-confessed "know-it-alls," and against the futility of Greek wisdom to understand and appreciate divine truth may have been in Paul's mind when he urged young Timothy to guard against false doctrines (I Timothy 1:4; 4:3; II Timothy 1:14, 16).

The father of modern philosophy — the science of sciences, representing the investigation of truth and nature — is supposed to have been Albrecht von Haller, of Berne (1718-1772). Solomon's Book of Ecclesiastes, teaching that "all is vanity under the sun," can be regarded as "an answer to modern philosophical naturalism." Shakespeare in *Much Ado About Nothing* says, "There was never yet philosopher that could endure the toothache patiently, however they have writ the style of gods, and made a push at chance and sufferance."

The Physician

Under the cameo of THE DOCTOR — which see — we drew attention to the fact that wherever "doctor" is used in the Bible it implies a teacher of God's law, and never a "physician" — commonly known as a "doctor" today. The Greek word for physician means, "to heal." The Italian word for doctor is "medico," from which we have "medicine." In the Old Testament physicians were Egyptian embalmers (Genesis 50:2), who knew of a wonderful process of embalming dead bodies preserving them, thereby, from decay. In our time physicians attend only to the living unless they conduct a postmortem to ascertain the cause of death. There are evidences, however, that at an early date in Egypt and Babylon there were those having medical and surgical knowledge. Egypt had its god of healing. Some 700 years after Joseph's embalming by the physicians Homer could write, "Such cunning drugs had Helen, drugs of healing virtues, which Polydamna gave, the wife of Thon in Egypt, where the fruitful soil yields drugs of every kind. . . . There everyone is a physician, skillful beyond humankind." With the founding of the Grecian School at Alexandria, Egypt became a center of medical education and research.

Among the Jews there were those capable of dealing with various physical maladies (Exodus 21:19; II Kings 8:29; 9:15; Isaiah 1:6; 3:7; Jeremiah 8:22; 33:6; Ezekiel 30:21). During the ministry of the prophets, healings are recorded as miracles. To the pious Jew, God was the Healer (Deuteronomy 32:39), and it was of greater value to trust in Him than to consult physicians who, although they had skill in dealing with the dead, did not know very well how to treat the living.

The most terribly afflicted man in the Bible was Job whose body was so loathsome that friends would not go near him. No one suggested that he should see a physician. Had he sent for one, it might have been said of him, as it was of King Asa, "yet in his disease he sought not to the Lord but to the physicians" (II Chronicles 16: 12).

King Solomon evidently had a certain amount of scientific and medical knowledge and under the Spirit's inspiration used symbolic language of medical facts (Ecclesiastes 12:6). "The silver cord" is the spinal marrow, white and precious as silver, attached to the brain which is "the golden bowl" says Jamieson. "This fountain" may mean the right ventricle of the heart, the "cistern" the left; "the pitcher" the veins, the "wheel" the aorta or great artery. The "wheel" however may mean life in its rapid motion, as in James 3:6 "the wheel of nature. The circulation of the blood is apparently expressed."

Approaching the New Testament we know that there has never been a Physician like Jesus who, as the Sun of Righteousness, arose upon this sin-sick world of ours with healing in His wings. Egyptian physicians preserved dead bodies. Jesus brought the dead back to life. To the sick before Him, He offered no medicines, and for the physically handicapped He had no surgical instruments to relieve them. "He spake, and it was done." Years ago healing was by magic, but Jesus used no magic. Before His august person and omnipotent word, sickness, disease, blindness and death fled He lived in the days of the Roman Empire when physicians were numerous in Palestine. In Nazareth, Jesus quoted the proverb, "Physician, heal thyself" (Luke 4:23); and the physicians of Galilee would understand His saying,

"They that are whole have no need of a Physician" (Matthew 9:12; Mark 2:17; Luke 5:31).

We are interested in Mark's story about the woman with an issue of blood, "who suffered many things of many physicians, and spent all that she had and was nothing better, but rather grew worse." (Mark 5:28; Luke 8:43). Job, irritated by the platitudes of his friends, called them "physicians of no value" (13:4). Among the "many things" that were tried to cure this woman of her infirmity were these — she was set in a place where two ways met, with a cup of wine in her hand. Then someone came up behind and frightened her and said, "Arise from thy flux!" Another method of healing practiced was to fasten several strips of rag to a tree — bits of the clothing of sick persons — the belief being that through the fluttering strip the disease would pass into the tree and the health of the living tree would pass into the patient's body. But all the woman had to do was to touch the seamless robe of Christ, and instantly she was healed. For a fuller study of the methods He used in His healings, the reader is referred to a companion volume, *All the Miracles of the Bible*.

What must not be forgotten is that it was Christ's interest in the sick that created hospitals. Through the centuries His healing ministry has inspired an unnumbered host of physicians and nurses. Calvary gave the name of Red Cross to the greatest healing organization in the world. The most talented physicians know that their skill and medicines are only means and that all life is in the hands of *Jehovah Jireh*, The Lord the Healer.

The only named physician in the Bible is Luke the companion of Paul whom he called "the beloved physician" (Colossians 4:14). Origen reckoned that this renowned physician was the unnamed brother whose praise in the Gospel is spread through all the churches (II Corinthians 8:18). There may be something in the suggestion that Luke first became acquainted with Paul at Antioch or at Troas when the apostle was sick and needed medical attention, and that Luke gave up his practice to accompany Paul and guard his health. Toward the end of his life, Paul wrote to Timothy, "Only Luke is with me." In the two books Luke wrote, the third gospel and the Acts, there are evidences of his medical knowledge in the language he used, as Sir Wm. Ramsey elaborates upon in his study, *Luke the Physician*.

The *Talmud* has references to physicians at the temple to care for the priests, and that to practice, physicians were required to have a license from the local authorities. Limited praise for their skill was given them in the Apocrypha, "There is a time when success lies in the hands of physicians. . . . He who sins before his Maker may he fall into the care of a physician" (Ecclesiasticus 38:13, 15, RSV). As to the medicines and means of healing employed, Scripture has much to say. Apart from magical rites and exorcisms, there was the use of natural remedies. That the Jews knew the virtues of certain plants and of many substances of animal and mineral origin is evident from their use of them. The myrtle, for instance, was much sought after, not only for its scent, but because its leaves and berries were used in medicine since they contained an aromatic, volatile oil (See Revelation 22:2). In the time of Moses there were midwives and regular physicians (Exodus 21:19), and from Egypt the Israelites took with them some knowledge of medicine received from the renowned Egyptian physicians. Albert E. Bailey says that Egyptian "materia medica included powders and decoctions made from sycamore figs, dates and other fruits, the pith of certain trees, salt, oil, magnesia, honey and sweet beer; often mixed with such unpleasant ingredients as rancid fat, bone dust and the droppings of animals." Here for example is a prescription for the inflammation of the eye:

> Parts — 1 myrrh, 1 "Great Protector's" seed, 1 oxide of copper, 1 citron pips, 1 northern cypress flowers, 1 antimony, 1 gazelle droppings, 1 oryx offal, 1 white oil. Place in water, let it stand overnight, strain through a cloth and paint it on the eye four days with a goose feather. Physicians please take notice!

In the Bible we read of oil lotions (Isaiah 1:6), anointings of balm (Jeremiah 8:22; 46:11; 51:8) (Gilead was a place resorted to for medical treatment), fig poultices (II Kings 20:7; Isaiah 38:21), eye-salves (II Kings 9:30; Jeremiah 4:30; Ezekiel 23:40; Revelation 3:18) not only to improve the eyesight but to beautify the eyes, oil and wine (Luke 10:23; I Timothy 5:23).

The Bible recognizes the close connection between physical health and moral health. "A cheerful heart is a good medicine," says Solomon, "but a downcast spirit dries up the bones" (Proverbs 17:22). Israel's general exemption from epidemics and remarkable healthiness can be traced not only to the healthful climate of Palestine but also to the washings, cleanliness of the camp, restriction in diet of clean animals, the prohibition of pork, separation of lepers and laws of marriage (Leviticus 15; Deuteronomy 23:12-14). One of the oldest names of God in the Bible is *Jehovah-rophi*, the Lord that heals, and He made it clear to His people that He was among them as One able to heal them. Among the five subjects of praise for which David called upon his soul to bless God for, the second was — "Who healeth all thy diseases" (Psalm 103:1-5). There is not a disease of the soul or of the body with which He is not acquainted, and for which He has not a specific remedy (Matthew 8:16, 17; Philippians 3:21). "Lord, . . . heal my soul; for I have sinned against Thee" (Psalm 41:4). Often a sick person's first need is not medicine but mercy. The cause of their physical malady is sin, and once this is dealt with by the Great Physician, physical health follows. "Thy faith hath made thee *whole*," and holiness is just wholeness, haleness, health. It is comforting to know that —

> The Great Physician now is here
> The sympathizing Jesus.

The Pilot

Although the term pilot is used in many ways — our gas stove has a *pilot* light — this English word is said to have come from an old French word, *pile*, meaning, "a ship." As used by Ezekiel (27:8, 27-29) it implies a "sailor" or "rope-puller," and represents the skillful nautical craftsmen from Tyre. As then, so now, a pilot was one duly qualified to conduct vessels into port and out of a port. Accustomed to storms, pilots had to know how to control their vessels.

> O pilot! 'tis a fearful night,
> There's danger on the deep.

John Dryden wrote of —

> A daring pilot in extremity,
> Pleased with the danger when the waves ran high.

John Milton referred to Peter as, "The pilot of the Galilean Lake."

The boats, ships and shipwrecks of the Bible form a profitable line of study. In the early years of their history, the Jews were a pastoral and agricultural people, having little inclination to follow a seafaring life. During the Monarchy, however, they came to the fore as a commercial people, with both David and Solomon becoming dependent upon "a navy of ships" (I Kings 9:26-28; 10:22; See Job 9:26; Mark 3:9; Luke 8:23; Acts 27:37, etc.).

William Pitt, the English statesman, was spoken of as "The Pilot that weathered the storm," seeing he steered the country through the European storm stirred up by Napoleon. In 1802, George Canning wrote a complimentary poem on Pitt's piloting of the ship of State —

> When our perils are past, shall our gratitude sleep?
> No, — here's to the pilot that weathered the storm.

It was Tennyson who bade us think of the Lord as our infallible Pilot. In his great poem on *Crossing the Bar* we have the verse —

> For tho' from out our bourne of time and place
> The flood may bear me far,
> I hope to see my Pilot face to face,
> When I have crossed the bar.

How comforting it is to know that amid the storms of life we have the Lord so near at hand to guide and preserve our frail vessels.

> Jesus, Saviour, pilot me
> Over life's tempestuous sea;
> Unknown waves before me roll,
> Hiding rock and treach'rous shoal;
> Chart and compass come from Thee:
> Jesus, Saviour, pilot me.

The Planter

The only reference in the Bible to this occupational name is found in Jeremiah. "The planters shall plant, and shall eat vines as common things" (31:5).

But all that this term implies permeates the Word. For a study of what the planters planted reference can be made to the section in *The Zondervan Pictorial Bible Dictionary* on flowers, plants and trees, or to *All the Plants of the Bible* by Winifred Walker. Jesus taught us to think of His Father and ours, as the divine Planter — "Every plant, which my heavenly Father hath not planted, shall be rooted up" (Matthew 15:13). Saved by His grace, we are planted as trees by rivers of water (Psalm 1:3), to bear fruit to His glory. Paul, likewise thought of himself as a "planter." With the churches in mind he had brought into being he could say, "I have planted" (I Corinthians 3:5-10).

The Plowman

As husbandmen and plowmen (or ploughmen) are used synonymously in Scripture, and often plowmen were farmers, compare material found under THE FARMER and THE HUSBANDMAN (Deuteronomy 22:10; Psalm 129:3; Isaiah 28:24; 61:5; Jeremiah 14:4; Amos 9:13; Luke 17:7). The plow and plowing are often mentioned in the Bible, and are used to enforce many spiritual truths. An ancient proverb reads, "The first men in the world were a gardener, a ploughman and a grazier."

Egyptian, Babylonian and Palestinian bas-reliefs and drawings of plowmen and plows with a metal plowshare (I Samuel 13:20, 21) reveal, more or less, a uniform pattern of the implement drawn by oxen (I Kings 19:19), and usually handled by laborers or slaves. In backward countries today the implements and methods of plowing have changed very little from ancient times. The Philistines probably played an important part in the introduction to Palestine of iron plowshares.

Modern, mechanical plows cut deep into the soil and turn it over, but Eastern plows with their broad point broke up the soil without turning it over. Simple, light and wheelless, the plow scratched the soil some six to eight inches deep, leaving small furrows (Psalm 65:10. See Isaiah 28:24). Drawn by oxen or other animals, the plow was of flimsy construction and required the least possible skill or expense. Generally, it consisted of two poles, crossing each other near the ground: the pole nearer the oxen was fastened to the yoke, while the other served, the one as the handle, the other as the plowshare. Similar, lightly built plows, are still used by Arabs today.

As for the plowmen, they had to be strong and skillful enough to hold the handle of the plowtail firmly in their grip and steer the plow and at the same time drive the oxen. The goad they used not only urged the oxen on, but also was helpful in breaking up clods of earth. Plowmen also had to keep a close lookout in order to avoid rocks and bushes which could break the primitive construction of the plow. Only a bad plowman would look behind (Luke 9:62). This saying is credited to Benjamin Franklin, "Plow deep while sluggards sleep." The "honest plowman" which Robert Burns — himself a plowman — wrote about was one Wordsworth eulogized thus:

> Of him who walked in glory and in joy
> Following his plough, along the mountain side.

Those plowmen of old had to observe certain conditions. For instance —

The law forbade Jews to yoke to the plow two animals of different species (Deuteronomy 22:10). This prohibition is disregarded in the East today.

Plowing was usually done by bondservants (Luke 17:7), and was not performed before the rains (Jeremiah 14:4).

In winter time the soil was too sticky to plough (Proverbs 20:4).

The law required one day of rest in every seven for plowing, as well as from occupation (Exodus 34:21).

An interesting feature of the subject before us is that both plowman and plowing are used often in a figurative sense in the Bible. For the preacher, these aspects can be noted:

"The plowers plowed upon my back" (Psalm 129:3) typifies deep affliction, particularly that which Jesus endured.

"Plow iniquity" (Job 4:8; Micah 3:12) is urged in the sense of "plant iniquity." Evil doing brings evil consequences. Robert Burns, the Scottish bard wrote of

> Stern ruin's ploughshare drivers, elate
> Full on thy bloom.

Further, as planting follows plowing, so surely will God carry out His decree of destruction (Isaiah 28:23-25). Many figures of destruction are used. "Judah shall plow" or become enslaved (Hosea 10:11) — "Foreigners shall be your plowmen" (Isaiah 61:5) — "Will one plow there with oxen" (Amos 6:12) — "neither plowing nor harvest" (Genesis 45:6) — "Zion shall be plowed like a field" (Jeremiah 26:18).

Plowing is also typical of divinely bestowed abundance. "The plowman shall overtake the reaper" (Amos 9:13). Here we have a glimpse of the

Millennium, when the soil shall be so fertile as to require no rest. Abundance of peace during Christ's millennial reign is typified by men beating their "swords into plowshares" (Isaiah 2:4; Micah 4:3). Alas, when men "beat their plowshares into swords" (Joel 3:10), war plagues the earth!

The plowman who puts his hand to the plow, and looks back (Luke 9:62), represents one who unfits himself for God's use if he longs for evil things after having set his face Godward (See Genesis 19:26; Philippians 3:13).

Plowmen expect to share in the fruits of harvest, and who are called to serve God can expect their temporal needs to be met (I Corinthians 9:10).

Plowmen were forbidden to yoke an ox and an ass together in a plough (Deuteronomy 22:10), and believers are forbidden to be yoked together with unbelievers (II Corinthians 6:14).

What is true Christian discipleship? Is it not the willingness to "plow the fields, and scatter the good Seed on the ground"? Plowing is hard work, and a sincere witness for Christ needs courage of heart. Opposition and persecution may have to be faced, and, as it has been expressed, "We need to bring our backbone to the front." Too many of us want to be comfortable Christians, no plowing of fields at home or abroad for us; no cross for our shoulder; no risks, when we can take it easy.

Napoleon is credited with having said: "Brave soldiers never fear death; they drive into the ranks of the enemy." Are we forever on the defensive against the forces of darkness, or are we among the number daring enough to take the offensive in the warfare against evil?

The Poet

The only time poet is mentioned in Scripture is in connection with Paul's speech to the men of Athens on Mars' hill — "As certain of your own poets have said" (Acts 17:28). The saying of this poet, "For we are also his offspring" is ascribed to the great poet, Aretus of Soli in Cilicia who lived around 270 B.C. who in his poem which Paul quoted from, endeavored to prove Jupiter as the father and controller of all things, and worthy of human worship. But Paul takes the praise and devotion offered by the Greek poet to an unknown and false god and associates the same with the one true God whom the apostle declared to the Athenians.

Other quotations from pagan poets by Paul who was well versed in them, include "Liars, evil beasts, slow bellies" (Titus 1:12), which Clement of Alexandria affirmed was from the poet Epimenides. "Feel after" (Acts 17:27) may have been taken from *Odyssey* O: 416 — the verb being used of the groping of the blind Cyclops. "A citizen of no mean city," referring to Athens (Acts 21:39), is an echo of a line from Euripides. "Evil communications corrupt good manners" (I Corinthians 15:33) is said to be "an iambic senarius from the poet of the New Comedy, Menander (342-291 B.C.)." That Paul was also acquainted with the Christian hymnology of his own times is evident from fragments found in Ephesians 5:14 and I Timothy 3:16.

The word poet is a Greek term meaning maker or creator, and many poems are indeed superb creations. Shelley, the renowned English poet wrote that, "Poets, not otherwise than philosophers, painters, sculptors and musicians, are, in one sense, the creators, and, in another, the creations, of their age." Shelley gave us the expressive lines —

> Most wretched men are cradled
> into poetry by wrong,
> They learn in suffering what they
> teach in song.

A forceful illustration of Paul's original flashes of poetic inspiration and utterances can be found in Romans 8:31-37. Another derivation of *poietes,* the classical Greek for an author, especially a poet, is *poiema* from which we have "poem," used twice in the Bible. "Things that are made" (Romans 1:20, *poiema*). "We are his workmanship" (Ephesians 2:10, *poiema*). That God the Creator should be a poet is not surprising. What does amaze us is that He is able to fashion poor, hell-deserving sinners into an appealing poem. Thus God has two poems to His credit, *creation* and His *church.* Shelley wrote that "A poem is the very image of life, expressed in its eternal truth." How true this sentiment is of God's poems — the first costing Him only His breath, for "He spake and it was done"; the second costing Him His blood for "with His blood He bought her."

> Turn great to call a world from
> nought;
> Turn greater to redeem.

Because the poetry of the Bible is of a very high order, one is sorely tempted to linger over this most fascinating aspect of the study of the Bible as literature, and show how the majority of its writers present the kinship between spirituality and poetry in many harmonious and beautiful forms. All that we can do, however, in this section is to touch upon the fringe of such an appealing subject. For a fuller and exhaustive treatment, the reader is urged to consult the *Zonder-*

van Pictorial Bible Dictionary and the two articles under "poetry" in *The International Standard Bible Encyclopedia.* Perhaps the most outstanding expositions of the poetic inspiration characteristic of the Bible as a whole is that by George Gilgillan, *The Bards of the Bible.* This classic, written over 100 years ago, is hard to secure, being long out of print. How worthy it is of a new edition! In the Preface of the first edition of this most enlightening volume of his, Gilgillan tells us that the main object of his book was not "to give an elaborate or full account of the mechanical structure of Hebrew poetry, but to be a prose poem or hymn, in honor of the poetry and the poets of the Bible." And in a captivating, poetical style he admirably succeeded in his purpose. The author rightly affirms that "the language of poetry is the language of the inspired Book, and is that into which all earnest natures are insensibly betrayed, so it is the speech which has in it the greatest power of permanent possession."

Dealing with the influences and effects of Scripture poetry, Gilgillan in dealing with all the writers of Holy Writ as "bards" extols their supremacy over all others in their poetical method of contemplating nature in its relation to God. "The superiority of the Bible poets to the mass of even men of true genius will not be disputed." These Bible poets, under "the quick Spirit of the Book ransacked creation to lay its treasures on Jehovah's altar — thus the innumerable rays of a far-streaming glory have been condensed on the little hill, Calvary — and a garland has been woven for the bleeding brow of Immanuel, the flowers of which have been culled from the gardens of a universe. This praise may seem lofty, but it is due to the Bible, and to it alone — because it is only, of all poems, uttered in broken fullness, in finished fragments that shape of the universal truth which instantly incarnates itself in living nature — impregnates it as a thought, a word — peoples it as a form, a mirror."

Enumerating many subsequent poets, Gilgillan shows how their poetry is colored by that of the Bible's poetic language. The charm of Scripture quotation adds to other classics of the heart. According to the Scotch writer, Hebrew poetry can be arranged under the two general heads of song and poetic statement. Under song we have —

Exulting — in order of triumph e. g. Psalm 105.

Insulting — in strains of irony and invective e. g. Psalm 109.

Mourning — over calamities e. g. Psalm 81 and Lamentations.

Worshiping — God e. g. Psalm 104.

Loving — in friendly and amatory songs e. g. Psalm 45

Reflecting — in gnomic or sententious strains e. g. Psalm 139 and Proverbs.

Interchanging — in the varied persons and parts of the simple drama, e. g. Job and Song of Solomon.

Wildly luxuriating — in Psalm 7 and Hebrews 3.

Narrating — the past deeds of God to Israel: the simple epic e. g. Psalm 78 and Exodus.

Predicting — the future history of the church and the world — prophetic writings.

Under poetical statement we have —

Poetic Facts — Creation, etc.

Poetic Doctrines — God's spirituality, etc.

Poetic Sentiments, with or without figurative language e. g. the Golden Rule, etc.

Poetic Symbols as in Zechariah, Revelation, etc.

In a unique way, Gilgillan sketches the outstanding character of Scripture and provides us with striking evidences of the poetic inspiration of each and of the influence which has radiated upon the works of both ancient and modern poets. We conclude with this arrestive paragraph —

In the poetical beauty and grandeur of Scripture, we have, as it were, a perpetual miracle attesting its divine origin. After the influence of its miracles has in a great measure died away, and although all now be still around Sinai's mount, and upon Bethlehem's plains. . . . Scripture poetry has refined society, softened the human heart, promoted deference and respect to women and tenderness to children, cleansed to a great degree the temple of our literature, and especially of our poetry and fiction — denounced licentiousness, while inculcating forgiveness and pity to those led astray, and riotous living, while smiling upon social intercourse — suspended the terrors of its final judgment over high as well as low, over the sins of the heart as well as of the conduct, over rich and respectable children of hell as well as over its pariahs and poor slaves and has branded such public enormities as slavery and capital punishments with the inexplicable mark of its spirit, and is destroying them by the breath of is power. We say Scripture *poetry* has done all this.

The Porter

The Levites, who were the Old Testament porters, or gate-keepers, were not burden-bearers. They were given charge of the various entrances to the temple. These officers, 4,000 in all, had control of every gate, to open and shut them, and were not permitted to leave their service. They not only prevented the unworthy and lepers from entering, whether by day or night, but they also had care of the offerings and treasure of the temple. They were more or less of a military order, and as soldiers of the Lord, guarded His house. Their office was evidently one of importance and dignity, and they were superintended by a superior officer who inspected the porters as often as he pleased. "Blessed is he that watcheth, and keepeth his garments" (Revelation 16:15), is supposed to refer to the custom of the head porter passing a sentinel, intent on duty and saluting him with "Peace be unto you." But if he found a porter asleep, he smote him and was at liberty to burn his clothes.

In many cases, porter signifies a gate, or doorkeeper. The psalmist declared that he would sooner be a doorkeeper (porter) of the house of the Lord than dwell in the courts of wickedness (Psalm 84:10). Doorkeeper here means to keep one's self at the threshold, and the term is used of females as well as males (See II Samuel 18:26; I Chronicles 9:17, 22, 26; 15:18, 23, 24; 26:1; II Chronicles 23:19; 35:15; Acts 12:13). Coming to the New Testament, porter again implies one who guards and opens doors. As used by our Lord, the term applied to John the Baptist who opened the door of repentance to the lost sheep of the house of Israel, and admitted the true shepherds, with baptism as the mode of admission to His fold. Among shepherds, the porter was responsible for keeping the door of the sheepfold. In the morning he opened the door, and the shepherds called their sheep, and at night he lay across the threshold of the fold guarding the sheep within the fold with his life. In our time, a porter represents a two-fold occupation, namely, one who carries burdens or packages, such as railway porters, and doormen usually liveried as they function at hotel entrances.

Symbolically, the Holy Spirit is the divine Porter who opens gospel doors for Christ (Acts 14:27; I Corinthians 16:9; II Corinthians 2:12; Colossians 4:3), and shuts them (Acts 16:6, 7). He, it is, who opens the hearts of men to the saving truth of the Gospel (Acts 16:14; Revelation 3:20). The servant of God, whether preacher, Sunday school teacher, Christian worker or godly parent who watches constantly for opportunities of witness, or opening doors for Jesus is likewise a porter. As believers it is not only incumbent upon us to guard the Shepherd's interests while He is absent, but to persuade lost sheep to enter the door while it is open.

The Postman

Although in ancient times the postal system and service was not as highly organized and efficient as it is today, nevertheless, people long ago eagerly anticipated the arrival of the postman just as they do today. From the several references to post, or mailmen in the Bible we discover that there were very early means of communication and that men were able to convey messages to each other somewhat speedily (Job 9:25). The first postmen went by foot, and as the Hebrew for "post" implies they were known as "runners." These men formed the bodyguard of the king and were used as couriers to carry royal letters and dispatches throughout the kingdom. It would seem as if they had the right to command the service of either men or animals in order to expedite their progress (I Samuel 22:17; I Kings 14: 27; II Kings 11:4, 13; II Chronicles

30:6, 10; Jeremiah 51:31; Matthew 5: 41; Mark 15:21). Letters from private persons were conveyed by private hands, and were confined for the most part to business of sufficient urgency. Some of Paul's letters on spiritual matters were personally delivered (Ephesians 6:21, 22; I Peter 5:12, etc.).

While the earliest Bible reference to posts is that which Job uses as a simile, Egyptian, Babylonian and Persian letter seals still in existence prove that the communication of correspondence goes back to ancient times. Job's declaration, "My days are swifter than a post," (9:25) suggests that in remote times reliable men were retained as couriers. As used by the patriarch, the simile implies that instead of passing away with a slowness of motion like that of a caravan, his days of prosperity disappeared with a swiftness like that of a runner carrying dispatches. Some of those old time foot runners could cover 150 miles in less than twenty-four hours.

When King Hezekiah decided to summon all the descendants of Israel to the great passover which he planned to celebrate at Jerusalem, he sent his couriers to gather the people (II Chronicles 30:6). These swift runners passed from city to city, through the country of Ephraim and Manasseh to Zebulun (II Chronicles 30:10). "Regular lines of couriers carried official dispatches, with posting stations at fixed intervals, and the merchants maintained a similar service." Another instance of royal, postal communication is found in the Book of Esther. When Ahasuerus, at the request of Haman determined to destroy all the Jews in his vast empire, "letters were sent by posts into all the king's provinces" (Esther 3:13, 15). A further order countermanding the planned atrocious massacre was expedited in the same way, whether on foot or

by horses, mules or camels we are not told. The Persians and Romans used horses, as well as men, for the delivery of government dispatches.

In Jeremiah's time there was a regular service of postal communication, with posts or meeting places at fixed intervals. In his prophecy of Babylon's destruction, Jeremiah speaks of one post running to meet another (51: 31). Because of the vast extent of Babylon, relays of special messengers had to be organized for the purpose. Babylon was taken at each end at the same time, so that the messengers who carried the tragic news to the king, at his palace in the middle of the city, did run to meet each other, coming as they did from opposite quarters.

Louis XI, of France, by an edict dated June 19, 1464, established an approximation to our modern postal system, in order that he might be the better and sooner informed of what happened in his own or in neighboring kingdoms. This practice soon spread throughout the rest of Europe and by 1619 a post office for private letters was set up. Today we have jet planes, electricity and fast ships and trains to speed the delivery of letters from near and far. In Britain, the first private carriers went on horseback. In 1635, during the reign of Charles I, the government established postal service between London and Edinburgh to go and come in six days. Cowper describes such a mail carrier arriving at a village in winter —

He comes, the herald of a noisy world,
With spattered boots, strapped waist,
    and frozen locks,
News from all nations lumb'ring at his
    back.

How different it is today, when a letter postmarked at night in London, is delivered in Edinburgh the next morning! It was in 1840 that the idea of a postage stamp was conceived. Engraved upon the outer wall of the post office in Washington D. C. is the following tribute to the ministry of a letter —

The messenger of sympathy and love,
Servant of parted friends,
Consoler of the lonely,
Bond of the scattered family,
Enlarger of common life,
Instrument of trade and industry,
Promoter of mutual acquaintance of peace, of goodwill among men and nations.

Several years ago I came across these lines in *The Christian*, London —

A postman makes his daily round
A walk in the temple of God.
To all of these each daily happening
Has come to be a whisper from the lips of God,
And every common circumstance —
A wayside shrine.

The Potentate

The Greek word here is used both of Christ and men, and means "the mighty one," and implies a monarch or person possessing great power and authority. The same term is used of Zeus in Sophocles (*Ant*, 608). It is applied to men (Luke 1:52, ASV, "princes") and of rulers or officers with great authority (Acts 8:27). In his stately and rhythmical doxology with which Paul closes his solemn charge to Timothy, the apostle presents Christ returning to earth with glory and power inconceivably greater and grander than any earthly potentate before Him possessed. In fact, He is the only One entitled to such a designation — "the blessed and *only* Potentate, the King of kings, and Lord of lords" (I Timothy 6:15). The hymn speaks of Him as —

The Creator of the rolling spheres,
The Potentate of time.

But when He returns to earth, He will be more than "the Potentate of time." He will be seen, revered and obeyed as the Potentate of potentates — supreme as the divine Monarch having all power and authority to exercise His universal reign of peace and righteousness. What earthly potentates seem to forget is the fact that the powers are all derived from Him. Is is not by Him that princes rule? "What hast thou that thou didst not receive?"

The Potter

Archaeological discoveries of Babylonian and Egyptian ceramics consisting of earthenware jars, baked clay records, vessels for holding liquids, fruits and other foods, indicate that the making of pottery is among the very oldest of the crafts. The Egyptians, who became famous for their beautiful glazed earthenware, are credited with having invented the potter's wheel. Among the Hebrews pottery was a known art and, once settled in Canaan, they developed distinctive forms of their own. Before the potter's wheel came into being, all vessels were shaped by hand. By Jeremiah's time, the wheel was in general use (Jeremiah 18:1-6). Dry clay, dug out of the field (Matthew 27:7), was steeped in water, and further softened by the potter's feet (Isaiah 41:25). After being shaped, vessels were dried and then baked in a furnace or kiln. Often jars were decorated in different ways, the decorations being burned in, or painted on, once shaped and ready for use (Ezekiel 4:1). Ceramic is from the Greek word for "potter."

Although regarded as an inferior craft, the potter yet met a universal need. In bondage, Israel was forced to accomplish this task (I Samuel 2:14; Psalm 81:6). Potters usually lived around parts where good clay was plentiful, thus we have settlements in Jerusalem (Jeremiah 18:2-4), and in the neighborhood of Hebron where the royal potteries were likely situated (I Chronicles 4:23; Matthew 27:7, 10). We can imagine how each potter was proud of his productions for "every potter praises his own pot." The royal establishment of potters under the sons of Shelah, carrying on their trade for the king's revenues doubtless vied with each other in the manufacture of the best vessels in all kinds and sizes. "The potter is envious of the potter, the smith of the smith." Another proverb implying that two of the same trade seldom agree reads, "The potter is at enmity with the potter." For illustrations of finished pottery styles belonging to successive periods, the reader is directed to the comprehensive articles under "Pottery" in *The Zondervan Pictorial Bible Dictionary* and *The International Standard Bible Encyclopaedia*.

"The potter's field" (Matthew 27:7), purchased with the money Judas received for betraying his Master was likely a field that had been worked out by a potter, and was good for nothing but a burial place where strangers, such as Romans and proselytes were buried. Luke called the field "Aceldama" meaning, "the field of blood" (Acts 1:19). J. T. Shipley in his *Dictionary of Words* informs us the potter's field was once, "a field where potters drew their clay; the soil rapidly decomposed bodies." The free burial ground was later called "God's acre." The purchase of the field by Judas was a fulfillment of prophecy (Matthew 27:9. See Zechariah 11:12, 13). A potsherd was a piece of a broken pot, and is referred to in Job as being used by the patriarch to scrape his body in his affliction (2:8. See Psalm 22:15; Proverbs 26:23).

Some of the most expressive of Biblical metaphors are taken from the craft of the potter, as a survey of the twenty-two times he is mentioned shows. First of all, the potter's mastery, as he molded the clay to his will, typified the sovereignty of God in shaping the characters and destinies of both nations and individuals sometimes without their knowledge. The facility of the potter to mold the clay in his hands to any pattern or purpose he might please is used by many writers to symbolize God's mind in dealing with His own (Job 10:8, 9; 33:6; Isaiah 29:16; 45:9; 64:8; Jeremiah 18:1-6; Lamentations 4:2; Romans 9:20; II Timothy 2:20, 21). It is God's right to deal with saints and sinners alike according to His own perfect counsel.

> Thou art the Potter,
> I am the clay.

Then there are several allusions to the fragile nature of clay, symbolizing as it does man's brittle frailty. As a vessel, no matter how beautifully formed, is quickly broken, so God, as the divine Potter who formed Adam from the dust, is able to smite the wicked as one would smash a piece of pottery. It was in this capacity He caused Jerusalem to be destroyed (Psalm 2:9; Isaiah 30:14; Jeremiah 19:11; Daniel 2:41; II Corinthians 4:17; Revelation 2:27). Are you familiar with the moving poem by William L. Stidger, founded on the lament "I am like a broken vessel" (Psalm 31:12)?

> I am like a broken vessel;
> Blind and deaf and desolate;
> Broken, wounded and misshapen
> On the tragic wheel of fate.
>
> I am like a broken vessel
> Full of hopelessness and pain;

I return, a wounded pilgrim
Father make me whole again.

The Praetor

While this particular, occupational term is not found in the Bible it is implied by the expression, praetorium, which was the quarters of the praetorian troop who formed the emperor's bodyguard and who became, in later Roman history, the virtual masters of the empire. These praetorian guards (Philippians 1:13, ASV), numbering ten thousands, were instituted by Augustus. Paul was kept in the custody of a praetorian soldier. As the guard constantly changed, it became manifest to the whole guard that the apostle's bonds were for the sake of Christ (Philippians 4:22).

The Latin word, *praetorium,* originally denoted the headquarters of the Praetor, or commander-in-chief in a Roman camp, or the official residence of a governor of a province, or a provisional seat of government. The Praetor himself was the official elected to administer justice. Its Greek expression *strategoi* (Acts 16:20-38), gives us the English word "strategy" (Mark 15:16; Acts 23:35). The term means, "to go before," or "to lead," and distinguished originally the highest Roman magistrate. In the early days of the empire, it was the equivalent of a consul. Merrill T. Unger in *Archaeology and The New Testament* remarks —

> Inscriptions reveal that the term *praetor* was employed as a "courtesy title" for the chief magistrate of a Roman colony. It was an office of great dignity and showed respect for the duumviri.

Of the praetorium, Unger says that it was "the sumptuous palace erected by Herod the Great which was taken over by the Roman authorities and used as the headquarters of the Roman procurators in Palestine, just as the palace of Hiero at Syracuse became the *domus praetoria.*"

The President

Daniel is the only one in the Bible to mention this office (6:2-7). President itself means "chief" or "head," and implies one who presides over, or who is the head of a country, university, council, or any society or institution. A president is the elected chief executive officer of a republic. The most powerful president of modern times is the titular head of the United States of America. In Britain, the Lord President is the presiding head of the Court of Session, and the Lord President of the Council, a member of the House of Lords who presides over the privy council. A presiding officer is an appointed person in charge of a polling place.

The significance of the term as used by Daniel is self-evident. The title refers to the appointment of the prophet by Darius to be one of the three princes who were to rule over the 120 satraps, or viceroys who ruled over small parts of the Persian Empire. The Bible is silent as to the nature of the duties of these administrative officers.

The Prince

Used around 400 times in the Bible, the English term "prince" represents different Hebrew and Greek words, the meaning of which vary with the context. Among the shades of meaning we have, "king," "chieftain," "ruler," "governor," "noble," "deputy," "captain," "author." From these implications we gather that a prince was a leader, one who was high, conspicuous and outstanding, an exalted person clothed with authority and able to bear rule. William Baur observes that, "while the term is never used to denote royal parentage (see I Chronicles 29:24), it often indicates actual royal or ruling power, together with royal dignity and authority."

A perusal of the numerous passages where the title is found reveals that it is applied to divine, human and satanic beings. For instance —

1. Prince is applied to God, who is the Supreme Ruler and Governor of men and nations (Daniel 8:11). He is the Prince, or Ruler of the vast host of heaven, and also of earth. Proud princes among men cannot treat the heavenly Prince with impunity. God is "the Prince of princes." The highest human title in its absolute sense is attributed to Him (Daniel 8:25). It is only by Him that earthly princes rule (I Kings 11:34; Proverbs 8:16; 31:4; Isaiah 32:1; 40:23).

2. Prince is also among the royal titles ascribed to Christ. He is — "the Prince of peace" (Isaiah 9:6), denoting His eminent position and peaceful reign. As the Prince of peace, He is the only purchaser and procurer of peace between God and man; and of peace between men and men (Isaiah 53:5; Ephesians 2:15). He bequeathed peace as His legacy to His own (John 14:27). He is called "the Prince of life" (Acts 3:15). He is the Source of our temporal life (John 1:12; Acts 17:28). As our Mediator, Christ is also the Source and Guide to eternal life (John 14:6). "The Prince of life" permitted the princes of this world to kill Him (I Corinthians 2:6, 8). Called "Prince and Saviour" (Acts 5:31), He is indeed a princely Saviour. The highest royalty was in the blood He shed for the sins of the world. He is also "Prince of the kings of the earth" (Revelation 1:5). When He returns as the King of kings to reign over all, even His most powerful enemies will be forced to honor Him. This term prince is also rendered as "captain' or "author" (Hebrews 2:10; 12:2).

3. Prince is a title ascribed to the devil. Out of the fourteen appearances of the term in the New Testament, eight references are associated with him who is "the prince of demons" (Matthew 9:34; 12:24; Mark 3:22) — "the prince of this world" (John 12:31; 14:30; 16:11) who has the kingdoms of this world at his disposal (Matthew 4:9) — "the prince of the power of the air" (Ephesians 2:2) ruling over all hellish principalities and powers (Ephesians 6:12). Air denotes the jurisdiction of the fallen angels of whom the devil is prince, and the seat of his authority.

4. Prince is likewise used of good and beneficent angelic beings. This high military title is applied to the mysterious, superhuman stranger who appeared to Joshua (5:14). It is a designation given to the guardian angels of nations (Daniel 10:13, 20, 21), and to the archangel Michael (Daniel 12:1). It represents "the princely representative of God's people in the sight of God, a royal title suggesting high power and alliance with God in the great struggle going on between Him and the powers of darkness."

5. Prince applies to human beings in different walks of life. As an honoring title it was conferred upon Abraham by the children of Heth. "Thou art a mighty

prince of God among us" (Genesis 23:6). A study of the numerous passages where the term is found reveals that "prince" was used of —

Rulers (Numbers 21:18; Isaiah 21:5)

Royal Officials (Genesis 12:15; II Kings 24:12; Isaiah 10:8)

Leaders of war (I Samuel 22:2)

Tribal chieftains (Numbers 17: 6; I Samuel 18:30)

Chief butler and baker (Genesis 40:2, 16)

Keeper of prison (Genesis 39:21)

Man of wealth (Job 34:19)

Taskmasters (Exodus 1:11)

Governor of eunuchs (Daniel 1: 7)

Foreign potentates (Ezekiel 26: 16; 28:2; 30:13; 32:29)

Chief priests — "Princes of the sanctuary" (Isaiah 43:28; Daniel 9:25)

Governor of a palace (II Chronicles 28:7)

Keeper of treasures (I Chronicles 26:24)

Chief of temple (I Chronicles 9: 11; II Chronicles 31:13)

Chief of Tribe (Genesis 17:20; 23:6; 34:2; II Chronicles 19:11; Ezra 1:8)

Son of a king, and the king himself (I Samuel 25:30; II Chronicles 11:22; Ezekiel 34:24)

Gentile rulers (Matthew 20:25)

Bethlehem (Matthew 2:6).

"Prince of Judah" because the Davidic dynasty had its origin there.

The Principal

In our time a principal is the chief or presiding, executive officer of a college or academy, but in the Bible days the term implied a person, highest in rank, authority or importance. As used in the New Testament, principal from *protos* denotes the first, whether in time or space. Zabud, the son of Nathan, was principal officer, and the king's friend (I Kings 4:5), meaning that he was the king's chief minister, as well as his confidant. The principal men of the city were its chief men. The phrase, "chief estates of Galilee" (Mark 6:21) imply "the principal persons." The three officers, lords, high captains, chief estates mean respectively —

1. Lords — magnates, or chief officials of the court.

2. High captains — *chiliarchs,* literally "captain of a thousand" — the same word as in Acts 21:31; 26:26 in the Roman legion.

3. Chief estates—not land, but men. Probably the large landowners of estates in a province.

The Proconsul

Two words go to make up this title, *pro* and *consul,* and together stand for a magistrate with the insignia and powers of a consul. Proconsuls were men of praetorian or consular rank, and administrators of the more important Roman provinces. As Roman territory increased, more of these senatorial governors became necessary. Their mandate usually lasted for one year, with their official power being exercised in provinces having no standing army. Provinces with a standing army were governed by an imperial legate (Luke 2:2). Paul's convert, Sergius Paulus was the proconsul in Syprus (Acts 13:7), and Gallio governed the less important province of Achaia (Acts 18:12. See 19: 38).

The Procurator

In our time a curator is a person having the care or guardianship of anything, such as the custodian of a museum or art gallery. *Pro* is a prefix meaning instead of or in place of, and thus a *procurator* was a selected person who acted in the place of his master. In Roman times, procurators were administrators of the emperor's revenues, whose term of office was subject to the emperor's will. Sometimes they had a bodyguard of soldiers (Matthew 27:27), visited great festivals when riots were frequent, and when in Jerusalem, resided in Herod's palace (John 14:9; Acts 23:35). They were military commanders with powers of life and death, charged also with the administration of justice and finance. Their importance depended upon that of their master. Thus, the emperor's stewards were men of consequence and like Theophilus (Luke 1:3; Acts 1:1), whose title "most excellent" implies equestrian rank.

Originally, however, a procurator signified in a general sense a steward of private property who had charge of slaves and also of his master's financial affairs with power of attorney. But by the time of Augustus, procurators were mostly imperial freedmen, and came to exercise the official activity of Roman knights. Among the fourteen procurators of Palestine only Pontius Pilate, Felix and Festus are mentioned by name in the New Testament (Matthew 27:2; 28:14; Mark 15:1; Luke 3:1; 23:1; Acts 23:24; 24:1, 27; 25:1). Because of his association with the trial and death of Jesus, Pilate stands out as the best remembered procurator. Unger points out that "important archaeologically are the coins which date back from the period of the Judaean procurators. Coins struck by the procurators from Coponius to Antonius Felix are extant. Of special interest are examples from the second to the sixth year of Pontius Pilate A.D. 27 - 28 to A.D. 31 - 32."

The Prognosticator

The monthly prognosticators are men who professed to know the omens of the new moon, and made their predictions accordingly. Pretense, however, to tell future events from the heavenly bodies is condemned (Isaiah 47:13). Ellicott observes that the three terms describe two aspects of the same false art —

1. *Astrologers* or dividers of the heavens, assigning stellar influences to the signs of the Zodiac:

2. *Stargazers* or *monthly prognosticators* are those who make known things to come at the new moon. Almanacs were compiled in which the days of the month were noted as lucky or unlucky for the incidents of war or of home-life, as the same might be. They were similar to the horoscopes of today which multitudes foolishly follow. (See material under THE ASTROLOGER, THE CHARMER and THE MAGICIAN).

The Publican

In English speaking countries a publican is a saloonkeeper, and owner or manager of a "public house," or "pub," where beer and spirits are sold. But in New Testament times, publican was a detestable term used to cover several grades of minor officials engaged in customs services. The word itself is from *Publicanus,* the farmer-general of a province and also his subordinate local officials, who collected customs duties or taxes on exports and imports (Matthew 9:9-11; Mark 2:14). Goods were examined and tolls collected at the city gates, on the roads or bridges at Caesarea, Capernaum and Jericho. Zaccheus, the chief publican lived at Jericho, the city of the balsam trade.

The occupation of tax-gathering was greatly hated by the Jews, whose pride was mortified by having to pay tribute at all. Some Jews, however, found it profitable to serve the Roman State in such sordid business and thus became objects of detestation to the rest of their fellow-Jews who manifested an important dislike of Roman supremacy. These Jewish tax-gatherers of Roman customs were regarded as traitors and apostates, and as being defiled by their frequent intercourse with the heathen and by functioning as willing tools of the Romans. "To be spoiled by foreigners was bad, but to be plundered by their own countrymen was far worse." Even the chief publican took from his own countrymen by false accusation, meaning that Zacchaeus unfairly exacted or extorted customs from Jews. Along with others he exacted more than that which was appointed (Luke 3:13). Louis Matthews Sweet in his summary on "Taxes, Taxing" in *The International Standard Bible Encyclopedia* shows that sufficient cause for the unpopularity of publicans is not far to seek —

> Hatred of paying duties seems to be ingrained in human nature. Customs officials are always unpopular. The method is necessarily inquisitorial. The man who opens one's boxes and bundles to appraise the value of what one has, is at best a tolerated evil. In Judea, under the Roman system, all circumstances combined to make the publican the object of bitter hatred. He represented and exercised in immediate contact, at a sore spot with individuals, the hated power of Rome. The tax itself was looked upon as an inherent religious wrong, as well as civil imposition, and by many the payment of it was considered a sinful act of disloyalty to God. The tax-gatherer, if a Jew, was a renegade in the eyes of his patriotic fellows. He paid a fixed sum for the taxes, and received for himself what he could over and above that amount.

The ancient and widespread curse of arbitrariness was in the system. The collector was thus always under the suspicion of being an extortioner and probably *was* in most instances. The name was apt to realize itself. The usual combination in the publican of petty tyrant, renegade and extortioner, made by circumstances almost inevitable, was not conducive to popularity.

Naturally hated intensely by the people, publicans were coupled habitually with "sinners," a term of deepest contempt (Matthew 9:10, 11; 11:19; Mark 2:15, 16; Luke 5:30; 7:34; 15:1); with "harlots" (Matthew 21:31, 32); with the heathen or Gentiles (Matthew 5:47; 18:17). The rabbis declared that one publican in a family disgraced the whole family. As the Scribes and Pharisees were the respectable and outwardly religious class, so the publicans were the vile and degraded.

Publicans and Sinners on the one side;
Scribes and Pharisees on the other.

But the gospels make it clear that Jesus came to give all men — even publicans — new hope. Abhorred by all others, it was a wonderful event in the eyes of the publicans themselves to find a Holy One "a Friend of publicans" (Matthew 11:19; Luke 15: 1). When Jesus supped with publicans, He revealed His love for sinners (Matthew 11:19). In fact, the references He made to publicans are most expressive of His compassion for the lost.

Without doubt His disciples, as Jews, shared the popular estimation of the despised publicans, but in genial irony Jesus reproached His followers for their low standard of love and forgiveness (Matthew 5:46, 47).

Then He employed the current combination, "an heathen man and a publican" (Matthew 18:17) when giving directions about excommunicating a persistently unrepentant member of the church (Matthew 18:17).

Further, Jesus was not ashamed to be known as "the friend of publicans and sinners." He was indifferent to the condemnation of the Scribes and Pharisees regarding His social fellowship with such a despised class (Matthew 11:19; Luke 7:34; 15:1).

Most impressive of all, Jesus used the publican, as He did the Samaritans, in a parable in which the despised outcast shows to advantage in an attitude to God. "It was His choice of Matthew as an apostle, and His parable in which He justified the penitent self-condemned publican and condemned the self-satisfied Pharisee" (Luke 18:9-14. See *All the Parables of the Bible*). Zacchaeus was the chief among the Publicans, who came to experience Christ's transforming grace and power (Luke 19:1-10). Probably many other repentant publicans became disciples of the Lord (Matthew 21:31). This we know —

> His blood can make the vilest clean,
> His blood avails for me.

The Publisher

The word "publish" means to be a herald, to proclaim, to preach (Mark 1:45; 5:20; 7:36; Luke 9:6; Romans 9:17, etc.). "The word of the Lord was published (spread abroad) throughout the region" (Acts 13:49). A preacher is one who heralds, publishes, or proclaims the good news of salvation. Noah is the first one named as a "preacher" or "publisher" of righteousness (II Peter 2:5). Man, by lip and literature, is the human channel through which God sends His truth to others. To publish, then, is to make public or to proclaim either by preach-

ing or publication a given message. Evangelical publishers are those who print books based on evangelical truths. The striking phrase of the psalmist, "The Lord gave the word: great was the company of those that published it" (68:11), covers not only preachers but their publishers also. As we think of the colossal number of religious books still coming from publishers it would seem as if there is no end of the making of such books (Ecclesiastes 12:12). John declared that the world could not contain all the books that could be written about Jesus (John 21:25). Moses, John and others were commanded to write in a book, truth revealed to them by the Spirit.

The Bible itself leaves us in no doubt as to what we are to publish both from the pulpit and from the press — His glorious name (Deuteronomy 32:3) — peace and salvation (Isaiah 52:7; Nahum 1:15) — affliction (Jeremiah 4:15, 16) — great things Christ has accomplished for us (Mark 5:20) — the word of the Lord (Mark 13:10; Acts 13:49). Ezra speaks of "the copy of the writing for a commandment to be given in every province published unto all the people" (Esther 8:13). Such copies were likely handwritten and distributed. Just when the publication of Christian literature began may be hard to determine. Albert E. Bailey in his most informative volume on *Daily Life in Bible Times* speaks of the Septuagint — the Greek translation of the Hebrew Old Testament — "the first translation ever to be made of so extensive a body of literature became the most influential book in the world." The author then goes on to describe how the rabbis of Alexandria were the editors of the Greek editions of their scriptures, and the copying establishments — or as we say today, the publishing houses — were probably connected with their homes.

> Passing through the rear of the home and crossing a small court with fountain and garden, we come to a separate building where the copying is done. A battery of five to ten transcribers, and professionals, sit at desks facing a reader. Each writer has his roll of papyrus, his pens and ink. As the chief scribe who is also a rabbi and a scholar reads slowly from his Septuagint roll all the others write in concert swiftly but carefully lest they change one jot or tittle of the inspired Word. All copies are afterward proofread to make sure that every transcriber has both heard and written accurately. The results are marvels of exactness and of beauty.

Coming to the post-Pauline church, Dr. Bailey affirms that "recent examination of the evidence seems to prove that Ephesus at the end of the first century became the focal point of the publication and circulation of Christian literature. Within twenty years there came from the Ephesian church not only the gospel, the three epistles of John, the Revelation, the two-volume work known as Luke - Acts, the fourfold gospel as we now have it, and the first published edition of the letters of Paul."

The author then goes on to credit the Ephesian church with the mechanical innovation of far-reaching importance. "Hitherto books had been written on rolls of parchment or papyrus. This was an inconvenient format and an expensive one in that only one side of the material could be written upon. At some time during the first century B.C. some bright mind devised the format which we know as a Codex, in which sheets of moderate size were written on both sides and bound up along the left edge — in other words, someone invented the book as we know it today. The publishing house of the Christian church at Ephesus decided that the new book form was the one to use for Christian literature .... The oldest fragment we have of any Christian work is the Ryland's Library bit of the Gospel of John in Codex form, which dates before the year 150 A.D. Most Christian books from the start were put into Codex form."

Today superb productions of the publisher's art pour from religious and secular publishing houses. Never were there so many books written and published as there are today. Alas, a quantity of them are not worth the paper they are printed on! How grateful we should be for evangelical publishers who endeavor to print books that publish the glorious truths of the infallible Book itself! Would that the Christian public could be persuaded to invest more of their money in beneficial Christian literature!

The Reaper

Much under this occupation has been touched upon already under THE FARMER and THE HARVESTER. Lacking modern mechanical combines for reaping and binding, reapers of ancient times had to rely upon the sickle which was used by the right hand, the left hand thus being free to hold the stalks (Deuteronomy 16:9; 23:25; Joel 3:13). Among the laws regarding reaping was the one relating to the corners of fields which had to be left for the poor to glean (Leviticus 19:9; 23:10; 25:5, 11; Deuteronomy 16:9; 24:19; Ruth 2:2). Samuel mentions the task of harvest reaping as one of the requirements which could be made by the king for whom the people were clamoring (I Samuel 8:12). Among the reapers of the Bible, Ruth the Moabitess has honorable mention

(2:3-14). Think of the lines of Thomas Hood on *Ruth* —

Sure, I said, Heaven did not mean,
Where I reap thou shouldst but glean,
Lay thy sheaf a-down and come,
Share my harvest and my home.

In many profitable ways the Bible figuratively employs the reaper. For instance —

1. Deeds, whether good or evil, produce their own harvest (Job 4:8; Proverbs 22:8; Hosea 8:7; 10:12, 13; II Corinthians 9:6; Galatians 6:7-9) "They that sow in tears shall reap in joy" is found in the captives' song of liberty (Psalm 126:5).

Sow a thought, reap an act;
Sow an act, reap a habit;
Sow a habit reap a character.

2. The lesson of faith in God's care is illustrated by sowing and reaping (Ecclesiastes 11:4; Matthew 6:26; Luke 12:24). Sowing and not reaping the harvest is mentioned as a punishment for disobedience (Job 31:8; Jeremiah 12:13; Micah 6:15) — reaping where he sowed not showed the injustice of the landlord (Matthew 25:26), as did also the withholding of the reapers' wages (James 5:4).

3. Sowing and reaping are also figurative of the discriminating separation divinely undertaken at the end of this age. When God judges the earth, angels who can discern the true condition of the heart are to thrust in the sickle and reap (Matthew 13:39, 41; Revelation 14:15, 16). Longfellow wrote of death as a reaper —

Oh, not in cruelty, not in wrath,
The Reaper came that day;
'Twas an angel visited the green earth,
And took the flowers away.

In the age to follow millennial prosperity is illustrated by the sower overtaking the reaper (Amos 9:13).

4. Gathering results in service for the Master is likened unto sowing and reaping. Division of labor is gathered for His word, "He that soweth and he that reapeth may rejoice together" (John 4:36-38, see Matthew 25:24; Luke 19:21, 22). Reaping, of course, is always proportionate to the sowing (II Corinthians 9:6). Both in life and service we reap what we sow (Galatians 6:7-9).

Sow blessings, and blessings will ripen,
Sow hatred, and hatred will grow;
Sow mercy, and reap sweet compassion,
You'll reap whatsoever you sow.

The Recorder

This was a responsible occupation in the courts of Jewish kings. The term really means, "one who calls to remembrance" — a remembrancer. Among royal officials, the recorder had an influential position. As a court counselor he was entrusted with the responsibility of chronicling the events of the sovereign's reign, and of reminding the king of affairs needing attention. He was among the chief ministers, the grand vizier of modern times (II Samuel 8:26; 20:24; I Kings 4:3; I Chronicles 18:15).

As the recorder is frequently mentioned along with the Scribes, he must have been a high functionary. He was associated with other royal offices in the representation of Hezekiah before Rabshakeh (II Kings 18:18); and also superintended in the reign of Josiah in the repairs of the temple (II Chronicles 34:8). He was not simply an annalist, but chancellor or president of the privy council (Isaiah 36:3, 22). Although an historiographer with charge over the public registers, to see that fit persons were put on record for future remembrance, he was always around the king to record what took place. The margin says he was "at the hand of the king" (II Kings 18:18, 37; I Chronicles 18:15).

We are reminded that our record is in heaven where the Lord as the divine Recorder registers the services of saints, and also the sin of sinners. For the saints, the Recorder will reward all faithful service in His register (I Corinthians 3:14; II Corinthians 5: 10); and ratify the condemnation of the wicked when the books are opened at the Great White Throne (Revelation 20:11-15). All who are not registered in the Book of Life are to be cast into the lake of fire.

The Redeemer

The foundational idea of redemption in the Bible is found in the purchase of both property and people, and was associated with the physical and material realms. Money or goods were paid according to law to buy back someone or something, who or which had to be rescued or delivered (Leviticus 25:26, 48-55; Ruth 4:4). Redemption, or deliverance, from oppression, violence, sickness, captivity or death was by power — the typical illustration being that of Israel's deliverance from Egypt (Exodus 13:17-20; Isaiah 51:9-11). Hebrew words for Redemption mean —

1. To buy back, by paying the price, what has been sold (Leviticus 25:25).
2. To redeem what has been devoted, by substituting something else in its place (Exodus 13:13; Leviticus 27:27; Psalms 72:14; 130:8; Isaiah 63:9).

The original word for redeemer is sometimes translated as "avenger" and "revenger" (Numbers 35:12, 19, 21; Deuteronomy 19:6, 12). God is the avenger or vindicator of His people (Isaiah 41:14; 43:14). Boaz, was the *goel* — the kinsman-redeemer of Ruth (Ruth 3:9, 13; 4:6, 7). Jeremiah gives us another example of redemption by purchase (Jeremiah 32:7, 8).

Fausset observes that the Old Testament goel, or kinsman-redeemer had three rights, namely —

1. To purchase back the forfeited inheritance for an Israelite who, through poverty, had sold his land, as Boaz; or to hold in possession for an impoverished kinsman till the year of Jubilee, when it should revert to the original owner (Leviticus 25:10, 13-16, 23-28).

2. The goel ransomed his kinsman from bondage to the foreigner (Leviticus 25:47-49).

3. The goel avenged the death of his slain kinsman as a point of honor (Ruth 2:10; Job 19:25-27). In a convincing way Fausset shows how these three rights are but types of our full redemption in and through Christ. First of all, man, the heir of all things bartered his magnificent birthright for vanity. Christ, by assuming our manhood, became our Goel, and saved us from being disinherited forever (Hebrews 9:15); the full restoration of the inheritance to be at "the times of restitution of all things" (Acts 3: 21), the grand last jubilee, ushered in as the Israelite jubilee, with the great trumpet (Isaiah 23:13; 61:2-4; I Corinthians 15:52; I Thessalonians 4:16; Revelation 11:15).

Secondly, man sold himself to Satan's bondage; Jesus has — at the price of His own precious blood (I Peter 1: 18, 19) — ransomed "the lawful captive delivered" (Isaiah 49:24). Thirdly, our Redeemer "through death has destroyed Satan — man's *murderer* from the beginning (John 8:44) — who had the power of death" and has delivered us from everlasting bondage to him (Hosea 13:14; Hebrews 2:14, 15).

In the New Testament, redemption, associated as it is with the spiritual realm, has a far deeper significance. The fundamental idea of the term is a double one — a redemption *from,* and a redemption *to,* and we must not neglect this double element. First, there is deliverance from the penalty and curse of the law which has bound the sinner. Through the Redeemer, the sinner is relieved of such a load (Romans 7:23; Galatians 3:13). Second, being freed from sin there came the positive movement of the delivered one toward the Deliverer. There comes a new relationship to God, a new life in Christ, a new hope in eternity. Because the Redeemer offered Himself as the payment for our redemption (Ephesians 1:7; I Peter 1: 18), redeemed, we are no longer our own but the property of the One who gave Himself as the ransom on our behalf (I Timothy 2:6).

Christ has for sin atonement made,
    What a wonderful Saviour!
We are redeemed! the price is paid!
    What a wonderful Saviour!

The Registrar

As the Bible speaks of a register of genealogies (Nehemiah 7:5, 64; See Ezra 2:62), the same implies a registrar whose work is to keep a register or record, principally of names. We know that registers of names were carefully kept by the Jews. Such meticulous recording of genealogies received its main impetus in the time of Ezra, when the line between the Jews and other nations was sharply drawn, and stress was laid on purity of descent, whether real or fictitious (Ezra 2:62). After the return from the Babylonian captivity, it was more important to be able to trace descent from the Exiles than to be a native of Judah (Ezra 9). Certain families

were excluded from the priesthood for lack of the requisite genealogical records (Nehemiah 7:63). It is quite probable that Jewish kings, like those of Persia, kept a register of the events of their respective reigns (Esther 6: 1, 2). It was not difficult to erase a name, if the ink resembled that which is now used in Syria, for it can soon be washed off by water (Exodus 32: 33).

For a thorough study of the registered genealogies of Scripture, the reader is referred to the remarkable survey under "Genealogy" in *The International Standard Bible Encyclopedia.* Benjamin Keach says, "It appertains to a judge in this world, to have not only rules of law, but a register of bypassed actions, that he may know what to do, if like cases fall in future times. God hath not only made laws, and published them, and will judge men for willful and reiterated rebellions; but keeps a register for the great day, to be then opened; as it is written, 'Some men's sins go beforehand to judgment, and they that are otherwise cannot be hid.' The dead shall be judged out of those things which are written in the books."

The Repairer

The bulk of repair work in the Old Testament is related to that of cities ravaged by war, and also to the restoration of the temple (Judges 21:23; Nehemiah 3). After seventy years in exile, the special task of new Israel, which would result in enduring fame, was the rebuilding of the ruined habitations. The remnant of the nation was to be called, "The repairer of the breach, The restorer of paths to dwell in" (Isaiah 58:12). Parallel lines are to be found in a later chapter, "They shall build the old wastes, they shall raise up the former desolations, and they shall repair the waste cities, the desolations of many generations" (Isaiah 61:4). Such rebuilding was to be Israel's own task, and once finished, she would enjoy her restored heritage.

In the highest sense God is "The repairer of the breach, the restorer of paths to dwell in." Joel says, "The Lord will be the hope of his people" (3:16). The margin has it, the place or haven of repair for His people (ASV "refuge"). In a world broken by war, sin and sorrow we certainly need Him as "the Repairer." What a breach has come into our national family life! The Lord is able to repair the multitudinous breaches represented by threatened divorces. Strained relationships in national and international life require the skillful handling of the divine Repairer of the breach. We read of the repair, or healing, of the altar, and of the house of God (I Kings 18:30; II Chronicles 24:27). The divided, apostate and impoverished of the church likewise require the Lord's expert work as the Repairer.

The Restorer

The word "restore" can mean "to make alive." Elisha restored or brought back to life the woman's dead son (II Kings 8:1-5). It also implies "to cause to turn back," and is the term used to describe our Lord's miracles in the restoration, or bringing back to their normal function, diseased eyes and hands (Matthew 12:13; Mark 3: 5; 8:25; Luke 6:10). As the Restorer of the soul, the Lord brings it back from its wanderings to full fellowship with Himself (Psalm 23:3). Obed is said to have been the restorer of the life of Naomi (Ruth 4:15), meaning, that the birth of her grandchild set back in the hands of the clock and made her feel young again. In a true sense the Lord is the Restorer of paths

to dwell in (Isaiah 58:12). These are days when many are departing from the old paths.

The spiritual restoration of Israel is the theme of Old Testament prophets, of Christ and His apostles. Peter speaks of this restoration in no uncertain terms (Acts 3:21, ASV.). W. E. Vine says that the word Peter used is that employed in "the papyrus of a temple cell of a goddess, a repair of a public way, the restoration of estates to rightful owners, a balancing of accounts. Apart from papyri illustrations the word is found in an Egyptian reference to a consummating agreement of the world's cyclical periods, an idea somewhat similar to that in the Acts passage." It is indeed wonderful to know the Lord as the Restorer. Do you need Him in this capacity?

The Roadmaker

Although the actual term "roadmaker" does not appear in the Bible, and the English word "road" occurs only once, and then means an "inroad" or "raid" made by David on surrounding nations (I Samuel 23:27; 27:10), yet the Hebrew root is used in many ways. Paths, bypaths (Judges 5:6; Jeremiah 18:15), highways, and ways all imply the occupation of the roadmaker. For an illuminating study on ancient roads in Old Testament history, the reader is directed to G. A. Smith's exhaustive treatise on the *Historical Geography of the Holy Land*.

The earliest reference to a roadway is that of "the king's highway" in the country of the Edomites by which the Israelites could travel without turning to the right hand or to the left (Numbers 20:17). A similar expression is used in the next chapter in reference to the roads of the Amorites (Numbers 21:22). Moses ordered that the roads giving access to the cities of refuge be maintained (Deuteronomy 19:3). Many of the roads were cared for by the king of the countries at the expense probably of the travelers, who paid dues or tolls on entering each territory. They were then called "King's Highways." Josephus says that King Solomon paved the roads leading to Jerusalem with black stones.

Originally, roads were mere tracks. Later roadways were thrown up, stones being erected to make their course, and caravanserais established at definite intervals. That the upkeep of ways of communication were neglected necessitating restoration for the arrival of an important personage, is implied by the prophet Isaiah (40:3; 57:14; 61:10; Jeremiah 31:21). In addition to main highways, there were secondary roads for the use of travelers and beasts of burden (Judges 19: 11; I Samuel 15:20; II Kings 4:24). These were mere tracks with landmarks and signposts indicating direction (Jeremiah 31:21). These paths naturally linked surrounding places together (Matthew 13:4).

The process of roadmaking, with allusions to the operations of mounding and excavating, possibly of paving, all of which operations the Israelites learned from Babylonian or Persian roadmakers, for under Persian domination a network of roads developed significantly, is referred to by Isaiah when he urged the people to make straight in the desert a highway for God (40:1-5). "Cast up the highway" (62:10). The image used is drawn from the march of Eastern kings who boasted of the roads they made in trackless deserts for military expeditions and commercial purposes. Says Ellicott, "The figure is taken from the titanic engineering operations of the kingly roadmakers of the East, but the parable is hardly veiled. The meek ex-

alted, the proud brought low, wrong ways set right, rough nations smoothed, and therefore the true work of every follower of the Baptist is preparing the way (See Matthew 3:3-5; Luke 3:3-9)."

Before the emergence of the Roman Empire roads were unpaved, but the Romans developed transportation and these roads — all of which led to Rome — became famous. Regular, paved roads with milestones to mark out distances were introduced, being constructed and maintained largely by the soldiers when not engaged in fighting or on guard duty. Traces of these magnificent highways which became the lifeblood of the Roman Empire are still traceable today. These great highways opened the way of Christianity. Says S. Angus this "great system of roads that knit the then civilized world together served not only the legions and the imperial escorts, but were of equal service to the early missionaries and when churches began to spring up over the empire, these roads greatly facilitated that church organization and brotherhood which strengthened the church to overcome the empire." To which we can add the observation of Albert E. Bailey that, "Paul showed his generalship by thus planting his Gospel at the crossroads of traffic. One great road began at the Cicilian Gates and was really the western communication of that almost prehistoric road from Mesopotamia. Paul was born in a city that lay on that route and he used the road himself more than once in his missionary journeys."

Now, roadmaking is not only an art, but big business; and our modern roads, highways, and boulevards, stretching in many cases for hundreds of miles, so necessary for motor transportation, are the wonder of those who still live on dirt track roads.

Years ago, narrow paths in the East were made by the feet of animals traveling them. Camels generally follow one another, and thus made many narrow paths in one broad way. Verdure and wild fruits often grew between those paths so that the camels would frequently bend their long necks to feed as they journeyed — which characteristic Solomon had in mind when writing of wisdom he said, "She . . . standeth by the way *in the places of the paths*" (Proverbs 8:2). "Ways" and "paths" are often used in a spiritual sense. The divine Shepherd, for instance, always leads His sheep in paths of righteousness (Psalm 23:2).

When Jesus said, "I am the way" (John 14:6), He actually inferred that He was the only Road, or King's Highway to God. "No man cometh unto the Father, *but by me.*" If, therefore, He is the appointed Road to God, how are we to reach the end of the Road if our feet are not on it? Is He not, in all that He accomplished on our behalf, the narrow Way leading to life eternal? All other ways end in death (Proverbs 1:15-18). But if we are on the Road God Himself fashioned for sinners to travel from the city of destruction to the celestial city, then when we reach His abode we will walk forever over streets that are paved with gold.

The Robber

The annals of ancient times prove that robbery was a common occupation with individuals, tribes and nations adopting it as an acknowledged and by no means discreditable mode of obtaining a livelihood. The Ishmaelites, for instance, esteemed robbery as creditable (Genesis 16:12). Robbers, or thieves, are parasites, snatching a living on what is not their own. Stealing was forbidden by law, and is often referred to as a most despicable occupation (Leviticus 19:13; 26:22; I Samuel 23:1; Proverbs 22:22; Isaiah 10:2, 13, etc.). For this reason property had to be protected against theft and burglary (Exodus 20:15; 22: 2). The broad word used for thief in the Old Testament includes that of a "kidnapper" as well (Deuteronomy 24:7).

Among the frequent allusions in the Bible to thieves and robbers we have—

The Shechemites who "set liers in wait . . . robbed all that came along that way by them" (Judges 9:25).

"The Chaldeans made out three bands, and fell upon the camels, and have carried them away" (Job 1:17).

David plundered the Amalekites who, in turn, made reprisals (I Samuel 27:6-10).

Hosea prophesied of apostate priests as troops of robbers that wait for a man (Hosea 6:9). In Israel's disorganized state in the northern kingdom, robbery was prevalent (Hosea 4:2).

Malachi says that man is capable of robbing God as well as man (chapter 3).

Although the advance of civilization and the might of Roman power had much to do with the suppression of highway robbers, they were still a menace in the time of our Lord. Because of the corrupt administration of Roman governors, and "the facility of collecting and hiding bandits in the natural caves of Palestine, robbers infested Judaea in Christ's day and after" (Luke 10:30; John 18:40; Acts 5:36, 37; II Corinthians 11:26). Armed bands were required to encounter thieves (Luke 22:5). "Fanatical zeal for emancipating the Jewish nation often accompanied robbery when Barabbas and his companions in insurrection and murder enlisted popular sympathy (Mark 15:7)." The parable of the good samaritan (Luke 10) describes how dangerous it was to travel from Jerusalem to Jericho.

Paul speaks of perils of robbers that he had doubtless encountered passing through Pisidia (II Corinthians 11:26). There were "robbers of temples," the reference being to the temple of Diana which had great treasure-chambers which possibly had been plundered (Acts 19:37. See Romans 2:22 "guilty of sacrilege").

Punishment for robbery was severe (Exodus 22). Crucifixion was the Roman penalty for robbers and rebels alike. Thus Christ's two companions at Calvary were thieves one of whom confessed that they deserved such a penalty for their crimes (Luke 23:40). The divine bearing of Jesus amidst all taunts and agonies, and His prayer for His murderers touched the heart of one of the two robbers with sympathy and awe (Luke 23:39-43), and, looking beyond his dying state to the eternity before him, he sought and found salvation. The last kind word of Jesus was addressed to a thief.

> The dying thief rejoiced to see,
> That fountain in his day.
> And there may I, though vile as he,
> Wash all my sin away.

Figuratively, thieves and robbers are used in various ways. Christ thought it not robbery to be counted equal with God (Philippians 2:6). Then His use of a thief as one coming without warning needs no explanation as we think of the suddenness of His return (Matthew 24:43). Thieves and robbers climbing up some other way (John 10), describe the futility of trying to enter the Shepherd's fold apart from the appointed way. As for the treasure we send on to heaven in advance, thieves can never break through and steal all we lay up there.

The Ruler

This occupational name, and its cognates, occurs almost 300 times in the Bible, and is translated by several Hebrew and Greek words implying many different ocupations. For the original words themselves consult Zondervan's *Expanded Concordance*. We herewith cite the meanings of the various terms used in Scripture.

1. Ruler — king, prince, master (tyrannical kind), supervisor. This particular term is applied to Joseph in Egypt (Genesis 45:8, see Psalm 105:21) — to the Philistines (Judges 15:11) — to David's descendants, the succeeding kings of Israel (II Chronicles 7:18, see Jeremiah 33:26) — to Pha-raoh (Psalm 105:20) — to a wicked, tyrannical prince (Proverbs 28:15, see Isaiah 14:5; 59:7) — to the Messiah the coming theocratic King (Micah 5:2) — to rulers in general (Proverbs 6:7; 23:1; 29:12; Ecclesiastes 10:4; Isaiah 16:1 etc.).

2. Ruler — leader, nobles, overseer, prince. This Hebrew word is used of Azrikam who had charge of the palace of King Ahaz. He was "governor" of the king's residence (II Chronicles 28:7) — of Azariah, or Seraiah, who is called "the ruler of the house of God," and who was the leader of a group of priests (I Chronicles 9:11; II Chronicles 31:13). Hilkiah, Zechariah and Hehiel were other rulers.

3. Ruler — head, prince. The spies to search out Canaan had to be "every one a ruler" (Numbers 13:2). This word describes a public authority (Exodus 22:28) — a ruler of the congregation (Exodus 16:22; 34:31). Such rulers had to be men of social standing and financial ability (Exodus 35:27). If any of these rulers sinned an offering had to be presented unto the Lord (Leviticus 4:22).

4. Ruler — royal representative, a

vice-regent, a deputy. During the leadership of Ezra and Nehemiah, leaders or principals of the people of Jerusalem were deputies under the general supervision of their leaders (Ezra 9:2; Nehemiah 2:16; 4:14, 19; 5:7, 17, etc.). In most cases this term is given in plural form (Isaiah 14:5; Ezekiel 23:6; Jeremiah 51:23, 28, 57).

5. Ruler — judge, magistrate, a military chief. It is used in these days (Joshua 10:24; Isaiah 1:10; 3:6, 7; 22: 3; Micah 3:1, 9). A similar term in the New Testament signifies "a person in authority," "a judge or magistrate," "authoritative person." A member of the supreme council of the Jews was a man of influence and authority (Matthew 9:18), as was a ruler of the Pharisees (Luke 14:1; 23:13, 35; John 3:1, etc.). Police magistrates or public authorities had to be obeyed and not evil spoken of (Acts 7:27, 35; 23:5, see Exodus 22:28; Romans 13:3). "The rulers of this world" (I Corinthians 2:6, 8) were those who, being mentally superior to their fellow-men, were appointed to shape their opinions and direct their actions.

6. Ruler of the synagogue (Mark 5:22, 35, 36, 38; Luke 8:41, 49; 13:14; Acts 13:15; 18:17). The Greek word here for ruler denotes an administrative official whose duty it was to preserve order and to invite persons to read or speak in the assembly. He functioned as the presiding officer with disciplinary power (John 9:22; 12:42; 16:2).

7. Ruler of the feast (John 2:8, 9). Here the word, meaning, steward, governor, head waiter occurs in the marriage feast in Cana of Galilee. It was an ancient custom to appoint one of the prominent guests — an intimate friend or relative of the host — to act as "master of the ceremonies" whose duty it was to generally supervise arrangements such as the placing of guests, superintending food and tables and the observance of the ordinary rules of etiquette.

8. The ruler of the city (Acts 17: 6, 8). Luke is the only Bible writer to give us this particular word for those prefects or magistrates of the city who became the tools of the unscrupulous Jews. Thessalonica being a free city, the citizens had liberty to choose their own politarchs. Vine has the following observation on the peculiar term Luke uses for "ruler" —

"The accuracy of Luke has been vindicated by the use of the term, for while classical authors use the terms *poliarchos* and *politarchos* of similar rulers, the form used by Luke is supported by inscriptions discovered at Thessalonica, one of which mentions Sosipater, Secundas, and Gaius among the politarchs, names occurring as those of Paul's companions. Professor Burton of Chicago, in a paper on *The Politarchs*, has recorded seventeen inscriptions which attest their existence, thirteen of which belong to Macedonia and five presumably to Thessalonica itself, illustrating the influence of Rome in the municipal organization of the place."

9. "The rulers of the darkness of this world" (Ephesians 6:12). These world-lords are not human beings made of flesh and blood, but fallen angelic beings. They are not earthly potentates, but spirit powers, who "under the permissive will of God, and in consequence of human sin, exercise Satanic and therefore antagonistic authority over the world in its present condition of spiritual darkness and alienation from God." They are "the angels of the devil" who is the prince of this world, and as his tools participate in his power in the morally corrupt state of this world (Matthew 12: 45; 25:41; John 12:31; 14:30; 16:11; II Corinthians 4:4).

10. The ruler of the kings of the earth (Revelation 1:5). The word John uses for prince means "ruler," and as such His dominion is to be universal (Revelation 17:14; 19:16). Now the rulers of the earth take counsel against Him as God's anointed Ruler (Psalm 2:2), but His day is coming when the destinies of all men will be in His hands (Revelation 1:18; 3:17). Complete sovereignty is to be His, and when He rules without a rival, then, clothed with all divine attributes, this bloodsoaked earth of ours, which human and satanic rulers have produced, will be resplendent with His peace and glory.

The Safeguard

When David said to Abiathar — "Abide thou with me, fear not: for he that seeketh my life seeketh thy life: but with me thou shalt be in safeguard" (I Samuel 22:23) — did he imply that he himself would be the safeguard or defender of Abiathar, or that he would see to the safety of the priest? It would seem as if David offered himself as Abiathar's protector. "Abide thou with *me* . . . with *me* thou shalt be in *safeguard*." Webster explains such means of protection in a fourfold way —

1. A convoy or escort
2. A pass: safe conduct
3. A precautionary measure or stipulation
4. A technical contrivance to prevent accident.

We like to think of the first meaning of "convoy" or "escort," in David's pledge. Assured of his own safety, the exile king promises Abiathar the full benefit of his protection. Had not the psalmist himself thought of God as His constant Safeguard? "Thou, Lord, only makest me dwell in safety"

(Psalm 4:8). Did he not write for the consolation of oppressed saints the word of the Lord, "I will set him in safety from him that puffeth at him" (Psalm 12:5)? Confident, then, of divine protection David offers Abiathar all necessary safety.

Do we think of God as our strong, invincible escort, or safeguard, or bodyguard? Has He not said, "Touch not mine anointed, and do my prophets no harm" (Psalm 105:15)? Did not Martin Luther have this aspect of divine safety in mind when he wrote that "battle hymn of the reformation" —

"A mighty Fortress is our God."

Sovereigns, rulers, and the rich who want protection, have their safeguards or bodyguards. The humblest, poorest child of God has One who is always near and about him. David made one condition in offering himself as Abiathar's safeguard, "Abide thou with me." Abiding in our Almighty Lord who can possibly harm us? In Him, we have not only salvation but safety, not only pardon but protection.

The Sailor

Up to now all the occupations we have considered have been land occupations with the exception of THE FISHERMAN (which see). Now we come to think of a sea occupation, namely that of sailors and ships, of which, surprisingly, the Bible has a good deal to say. Where can we find finer descriptions of a storm at sea and the difficulties sailors have to face than those to be found in the Psalms, Jonah, and The Acts? Fairbairn in introducing his article on "Ships" says that, "Ancient literature is singularly deficient in everything which relates to ships or navigation. No work written expressly on the subject has come down to us; and we are dependent for our knowledge on the subject to the incidental notices in poets and historians, or to the figures on coins, marbles, or paintings, often the works of ignorant artists (which are calculated to mislead)."

The Bible, however, is ancient literature and is not "singularly deficient" in matters relating to those who go down to the sea in ships. It is true that originally the Jews as a pastoral people had no inducements to follow a sea-faring life. Although the coast by which Palestine was bordered was long, the large part of the coast was occupied by the Phoenicians in the North and the Philistines in the South, who were foremost in shipbuilding. The extent of the skill of the Jews in shipbuilding was confined to fishing boats. But under the Monarchy they developed as a commercial people. "To the Israelites the sea was a mystery like the judgments of God (Psalm 36:6), and the finest picture they have given us of it represents the terror of storm and the thankfulness of deliverance" (Psalm 107:23-32; Jonah 1). Shipping, however, which began on the great rivers of Mesopotamia and Egypt in the simple form of a raft, helped to shape Israelitish history, culture and destiny. Let us take a brief look at the development of ships and sailing in the Bible:

The first record of any semblance of shipbuilding was the construction of the Ark by Noah according to divine specification (Genesis 6). Its unique form was calculated to keep it steady on the water without rolling. Between 450 to 550 feet in length, ninety feet in breadth and fifty feet in height, the Ark must have been a colossal vessel, which it had to be because of its tremendous tonnage.

The tribes of Zebulun and Dan had earlier engaged in sea commerce

(Genesis 49:13; Deuteronomy 33:19; Judges 5:17). "By Abraham's time large river and sea-going ships had been evolved. Practically all transportation with the alluvium was by water, on river or canal." Issachar with Zebulun derived much wealth from naval commerce.

Ships with destructive power came from Chittim (Numbers 24:24; Isaiah 23:12; Jeremiah 2:10; Ezekiel 30:9; Daniel 11:30).

The ferry boats, cut out of cedar and cypress wood and fashioned as floats or rafts, were used not only for ferrying people across Jordan, but also to carry cut stones to Joppa and essential goods to other parts.

Under Solomon commercial activities were intensified and so we have his navy of ships navigated by Phoenician sailors (I Kings 5:9; 9:26-28; 10:22; II Chronicles 2:8-18). The ships of Hiram and Solomon made distant voyages and developed considerable trade by sea, chariots and horses coming from Egypt (I Kings 10:11, 28, 29). Navy is derived from Latin *navis*, meaning "ship," and originally the term referred to all of a nation's ships, whether for commerce or war. The use of navy by the English translators indicates that they referred to merchant ships.

Dr. A. Van Deursen in his *Dictionary of Bible Customs* reminds us that in "early times the Nile teemed with barques and all kinds of different vessels." "The Daytime and the Waters," one of the songs of Ichnaton exclaims:

The barques sail upstream and downstream,
Every route is open, because thou art risen,
The fish in the river leap up before thee.
And thy rays are in the midst of the great sea.

Ships carried cedar and fir from Tyre (II Chronicles 2:16; Ezra 3:2), gold and precious stones from Ophir (I Kings 9:26-28; 22:48). Ships of Tarshish figure prominently in Scripture. These sturdily built vessels not only carried commerce but also exiles back to Jerusalem, their natural home. These ships made a deep impression upon the imagination of the Hebrew people (Psalm 72:10; II Chronicles 20:36). God's power was seen in the breaking of these worthy ships with an east wind (Psalm 48:7). Scriptures record a similar manifestation of divine power and glory (Isaiah 2:16; 33:21, 23; 60:9; 66:19; Ezekiel 38:13; Jonah 1:3).

A word is necessary regarding "the vessels of papyrus" which the Egyptians used for navigation on the Nile (Isaiah 18:2). Papyrus reeds were bound together to make a stem and a stern. (The margin has "bulrushes" instead of papyrus.) These original vessels were swift-going, and "the swift ship" or "ship of reeds" Job mentions were most likely these skiffs with a wooden keel and the rest of bulrushes, sufficient to carry one person, or at most, two, and light, to travel quickly (Job 9:26).

Coming to the New Testament, particularly the gospels, ordinary fishing boats for use on the Sea of Galilee occupy our attention. On the shores of Galilee there was quite a thriving fishing industry (Matthew 4:21,22; 14:24; Mark 3:9; 4:1, 38; 6:48; Luke 8:22, 23; John 6:22; 21:8), and the shore being densely populated, the fisherman would have a brisk trade for their harvest of the sea. It could seem as if Jesus had a special fondness for those Galilean boats for more than once He made special use of one. Two of the most picturesque incidents of His Galilean ministry are the miracle of the stilling of the tempest, and the miraculous draught of fishes. These miracles prove that the boats were small enough to be in danger of sinking from a heavy load of fish, yet large enough to carry Jesus and the majority of His disciples, and also to weather the frequent storms so characteristic of the Sea of Galilee. It was in a boat that Jesus, weary and tired, fell asleep. He also turned a boat into a pulpit and preached there from the message of life to a great concourse of people gathered on the seashore.

We cannot read of Paul's missionary journeys, and peruse his epistles, without realizing that ships played a most important part in his service for the Master. It is often necessary for him to use these large seagoing vessels to cross the Aegean Sea, and sometimes make longer voyages to and from Syria. That these were large ships is proven by the fact that in addition to the cargo carried, they were able to carry 276 persons (Acts 27:37). At least two of these ships the apostle sailed in were ships of Alexandria engaged in wheat trade with Italy (Acts 27:6, 38; 28:11, 13). Frequently, Paul was exposed to great danger on the sea. He suffered shipwreck three times, and at one time spent a night and a day in the deep. He was truly in "perils oft" (Acts 20:13; 27; 28; II Corinthians 11:25).

The apostle certainly had spiritual intuition coupled with the sixth sense of the seamen, when he declared that although the ship would be lost all on board would be saved, and the ill-assorted crew were somehow consoled by the confident assertion of Paul, "I believe God."

What is known as the sixth sense of the sailor is born out of long familiarity with the elements as he sails the seas. As Christians, do we have a "sixth sense" coming as the result of long familiarity with God in whom we "live, move and have our being"? "Whom having not seen, we love," and trust Him in the dark.

Going back over all the references to ships it is profitable to notice what is said regarding the necessary accessories used. Lacking modern, mechanical means of ship propulsion, oars and sails were used. Egyptian ships had both oars and sails, whereas the Philistine ships depended on sails alone (Isaiah 33:21, 23; Ezekiel 27:7). Galilean boats were propelled by oars, with sails being used when the wind was favorable (Luke 8:23). The boatmen rowing in the teeth of a gale, and struggling with the threatening waves, must have had anxious moments (Matthew 14:24; Mark 6:48). The only time the sides of a ship are mentioned is the reference to "the innermost parts of the ship" which Jonah met disaster in (1:5). From time immemorial ships have displayed ensigns or flags of ownership or nationality. The brightly colored sail Ezekiel mentions likely served the dual purpose of sail and sign. The name or sign of the ship Paul sailed in was *The Twin Brothers.* An ancient painting or relief represents "the Twin Brothers" as a figurehead of the ship (Acts 28:11).

Luke, who wrote the Acts, with his true Greek feeling for the sea gives us many "nautical terms, peculiar to him, used with great exactitude and precision." He makes use of no less than fourteen different verbs to describe the progression of a ship (See Luke 8:23, 26; Acts 13:4; 14:26; 15: 39; 16:7; 20:15, 16; 21:1-3; 27:1, 4, 5, 7, 8, 13, 15, 16, 27). Of the ship's equipment we have mainsail and foresail used for the ship's course (Acts 27:40) — the one small boat usually towed behind the larger vessel, but taken up on board for security reasons during a storm (27:16) — the helps or undergirders or chains which were passed under and across the ship and tightened to prevent the boards from springing (27:17) — the anchors made of stone, iron, lead or some other metal, held by a cable or chain (27: 29, 40) — the rudders of which were two used for steering and which could be lifted up out of the water and made fast to the side of the ship if emergency arose — lightening the load of the ship by throwing wheat and other cargo into the sea (21:3; 27:19, 38; Revelation 18:11). Soundings were taken to test the near approach to land (27:28).

As to the various persons handling the ship we have the two principal officers namely, the master and the owner (Acts 27:11). The rank of the former would be the equivalent of captain, or principal officer in command — the sailing master (Jonah 1: 6). The latter spoken of as the owner would be more probably the pilot. The same word is translated governor, or the man at the helm (Ezekiel 27: 27; James 3:4). Then we have the sailors or mariners (Ezekiel 27:8, 27-29; Jonah 1:5; Acts 27:30; Revelation 18:17). These "shipmen" forming the crew, or common seamen, (I Kings 9:27) were heathen men, and as strong as they were coarse. Others, like rowers and carpenters are mentioned. A bas-relief of a Phoenician war galley, about the time of Sennacherib, 700 B.C., depicts thirty-four rowers, arranged in two tiers, as well as deckspace for soldiers whose shields were hung along the sides of the ship. There were also the calkers (see THE CALKER), whose work it was to fill up seams or cracks in the timbers with tow and cover them with tar or wax, after the instruction given to Noah regarding the Ark — "Thou . . . shalt pitch it within and without with pitch" (Genesis 6:14; Ezekiel 27

— in which we have the authentic features of a ship of antiquity).

Shipping provided Old and New Testament writers with some striking similes. Job speaks of God breaking him as with a tempest (9:17), and of his days being passed away as the swift ships (9:26). Among the four wonderful things beyond the mind of Solomon to fully comprehend was "the way of a ship in the midst of the sea" (Proverbs 30:19), which symbolizes the remarkable guidance of God as He directs His own through seas and storms of life until the desired haven is reached. The seaman or pilot who knows all the treacherous currents, and how to cross the bar suggests the need of the heavenly Pilot to guide us over life's tempestuous sea (see THE PILOT)

> Jesus is our Pilot!
> No one else can guide
> Our frail barque in safety
> O'er life's stormy tide.

James compares the tongue, "in the control which its constraint exercises on the character to the very small rudders by which ships, though they be so great, are turned about" (3:4). The Christian hope is presented as "an anchor . . . sure and stedfast, and entereth into that within the veil" (Hebrews 6:19). Knowing that his end was near, John Knox, the great Scottish Reformer said to his wife, "Go read where I first cast my first anchor," which was the seventeenth chapter of John. Jamieson gives us this assuring paragraph on the anchors symbolizing as they do our hope in Christ —

> The soul is the ship; the world the sea; the bliss beyond, the distant coast; hope resting on faith, the anchor which prevents the vessel being tossed to and fro; the consolation through

God's promise and hope is the cable connecting the ship and the anchor. The soul clings, as one in fear of shipwreck, to the anchor, and sees not whither the cable runs, where it is fastened; she knows it is fastened behind the veil which hides the future glory; if only she holds on to the anchor, she shall in due time be drawn in where it is, into the holiest, by the Saviour.

> We have an anchor that keeps the soul
> Steadfast and sure while the billows roll,
> Fasten'd to the Rock which cannot move,
> Grounded firm and deep in the Saviour's love.

Warning young Timothy to be on his guard against false teachers responsible for evil work against believers at Ephesus, Paul uses nautical terms to describe their pernicious influence. The "good conscience" represents the ballast, or cargo, of the ship, while "having put away" actually means, "tossing overboard" — the vessel becoming unmanageable, thereby tossed about, the plaything of the boisterous waves, and in the end wrecked. Hymenaeus and Alexander were guilty of the utter shipwreck of all true faith. In our apostate days, there are too many who have tossed overboard the fundamental truths of the Christian faith and yet have the audacity to remain within the fold of the Christian church.

Then there is also the symbolic fall of Babylon reminiscent of the fall of Tyre (Ezekiel 27), in which woes arise from the merchants of the earth who can no more purchase profitable cargo (Revelation 18:12-18, ASV), and from the shipmasters and passengers and seafaring people who look in terror and grief upon the smoke of burning Babylon.

The Scholar

Twice over in Scripture we read of the scholar —

"The Lord will cut off . . . the scholar" (Malachi 2:12)

"The teacher as the scholar" (I Chronicles 25:8)

In the first reference scholar means "to answer," or "to respond," and the Hebrew word occurs many times in the Bible. The second reference gives us a different Hebrew word for scholar namely, "one who is being taught," and is found nowhere else in Scripture. Ellicott says of the phrase, "The teacher as the scholar" that it literally means, "cunning with learner" (See I Chronicles 25:7). According to a previous verse (33:5), the entire number of Levites appointed for the service of song was 4,000. These were all included in the twenty-four classes, 288 of them being "cunning" men, that is, masters in their art, and the remaining 3,712 forming the rank and file of the choir under the training of the professionals. The Aramaic word *talmid* — scholar — occurs nowhere else in the Old Testament. It is the term used of the disciples of the rabbis in the Talmud, and is the exact equivalent of the New Testament word, disciple, which is found well over 250 times (Matthew 10:24).

The margin of the former reference — the master and the scholar (Malachi 2:12) — has the alternate reading "him that waketh, and him that answereth," and applies to the entire nation of Israel rather than to those who were their appointed scholars and teachers. It can be better rendered, "watchman and answerer." Gesenius, supporting this interpretation quotes the Arabic expression from the life of Timur-lang, "When he left the city, there was not a crier or an answerer in it."

There is the wider application, however, of the phrase from Malachi. Is our blessed Lord not the perfect and patient Teacher, and those who profess to be His followers, scholars or learners in His school? Did He, Himself, not say, "learn of me" (Matthew 11:29)? And from the context we discover that lowliness is one of the most important virtues He would have us emulate — a meekness learned of Him that does not murmur and does not shrink. Among the dictionary definitions of a scholar we have a scholar who is keen in the pursuit of knowledge; and a most learned and literate person. As Christ's scholars, we are but learners with a passion to grow in the knowledge of Him who is incomparable as a Teacher, "I am the Lord thy God which teacheth thee to profit" (Isaiah 48:17). Knowledge received from Him improves our manners, as well as our minds. Shakespeare in Othello wrote —

Mere prattle with our practice,
Is all his scholarship.

What is the use of all we learn from, and about, Christ, unless study results in sanctification? Scholars in His school must become saints in His service.

The Schoolmaster

Such an occupation is mentioned twice as "schoolmaster" (Galatians 3:24, 25), and once as "instructor" (I Corinthians 4:15). Our understanding of a schoolmaster is one who teaches in, and masters a school — a headmaster, but the word Paul uses does not have this modern connotation. It simply means a guardian or trainer of boys, responsible for discipline and not for the impartation of knowledge (See more fully THE INSTRUCTOR).

There is only one mention of a

"school" in the Bible (Acts 19:9), where the reference is to the lecture hall of Tyrannus, the renowned Greek teacher of rhetoric or philosophy. In the Old Testament times, there appears to have been a school for prophets, where "the sons of the prophets" studied the Law and its interpretation (I Samuel 19:19-23; II Kings 2:3; 4: 38). For Jewish children in general there were no public schools. Education of a religious and ethical nature (Proverbs 1:7) was received in the home, religious parents being a child's only instructor. The ultimate aim of Hebrew education was the formation of character. With the advent of the synagogue, the same became the meeting place for religious instruction with elementary teachers to instruct the young in the Law (Matthew 4: 23; Mark 1:21; Luke 5:17), their only textbooks being the rolls of the sacred Scriptures. "After the letters were mastered," says Hastings, "the teacher copied a verse which the child had already learned by heart, and taught him to identify the individual words. The chief feature of the teaching was by rote, and that audibly, for the Jewish teachers were thorough believers in the Latin maxim — *repetitio mater studiorum . . . .*" The subjects taught were "the three R's — reading, writing, arithmetic, the latter in elementary form." As Saul sat at the feet of Gamaliel (Acts 22:3), it would seem as if pupils sat on the floor before their tutors. What precious lessons Mary learned as she sat at her Master's feet!

The Scientist

Because it is affirmed that this term was not coined until 1840, by William Whewell of Cambridge, we cannot expect to find it in the Bible. The word "science," however, is found twice in Holy Writ, and means knowledge, wisdom and understanding.

"Children . . . understanding science" (Daniel 1:4). While science in the modern sense of the word, implying the discovery and orderly classification and exposition of the phenomena and of the laws of nature may not be found in the Bible, it is quite possible that the scientific knowledge possessed by the learned men of Babylon, included mathematics and astronomy (Acts 7:22). "To the Hebrew mind all natural phenomena meant the working of the hand of God in the world, directly and immediately, without the intervention of any secondary laws." An understanding of divine Providence then, and not philosophy, is "the science of sciences." Between the Bible and true science there is no conflict. It was Charles Kingsley who wrote, "No true science without religion." W. Corswant writes, "Science, which is supposed to delve into the secret and mysterious relationships of events, is out of man's reach; God alone possesses it. This is what the last speech of Job to his friends expresses throughout" (Job 38-42).

"Oppositions of science falsely so called" (I Timothy 6:20). Paul is here warning against the vain and corrupt speculations of heathen philosophers. The apostle valued true, full and accurate knowledge, and utilized secular knowledge (Acts 17:28; Philippians 1: 9; 4:8; Colossians 2:3; 3:10). He had a well-trained mind and one of the master intellects of his time. He could subscribe to the couplet Alexander Pope wrote to the Earl of Burlington —

> Good sense, which only is the gift of Heaven,
> And though no science, fairly worth the seven.

The Greek word Paul uses for "science" is *gnosis*, the general word for "knowledge" about thirty times in the

New Testament. It was from this word that the Gnostics derived their name. An old English phrase in Barlow's *Dialoge* reads, "There is no truthe, no mercye, nor scyence of God in the yerth." The science which the false teachers Paul exposed boasted of, and which became known as "Gnosticism," and which was in opposition to the Gospel, consisted of a denial of Christ's divine dignity. Belittling Christ's exalted rank and redeeming work, the Gnostics "assigned to Him merely the highest rank in the order of spirits, while they exalted angels as concerned in bringing in the Messianic salvation" (Colossians 2:18, 19). Paul's characteristic word in Colossians for the divine revelation is not *gnosis* but *epignosis,* meaning, "full-knowledge" (Colossians 1:9; 3: 10), as against the pretended "knowledge" of the erroneous Gnostics and Ascetics (Colossians 2:20, 23).

The Scribe

Frequently mentioned along with the "recorder," the scribe represented a most important occupation. He attended to royal correspondence, and functioned as THE CHANCELLOR (which see), or rather as secretary of state. Under David and Solomon these scribes or royal secretaries ranked with the high priest and the captain of the host (II Samuel 8:17; 20:25; I Kings 4:3; II Kings 12:10; 18:18, 37). The word "scribe" is from a root meaning to write, order, count. The Greek word is *grammaticus* from which we have "grammar." Among these legal experts, jurists, teachers of the law, we have the godly scribe Ezra (Ezra 7:6), "a scribe of the Lord God of Heaven," who, under the guidance of the Holy Spirit, probably compiled, from authoritative histories, Chronicles (I Chronicles 29:29; II

Chronicles 9:29; 13:22). Zadok is another scribe who is named. Jonathan, David's uncle was likewise a scribe (I Chronicles 27:32). Then we read of Shebna the secretary and Joah the recorder (Isaiah 36:3). We read of the "king's scribes" (Esther 3:12). Baruch and Shaphan were others (Jeremiah 36:4, 10, 20). In the New Testament Zenas and Apollos were the equivalent of spiritually-minded scribes (Titus 3:13).

Writing ranked as a profession in Eastern countries and thus scribes were employed by kings, magistrates and merchants to keep registers of national and commercial affairs (II Samuel 8:17; 10:25; I Kings 4:3; II Kings 19:2; 22:8; Psalm 45:1; Isaiah 33:18; Jeremiah 36:26; Matthew 7: 29). From the gospels it would appear as if there was an inseparable connection between the scribes and the Pharisees seeing that they are often grouped together — "The scribes and of the Pharisees" (Matthew 12: 38; Mark 2:16; 7:5; Luke 6:7). If any distinction can be drawn between them, the Pharisees were a religious party, while the scribes, although professedly religious, held an office.

Scribes are to be distinguished from the Roman lawyer or modern judge (See under THE CLERK, THE LAWYER, THE DOCTOR, THE RECORDER). Because of the intricacies of the law which they had to master, then administrate, they became a combination of scholar, writer, preacher, lawyer and magistrate. Their original task was to write nothing themselves but to let the sacred Word they transcribed speak for itself (Nehemiah 8: 8). Any interpretation was done orally for instance, as Ezra gave the sense of what he read (Nehemiah 8:1-9). Because of his authoritative function as an interpreter the scribe came to occupy a high position in Judaism. He sat in Moses' seat (Matthew 23:2) having power to bind or loose, to pronounce authoritative judgments upon the legality or illegality of all Jewish matters. They had "the key of knowledge" wherewith to open or shut the treasures of wisdom (Luke 11:52). At times, vain scribes fought for their prerogative as "teachers." Ambitious of honor, they loved the title of "rabbi" — a title Christ urged His disciples to refuse (Matthew 23:7, 8). Their dress equalled their nobility, and their families had their own special residence (I Chronicles 2:55). They were considered naturally qualified to teach in the Synagogue (Mark 1:22).

There were, of course, many noble scribes, whose life and learning were commensurate with their important task, such as Gamaliel (Acts 5:34; 22: 3). The most conscientious among them accepted no salary for their educational and judicial work — a rule associated with the impartial judge (Exodus 23:8; Deuteronomy 16:19). Yet fees were paid or extracted for certain services (Matthew 23:14; Luke 8:2, 3; 12:14). It is to be regretted that the precise training received unfitted many proud scribes to understand the Messiahship of Jesus. They were totally blind to the creative force in spiritual things, hence, their rejection of John the Baptist and Jesus, whose fearful denunciations of the Scribes was an evidence of His righteous indignation (Matthew 23). As the *Zondervan Pictorial Bible Dictionary* expresses it —

> Because Jesus refused to be bound by the scribal accretions to the law (John 5:10-18; Mark 7:1-13), the scribes soon fiercely opposed Him. Throughout His ministry they were His most watchful and determined opponents (Mark 2:6; Luke 5:30; 15:2). Their hypocrisy and unrelenting hatred drew forth Christ's devastating denunciation of them (Matthew 23). They played an important part in the death of Jesus (Matthew 26:57; 27:41; Mark 15:1, 31; Luke 22:66; 23:10), also in the persecution of the early church (Acts 4:5; 6:12). Not all the scribes were wholly bad, for Nicodemus and Gamaliel were scribes, but as a whole they were marked by spiritual corruption and were the very quintessence of Pharisaism.

Jesus urged them to find Him in their search of Old Testament Scriptures, and that if they found Him they would discover life (John 5:39). Some, there were, who were not far from the kingdom (Mark 12:32-34, 38-44). But alas, as a body the scribes strove for external formalism. They made life a burden, and evaded their own precepts (Matthew 23:16; Luke 11:46). "By their traditions of the law, instead of being a help in moral and spiritual life, they became an instrument for preventing true access to God" (Luke 11:52).

What a striking contrast there is between the life and teaching of Jesus, and that of the scribes! The latter depended on "them of old time" (Matthew 5:21, 27, 33) — Jesus "taught as one having authority and not as the scribes" (Matthew 7:29). The scribes taught only their disciples in scribal schools — Jesus "had compassion on the multitudes" and through "all the cities and villages" (Matthew 4:23; 9:35, 36).

Today there are a vast company of scribes — Christian men and women, who, with a love for the Word, endeavor to expound it by means of the printed page. In his inaugural lecture as the Norrisian Professor of Divinity at Cambridge in 1899, Dr. Handley C. S. Moule had this to say in the introduction to his lecture on Second Corinthians, and his words should be heeded by all God's scribes —

There is one word of our divine Lord's which has often, in the life and labor of a religious teacher, been a help and cheer to my thoughts. It is found in a dark context, in the twenty-third chapter of St. Matthew, verse 34, but it has a pure ray of light to shed upon vocation in a University, "Behold, . . . I send unto you scribes."

He speaks in the same sacred breath of sending prophets, and of sending wise men to act, and also if need be to suffer. But the word I fasten upon is, "I send unto you scribes"; the men of the library, the pen, the teacher's chair. Their function lacks from many aspects the possible grandeur of the life which is called into the field of open action for the Lord; the life for example of the pastor or of the missionary. As one has said, it is the life whose business is rather to sharpen the sickles of others than to go out armed into the standing corn, and reap, and reap, till the evening comes, and with it the call home to the reward.

Nevertheless, the life of the scribe is a life that is capable of mission; "I send unto you." And that is enough to furnish matter from devotion and hope.

The Secretary

From what we have just written on THE SCRIBE, it will be remembered that the same was originally a secretary which kings and important officials employed as official writers to compose letters and deal with correspondence. Baruch was secretary to the prophet Jeremiah, and Paul usually dictated his letters (Jeremiah 36: 18; Romans 16:22; I Corinthians 16: 21; Colossians 4:18, etc.). All references under THE SCRIBE can be added here. Shipley in his *Dictionary of Words* says that "When we speak of a private secretary, we are going back to the first sense of the word: Latin *secretarius* is from *secretum, secret.*"

The Seducer

This is one of the despicable, dishonorable occupations of the Bible. Although the noun "seducer" is not found in its specific sense of "to entice a female to surrender her chastity," such a crime is referred to and condemned. Among the crimes marring the sanctity of life was that of seduction, three aspects of which are dealt with under the Mosaic Law.

1. The seducer of an unbetrothed virgin was compelled to take the virgin as his wife, and if her father consented to the union, the seducer had to pay him the usual purchase price or dowry of fifty shekels, and forfeit any right of divorce (Exodus 22:16; Deuteronomy 22:28).

2. The seducer of a betrothed virgin was deemed guilty of adultery. Such a virgin was regarded as pledged to her future husband as fully as if she were formally married to him. The penalty for the seducer was death (Deuteronomy 22:23-27).

3. The seducer of a betrothed bondmaid (Leviticus 19:10-22). Here there is no infliction of death, because the girl, being a slave, was not free. The seducer, however, was required to pay a fine, and make a tresspass offering.

Elsewhere in Scripture "seduction" is related to truth and morals, as the following references clearly show —

"Manasseh seduced them to do more evil" (II Kings 21:9). In the history of God's ancient people, Manasseh is the most conspicuous seducer, whose constant endeavor was to lead the children of Israel astray.

"The way of the wicked seduceth them" (Proverbs 12:26). Solomon presents a sharp contrast in the verse as a whole. The righteous, although inferior to his neighbor in worldly advantages, is yet a guide to him, showing him "the way wherein he should walk." But the wicked, so far from guiding others in the way of truth, hopelessly wanders from it himself, and seduces others from it.

"The princes of Noph are deceived; they have also seduced Egypt" (Isaiah 19:13).

Themselves deceived, they become deceivers. These princes were deluded into believing that their country was secure from Assyrian invasion, and then proclaimed to Egypt that there was peace, when there was no peace.

"Because they have seduced my people" (Ezekiel 13:10). What heartless seducers those lying prophets were. The repetition because . . . because, heightens the divine emphasis of condemnation. The illustration of deception the prophet uses is apt. Mortar was mixed with sand and water only, the lime being left out. It was a common practice to cover walls with stucco. The false prophets are described as joining with those who built a wall but covered over its defects and weaknesses with a fair-seeming plaster (Ezekiel 13:10-16; See Matthew 23:27; Acts 23:3). By giving delusion the weight of their influence, and persuading the people to believe a lie, the false prophets were guilty of cruel seduction.

"To seduce, if it were possible, even the elect" (Mark 13:22). Because of the manifestation of miraculous power by the man of sin during the Great Tribulation, many will be deceived. Our Lord, however, forewarns His own, and in the time of satanic delusion will preserve then from following the false Christ and His seducing prophet. "These things have I written unto you concerning them that seduce you" (I John 2:26).

"Giving heed to seducing spirits" (I Timothy 4:1). These spirits are evil ones working in heretical teachers as they propound "the spirit of error" as opposed to "the spirit of truth" (I John 4:2-6). "Doctrines of devils" represents the teachings suggested by demons who are "Satan's monsters" (II Corinthians 11:15; James 3:15).

"Evil men and seducers shall wax worse and worse" (II Timothy 3:13). This phrase flatly contradicts the gospel that the world is getting better. Materially, we never had it so good; but morally, we never had it so bad. The word Paul uses here for "seducers" is found nowhere else in the Bible. It means "imposters" (ASV), and denotes a wailer from the howl in which spells were chanted — a wizard, — sorcerer — enchanter, hence, a juggler, a cheat. Possibly the false teachers Paul referred to practiced magical arts (II Timothy 3:8). The Amplified New Testament translates "divers lusts" (II Timothy 3:6), as "seductive impulses."

"To teach and to seduce my servants" (Revelation 2:20). Jezebel, the false prophetess, is used to symbolize those in the church at Thyatira who lacked zeal for godly discipline and doctrine. Error in belief led to evil in behavior. In these apostate days there are far too many theological seducers in the church. Leaders openly deny the fundamental truths of Scripture, and thereby open the flood gates of adultery and idolatry. Shakespeare, in *Julius Caesar*, says,

> Therefore 'tis meet
> That noble minds keep ever with their likes;
> For who so firm that cannot be seduced.

For those of us who like and love the truth, may we be so established in it that no one and nothing could ever possibly move us from such a sure and firm foundation.

The Seer

Found almost thirty times in the Old Testament only, this term actually means a "prophet," who sees the message God would have him declare, the seeing probably to be conceived as having taken place in a vision. He both sees and speaks forth a divine revelation (I Samuel 9:9; II Samuel 15:27; 24:11; I Chronicles 21:9; 25:5, etc.). By the Holy Spirit the prophets had insight and vision, enabling them to testify beforehand the mind and message of God (I Peter 1:11; II Peter 1:21). At times, distinction is preserved between "prophets" and "seers" (II Kings 17:13; I Chronicles 29:29). Some scholars suggest that "seer" denotes one who did not belong to the regular prophetic order. We feel, however, that all true prophets were "seers," because of their ability to foresee and declare future events. Spiritual vision gave them knowledge of the divine mind and will, and power of utterance was bestowed upon them to declare the revelation with power.

The Senator

Although this occupational name is found only once in the Bible (Psalm 105:22), "the senate" (Acts 5:21) implies the provision of senators — a term meaning "aged" or "senior." The notion of age was merged in dignity. The Sanhedrin of New Testament times was the senate and was the supreme court with the elders, or senators having governing powers as well as judicial functions (II Chronicles 19:8; Matthew 5:22; Acts 4:15; 5:21, etc.). The tenure of service was ordinarily for life.

The Sergeant

From a root meaning "to serve," a sergeant (Acts 16:35, 38) was a "rodbearer" or "lictor" (ASV margin *lic-tors*). These "rod-bearers" were Roman officials whose duty it was to attend the magistrates, to carry out their orders, and especially to administer the punishments of scourging and execution. For this purpose they carried their mark of office, the "fasces," a bundle of rods with an axe inserted. At Philippi, the sergeants served under THE PRAETORS (which see), and Paul and Silas as Roman subjects refused to be "privily" set free by them.

In Britain, the sergeant-at-law is one of a former ranking order of barristers acting for the sovereign in the deciding of cases in the royal courts. A sergeant is an office in the armed and police forces distinguished by three stripes on the sleeves. Such a commanding officer has been used to describe death. Shakespeare in *Hamlet* speaks of —

This fell sergeant, death,
Is strict in his arrest.

William Alexander, of the fifteenth century, has a similar thought —

"That fatal sergeant, Death,
spares no degree."

The Servant

In the ancient world, service and slavery were closely related, so much so that one can scarcely distinguish the one from the other. The original words used for "servants" and "service" carry a variety of meanings between which it is not always easy to determine what is meant. As servant and its cognates, "servants," "serve" and "service" occur well over 1,000 times in the Bible, it can be seen what a task it would be to set forth all the different terms used. There are two words, however, that we can separate for general purposes. One word implies free, voluntary service, meaning a kind of service involving no slavery, but which was the result of mutual agreement between contracting parties. For instance, Jacob's double term of servitude for his two wives was a matter of arrangement between Laban and Jacob (Genesis 29). Joshua was the servant, or minister of choice by Moses, just as Elisha was the servant of the prophet Elijah. Servants in attendance on guests afford another example of voluntary service. Their strict, reverential attendance, with eyes fixed on the several guests, ready to obey the slightest gesture is alluded to by David as a lesson for the servants of God (Psalm 123:2. See Luke 17:8).

Another common word *ebed* indicates a greater or less degree of inferiority and want of freedom and is the frequent equivalent of a slave (Genesis 9:25; 24:9, etc.). Yet this term is associated with higher relations, for example, a rich man's steward (Genesis 15:2), but we are not presently concerned with the slavery connotation of service. Under THE SLAVE the reader will find a study of this degraded form of service. Slaves were actually reckoned as property, held to be as strictly the property of those whose slaves they were, as house or furniture, land or estate. Servants on the other hand are free, and more or less their own masters. God's servants realize that they are not their own. They have been bought with a price. It is these we are taken up with in this section.

In the New Testament, servant represents various Greek words, three of which we distinguish. There is *doulos,* the most common and general word for "servant," and frequently implying subjection without the idea of bondage. This particular word is used —

1. Of natural associations (Matthew 8:9; I Corinthians 7:21, 22; Ephesians 6:5; Colossians 4:1, etc.).
2. Metaphorically of spiritual, moral and ethical conditions, servants of God (Acts 16:17; Titus 1:1; I Peter 2:16; Revelations 7:3; 15:3).

Christ, the most perfect example (Philippians 2:7). Servants of Christ (Romans 1:1; I Corinthians 7:22; Galatians 1:10; Ephesians 6:6; Philippians 1:1).

Servants of sin (John 8:34, ASV. bondservant, Romans 6:17, 20, etc.).

Servants of Corruption (II Peter 2:19, ASV, bondservants).

Then there is *diakonos,* meaning, deacon, minister, or servant, and from which we have "diaconate" or Board of Deacons (Matthew 22:14 ASV; Mark 9:35 ASV; John 2:5, 9; 12:26; Romans 16:1). *Doulos* views the servant in relationship to his master — *diakonos* views his relationship to his work. Another word for "servant" is *pais,* one of the terms for "child" and in many cases denotes a spiritual relation to God — Israel (Luke 1:54); David (Luke 1:69; Acts 4:25) Christ (Matthew 12:18. See Acts 4:27, 30 ASV).

Hired service was not common in Old Testament days, slavery being the recognized form of service. But from the parable of the vineyard (Matthew 20:1-15), we learn these facts about servants in our Lord's time —

1. They gathered early in the morning and stood in the marketplace to be hired.

2. The usual daily wage of a servant, or laborer was about eight pence or ten cents.

3. That the hours of working were till six at night.

A servitor (II Kings 4:43), was one who ministers to, or serves, but not in a menial, degraded capacity as a slave.

Among the servants of Scripture, the Lord Jesus has the place of preeminence. He came as "the Righteous Servant of Jehovah" (Isaiah 42:1; 53: 11; Acts 3:24-26; 4:27). This is one of the most notable designations of our Lord; and along with it occurs "the Holy and Righteous One" (Acts 3:14). Although the Son of God, He was the Servant of God, fulfilling every behest of the divine will. In His essential nature, Christ was very and eternal God, yet He took upon Himself "the form of a servant — or slave." In the context there is an allusion to the manner of His death. Crucifixion was a servile punishment inflicted on vile and incorrigible slaves. On the cross, Christ was numbered with transgressors (Isaiah 53:12).

Of other servants, Eliezer, the eldest servant of Abraham's household, certainly earned the title of a "good and faithful servant." His position can be compared with that of the prime minister (Genesis 14:2; 24:2). The preacher can find a wealth of sermonic material in "The Servants of the Bible."

Eliezer, as a servant, illustrates faithfulness in fulfilling a trust (Genesis 24:62, 63).

Deborah, Rebekah's nurse, as a servant, rendered long and loyal service (Genesis 35:8).

Phurah, Gideon's servant, is conspicuous as a partner in privileges (Judges 7:10).

Obadiah was the God-fearing servant of an ungodly master (I Kings 18:16).

The little maid and Gehazi, as servants of Naaman, teach us the use and misuse of opportunities (II Kings 5:2, 3, 20).

The servants at Cana remind us of the knowledge of those that draw.

What the governor of the Feast did not know, his servants knew (John 2:9).

The centurion's servant teaches us the necessity of affection for dependents (Luke 7:2).

Malchus, the servant, gives us an example of service in a sinful household (John 18:10).

Onesimus, a convert of Paul's was the offending servant reclaimed (Philemon 17).

As to service, such a term has a variety of meanings — servile work of slavery (Leviticus 23:7; Exodus 1:14) — military employment (I Chronicles 24:3) — ministration in the Tabernacle or temple (Exodus 36:1-5; I Chronicles 23:26, etc.) — service for Christ (Ephesians 6:7). If *diakonia,* one of the Greek words for "service" is from a root meaning "to run on errands," are we as the servants of the Lord ready to run His errands? "Here am I, Lord, send me." The Bible leaves us in no doubt as to the nature of service we are to render. It must be —

Consecrated Service (Romans 12:1).

Prayerful Service (Genesis 24:12; Luke 3:21; 5:16; 6:12; 9:28; Acts 4:31, etc.).

Humble Service (Matthew 11:29; Acts 20:19).

Joyful Service (Hebrews 12:2) "Serve the Lord with gladness."

Diligent Service (Romans 12:11; Hebrews 7:25 *ever.* See Proverbs 6:6; 22:29).

Stedfast Service (I Corinthians 15:58).

Rewarded Service (Matthew 25:21; I Corinthians 3:12-15; Revelation 2:10).

Ye servants of the Lord,
　Each in his office wait,
Observant of His heavenly word,
　And watchful at His gate.

O happy servant he,
In such a posture found!
He shall his Lord with rapture see,
And be with honor crowned.

The Sheepmaster

Sheep shearers were those employed for shaving, or cutting off the wool from sheep (Genesis 38:12; II Samuel 13:23, 24). Mesha, King of Moab is spoken of as a "sheepmaster" (II Kings 3:4). Owners, however, sheared their own sheep as well as employing regular shearers (I Samuel 25:2, 4, 7, 11; Isaiah 53:7). Mesha was both a shepherd and the owner of sheep, and paid as tribute to the king of Israel the wool of 100,000 lambs and 100,000 rams. In some parts the sheepmaster was one owning superior kind of sheep. Ellicott reminds us that in Arabic, *naqad,* allied to *noged,* the Hebrew for sheepmaster or herdsman (Amos 1:1), means a kind of sheep of superior wool; *naggad,* the owner or shepherd of such sheep.

The Shepherd

Although the first reference to shepherds is associated with Joseph's brethren (Genesis 46:32), such an occupation must have been in vogue long before then. At the beginning of the human race, pastoral work was naturally among the first and most important in which men could be engaged. Abel was "a keeper of sheep" (Genesis 4:2). Cain was older than Abel yet the latter's occupation is mentioned before the former, which is as it should be, because the shepherd comes naturally before the farmer. Tilling the ground must have been a later occupation than tending flocks. Some of the greatest and best men in Bible history were shepherds: Abraham, Jacob, Moses, David, Amos, etc. (See THE HERDSMAN).

The shepherd's task was both varied and arduous. Not only had he to protect his sheep from robbers and wild beasts, he had also to be constantly on the search for good pasture and sufficient water (Psalm 23:2). Jacob reminds us how hard a shepherd's life could be, "In the day the drought consumed me, and the frost by night, and my sheep departed from my eyes" (Genesis 31:40). Shepherding flocks, however, could be profitable. When the Bible speaks of a great or rich man, it does not tell us how much money he had, or how much land he owned, but how many sheep he possessed. Job was the greatest of all men in the East — he had 14,000 sheep. Nabal, "a very great man," kept 3,000 sheep and 1,000 goats on the slopes of Mount Carmel. Then reference has been made to Mesha, king of Moab. In the earliest stages of society the nomad state was regarded as honorable even to a chief (Genesis 4:20; 30:29; 37). The daughters of chiefs did not regard as unworthy the caring of flocks (Genesis 29:6; Exodus 2:19). Alas, the shepherds' occupation came to lose much of its dignity (II Samuel 7:8; Psalm 78:70; Amos 7:14).

Among the shepherd's simple equipment the following can be noted. His chief garment was a cloak woven from wool or made from sheepskins with fleece (Jeremiah 43:12). Sleeveless, and hanging from the shoulders like a mantle, this outer garment was gathered around the waist by a strong leather belt or girdle. At night, it formed his bedding, as he curled up under it, head and all. That some shepherds used tents at night (Song of Solomon 1:8) is evident from the same being employed to illustrate desolation (Ezekiel 25:4; Zechariah 2:6). The shepherd's scrip, made of goat's skin with legs tied, was used as a container for food, necessary articles and chief belongings (I Samuel 17:40). A sling, made of goat's hair, was carried to protect the shepherd himself and his sheep from wild animals. David, the shepherd lad was able to kill the giant Goliath with his sling. Then there was the rod or club, about thirty inches long, having a number of heavy iron nails driven into its round head and used for defense against attack. As for the staff, which was something like our walking cane, the same had a crook on the end to seize straying sheep by the leg (Psalm 32:4; Zechariah 11:7). The shepherd usually had a flute or pipe (Judges 5:16), made of reeds, to entertain himself and content his sheep (I Samuel 17:34; Isaiah 31:4). No shepherd would journey far without his dogs, so necessary in frightening wild beasts and robbers. Fearless, they were the best protectors of the sheep (Job 30:1; Isaiah 31:4; 56:10, 11). As for his wages, the shepherd was paid in money but more often than not in kind, in the form of milk, wool or sheep (Genesis 31; Zechariah 11:12).

The task of the shepherd was both demanding and dangerous. Shepherds would contend with one another for necessary water (Genesis 26:17-22; Exodus 2:17). Flocks had to be protected from poisonous serpents, beasts of prey, or thieves (Genesis 31:39; Exodus 22:13; I Samuel 17:34-36; Isaiah 31:4; Amos 3:12). Sick sheep had to be cared for, and the mother ewes spared too much walking, and the tired lambs carried (Genesis 33:13; Isaiah 40:11; Luke 15:4-7). Lovingly, the shepherd supervised his flock. He knew all his sheep by name, and they knew his voice and were attentive to it. How relieved he was when they were all safe in the fold at night! Yet the shepherd's life had its pleasures

as well as its hardships. The time of shearing was a season of feasting and merriment (Genesis 38:12; I Samuel 25:2, 36; II Samuel 13:23). The days included pleasant hours of conversation and musing, with the sling being an instrument of amusement as well as defense (I Samuel 17:40). While a shepherd, David received many of his deepest impressions, and most poetic images, and in later years expressed them in some of his sweetest psalms (Psalm 23, etc.).

Is it to be wondered at that the vocation of the shepherd is one of the most expressive metaphors used in so many ways in the Bible? We have constant reference to the shepherd's activity. Kings, priests, prophets, leaders in temporal affairs and teachers must feed and care for the people as faithful guardians of the flock (Isaiah 44:28; 63:11; Jeremiah 3:15; 23:4, 25; Ezekiel 34:2-10; Zechariah 10:2 etc.). Spiritual overseers are "shepherds" or "pastors." *Pastor* is a Latin word for "shepherd" (Psalm 23:1; 80:1; Ecclesiastes 12:11; Isaiah 40:11; Ephesians 4:11). "Sheep without a shepherd" typified individuals or nations who had forgotten God (Numbers 27:17; I Kings 22:17; Ezekiel 34:5, 8; Zechariah 10:2; Matthew 9:36; Mark 6:34).

There are numerous metaphorical allusions to the shepherd's vocation, descriptive of the care of God for His children (Psalms 23:1; 77:20; 78:52, 53; 80:1; Jeremiah 33:3; Ezekiel 34:14-29; Micah 7:14). As their Shepherd, He "lifts up his staff against" His people's foes (Isaiah 10:1, 24). Some shepherds counted their flocks by admitting them one by one into a pen — a custom to which Jeremiah alludes (33:13). "The Lord knoweth them that are his" (John 10:2-5). "A strong sympathy for helpless animals, though sometimes misdirected, is a marked characteristic of the people of Bible lands. The birth of offspring in a flock often occurs far off on the mountain side. The shepherd solicitously guards the mother during her helpless moments and picks up the lamb and carries it to the fold. For the few days, until it is able to walk, he may carry it in his arms or in the loose folds of his coat above his girdle." Did Isaiah have his precious glimpse of the shepherd's care in mind when he wrote of God as the Shepherd, carrying the lambs in His bosom (40:11)?

Our Lord identified Himself with the prophetic, mysterious shepherd of Zechariah, who is the fellow of the Lord of hosts (Zechariah 13:7; 14:21; Matthew 26:31), and applies the simile of the shepherd to His mission among men (Luke 15:4-7). He is the one and only Shepherd of the sheep who have gone their own way (Isaiah 53:6; John 10:16). He is "the Good Shepherd" who was willing to lay down His life for the sheep (John 10:11-14); "the Great Shepherd" who not only purchased the sheep with His blood, but rose again and ever lives on their behalf (Hebrews 13:20). In, and from heaven, He cares for His sheep as "the Shepherd and Bishop of their souls" (I Peter 2:25). When He returns, it will be as "the chief shepherd" to reward His under-shepherds, or those pastors and teachers He called to minister to the spiritual needs of His sheep (I Peter 2:25). The appropriateness of the title of shepherd can be gathered from the fact that —

He knows His own sheep — the ground of security (Ezekiel 9:4; John 1:48; 10:11, 14; II Timothy 2:19).

He calls His own sheep. He has a unique call (Psalm 85:8; Matthew 9:9; John 10:3; Romans 8:30).

He gathers His own sheep, no matter where they are (John 4:29; 10:16. See Luke 23:42; Acts 16:34).

He sacrificed His life for His sheep (Matthew 26:31; John 10:11, 15; Romans 5:7).

He gives eternal life to His own sheep. This is part of the grand covenant arrangement between the Father and the Son (John 10:28, 29; 17:2).

As sacrifice is the supreme test of love, loyalty and devotion, the preposition used in the phrase, "He gave his life *for* his sheep," is of the utmost importance. This common three-letter word *for* summarizes the doctrine of vicarious sacrifice and teaches us that Jesus died that we might live. Our sin, deserving eternal death, He took and made His own.

> Jesus is our Shepherd;
>   For the sheep He bled;
> Every Lamb is sprinkled
>   With the blood He shed.
> Then on each He setteth,
>   His own secret sign: —
> "They that have My Spirit,
>   These," saith He, "are Mine."

The Shipmaster

Under THE PILOT and THE SAILOR, the reader will find references to the "shipmaster," the original of which means a "master of the pilots" (Jonah 1:6); a pilot, steersman, governor (Revelation 18:17); master or owner of a ship (Acts 27:11). Along with sailors (Ezekiel 26:17; Acts 27:27, 30), the shipmaster was the "shipman" with knowledge of the sea (I Kings 9:27), and who, going down to the sea in ships, beheld the wonders of the God who made the sea (Psalms 95:5; 107: 23).

The Silversmith

The many objects made of silver referred to in the Bible imply the good craftmanship of silversmiths. The only one named is Demetrius, the silversmith of Ephesus, who had a lucrative business making silver shrines for Diana (Acts 19:24, See LXX for Judges 17:4; Jeremiah 6:29). Drinking cups (Genesis 44:2), and the sockets, hooks, chargers, bowls, trumpets, basins, candlesticks, and cords of the Tabernacle were fashioned of silver. From ancient times silver was used in Palestine in making jewelry by silversmiths (Genesis 24:53; Exodus 3:22). A shekel and the talent of silver formed the medium of exchange (Genesis 23: 16; I Samuel 9:8; Job 28:15; Matthew 10:9; 22:19, 20; 27:9). As a precious metal silver is mentioned over 200 times in the Bible. Prophets and poets often allude to the silversmith's art (Psalm 12:6; Proverbs 25:4; 26:23; Isaiah 1:25; Ezekiel 22:18, 22; Zechariah 13:9; Malachi 3:3). Silver is likewise used in a figurative or symbolic sense for something refined and pure, free from dross such as the Word of God (Psalm 12:6), and His saints (Malachi 3:3). Commenting on this verse Fausset says, "The Lord, with perfect wisdom and love, leaves His people in affliction till, their dross being purified, He sees them reflecting His holy image; just as a 'refiner of silver' sits watching the melting silver until he sees his own image reflected when he knows the silver has been long enough in the furnace and withdraws it."

> Work on, then, Lord, till on my soul
> Eternal light shall break
> And, in Thy likeness perfected,
> I "satisfied" shall wake.

The Singer

The fifty odd mentions of singers, and the 100 or more references to singing in the Bible surely imply that our happy God means His people to be likewise happy. What a fascinating study "Bible Singers and Their Songs" would make! There is the notable Song of Moses; and the Song of Israel about the springing well. God is said to joy over His own with singing (Zephaniah 3:17), and, in turn, they are to come before Him in singing (Psalm 100:2). The loss of divine favor results in the absence of singing (Isaiah 16:10). Our incarnate Lord joined with His disciples in song, "When they had sung an hymn, they went out to the Mount of Olives." Was ever hymn sung under such tragic circumstances? Under the deepening shadows of Gethsemane and Calvary, they sang praises unto God. Dr. Andrew Bonar, in his comment on the above verse said, "Never man spake like this Man, and possibly the same might be true of Christ's singing — 'Never man sang like this Man'." How thrilled the singing angels must have been at that song of triumph! Midnight in prison did not deter Paul and Silas singing hymns, to which the prisoners listened with admiration. What a marvel of grace to sing under such circumstances! Perhaps some of the prisoners were saved that night through those songs of salvation. A pagan testimony of old reads, "The Christians sing hymns to Christ as God, at daybreak." Often the Gospel flies victoriously on the wings of song. "A song may reach him who a sermon flies" (See THE MUSICIANS). The proverb has it, "God giveth speech to all, song to few."

Temple choirs were "instructed in the songs of the Lord" (II Samuel 19: 35; I Chronicles 25:7), and the choristers themselves were called "workers" (I Chronicles 25:1), and like the "workman" Paul speaks of, they had to be worthy of such a strenuous designation. It would appear as if singers and musicians belonged to a particular guild (I Chronicles 9:33; Nehemiah 12:29, 35, 46; Ezekiel 40:44). The first song in the Bible was sung by Lamech (Genesis 4:23, 24). Songs were composed to celebrate some special victory or significant religious experience (Exodus 15). Believers are urged to sing (Ephesians 5:19; Colossians 3:16). Reference is made to singing in heaven (Revelation 5:9; 14:3). The value of singing was so appreciated that it was considered to be of the nature of prophecy (I Chronicles 15:16). We gather from Isaiah that it was not uncommon for foreign female singers of questionable character to make "sweet melody" as they sang songs along the streets and highways of Judaea (Isaiah 23:16). In the majority of references to "singing" it is used always of praise to God (Romans 15:9; I Corinthians 14:15; James 5:13; Revelation 15:3). As an ordinance of divine worship, singing expresses our joy in God, and gratitude for His mercies (Psalm 13:6; 30:4; 68:32, etc.).

> Sing on; oh! blissful music!
> With every note you raise
> My heart is filled with rapture
> My soul is lost in praise.

The Slave

While the word slave occurs only once in the KJV (Revelation 18:13), yet it is present in both Hebrew and Greek words for "servant" (Genesis 9:25; Matthew 8:9 etc.) See THE BONDSERVANT for a full treatment of slaves and slavery. Also consult material under THE SERVANT.

> He is the free man, whom the truth sets free;
> And all are slaves beside (John 8:32-36).

The Smith

As used in the Bible, this occupational term covers all artificers and engravers in the metals Moses named — gold, silver, brass (copper), iron, tin and lead (Numbers 31:22). The smith's trade goes back to Tubal-Cain who is described as "a whetter of every instrument of copper and iron" (Genesis 4:22), in other words as a smith endowed to construct agricultural, household and warlike articles. The fearful havoc wrought by some of the weapons is immortalized in "The Song of Lamech" (Genesis 4:23, 24). From then on the smith's art took precedence over all other occupations, inasmuch as he furnished the tools necessary for an advancing civilization. Metal work, carpentry, building and other useful arts were greatly developed before the Flood.

All the vessels used in the Tabernacle involved a knowledge of every kind of handicraft, and great skill in the fashioning of all that was required (Exodus 25:10, 11, 17, 18; 31:4, 5). We read of the goldsmith (see under his cameo), the silversmith (see under his cameo). These particular smiths were skillful in making ornaments for adornment, vessels and images (Genesis 24:22; 35:4). Then there is the coppersmith, artificer or worker in brass (Genesis 4:22; I Kings 7:14, 45; see under this occupation). Mention is also made of the ironsmith, or worker in iron (I Samuel 13:19; II Chronicles 24:12; Isaiah 44:12). So highly were those smiths skilled in the manufacture of war weapons that conquerors removed them from a conquered nation, as those smiths were by Nebuchadnezzar, to more certainly impoverish a defeated people (II Kings 24:14; Isaiah 44:12; 54:16; Jeremiah 24:1).

For the making of helmets, breastplates, greaves, javelins, fetters, cult objects and implements, plates and bars for city gates, various musical instruments, farming tools with iron fittings, flails, plowshares, coulters, mattocks, saws, chariots, swords, prison bars, household utensils like pots and pans and cauldrons and forks, pens and razors (Judges 16:21; I Samuel 2:13, 14; 13:19-21; 17:5-7; II Samuel 12:31; I Kings 7; II Kings 6:5; 9:27; I Chronicles 15:19-24; Job 19:24; Psalms 105:18; 107:16; Isaiah 7:20; 28:24, 27; 45:2; Jeremiah 17:1; 50:16; Ezekiel 4:3; 5:1; Amos 1:3), various processes and tools were necessary. Thus we have references to smelting (Job 28:2), to the bellows for blowing the coals in the fire (Isaiah 54:16), and to the blacksmith who fashions heated iron into axes, and saws with his hammer (Joshua 17:15, 18; Isaiah 41:7; 44:12; Jeremiah 6:29). Hammers (Isaiah 41:7; 44:12), tools for carving and engraving (I Kings 6:29, 32-36), tongs (Isaiah 44:12), are among the implements a smith required. We can imagine how smiths readily plied their trade from place to place in order to repair farming implements and household utensils, or to supply new ones. Archaeologists have found traces of an Israelite smithy, complete with plowshares in the Palestine area. An Egyptian mural represents two smiths working the bellows. A somewhat complete picture of a smith working at his anvil is to be found in Ecclesiasticus (38:28) —

> So is the smith sitting by the anvil, and considering the unwrought iron: the vapor of the fire will waste his flesh: and in the heat of the furnace will he wrestle with his work: the noise of the hammer will be ever in his ear, and his eyes are upon the pattern of the vessel; he will set his heart upon perfecting his works, and he will be wakeful to adorn them perfectly.

The Soldier

As the Bible records many wars, we should expect frequent mention of soldiers. In fact, the first time they appear in Scripture is in connection with war (I Chronicles 7:4). With "battle" occurring about 170 times, "war" over 200 times, and "soldiers" thirty-two times, the Bible is a warlike Book. It contains many descriptions of campaigns, conquests and captives from the time when Abraham pursued the five kings down to "War in Heaven" and the manifestation of Christ as the mighty Conqueror.

Throughout the whole of the national existence of the Jews, around which the Bible revolves, there were but brief intervals when they were not either actually engaged in war or in danger of it, their most powerful enemies being the Egyptians, the Assyrians and the Romans. It was because of this constant threat of warfare that every male adult "from twenty years old and upward" (Numbers 1:3) was obliged to serve as a soldier. The tribes were formed as an army ready to take the field against an enemy when summoned to do so by the call of the trumpet or by the hoisting of a standard on some conspicuous height. Summarizing what the Bible has to say about armies, soldiers, and warfare, we trust the following aspects will prove to be instructive.

Nimrod is the first conqueror we have any knowledge of (Genesis 10: 8, 9). All war lords whose prowess has dazzled the eyes of men amid the terrible slaughter and destruction due to their ambitions, find their prototype in Nimrod, the earliest war lord of whom we have any record. The rise and fall of empires founded on brute force illustrate the dictum of our Lord that "all they that take the sword shall perish with the sword" (Matthew 26:52). Let us consider first army regulations under the law of Moses, distinguishing the following features.

1. All males fit for war had to be numbered. All of Israel formed a great body of militia, and were liable to be called into active service from twenty years old and upward to play the part assigned to them in furthering God's righteous cause (Numbers 1; 26; II Chronicles 25:5). Immaturity exempted men from serving as well as did other exemptions mentioned in Deuteronomy 20:5-8. Length of service lasted for twenty-five to thirty years (Numbers 4:23 margin; II Chronicles 25:5). Although the Levites were ordinarily exempt from material warfare (Numbers 2:33), we yet read of Levitical and priestly warriors (I Chronicles 12:26-28; 27:5, 6). Special soldiers were selected according to the necessities of any particular case (Exodus 17:9; Numbers 31:2-5; Judges 21:10; II Samuel 17:1). The whole available force could be called out if necessary (Judges 20:1, 2; I Samuel 11:7, 8).

2. The camp had to be ordered according to the tribes (Numbers 1:4) to which the men belonged — each tribe marshaled under its own standard or flag (Numbers 2:2) and serving under its own God-appointed "prince" (Numbers 2:3; Deuteronomy 20:5; 33:17; I Kings 22:11). Under the Monarchy, war became the affair of the whole nation, and so under Saul, David and Solomon we have the establishment of a standing army (I Samuel 13:2; 14:52). David had a permanent bodyguard of 600 "mighty

men" who shielded him while in exile (I Samuel 23:13; 30:9; II Samuel 10: 7; 16:6). Archers, carrying sword and buckler (I Chronicles 5:18), and slingers (II Chronicles 26:14) made up the light infantry. Chariots and horsemen were likewise prominent in battle (Judges 4:3; I Kings 4:26; 9:22; 10:26).

3. Private war was not allowed. The right and duty of calling out the troop by trumpet for war belonged to the civic ruler. In Moses' time, God was King of Israel (Deuteronomy 33:5), and His help against enemies was invoked by blowing an alarm on silver trumpets (Numbers 10:1-10; Judges 3:27; 6:34; 7:16; Joel 2:1-15). The most striking instance with reference to the leading of God can be found in the directions for military operations being communicated to Joshua by the "captain of the host of the Lord" (Joshua 5:13 - 6:5).

4. The dangerous but not sinful mission of spies (ASV "watchers") or scouts, was assigned to princes. Where the element of secrecy enters, we may call them spies. Of the twelve spies sent to search the land of Canaan and ascertain the enemy's position and strength, only two came back with a true report of the land — which minority report was rejected (Numbers 13; 14:6-10; Joshua 2:1; Judges 1:24; I Samuel 26:4; II Samuel 15:10).

5. As to war with her enemies, Israel had to distinguish between votive war (Numbers 21:1-3), vowed to the Lord on the spur of a disaster, religiously performed and accepted of Him (Numbers 21:21-35; Deuteronomy 2:3; 3; Psalm 135). See the conquest of eastern Palestine (Deuteronomy 33:20, 21). Then there was punitive war waged to avenge, not Israel, but the Lord who suffered through the seduction of His people (Numbers 25: 2; 31:3, 8, 16). So deep was the pol-

lution of foreign vices that on their return from war Israelite soldiers had to purify themselves and their clothes (Numbers 31:19-24), and metal articles taken as spoil were purified by fire.

6. Booty taken in war had to be equally divided between the soldiers and the congregation (Numbers 31: 42, 43; I Samuel 30:24). Apart from maintenance, the soldier's recompense consisted in his share of the loot. "The first mention of regular pay is in connection with the army of Simon Maccabaeus (I Maccabees 14:32). The Lord's portion of the spoil went to the priests and the Levites (Numbers 31: 41, 47). In addition to this the officers, grateful that none of their men had fallen in battle, had to bring an oblation out of what each had gotten in the way of spoil."

7. The rights of other nations to their land had to be recognized. Nations, as well as individuals have their rights. International law which power-thirsty dictators outrage, has its sanction from God's Word (Deuteronomy 2:1-22; Psalm 83:8; Acts 17:26).

8. As to the extermination of foes, Israel had to remember that punitive war was in the interests of religion and morality and that, therefore, her soldiers had to act, not as murderers, but as God-appointed executioners of divine judgment upon nations for their gross idolatry and iniquity (Genesis 15:16; Deuteronomy 7). Such cutting off of contaminated nations was a piece of divine surgery, impressive as an example to other sinners (Jude 7).

9. The nations had to be reminded that military success had its moral dangers, as well as its material gain (Deuteronomy 8:10-20; 9:1-7). Three dangers in particular are cited —

Forgetting God, and lapsing into disobedience to His precepts and rejecting the moral and spiritual truths found in His Word (Deuteronomy 8: 11).

Pride and boastfulness, as if their own arms had gotten them the victory (Deuteronomy 8:14).

Self-righteousness. The best warriors are sinners and at their best only did their duty (Deuteronomy 9:14; Proverbs 24:16; Luke 17:10).

10. Laws regulating the exercise of war had to be observed. First of all, war had to be conducted in a religious, believing, courageous spirit, with a lively remembrance of God's former mercies (Deuteronomy 20:1), which brings us to a consideration of the problem of God and war. Startling though it may seem, war in past Israelite history was deemed to be sacred — a religious duty begun and carried through under the highest sanctions of religion. Every soldier had to consecrate himself to God, and before and during hostilities had to submit himself to "the abstinences of sanctification" (Joshua 3:5; Judges 20: 26; I Samuel 21:5; II Samuel 11:11; Isaiah 13:3). Small matters making for decency and clean living were not to be forgotten (Deuteronomy 23:12, 13).

Religious ceremonies and sacrifices preceded wars and no campaign was undertaken without prayer for divine guidance and help. Prophets prayed before a campaign. Divine oracles had to be consulted before engagements (Judges 1:1; 20:8, 18, 28; I Samuel 7:9; 13:9; 14:37; 23:2; 28:6; 30:8; I Kings 22:5; II Kings 3:11; Psalm 20). God Himself is depicted as a "Man of war" and "strong and mighty in battle," Israel's enemies being His. From Psalm 144:1 we have the language, "Blessed be the Lord my strength, which teacheth my hands to war, and my fingers to fight" — "Gird thy sword upon thy thigh" (Psalm 45:3). Isaiah speaks of Him stirring up jealousy like a Man of war. From Sinai, God rushes to the fight, strikes His adversaries with terror, casts both horse and rider into the sea and causes huge stones to fall on the fugitives whom He has put to flight (Genesis 35:5; Exodus 15:1, 3, 21; 23: 27; Deuteronomy 32:41; Judges 5:4, 31; I Samuel 30:26; II Samuel 5:24; Psalm 18:14; Isaiah 31:4). The ancient song of Deborah curses those who did not come to the help of the Lord against His foes (Judges 5:23). The victorious army sang praise to God and were welcomed home with rejoicings (Exodus 15:1-22; Judges 5: 1-11). Read "The Song of the Sword" (Genesis 4:22-24), Jehoshaphat's "Alleluia Battle" (II Chronicles 20) and "Armies in Heaven" (Revelation 19).

Moses, Joshua and David fought the Lord's battles as they waged the national battles of Israel (I Samuel 18: 17; 25:28). The God of Israel's battle array (I Samuel 17:43) was at the head of His armies manifested by the pillar of cloud and fire. An ancient book since lost bears the title *The Book of the Wars of the Lord* (Numbers 21:14). The ark of the covenant indicated and secured the presence of the God of Israel in the ranks of those who fought with, and for, Him (Numbers 10:35; I Samuel 4:3, 6, 7; II Samuel 11:11). Soldiers became God's "consecrated ones" in campaigns to "consecrate war" (Isaiah 13:3, ASV; Jeremiah 6:4; Joel 3:9). Priests exhorted the people to lay aside fears of defeat, because in a just war, "the Lord goeth before them" (Deuteronomy 20:3, 4).

11. To the officers belonged the ordering of the troop, and they had to consider generously the circumstances and feelings of the males called to fight. Under no circumstances was the presence of the fainthearted considered lest their timidity and fear should prove infectious (Deuteronomy 20:5-8).

12. Regulations governing conquest and treatment of prisoners were explicit, with the exception of the Canaanites who had to be totally destroyed. Sometimes prisoners were sold into slavery. Certain fundamental principles had to be observed, namely, with the taking of a city, the conquered fighting men if not allowed to become slaves, had to be destroyed. Women and children, classified as spoil, were given up to the disposal of the conquerors who had to treat the defenseless ones in conformity with the moral law (Deuteronomy 20:10-20; 21:10-14). Delicate considerations had to be given for the sorrow, natural to married women taken captive, and protection afforded to their rights — a fine anticipation of chivalry to women which some aggressive nations have forgotten. Probably the conduct of Jewish conquerors was superior to those of surrounding nations. While, in some cases, treatment seems to be extraordinarily severe, righteous retribution must not be forgotten (Numbers 21; Judges 1: 6, 7; 7:25; 8:8-11; 9:45; 11:4-7; 21:6; I Samuel 11:2; II Samuel 8:2; I Kings 20:3; II Kings 6:20-23; 25:7; Isaiah 16:5). Every effort had to be made to relieve soldiers dying in battle (I Samuel 31:11-13). A beautiful direction is given as to fruit trees in the path of the conqueror — "Thou mayest eat of them" it is said (Deuteronomy 20: 19, 20). They had to be enjoyed not destroyed — a principle that ought to be applied to libraries, art galleries, noble buildings, as well as fruit gardens. Alas, however, warmongers have been guilty of terrible wanton destruction!

Victory in a righteous war such as Abraham waged against ungodly warrior kings should end in high acts of religious thanksgiving and offerings due to God for His aid (Judges 4; 5). There had to be devout prayer to Him for continuance of His mercies "in destroying all His and our enemies" (Judges 5:31). At the end of Deborah's Song, the historian adds a postscript telling of the happy fruits of deliverance.

"A righteous war, jealously carried on with stern determination, but not in malice, should bring in a lasting peace enjoyed in grateful obedience to the divine Giver of the victory" (See THE PRISONER, THE SLAVE.)

Coming to the New Testament, while it does not contain an account of an actual war, yet Roman soldiers are never far away with Christ and His apostles seeing a great deal of them. The term "legion" which our Lord used literally means "a gathering" and was associated with the Roman citizen army and represented a force of about 6,000 infantry, together with complements of other arms. The infantry proper were divided into ten cohorts, or bands, each containing about 600 men. A cohort itself was subdivided into six centuries, each commanded by a centurion (See THE CENTURION). Our Lord had contact with a good centurion (Matthew 8: 5-13; Luke 7:1-10), and Cornelius was the first Gentile Christian (Acts 10). The latter was a bodyguard of the governor, whose large household marks him out as a wealthy man with a superior social position. Although a soldier, Cornelius was sincerely religious, "devout" — "feared God"; ordered his household in religious ways; was very charitable "giving much alms"; looked to God Himself, praying to Him always. Yet he needed more and God gave him more through Peter. He came to know Christ, whom to know is life eternal. Legion became a proverb representing a large num-

ber of persons in orderly combination (Matthew 26:53; 27:27; Mark 5:9, 15; 15:16; Luke 8:30; John 18:3, 12; Acts 10:1; 21:31; 27:1).

Soldiers in the Roman army were seldom, if ever, Jews by birth. Roman emperors sometimes allowed non-Roman princes, whom they favored, to bear the title of "king" or "tetrarch." They could live in royal pomp, exercise certain restricted powers, and keep a small army for show or for coercive work over the natives. Romans allowed their ecclesiastical chiefs to have an armed guard of officers who could command the Jews and police the temple (John 7:32, 53; Acts 5:26). The association of John the Baptist with two classes in the service of Rome, soldiers and publicans, provides an interesting study. The mission of the Baptist was to prepare the way of the Lord, and not to overthrow the brutal and tyrannical Roman empire (Luke 1:17; 3:14, ASV). To soldiers on service to the emperor, the Baptist did not say that they were to quit such service because God had permitted Rome to be the existing power (Romans 13:11). What the Roman soldier had to do was to avoid those sins to which they were likely to succumb. For instance —

1. They must "do violence to no man" — not treat roughly any one, be he comrade, provincial, slave.

2. They must not exact, or accuse any one.

3. They had to be content with their rations and wages.

4. They must cease to do evil and learn to do good.

Our Lord, too, had intimate dealings with soldiers. Officers were sent to take Him to the high priest (John 7:32). Soldiers were present at the cross and at the resurrection (Matthew 27:26-36, 54; Luke 23:8-11, 47; John 19:1-3, 28-37). Soldiers put the crown of thorns on His brow, and then bowing the knee, mocked His claim to be a king. Soldiers reviled Him after they had nailed Him to the cross. It was a soldier who pierced His side, and soldiers gambled for the seamless garment of Christ. They committed the too common practice of soldiers — they plundered the dying (Psalm 22:18). These soldiers manifested the vices to which a wicked soldiery is prone. Soldiers guarded Christ's sepulchre, and became witnesses of His resurrection. It was well for them that they reported the opened tomb to the chief priests. A Roman commander would have put them to death for allowing Christ to escape (Acts 12:19). Our Lord's teaching on war and peace is a related subject one could pursue with profit. When questioned as to the payment of tribute to pagan Rome, He gave an answer that included soldiery as well, "Render therefore unto Caesar the things which are Caesar's; and unto God the things that are God's" (Matthew 22:15-21).

After Christ, His apostles had intimate contact with Roman soldiers. Peter, in his imprisonments, was subject to their discipline. Then the experiences which befell Paul were so ordered by the Lord not only for the furtherance of the Gospel among people generally, but among the soldiers particularly to whom the apostle was able to exhibit the grace of the Christian character and to teach the Christian message. In fact, we can look upon Paul as the first "army chaplain." The first record we have of Paul coming under military observation is described by him in a letter in which he enumerates the trials of his ministry (II Corinthians 11). The next occasion was when he was delivered from death by falling into the hands of Roman soldiers of the imperial army

stationed in Jerusalem in the castle of Anatonia (Acts 21:34; 23:23-25, 32; 24). Then there was Claudius Lysias who had a soldier's determination not to be outwitted. The two years' imprisonment, chained to soldiers, gave Paul great opportunities of winning many of them to Christ (Acts 24:27; 25; 26:29). Appealing to Nero, Paul was sent to Rome in the charge of Julius, the Roman centurion (Acts 27). The voyage to Italy, however, proved tedious and dangerous but Paul was the master of the situation and by his confidence in God, prayers and miracles was acknowledged as a true servant of God. Ultimately, Paul reached Rome and obtained the fulfillment of his desire to see it (Acts 19: 21). A prisoner in his own hired house for two years, he was always chained to a "soldier that kept him," and as the guard was changed continually, Paul's bonds in Christ were manifest throughout the whole of the praetorian guard (Philippians 1:13, ASV). Not only were the soldiers blessed through Paul, but the apostle also was the winner for his daily contact with armed soldiers provided him with those military metaphors characteristic of his writings (Ephesians 6:12-20, ASV).

The panorama of coming events found in the Book of Revelation is likewise couched in military language. The foes of God's people, the dragon, the beasts, and the false prophet (Revelation 12:1-18) are over against the rider on the White Horse, who "in righteousness doth judge and make war"; and the armies in heaven follow Him (Revelation 19), who must reign until all His enemies are under His feet.

As to strategical operations in campaigns, the tactics of the Hebrew generals were as simple as their strategy. Hostilities usually began in the Spring, and were generally prepared by secret investigation of the power and position of the enemy (Numbers 21:32; Deuteronomy 1:22; Joshua 2:7; 6:3, etc.). Sometimes a campaign would be preceded by a declaration of war or by acts of provocation, but more often war was released unexpectedly (Judges 11:12; I Samuel 11:1; II Kings 14:8). The battle "set in array" meant that the opposing forces were drawn up facing each other, and as the battle cry was raised the soldiers rushed into battle (Judges 7:18; Jeremiah 4:19; Amos 1:14). With the forces divided into three divisions, a cunning device was to pretend to flee, and by leaving a body of men in ambush, the unwary pursuers were hemmed in, front and rear (Joshua 8:15; Judges 7:16; 20:20, 36; I Samuel 11:11; II Samuel 18:27). Other strategical movements included the flank movement (II Samuel 5:22), the surprise attack (Joshua 11:7), the raid (II Chronicles 14:9), the foray (II Samuel 3:22), and the foraging to secure supplies (II Samuel 23:11). The recall of troops was sounded on the war-horn (II Samuel 2:28; 18:16; 20:22). Examples of more elaborate and cunning tactics can be seen in Joab's handling of his army before Rabbath-Ammon (II Samuel 10:9-11), and Benhadad's massing of his chariots at the battle of Ramoth-Gilead (I Kings 22:11).

As to the defensive and offensive weapons used by soldiers of antiquity, alongside of the now dreadful implements of war today they may appear simple yet were most effective when used expertly. Among the defensive weapons referred to in the Bible we have —

The Shield

Varying in form and material, Egyptian shields were usually formed of wicker-work and covered with bull's hide and were about half the soldier's height and generally double its own breadth. Shields also of metal were the ancient warrior's chief defense. To "anoint" these shields alludes to the practice of smearing the metal surface with oil, that hostile weapons might easily glance off (II Samuel 1:21; Isaiah 21:5). Several designations and applications are given of the shield (See I Samuel 17:7; II Samuel 8:7; I Kings 10:16; 14:26; II Kings 11:10; Isaiah 21:5; Ezekiel 39:9; Ephesians 6:16). Each Roman soldier had his name incribed upon his shield.

The Helmet

Head protectors or skull coverings assumed different styles in different ages. The earliest helmets were furnished with flaps, covered with metal scales to protect the ears and the back of the head. Made of brass they must have been heavy and cumbersome (I Samuel 17:38; Ephesians 6:17).

The Breastplate

Flaps of the helmet would fall over the shoulders, and then the breastplate took over to protect the body. The coat of mail consisted of a leather jerkin covered with small metal plates. Originally worn only by leading citizens (I Samuel 17:5; 31:4; I Kings 22:34), Uzziah was the first to prepare this body-protector for the whole army (II Chronicles 26:14; Romans 13:12).

The Greaves

Greaves, made of metal with a lining of leather, felt, or cloth, protected the calves and ankles. These gaiters were secured with straps (I Samuel 17:6).

The War-Shoes

Composed of leather and the sole thickly studded with large nails, shoes for the feet were pointed and turned up at the toes (Isaiah 5:27; Ephesians 6:15). The heavy, metallic armor of medieval knights is a development of body protection the Hebrews conceived.

As for the soldier's offensive weapons we have —

The Sword

Swords varied in size and shape according to nationality. Those of Egypt and Assyria were more like a dagger, and about two feet in length tapering to a fine point, and hung on the left side of the girdle (I Samuel 17:39). The soldiers "who draw the sword" had swords made of iron and sometimes were double-edged. When not in use they were sheathed (I Samuel 13:19; 17:51; Joel 3:10). This frequently mentioned weapon is described as a flashing sword (Nahum 3:3), an oppressing sword (Jeremiah 46:16), the devouring sword (II Samuel 18:8; Jeremiah 12:12), the sword which drinks its fill of blood (Isaiah 34:5, 6), the sword of the Lord executing divine judgment (Jeremiah 47:6; Ezekiel 21:9, 10).

The Spear

Between five to six feet long, the spear was made of wood, with a metal head of bronze or iron with a double edge. The head of one of these ancient spears can be seen in the British Museum. When the spear was struck in the ground it betokened the abode of the king for the time (I Samuel 17:7; 18:11; 22:6; 26:7; II Samuel 23:7; Nahum 3:3).

The Javelin

Lighter and shorter than the spear, the javelin was fashioned of wood and similarly armed with a two-edged metal head of an elongated diamond shape. This was the weapon Saul used

in his attempt to kill David. Spears and javelins are sometimes used interchangeably (I Samuel 13:22; 18:11; Joel 3:10).

The Bow and Arrow

Bows and arrows were the principal weapons of Egypt and Assyria, as they were of soldiers in later Saxon times. Made of reed, sometimes the arrows were poisoned (I Samuel 31:3; II Samuel 22:35; Job 6:4; Psalm 7:12; Isaiah 22:6; Habakkuk 3:11; Ephesians 6:16). For further reference see THE ARCHER, and THE HUNTER.

The Sling

The light infantry commonly used slings which were the favorite war-weapon of the Benjaminites who could sling equally well with either hand. Made of leather, or of a double rope, with a broad thong in the middle to receive the stone, the sling was used by shepherds to drive off beasts. The precision with which the stone could be cast, appears from David's slaughter of the giant. The sling provides a powerful figure of divine judgment (Judges 20:16; I Samuel 17:40; 25:29; II Kings 3:25; Jeremiah 10:18).

The Battle Axe

The Egyptian battle axe appears frequently on their sculpture. About two feet in length and with a single blade, soldiers on the march either held it in their hand, or had it suspended on the back, with the blade downward (Jeremiah 51:20).

The armorbearer was a chosen soldier who carried the armor — shield and other weapons — for the king or captain. All warriors had such attendants (Judges 9:54; I Samuel 14:7; 31:4; II Samuel 23:37, see THE ARMORBEARER). Among the notable soldiers and war leaders in Old Testament history, Joshua is prominent as the example of the finest soldierly virtues.

War, soldiers and their accouterments provide Biblical writers with some of their most expressive similes of spiritual truth. First and foremost, Christ is our courageous Captain (Joshua 5:13-15; 24:1-25; Hebrews 2:10) who overcame all His foes. In Joshua, as a type, we are shown what the Captain of our salvation is. He was marked —

1. By His faith and decision for God (Joshua 14:8; 24:15)
2. By His uncompromising warfare against God's enemies (10:28, 30, 37, 39, 40)
3. By His strict adherence to the guidance of God's Word (1:7, 8)

These are three virtues every Christian warrior should lay to heart (Philippians 3:16, 17). Fully armed with spiritual weapons we can go forth to conquer under our invincible Commander (II Corinthians 10:4, 5; I Thessalonians 5:8; I Timothy 6:12; II Timothy 2:3; Revelation 6:2; 17:14; 19:11-21).

We have already noticed that soldiers, going out against the enemy, were admonished to keep themselves from evil (Deuteronomy 23:9-14), the exhortation to sanctity of life being based upon the highest ground of all, "The Lord thy God walketh in the midst of thy camp . . . therefore shall thy camp be holy" (23:14). Would that these words could be written not only on the quarters of all our fighting forces, but upon our schools, places of amusement, our homes, even upon the bells of the horses (Zechariah 14:20). Because God indwells us, and walks in and with us, we must heed the command, "Touch not the unclean thing" (II Corinthians 6:17, 18).

The shield which the soldier carried hanging from his shoulders is often employed as a figure for divine protection. God speaks of Himself as the Shield and Protector of His people (Genesis 15:1; Deuteronomy 33:29; Psalm 18:2, 30, 35; 35:2; 84:11, etc.). In some references the large Greek-Roman shield is implied, and the great shield of faith is the weapon the Christian must arm himself with, and by it quench all the fiery darts (poisoned arrows) of the evil one (Psalms 5:12; 91:4; Ephesians 6:16). Princes of the people, or the chief men of Israel are sometimes called "the shields of the land" (Psalm 47:9; Hosea 4:18, ASV margin). The Prince of Life is the believer's impenetrable Shield.

The well-known helmets of Greek and Roman soldiers fashioned as they were of leather and brass provided Paul with another striking simile, namely, the helmet of salvation for the Christian soldier (Ephesians 6:17; I Thessalonians 5:8).

Body armor for the protection of soldiers in battle, "the coat of mail" Nehemiah's workers wore (4:16), as well as others (I Samuel 17:5, 38; I Kings 22:34; II Chronicles 26:14), is employed by Isaiah to illustrate the covering of divine righteousness (59:17) — a figure Paul borrowed when he wrote about the armor of light and the "breastplate of righteousness" (Romans 13:12; Ephesians 6:14).

The sword, the most frequently mentioned weapon in the Bible symbolizes the execution of divine judgment and the calamities accruing from war (Jeremiah 47:6; 50:35-37; Ezekiel 21:9, 10, 25). The Bible as a whole is the sword of the Spirit — and a sharp two-edged sword at that. If the truth does not convert, it condemns; if it does not save, it slays (Ephesians 6:17; Hebrews 4:12; Revelation 19:15).

The strong shoes of ancient warriors likewise come under Paul's notice.

Thus he used the shoe as a part of the Christian's armor as a symbol of eagerness to proclaim the Gospel of peace (Ephesians 6:15). As a prisoner and in daily contact with the armed soldiers of Rome, Paul wrote his epistle to the Ephesians and in it reminds Christians of their constant warfare with satanic foes and of the necessity of having on the whole armor of God (Ephesians 6:12-20, asv.). Writing to young Timothy, Paul urged him to endure hardness as a good soldier of Jesus Christ (II Timothy 2:2, 3).

> Am I a soldier of the Cross,
>   A follower of the Lamb,
> And shall I fear to own His cause,
>   Or blush to speak His name?
> Since I must fight if I would reign,
>   Increase my courage, Lord;
> I'll bear the toil, endure the pain,
>   Supported by Thy Word.

Returning to soldiery and war, many are troubled as to whether a Christian can be a soldier and go to war. Many Christians and non-Christians are pacifists or conscientious objectors who refuse to take measure to defend their home and nation from enemy attack. Perhaps the most enlightening study of this question is by a renowned soldier himself, General Sir William G. S. Dobbie, C.B., C.M.G., C.S.O. — the hero of Malta. His booklet, *Christianity and Military Service,* tests his position as a soldier from the Bible and reaches the conclusion that —

> The profession of arms is an honorable and lawful one, that the use of force and material weapons is not incompatible with faith in God, that God is a God of order and that in this present dispensation He has ordained that human governments shall maintain order by force; that the time is not yet, though it will surely come when "the government will be on His shoulder," and mankind will "then be able to beat his sword into a plough-share."

The gospels make it clear that Jesus accepted war as an inevitable aspect of the present sinful order, but warned that those who take the sword must perish by it (Matthew 24:6; 26:52).

The Soothsayer

Soothsayer is from an old Anglo-Saxon word meaning, "sayer of the truth." As a class, however, soothsayers were not always truthful in their sayings. One Hebrew word for soothsayer implies "to observe the clouds" (Isaiah 2:6; Micah 5:12), and soothsayers pretended to foretell future events by the motion of the clouds, the position of the planets, the flight of birds, or magical arts (Daniel 2:6, 27; 5:7-11). Such a method of forecasting the future was futile for a knowledge of the future does not lie within the scope of man. There were those soothsayers who professed ability to interpret dreams (Daniel 4:7), reveal secrets (Daniel 2:27), and to unravel the mysteries of numbers. The term Luke uses for soothsaying (Acts 16:16), while it implies the practice of divination, is allied to another word meaning "to rave," and expresses the fury displayed by those who were demon-possessed as they delivered their oracular messages. Balaam is the only named soothsayer in the Bible (Joshua 13:22). All aspects of soothsaying or divination were forbidden under the Mosaic Law (Deuteronomy 18:9-15). See more fully The Astrologer, The Diviner, The Magician, The Necromancer, The Prognosticator, The Sorcerer.

The Sorcerer

Allied to the forbidden occupation just considered the cameos mentioned should also be consulted for further information on sorcery, seeing that magicians, enchanters and sorcerers are linked together (Daniel 2:2). One interpretation of sorcerer is "one who mutters incantations or magic formulae" (Isaiah 47:9-12), or one who speaks in ventriloquial whispers, as if under the influence of the spirits of the dead. These wizards practicing witchcraft were the equivalent of mediums, or consulters of the dead in spiritualism, and were regarded as an evil influence in Israel (Isaiah 47:9). Modern Spiritualism is an evident sign of these last days (Isaiah 8:19, 20; I Timothy 4:1). Sorcerers are especially mentioned as abounding with lying wonders and are to be judged and punished when Christ returns (Malachi 3:5; II Thessalonians 2:9-11; Revelation 21:8; 22:15, see I Samuel 15: 23; 18:3-20).

Another word used for sorcerer is *pharmakos* from which we have "pharmacy." The root meaning of this particular term is one devoted to magical arts, employed mixing potions, or drugs for magical purposes (Revelation 21:8; 22:15). Vine remarks —

> In sorcery, the use of drugs, whether simple or potent, was generally accompanied by incantations and appeals to occult powers, with the provision of various charms, amulets, etc., professedly designed to keep the applicant or patient from the attention and power of demons, but actually to impress the applicant with the mysterious resources and powers of the sorcerers.

Simon Magnus was renowned for the magic aspect of sorcery (Acts 8:9-11). Elymas was another pretender to magic powers, a professor of the arts of witchcraft (Acts 13:6-11). Although the practice of all forms of sorcery was widespread in Bible times, it is strongly and frequently denounced (Exodus 22:18; Deuteronomy 18:10; II Kings 21:6; II Chronicles 33:6; Isaiah 8:19, 20; Jeremiah 27:9; Galatians 5:20; Revelation 9:21; 21:8).

The Steward

In his *Dictionary of Words,* Joseph T. Shipley informs us that originally the English word "steward" meant styward, that is, the ward or keeper of pigs. As it appears in the Bible "steward" has varied meanings. As used of Eliezer, Abraham's steward, it implies "possessor." The American Revised Version expresses it, "he that shall be possessor" (Genesis 15:2). Here "steward" implies a son of requisition, hence "heir." Eliezer had charge of the persons in Abraham's household, as well as the oversight of his master's possessions. Every household of distinction or of sufficient wealth had a steward taking charge of food, raiment, money and property (I Chronicles 27:25). The word for David's stewards (I Chronicles 28:1) is given as "rulers" in the margin, just as the margin gives "steward" for ruler in John 2:9. In connection with Shebna referred to as treasurer, the margin gives us "steward" (Isaiah 22: 15). Shebna was a high official in charge of the city's funds and was responsible for their administration for the city's benefit. Joseph became a steward over Potiphar's household and in turn had a steward over his own house (Genesis 39:4, 5; 44:4).

In the New Testament, stewardship is prominent. Chuza was Herod's steward who possibly had charge of the king's children, received all the cash, kept regular accounts, and gave to all in the household their due. Erastus the chamberlain, can be translated the treasurer or steward (Romans 16:23). Some of our Lord's parables are taken up with stewardship.

In the parable of the vineyard, the steward is the one who paid the laborers at the close of the day (Matthew 20:8). In the parable of the unjust steward, dishonest stewardship was punished (Luke 16:1-13). In other parables, like the pounds, the talents, the wicked husbandman, similar truths are taught. Christ's disciples must act as stewards during His absence. As those following the occupation as stewards had to attend to receipts and expenditures, and portion out to each member of the household what they should have, so Christ has left us in charge of His Gospel and we are to use our gifts to the best advantage in the furtherance of that Gospel until He returns.

In the epistles, stewardship is largely confined to the proclamation of the Word. Dispensation is given in the ASV margin as "stewardship" (Ephesians 3:2; Colossians 1:25; I Timothy 1:4). As stewards of the mysteries of God, we must take scrupulous care of all He has entrusted us with (I Corinthians 4:1). As stewards we must act wisely and diligently in all our affairs — and His. A bishop or overseer is God's steward (Acts 20:28; Titus 1:7). Preachers, teachers and Christians generally must, by the Spirit, function as good stewards of the manifold grace of God (I Peter 4:10). See THE CHAMBERLAIN and THE HOUSEHOLDER. For a full study of our Lord's stewardship parables see the author's volume, *All the Parables of the Bible*.

The Stonesquarer

Although there is only one reference to this particular occupation (I Kings 5:18), the evidence of it is apparent in the magnificent buildings mentioned in the Bible. The same Hebrew word for "stonesquarer" is translated "Giblite," an inhabitant of Gebal, Phoenicia (Joshua 13:5; Ezekiel 27:9). It would seem as if the Giblites were experts in this branch of industry. Masonry, as we have already indicated (see THE MASON) was a regular trade (II Samuel 5:11) and stone hewing is often spoken of (I Kings 5: 17, 18; II Kings 12:12, etc.). A remarkable feature of the building of Solomon's temple was that all its huge stones were made ready in the quarry so that there was "neither hammer nor axe nor any tool of iron heard in the house, while it was in building" (I Kings 6:7, ASV). The massive stones of the modern Coventry Cathedral were all squared, prepared and numbered beforehand and then simply fitted together according to their numbers. No wonder God's servants took pleasure in the stones of the temple (Psalm 102:19), and the disciples evinced the same pride and joy over a later temple adorned with goodly stones (Matthew 24:1-3).

Israel's gorgeous temple perished long ago. The world's most enduring wonder is the Great Pyramid, which although "rifled, desecrated, stripped to its core, remains a monument to men's skill and longing for immortality." The facts of this colossal tomb are well-known. It covers almost thirteen acres of desert sand and rises as high as a modern forty-story building, and is built of stones ranging in weight from about two and a half to fifteen tons. Leonard Cottrell, the famous Egyptologist says, "There are nearly 2.5 million such blocks in the Great Pyramid, yet the men who quarried them and raised them into position had no mechanical aids except the lever, the roller and the inclined plane. These ancient architects had no fine measuring instruments, yet the corners of the Pyramids are almost perfect right angles and the sides face the four main points of the compass with astonishing precision. The blocks of limestone sheats, a few fragments of which remain at the base of the Pyramid, were so accurately cut and fitted that a cigarette paper could hardly be passed between them . . . The quarrymen used 'pounders' of dolerite, harder than granite, to cut the blocks roughly. At the site of the Pyramid masons trimmed them accurately to their final shape, using abrasives to obtain a high polish."

No wonder the traveler stands in awe at this monumental structure it took over thirty years to erect. The same can be said of The Sphinx, and many ancient temples with their remarkable figures still clear and distinct after centuries of exposure. How they testify to the expert craftmanship of those workers in stone who had little else than hammers (I Kings 6: 7; Jeremiah 23:29), saws (Isaiah 10: 15), and with a rule to cut and dress stones for building purposes (I Chronicles 22:15)!

Surpassing all superbly cut and squared stones, however, will be the Lord Jesus Christ, who, as the Stone cut out of the mountains without hands will break in pieces the final world-empire (Daniel 2:34, 35, 45). Although He came the first time in His perfection as the Stone, the builders rejected Him as such (Psalm 118: 22; Matthew 21:42), but this same Stone is to grind rejectors to pieces (Matthew 21:44, 45). For expensive, ornate structures, builders were at great pains to select stones of enormous size, such as those the disciples were perfectly justified in admiring composing the temple Jesus had just forsaken (Mark 13:1). But none can ever compare in symmetry, beauty and manificence to Him who is the chief Cornerstone (I Peter 2:6, 7), nor to the adornment of the foundations of the wall of the spiritual and heavenly Jerusalem (Revelation 21:19).

Through grace, all who are the Lord's should be as cornerstones, prepared and polished like those of a palace (Psalm 144:12). Peter's other name *Cephas* means a stone (John 1: 42) but what a man of rough, uncut stone he was. But the great Stonesquarer shaped and prepared Peter until he came to write of the saints as "living stones" like the living Stone Himself, built up into a spiritual house (I Peter 2:4, 5, see Ephesians 2:20-22), and built upon the Stone Himself (I Corinthians 3:11).

The Swimmer

In our time swimming and diving have become a specialized, competitive art, with schools and clubs teaching children how to swim. Surprisingly enough we read of swimmers in the Bible. Apart from the reference about the iron that swam (II Kings 6:6), and the psalmist's expressive illustration about swimming in tears (Psalm 6:6), the first mention of swimming as an art is the application of swimming to divine judgment. Orientals of ancient times swam in the manner the majority do today, namely, hand over hand. Assyrian tablets and sculptures represent swimming in this fashion, and the prophet, with this familiar stroke in mind says, "He shall spread forth his hands in the midst of them (the foes), as he that swimmeth spreadeth forth . . . to swim" (Isaiah 25:11) — the swimmer beating down with his hands, that is, bringing down each forcibly. The word Luke uses of swimmers (Acts 27:42, 43) implies to plunge or dive into the sea. Those who swam must have been good swimmers to reach land. The non-swimmers had to do the best they could on boards and broken pieces of the ship (Acts 27:44).

The other reference to swimming is likewise capable of expressing a deep spiritual truth. "Waters to swim in" (Ezekiel 47:5). The prophet's parabolic narrative (47:1-6), is full of profitable teaching on "The Fruitfulness of the Spirit-filled Life." How fascinating is the rapid augmentation of a petty stream into a mighty river as the result of a self-supply from the sacred, miraculous source in the Temple. In numerous passages, water is used as a symbol of the Spirit (John 7:37-39, etc.). First, there was the trickle (Ezekiel 47:2). Oozing forth, the water was hardly perceptible, but as it flowed it gathered volume until the water came to the ankles, then the knees, next the loins and ultimately, about a mile from its source, the trickle had become a torrent, "the waters were risen, waters to swim in." Has ours been a spiritually-progressive life, and are we now abandoned to the tide of the Spirit? "Ye living waters rise within me evermore." Like swimmers, are we out in the deep, allowing the waters to bear us along? The prophet asked a pertinent question, "Son of man, hast thou seen this?" (47:6). Are we experiencing what it is to swim the life-giving waters, and to be carried along irresistibly and joyfully by the Spirit? Have we left the shore line, and are we now out in the deep? If so, everything will live whither the river flows. Is this not the life more abundant Jesus offers His own (John 10:10)?

The Tanner

First among the workers in leather is the "tanner" who prepared the leather from the skins of domestic and other animals required for shields, helmets, shoes, girdles and other articles of leather such as skin-bottles for water, wine and milk (Exodus 25:5). Leathern girdles are mentioned (II Kings 1:8; Matthew 3:4), as are the bottles (Joshua 9:4, 13; Hosea 7:5; Matthew 9:17; Mark 2:22; Luke 5:37). Leather was extensively used among the Egyptians who understood the art of making stamped leather. Illustrations from ancient monuments and sculptures prove that methods were known of making leather into sandals, trimmings for chariots, covering for chairs, decorations for harps. On the tomb at Thebes is a drawing of one man immersing raw hide in a vase containing red dye, and of another man twisting strips of leather into ropes and shoes. Although the manufacture of leather as a mechanical art was practiced by the Egyptians at the time of the Exodus, the tanner is not mentioned in the Old Testament, even though the Israelites depended on his trade for many necessary articles. The phrase "rams' skins dyed red" (Exodus 25:5), proves the art of the tanner.

Possibly it was because the Jews looked upon tanning as an undesirable occupation because dead animals were regarded as unclean and because of its unclean accompaniments such as unpleasant odors and unattractive sights that they looked upon it with much disfavor. Like the fuller and the dyer (which see) the tanner was obliged to pursue his calling outside the town, which explains the threefold reference to Simon the Tanner (Acts 9:43; 10:6, 32), whose tannery was by the seaside. The tanneries of Joppa are now on the shore, south of the city. Tanner itself is from a word meaning "a hide." As to the method employed in tanning, the hair of the skins was removed by a paste of slaked lime, applied to the skins after they had been soaked for some time in water. Once dried, the softened skins were blackened on one side by rubbing on a solution made by boiling vinegar with old nails or pieces of copper, and by giving a dressing of olive oil. Curing processes in modern tanneries are more scientific.

The Taskmaster

This was a heartless occupation dreaded by the Israelites in their periods of captivity. The word itself means, "chief of the burden," "driver," "oppressor," "raiser of taxes" (Exodus 1:11; 3:7; 5:6, 10, 13, 14) and indicates "a class of men appointed by Pharaoh for the purpose of oppressing the Israelites and subduing their spirits and reducing their number lest they seek complete independence or organize a rebellion against the government." John Milton applied the designation to God. Reaching the age of twenty-three, he wrote that he wanted to live "as ever in my great Taskmaster's eye."

The Teacher

Teachers and teaching are frequently mentioned in Scripture. In the days of the apostles there were teachers good and bad (Titus 2:3; II Peter 2:1). By linking "pastors and teachers" together Paul implied that overseers of a flock must not only evangelize but educate. Once saved, converts must be instructed (Ephesians 4:11). Paul speaks of himself as "a teacher of the Gentiles" (I Timothy 2:7). Teaching was an important phase of the work of the early church (Acts 2:42; 4:1, 2; 5:21, 28). Along with Paul, Barnabas exercised a teaching ministry (Acts 11:26). The title of teacher is ascribed to many who filled the office of instruction and who had the ability and fitness teaching required (Romans 2:20; Hebrews 5:12).

1. To Jewish teachers in general (John 1:38).
2. To John the Baptist (Luke 3:12).
3. To Christ — used by Himself, applied by others (Matthew 23:8; John 3:2; 8:4, etc. "One is your Teacher" (Luke 3:12).
4. To expositors of the truth in the churches (Acts 13:1; Romans 12:7; I Corinthians 12:28, 29; Ephesians 4:1). "They that be wise (margin — *the teachers*) shall shine as the brightness of the firmament" (Daniel 12:3).
5. To Paul (I Timothy 2:7; II Timothy 1:11).
6. To both good and bad instructors (II Timothy 4:3; Titus 2:3; II Peter 2:1). "Itching ears" implies an eagerness to hear anything tickling the fancy.
7. To all the apostles (Matthew 28:19; Mark 16:15; Ephesians 4:1).

Teaching was fundamentally related to the creation of a missionary atmosphere (Acts 13:1), and religious instruction was deemed necessary to the development of Christian character and the highest efficiency in service (I Corinthians 12:4-11, 28, 29; Ephesians 4:11, 12). Pastors are to *teach* as well as *preach*. In his pastoral epistles, Paul emphasizes the necessity of the pastor-teacher being orthodox himself if he is to preach sound doctrine convincingly (Titus 1:9). He must also study the truth and be well informed regarding it (I Timothy 4:13, 15); have tactfulness as well as ability (I Timothy 3:2; II Timothy 2:2); practice the truth he teaches others (I Timothy 4:16; II Timothy 2:2). Daniel Defoe, writing on the influence of his tutor, Dr. S. Annesley said — "We loved the doctrine for the teacher's sake."

8. God Himself is magnified as the

220

Teacher, teaching us to profit. "Who teacheth like Him?" (Job 36:22, see 21:22). There is a Gaelic saying to the effect, "When God teaches not, man cannot." An ancient Greek saying has it, "Time is the great teacher."

Teachers imply a school, but school occurs only once in the Bible and is then used of the lecture-hall in which Tyrannus the Greek teacher instructed his pupils (Acts 19:9). Byron H. De Ment in his illuminating article on Teacher and Teaching in *The International Standard Bible Encyclopaedia* reminds us that the Bible employs a rich variety of words to describe the teaching process and that these words do not so much indicate an office and an official as a function and a service, although both ideas are often expressed or implied. The reader is directed to the full exposition of the leading educational terms as given by Dr. De Ment. These can also be studied with great profit by secular educationalists. (See THE SCHOOLMASTER and THE SCRIBE).

The Templekeeper

The Bible explains how a non-Israelitish class became sanctuary servants. After the conquest of Midian, Moses took sons of the Midianites and associated them with the Levites to keep the charge of the tabernacle of Jehovah (Numbers 31:30, 47). Similarly, when Joshua discovered the deception of the Gibeonites, he made them servants of the altar of Jehovah (Joshua 9:27). Later on, however, Ezekiel severely denounced the employment of uncircumcised foreigners to take charge of God's house (Ezekiel 44:7). The prophet directed that these should be displaced by those Levites "who had been degraded from priestly privileges for participating in idolatrous worship. They were

not fit to assist in the offering of sacrifice. This deposed class now given menial service had their own special quarters in the temple (Ezekiel 40:10-15, 44). Among the Nethinim meaning, "given ones" were the captives given for the Lord's service (Numbers 8:19; 31; Ezra 2:43-58; 8:20).

In the informative volume, *Archaeology and the New Testament,* Dr. Merrill F. Unger has this observation — "When the town clerk called the city of Ephesus the temple-keeper *(neokoros)* of Diana (Acts 19:35), he was employing a term widely used of individuals. An inscription from Priene in Asia Minor refers to a man who was 'templekeeper' (temple official) of Artemis in Ephesus. A later papyrus mentions a man who was 'temple-keeper of the great Serapis' (a famous Egyptian deity). Josephus refers to the Israelites as 'temple-keeper' (guardian) of the shrine of their God *(Wars of the Jews V, 9, 4).* This reference to a people as guardian of a temple is identical to the use by Luke where the people of Ephesus are called 'temple-keeper of the great goddess Diana,' as well as to various inscriptions where the city is spoken of as 'temple-keeper of the divine emperor.'" The psalmist confessed that he preferred to be a doorkeeper in the house of his God than to dwell in the tents of wickedness (Psalm 84:10).

The Tentmaker

The first nomadic tent dweller and originator or maker of tents for people to dwell in was Jabin, the sixth generation after Cain (Genesis 4:20; 9:27). As the patriarchs were tent dwellers they became skilled in the art of tentmaking, fashioning tents from hair, wool or skins. Noah, Abraham and Deborah, and the Israelites as a whole were originally tent dwellers

(Genesis 9:27; 28:4; Numbers 24:5; Judges 4:5; I Kings 12:16; Psalm 120: 5). Sometimes the word tent refers to a habitation generally (Genesis 9: 27; I Kings 8:66; Psalm 84:10). While in Egypt, Israel was weaned from movable dwelling places such as tents, and found fixed homes in Canaan, although some of the pastoral tribes retained their tent life (Joshua 22:8). After tents were abandoned for houses, worshiping in tents continued (II Samuel 7:1-6; II Chronicles 1:3, 4). Then, as now, military tents were indispensable. The phrase, "To your tents, O Israel," remained as a reminder of the nation's former nomad state when the people were no longer so (I Kings 12:16).

When tent-dwelling people, the Israelites had tents adapted to the size of the household. Those of the better kind were oblong and divided by a curtain into an outer apartment for males, and an inner one for females. The wives of the patriarch had separate tents. Jacob was rich enough to provide separate tents for his two wives and their maids (Genesis 24: 67; 25:27; 31:33). The making, pitching and striking of tents was looked upon as a woman's work, and women became expert in all phases of tent equipment. Both Priscilla and Aquila were tentmakers (Acts 18:3). The adjective "making" is from *piveo* from which we have "poem."

As for the tents themselves, those of antiquity were of the same material and same pattern. While the Bible gives us no clue as to the shape of the tents Israel used, the covering itself was made of black goat's long hair and could thus stand out in contrast against the lighter colors of the desert soil (Song of Solomon 1:5). Crude looms for weaving cloth were in use from ancient times (Exodus 35:25; Leviticus 13:48; Job 10:11; Psalm 139:

13, ASV, margin; Proverbs 31:19; Isaiah 19:9; 38:12; John 19:23). The strips of native goats'-hair cloth were sewn together and known as curtains (Song of Solomon 1:5; Jeremiah 4:20), and were held up by nine poles arranged in three rows of three, kept in position by tent-cord attached to the stakes or tent-pins driven into the ground (Song of Solomon 1:5; 4:1; Isaiah 54:2; Jeremiah 10:20). The corners of the matting where two ends met were turned back to make the door of the tent. The tents had to be erected in orderly array (Numbers 24:5, 6). At danger signals the people gathered together grouped in horseshoe formation, becoming a village of tents (Psalm 69: 25). Nails and mallets were used in connection with tent-pitching (Judges 4:21; Ezra 9:8). Tent mats were made of hair or wool (Judges 4:18). Hooks were fixed on the poles to hang articles on (Isaiah 22:23, 24).

Paul followed the craft of tentmaking and labored for a while with Priscilla and Aquila who by occupation were tentmakers. As a necessary part of their education, all Jewish boys were taught a trade.

We are accustomed to think of Paul as the eloquent scribe, the brilliant controversialist, the "apostle extraordinary," but brought up at the feet of Gamaliel, he must have heard him say: "He that has a craft in his hands, unto what is he like? He is like a vineyard that is fenced." Thus Paul, renowned as preacher, scholar, writer, had a trade to which he could fall back upon for support when he found himself in want. Tentmaking was one of the most laborious of tasks in the apostle's day, but of this we are confident, he knew his trade, and made the best tents available when he was not otherwise engaged in preaching and writing epistles. Even the greatest rabbis maintained themselves by a trade. Says Rabbi Jehuida, "He who does not teach his son a trade is much the same as if he taught him to be a thief." It is quite probable that Paul learned his craft as a lad from his father, just as Christ learned carpentry from His foster-father, Joseph. When we read of Paul's own hands ministering unto his immediate needs it means that when other means of support failed he returned to his tent-making, as, for example, when he abode with Priscilla and Aquila.

Tents are used figuratively throughout the Bible. The tent, or tabernacle, of David was used metaphorically of his people (Acts 15:16). The heavens are compared to a tent spread out (Isaiah 40:22). The tent represents the increase in numbers and prosperity of God's people (Isaiah 33:20; 54:2). Jesus used the word tent for the dwelling place of souls in eternity (Luke 16:9), and John employs the same figure for the future dwelling place of God (Revelation 21:3). Paul speaks of the tent or tabernacle of the soul and uses the same figure as a touching emblem of the transitoriness of life. The quickness and ease with which tents could be struck, leaving the dwellers without covering in a lonely desert supplied Paul with the expressive image of the speedy dissolution of one mortal body, and of the possibility of a more permanent abode (II Corinthians 5:1-4). James Montgomery has a similar thought in one of his hymns, where he says — "Yet nightly pitch my moving tent a day's march nearer home."

Longfellow, too, has the lines —

The cares that infest the day
Shall fold their tents like the Arabs,
And silently steal away.

Going to one's tent meant going home (Judges 19:9).

Hezekiah in his sickness speaks of life as being carried away as easily as a shepherd's tent. The removal of a tent is rapidly effected; all traces of its site quickly disappear and "the place thereof knoweth it no more." How apt an emblem of the fleeting and insecure nature of man's life, as Hezekiah appropriately confesses, "Mine age is departed, and is removed from me as a shepherd's tent" (Isaiah 38:12). Isaiah employs the absence of tents to typify utter desolation. "Neither shall the Arabian pitch tent there" (Isaiah 13:20). Tents are also symbolic of war (Jeremiah 6:3), and of the destruction of households as applied to Judah (Jeremiah 10:20). The various words for tent are translated as "booth," "tabernacle," "dwelling" (Numbers 25:8; II Samuel 11:11). One word means "to be conspicuous from a distance," implying that in a flat desert, tents are easily seen, and just as easily missed.

It is interesting to observe that in ancient times a special tent was pitched for a newly-wedded pair (Psalm 19:5; Joel 2:16) see II Samuel 16:22), and that this is still the custom around the Arabs. Further, the canopy under which Jewish couples wed in our times retains the name, seeing it is a survival of the ancient *chuppah* or bridal tent.

The Tetrarch

This title applied by courtesy, not by right, means "chief," or "ruler of a fourth part," that is, the fourth part of a region within the Roman Empire. It always implies a distinct and specific title, and in Bible times meant petty rulers in the empire. As time went by it lost its strict etymological force and came to be used of a petty prince, or ruler of a district. A tetrarch has the power, but not the crown or title of king (Mark 6:14, 22, 25, 26; Luke

3:19). While, however, he was a princeling inferior to a king or emperor, he yet enjoyed certain royal privileges. The Greeks were the first to use the term. A district ruled over by a tetrarch was known as a "tetrarchy" or kingdom.

Herod the Tetrarch, was Herod Antipas, son of Herod the Great, who governed Galilee and Peraea (Matthew 14:1; Luke 2:1, 19; Acts 13:11). Two other tetrarchs were mentioned, namely Herod Philip, brother of Antipas who ruled over the Ituraian and Trachonitic territory (Matthew 14:1; Luke 3:1). Antipas and Herod each inherited a fourth part of his father's dominion. Then there was Lysanias, of whom little is known, who was tetrarch of Asilene (Acts 13:1). Caligula annexed the three tetrarchies to the kingdom of Herod Agrippa whom he honored with the title of "king" (Acts 12:1).

The Thief

In these affluent times when thieving has become a most successful occupation, and clever crooks, like parasites, are living off what they rob others of, the Bible reminds us that thieves and robbers are almost as old as the human race. The Mosaic Law had severe punishments for thieves (Exodus 22:2, 7; Deuteronomy 24:7). Compare the material to be found under THE ROBBER.

The Town Clerk

When dealing with THE CLERK (which see), for material on THE TOWN CLERK, we pointed out that the Greek word implying a writer or scribe (See also THE SCRIBE) is the word from which we have "grammar."

The Trader

Trading (Ezekiel 27:12-17; Matthew 25:16; Revelation 18:17), and trafficking or hawking (Isaiah 23:8; Ezekiel 17:4), imply traders in various commodities. Trade products of Palestine and surrounding countries were numerous — grain, oil, wine, wool, flax, wood, spices and slaves, and were distributed through traders who were familiar figures in Palestine (Genesis 37:25, 28; I Kings 10:15; Nehemiah 13:16; Isaiah 2:6; Zephaniah 1:11, etc.). Now, as then, middlemen abounded. The words used for merchants are such as signify primarily "traveler," "trader," "trafficker" (I Kings 10:15 ASV.). Evidently the Canaanites excelled in this connection, so much so that "the land of Canaan" is given as "the land of traffic or trade" (Ezekiel 17:4; Zephaniah 1:11), and Canaanite and merchant or trader were convertible terms (See THE CHAPMAN and THE MERCHANT. There may be an allusion to the cumbersome process of bargaining in Solomon's expressive lines (Proverbs 20:14). For a full and exhaustive treatment of Trade and Travel the reader is referred to the illuminating study under this caption in *The Zondervan Pictorial Bible Dictionary*.

The Treader

Treaders were associated not only with vineyards (Nehemiah 13:15; Isaiah 16:10; Amos 9:13) but also with potteries (Isaiah 41:25). The potter softened the clay by means of his feet. As for treading the winepress perhaps no effectual substitute has been found for the human foot as the means of extracting the juice of the grape without crushing the seeds or "stones." "The treading of winepresses" goes back to ancient times (Nehemiah 13: 15). The famous reference in Isaiah's vision is well-known, "him that treadeth in the winefat. I have trod the winepress alone" (Isaiah 63:1-3). The grapes were brought for the vineyards in baskets, and either spread out for a few days in order to increase the amount of sugar and diminish the amount of water in the grapes, or thrown immediately into the press-vat where they were thoroughly trodden with the bare feet with the trodden wine flowing into a lower trough or gutter and channeled into a lower winevat (Jeremiah 48:33). From this the wine was taken and placed in jars (Haggai 2:16) or into new goatskin bags (Matthew 9:17).

As the treaders trampled on the grapes to the rhythm of songs and shouts, the crushing of grapes appeared to be a pleasurable occupation (Judges 9:27; Isaiah 16:10; Jeremiah 25:30; 48:33). "To tread down" symbolizes to overcome, to bring unto subjection (Psalms 60:12; 108:13). God's people are more than conquerors. Power is theirs to tread down their enemies (Joshua 1:3; Psalm 91:13; Luke 10:19). God Himself is a Treader, crushing His foes beneath His feet (Psalm 119:118; Isaiah 22:5). His day of "treading down" will be terrible (Isaiah 22:5; Revelation 19:15). It will be the day of His fierce wrath. Is it not better to sit at His feet and learn of Him, than to be crushed of those feet of brass in judgment?

The Treasurer

The word used of this occupation is represented by different original terms (Nehemiah 13:13; Ezra 1:8; 7:21; Isaiah 22:15; Daniel 3:2, 3). The Ethiopian eunuch who had charge of all the treasure of Queen Candace was her treasurer or "chamberlain" (See Romans 16:23, ASV. See also THE CHAMBERLAIN). From the above Old Testament references we gather that a treasurer was an important official in Eastern courts, having charge of the receipts and disbursements of public funds, "Treasurers over the treasuries" (Nehemiah 13:13). As a title, treasurer was considered superior to all others and was sometimes filled by the heir to the throne (II Chronicles 26:21). Daniel names treasurers along with judges and counsellors as recognized government officials. Isaiah's use of the term may suggest the idea of a "steward" (See THE STEWARD). The wealth contained in many treasuries must have been considerable (Joshua 6:19, 24).

The Trucebreakers

In an ancient record written, it would seem, for modern times, Paul lists characteristic features of the last days. Among those described are trucebreakers, of whom we have many in the last quarter of a century who came to treat solemn treaties as mere scraps of paper. The word the apostle uses here means "implacable," or not to be appeased, "irreconcilable." Literally, a trucebreaker is one "without a libation." As a libation or offering always accompanied the making of a treaty in Greek lands, the lack of a libation implied that no treaty had been made, or, by a natural extension of the meaning, could be made. In his *Expository Dictionary of New Testament Words* — an indispensable book for any Bible student — W. E. Vine says that "Paul's term means 'without a truce,' as a libation accompanied the making of treaties and compacts; then, one who can be persuaded to enter into a covenant. Some mms. have this word in Romans 1:31." Then Vine goes on to compare trucebreaking with covenant breaking noting the distinctions. Trench observes between *asunthetos*, meaning covenant breaking, faithless, the presumption of a state of peace interrupted by the unrighteous (Ezra 9:2, 4; 10:6; Psalm 73:15; Jeremiah 3:8, 11), and *aspondos,* the word Paul employs (II Timothy 3:3), which is derived from *sponde,* a sacrificial libation accompanying treaty-making. With the negative prefix *a,* the word implies "without a treaty or covenant," and denotes a person who cannot be persuaded to enter into a covenant. Dictators ruthlessly destroy covenants and pacts. "When they shall say, Peace and safety; then sudden destruction cometh upon them . . . they shall not escape" (I Thessalonians 5:1-4).

The Tutor

In modern English the word Paul uses for tutor represents a private instructor or guardian or trainer of boys. "Schoolmaster" and "tutor" appear as synonymous terms (Galatians 3:24, 25; 4:2, asv gives "guardian" for "tutor." For fuller·treatment compare material given under THE INSTRUCTOR, THE SCHOOLMASTER, THE TEACHER).

The Undertaker

In modern parlance, the occupation implied is a most necessary yet unpleasant one. Those who bury the dead are known as undertakers. Moses is the only man in the Bible to have had God as his Undertaker, "And God buried him in a valley . . . but no man knoweth of his sepulchre" (Deuteronomy 34:6). The two Old Testament saints who cheated the undertaker were Enoch and Elijah, both of whom were raptured without tasting death; and such will be the privilege of those who are living when Jesus returns (I Thessalonians 4:16, 17).

While the contrasts and comparisons between the burial customs of ancient Israel and those of surrounding nations forms an interesting study, and can be pursued in the material found under "Burial" in *The International Standard Bible Encyclopaedia,* it is with Israel that we are presently concerned. In the East, the dead were — and still are — buried somewhat hastily. Joseph of Arimathaea begged the body of Jesus for burial on the day of His death (Matthew 27:57, 58). One authority on ancient burial customs commenting on burials in Syria taking place not later than ten hours after death says, "The rapidity of decomposition, the excessive violence of grief, the reluctance of Orientals to allow the dead to remain long in the houses of the living, explain what seems to us the indecency of haste."

In most far-off days there were no funeral parlors or homes, or mortuaries such as have developed in our modern society. Although much is said in Scripture regarding preparations for burial, like washing the body and anointing it with aromatic ointments, and wrapping it with sheets, it would seem as if all other last rites were also undertaken by relatives and friends of the deceased. We have no evidence of hired people to prepare bodies for burial such as undertakers are responsible for today. The young men who wrapped Ananias up and carried him out and buried him were likely those who were friends of the deceased. From Acts 5:6 and 8:2 it would seem as if a group of young men made themselves responsible to care for the properties and preparations on behalf of the dead, as such last ministries usually devolved upon living friends (Mark 16:1; Luke 24:1; John 19:39, 40). There were, of course, professional embalmers (Genesis 50:2, 26). Embalming, however, was not the general practice among the Israelites (See THE EMBALMER). Then there were professional mourners hired to shriek and lament (Ecclesiastes 12:5; Jeremiah 9:17, 18; Amos 5:16). As for the act of burial itself, which undertakers or mortuaries care for today, Ezekiel seems to have an allusion to a class of buriers. "Set up a sign by it, till the buriers have buried it" (39:15), which implies that when exposed human remains were found some kind of a mark had to be displayed in order to attract the attention of the buriers who followed the searchers.

The Usurer

In his *Two Races of Men*, Charles Lamb wrote, "The human species, according to the best theory I can form of it, is composed of two distinct races, *the men who borrow*, and *the men who lend*." The French writer, Rabelais said, "Nature has only created man to lend and to borrow." Well, both lending and borrowing find space in God's most wonderful Word. Did He not say of Israel, "Thou shalt lend unto many nations, but thou shalt not borrow" (Deuteronomy 15:6; 28:12)?

Reference is made to the usurer (Exodus 22:25), who was one who loaned his money with or without usury or interest. The Mosaic Law governing interest on loans is very humane. A well-to-do Jew had to lend to his poorer brother without interest (Exodus 22:25; Leviticus 25:35-38; Deuteronomy 23:19, 20; Isaiah 24:2). While interest could be exacted from a foreigner, a Jew was commanded to help his needy brother without making a gain of his property (Psalm 15:5; Proverbs 28:8; Jeremiah 15:10; Ezekiel 18:8, 17). Nehemiah forced the people after their return from exile to return exactions on loans at the rate of one per cent monthly on what they took from their brethren

(Nehemiah 5:10): Among the many crimes of Jerusalem, the breaking of the law in respect to usury was bemoaned by Ezekiel (22:12). Christian sentiment still condemns interest charged on charitable loans. A good citizen of Zion then, was one who put not out his money, among poorer brethren to usury. To do so meant disaster (Psalm 15:5; Proverbs 28:8).

While in ancient Israel commercial loans were practically unknown, by Christ's time money-lenders were numerous among the Jews. The New Testament word for usury (Matthew 25:27; Luke 19:23) means "offspring," and implies interest springing out of the principal, and is used metaphorically of the gain on money lent out. In the parable of the talents, our Lord represents the lord of the unprofitable servants rebuking their laziness in not putting out his money to interest. The Old Testament word for usury comes from the root to eat, bite, vex or devour, and "gives plain indication of the malignant and hurtful nature of the thing signified by it: it points to such heavy exactions made for a temporary loan of money as trenches materially on the resources of the borrower, and even threatens wholly to devour his substance."

While, in the past, usury meant immoderate interest or oppression, in the New Testament era, when capital was required for many trading concerns, loans at moderate interest was apparently a lawful as well as required practice. This is why our Lord twice over introduces with approbation the investment of money with the bankers (Matthew 25:27; Luke 19:23. See THE BANKERS) so as to yield a proper "interest" or "usury." It was, therefore, not unlawful to live on reasonable interest accruing from invested money. Because the Jews were prohibited from taking usury from their poor brethren who, if no money could be secured would be sold as slaves, it must not be deemed unlawful to engage in the practice of usury. As *The Bible Companion* puts it, "It seems as lawful for a man to receive interest for money, which another gains with, improves, but runs the hazard of in trade, as it is to receive rent for our land, which another gains with, improves, but runs the hazard of in husbandry."

In our time money-lending has become a highly specialized art. Nations, as well as individuals, exist on what they can borrow. The unwary, however, whose straightened circumstances force them to borrow often find themselves in the tight grip of a merciless money-lender, or a money-shark in disguise. One loan leads to another loan, and the poor man finds himself in the web of the money spider with hardly any hope of extricating himself.

> Who goeth a borrowing,
> Goeth a sorrowing.

The Vinedresser

Noah appears as the first originator and cultivator of vines (Genesis 9:20). It is probable, however, that he gathered his knowledge of vines and their culture from other antediluvian vinegrowers who only ate the grape like other fruits. It would seem as if Noah was the first that extracted the juice of the grape, and preserved it until, by fermentation, it became a drinkable liquor. After the planting of Noah's vineyard we read of the vine of Egypt (Genesis 40:9-11; Numbers 20:5; Psalm 78:47). Plant and fruit figured on Egyptian monuments prove that the vine was grown in Egypt and Canaan long before the time of Abraham (Genesis 14:18; Numbers 13:20, 24). Metaphorically, we read of Is-

rael as "a vine out of Egypt." The vine leaf became a favorite design on Jewish coins. Palestine, because its climate is peculiarly suited to the culture of grapes — a climate reaching perfection during the prolonged sunshine and the dewy nights of summer — is spoken of as "the land of vineyards." The grapes of Hebron are still considered the finest produced in the Holy Land.

Wine, the fruit of the vine, is mentioned 141 times with certain verses praising the benefit of such wine (Judges 9:13; Psalm 104:15; Ecclesiastes 10:19; Zechariah 10:7). In his famous song about the vine, Isaiah reviews the labor of which the vine is the object (5:1-9). Jesus Himself, drank wine of grapes (Matthew 11:19; 26:29; John 2:1-11). Because of their importance, vines required constant care to keep them productive. Neglected, their fruit quickly degenerated. The ground had to be well-dunged and kept free from weeds. Each vine was trained as a separate stock, pruned back every spring, to the parent stem. Vines were propped up to keep the grapes above the soil, and nothing else was allowed to grow in the vineyard (Deuteronomy 22:9). Pruning was necessary because the flowering was over and the sap must make the grapes grow rather than increase still further the length of the shoots (John 15:2). Thorns and prunings were burned on the spot (Ezekiel 15:4, 5). By contrast, Solomon portrays the vineyard of the sluggard (Proverbs 24:30, 31). When in captivity, the vineyards of Israel lapsed into an uncultivated wilderness. When the leading people were carried into captivity, the poor were left as vinedressers (II Kings 25:12; Jeremiah 52:16; See II Chronicles 26:10; Isaiah 61:5; Joel 1:11; Luke 13:7). The culture of the vine provides us with many expressive metaphors. Christ made the vine always sacred in Christian symbolism when He portrayed Himself as the true Vine and His Father as the Tiller or Vinedresser (John 15: 1) — the thought here being that God is the Owner of the Vine and that He Himself cultivates, trains, prunes and purges His Vine to bring forth more and better fruit. In His parables and sayings, Christ often referred to vines and their culture (Matthew 9:17; 20: 1-6; 21:28-33; Mark 12:1; Luke 13:6-9; 20:9). The purging, or bleeding of the vine effected by making incisions in it with a knife which the vinedresser used with great skill and delicacy has been often used as an emblem of sanctified affliction. The heavenly Vinedresser always knows when it is the best to use His pruning knife (See THE HUSBANDMAN).

The Warrior

Two different Hebrew words are used of the English term warrior. The first means "to do war, or battle" (I Kings 12:21); and the second, "to equip, shoe, or prepare oneself for battle" (Isaiah 9:5). Warriors of old were men who prepared themselves in every possible way for battle and who, when the battle was begun, fought bravely and sacrificially. In early Israelite history, when the country was raided the people took to the caves, the forests and defiles of the wilderness (Judges 5:6, 7; I Samuel 13:6, 7; 14:11, 12), and under the leadership of a brave man, fought the enemy. "There was not much organization or strategy — mostly hand-to-hand fighting with clubs, stones, slings, bows and arrows, flint knives and bare fists." In Gibeah there were 700 lefthanded men, "all of them accustomed to sling a stone at a hair without missing" (Judges 20:16).

As personal bravery, physical strength, agility and endurance were the all-important qualities, the Bible has many warriors in its portrait gallery. Zebulun and Naphtali jeopardized their lives unto the death (Judges 5:18). "Home they brought the warrior dead." David praised Saul and Jonathan for their courage in battle (II Samuel 1:22-27). David's three warriors displayed wonderful devotion when they jeopardized their lives to bring the king a drink of his favorite water from the well of Bethlehem (II Samuel 23:16, 17; I Chronicles 11:19). What mighty warriors Paul and Barnabas were to hazard their lives for the name of our Lord Jesus Christ (Acts 15:25, 26). The annals of Christianity carry the names of multitudes of God's warriors who loved not their lives unto the death (Revelation 12: 11). Courageously they climbed the steep ascent to heaven, through peril, toil and pain. Returning warriors were welcomed home by the women with dance and song (Exodus 15:20; Judges 11:34; I Samuel 18:6, etc.), but no welcome to a warrior can ever exceed the welcome Christ gave to the first warrior-martyr of the church. Although seated on the right hand of the majesty on high (Hebrews 1:3), the warrior-Christ Himself rose to greet Stephen after his death at the hands of cruel men (Acts 7:54-60). When Stephen fell asleep, the lines of Charles Wolfe on *The Burial of Sir John Moore* were also true of him:

He lay like a warrior taking his rest
With his martial cloak around him.

All who are soldiers of Christ must endure hardness as they fight the good fight of faith, even though the battle may mean martyrdom. While the majority of us may never be called to seal our testimony with our blood, yet we must be fearless and courageous in our witness for Christ. Do you remember the words of Wordsworth on *The Character of the Happy Warrior?*

> Who is the happy Warrior? Who is he
> That every man in arms should wish to be?
> It is the generous spirit, who, when brought
> Among the tasks of real life, hath wrought
> Upon the plan that pleased his childish thought:
> Whose high endeavors are an inward light
> That makes the path before him always bright:
> Who with a natural instinct to discern
> What knowledge can perform, is diligent to learn.

Warrior is used figuratively. Did not Moses think of God in this way when he wrote — Jehovah is a man of war: Jehovah is his name (Exodus 15:3)? Christ was not lacking in warrior-courage when, as He died, He could cry with a loud voice, "It is finished!" That was the shout of a victor, not the wail of a victim. Under the figures of battle and war John conceives the age-long conflict between righteousness and sin, Christ and Satan, and the final triumph of the Lamb, who is King of kings, and Lord of lords (Revelation 16:14-16; 17:14; 19:14). (See THE SOLDIER).

The Watchman

A chronometer is simply a "watch" by which to tell the time of day, and a watch came by its name from the way men used to measure time which was known as "watches." Between prescribed hours were called a "watch" because of the length of time a watchman remained on duty. Thus, originally, a "watch" was actually a man or a number of men, as found in the chief priests "setting a watch" to guard the sepulchre in which Jesus was buried. One of the words used for watchmen is *custodia* from which we have custody and custodian (Matthew 27: 65, 66; 28:11; See THE GUARD). The Jews divided the night into three military watches —

The "first" or beginning of watches from sunset to ten o'clock (Lamentations 2:19).

The second or "middle watch" was from ten till two o'clock (Judges 7:19).

The third, "the morning watch" from two to sunrise (Exodus 14: 24; I Samuel 11:11).

Under the Romans the night was divided into four watches, a system the Jews came to recognize (Mark 13: 35). These four watches were styled as "even, midnight, cockcrowing and morning," and ended respectively at 9 P.M. — midnight — 3 A.M. — and 6 A.M. (Matthew 14:25; Mark 13:35; Luke 12:38; Acts 12:4).

In Bible times, the occupation of watchman was an important one. His duty was to keep awake while others slept; to keep his eyes open; to keep a sharp lookout in every direction. Nehemiah set a group of men to guard the city, while its walls were rebuilt (4:9; 7:3). The Jews raised dry-stone towers in their fields from which a watchman kept an eye on the fruit and crops to protect them against thieves, foxes and bears (Psalm 80: 13; Song of Solomon 2:15). Projected stones served as an external staircase and inside the tower was a storehouse for food (II Kings 17:9; 18:8; I Chronicles 27:25; Isaiah 5:2; Matthew 21:33; Mark 12:1). On the top of the tower was a booth in which, at harvest time, the whole family of the watchman could live (Isaiah 1:8; Amos 9: 11). Such a booth was used as the symbol of protection (Psalm 27:5).

Watchmen were also employed to guard a city. During the night they mounted guard on the ramparts, or went "about the city," patrolling the streets (Psalm 127:1; Song of Solomon 3:3; Isaiah 62:8). Besides protecting the city and its inhabitants from violence, watchmen were required to call out the hours of the night (II Samuel 18:24-27; Song of Solomon 5:7; Isaiah 21:11, 12). In Britain, before the days of policemen, watchmen used to patrol the streets during the night. George Sinclair writes of an old lady who remembered a watchman in Edinburgh calling out, "Four o'clock, and a fine frosty morning."

Prophets and teachers are referred to as watchmen, whose duty it is to warn God's people (Isaiah 22:11; 52:8; 62:6; Jeremiah 6:17). Twice over God said to Ezekiel, "I have set thee a watchman" (3:17; 33:2-7). Every preacher of the Gospel is a watchman, divinely trained to descry the enemies of men's souls at a distance. How apt are the words from the Apocrypha, "For a man's soul is sometimes wont to bring his tidings more than seven watchmen, that is set on high on a watchtower." May we be delivered from the company of "blind" watchmen the prophet speaks about! (Isaiah 56:10).

God wishes every child of His to function as a "watchman." Is not watching metaphorically used of moral alertness? "Watch thou in all things" (II Timothy 4:5). The word Paul employs suggests one who is watchful enough to possess a treasure. John Bunyan in his *Holy War* describes the town of Mansoul with its five gates, captured by Diabolus and recaptured by Emmanuel. Over every gateway was a tower, and the last word of Emmanuel's parting address was "watch." The pilgrim is to stand guard over Ear-gate, over Eye-gate, over Lip-gate. "Set a watch, O Lord, before my mouth; keep the door of my lips" (Psalm 141:3). The Moravians, when they crossed over the frontier of Austria into Saxony that they might have freedom to worship God, laid out a small settlement for themselves, and called it *Herrn Hut,* "The Lord's Watch."

The Christian must be vigilant to guard against spiritual foes and dangers. Watchfulness must be the keyword in a world of temptation. He must be constantly watchful against —

1. The temptations of Satan (Ephesians 6:11).
2. The allurements of the world (Psalm 39:1; Mark 8:15).
4. The erroneous doctrines of false cults, and also against whatever would hinder his piety and spiritual progress. God's watchmen are to watch for —

a. The teachings of providence (Psalm 5:8).
b. The fulfillment of prophecies (Revelation 16:15).
c. The righteous deliverance from trouble (Psalm 130).
d. The proper topics, spirit and seasons of prayer (Ephesians 6:18).
e. The salvation of the souls of men (Hebrews 13:7).
f. The declared death and judgment (Mark 13:37).
g. The promised Saviour from Heaven (I Thessalonians 5:6).

Watch, as if on this alone
Hung the issue of the day.
Pray that help may be sent down,
Watch and pray.

That there are divine watchers is evident from the dream Nebuchadnezzar had, messengers from God who with "holy ones" from heaven had joint authority to issue decrees. God

Himself is the thrice holy watchman (Jeremiah 44:27). The Moravian watchmen had a beautiful hymn, a verse of which reads —

> Lie still in the darkness,
>   Sleep safe in the night;
> The Lord is a Watchman,
>   The Lamb is the Light;
> Jehovah He holdeth
>   The sea and the land,
> The earth in the hollow
>   Of His mighty hand.

The Wizard

Mention has been made of the forbidden and severely denounced occupation of wizardry (Exodus 22:18; Leviticus 20:6; II Kings 9:22; Galatians 5:20). See under THE ASTROLOGER, THE NECROMANCER, THE PROGNOSTICATOR, THE SOOTHSAYER, THE WITCH. We have eleven references to wizards (Leviticus 19:31; 20:6, 27; Deuteronomy 18:11; I Samuel 28:3, 9; II Kings 21:6; 23:24; II Chronicles 33:6; Isaiah 8:19; 19:3), and in each case the word wizard implies "one who knows" or "the knowing or wise one," and represents one supposedly acquainted with the secrets of the unseen world. Witch was the name given to the woman and wizard the designation of the man practicing the form of witchcraft which professed ability to communicate with demons and spirits of the dead, by means of which future events were revealed, diseases cured, and evil spirits exorcised and banished.

The Worker

All kinds of craftsmen and laborers are spoken of as workers. We read of "a worker in brass" (I Kings 7:14), "a worker in stone" (I Chronicles 22: 15). "Men of work" or "them that did the work" (I Chronicles 25:1), represents "artificers" or men of various trades. For "cunning work" we can read, "the work of the skillful workman" (Exodus 35:35). The ASV of Proverbs 8:30 reads, "I was by him, as a master workman." Then we read of "workers of iniquity" (Job 31:3; 34:8, 22, etc.), "deceitful workers" (II Corinthians 11:13), "evil workers" (Philippians 3:2). As believers, we are "workers together with him," who is the Master Workman (II Corinthians 6:1). At the judgment seat of Christ, "every man's work is to be tried by fire of what sort it is" (I Corinthians 3:13). God grant that our workmanship will stand the test of the fire! The proverb has it, "At the end of the work you may judge of the workman." When our life's work is ended may we appear as workmen who have no need to be ashamed.

God instituted work before the Fall, when He placed Adam in the garden "to till it and keep it." After the entrance of sin work became more difficult and laborious (Genesis 2:15). The fourth commandment reads "Six days shalt thou labour" (Exodus 20: 9). Unless we are willing to work, we have no right to eat. Sluggards are to be despised (Proverbs 13:4; 20:4, etc.). God Himself is the Master Workman. Creation was His work (Genesis 2:1, 2). "My Father worketh hitherto, and I work" (John 5:17). Jesus also stressed the value of work. Faith in His finished work is "the work of God" (John 6:28-30). Work is used figuratively for the action of Jesus Himself (John 9:3, 4), and also for the evangelistic activity of His followers (I Corinthians 15:58; Philippians 2:16, etc.). Good works are the only evidence of our title to heaven (James 2:18-20). They also show our gratitude to God (Psalm 116:12, 13), and are profitable to men (Titus 3:8). As the shadows of judgment gather around a guilty world we must "work for the night is coming, when man's work is o'er." (See under THE LABORER). Labor in heaven will be different for there we shall serve the Lord day and night forever without any weariness of flesh.

The Wrestler

The Bible introduces us to three wrestlers. Wrestling, of course, is different from fighting. Fighting implies the use of instruments as in war; wrestling consists of two persons contesting without weapons, and striving to see which can overcome. The first wrestler is a woman, Rachel who, when her maid Bilhah bore Jacob his fifth son said, "With great wrestlings have I wrestled with my sister, and I have prevailed: and she called his name Naphtali" (Genesis 30:7, 8). The name, Naphtali, meaning, "wrestlings of God" or "mighty wrestlings" was a monument of Rachel's victory. She had won the favor and blessing of God for the yearning of the oriental heart for the birth of sons. Here, the word for "wrestling" is identified with a similar word meaning "to show self-froward or unsavory."

The next wrestler was the heavenly person who wrestled with Jacob until the breaking of the day (Genesis 32: 24-32). Rachel's wrestling was emotional and vocal rather than literal and physical, but Jacob's wrestling was intensely physical resulting in the dislocation of his thigh. The experience at Peniel was the turning point in Jacob's life. "What the revelation of the host of God had not sufficed to teach this faithless, anxious, scheming patriarch, that God sought to teach him in the night struggle with its ineffaceable physical memorial of a human impotence that can compass no more than to cling to divine Omnipotence." In spite of his strained muscle Jacob still resisted the heavenly Wrestler and could not be thrown down. Unable to gain further advantage in the wrestle, the *man* acknowledged Jacob's superiority and left at daybreak. The vanquished yielded the spoil to the victor, and Jacob received the requested blessing. That grim, midnight contest was for the purpose of giving Jacob courage and enablement to meet danger and difficulty in the power of faith. Because his will was so fixed that he simply would not be refused the blessing which came at daybreak, Jacob received a new name, "Israel," meaning a prince of, or with God. "For as a prince hast thou power with God and with men, and hast prevailed" (Genesis 32:28). It was Edmund Burke who gave us the thought — "He that wrestles with us strengthens our nerves, and sharpens our skill. Our antagonist is our helper." Out of his wrestling bout Jacob emerged as Israel, and his unknown antagonist became his constant helper, especially if the antagonist was God (Genesis 32:30).

The third wrestler is the Christian whose struggle is not with benign heavenly forces, but with the powers of hell. Public games in Greece and Rome provided New Testament writers, particularly Paul, with a rich source of material from which to draw spiritual truths. Among ancient contests between athletes was that of wrestling (Compare THE ATHLETE). Fairbairn says of this most popular sport —

> Wrestling was at first merely a trial of strength, in which the stronger of the two was sure to prevail, but Theseus converted it into an art by which men of skill were enabled to throw others far superior to them in bodily strength. The wrestler had to throw his adversary either by swinging him around, or tripping him up, and then

to keep him down. The joints and limbs were prepared for the struggle by being well rubbed and supplied with oil. The victory was adjudged to him who gave his adversary three falls.

The present spectacular, highly financed and often faked wrestling matches of today are far removed from the high standard of wrestling Paul doubtless witnessed.

One of the words for wrestle means not only "to clasp around," but also to "dust." Wrestlers were quickly involved in a cloud of dust. It was the custom in Greece for wrestlers to rub their bodies with dust.

Paul, who makes use of the spirit of many of the Grecian and Roman games to illustrate the self-denial, the strenuousness and the glorious issue of the Christian conflict, employs the metaphor of the wrestling match to emphasize the contest of the believer with evil forces (Ephesians 6:12). In our unconverted state we wrestled against God. The Spirit strove with us, but we resisted Him. Now it is our privilege to wrestle in His power against His and our enemies. Paul's simile reminds us of what we are *not* to wrestle against, namely "flesh and blood." The negative statement immediately identifies the nature of our opponent. There is always trouble and defeat when flesh and blood wrestles against flesh and blood, that is, when we strive against one another (Romans 13:13; Philippians 2:3), or strive "about words to no profit" (II Timothy 2:14). We know from the herdsmen of Abraham, Lot and Gerar that strife causes division (Genesis 13:7; 26:20). Too often our contest is with visible flesh and blood rather than with the invisible powers of evil.

Paul, then, exhorts us to remember that our conflict is not with the human and the visible, but with the superhuman and invisible. When we meet with opposition, in any form from flesh and blood, whether our own or otherwise, we must not wrestle with them. Human foes are the media of satanic attack, and our conflict is with the source, not the channel, of antagonism. In virtue of Calvary, we must gain the victory over the power of hell we cannot see. When resting in the victory of the cross over Satan, nothing flesh and blood can disturb us. When Peter tried to dissuade Christ from going to the cross, He did not answer Peter but immediately addressed Himself to Satan, "Get thou behind me, Satan" (Matthew 16:23). He did not speak to the flesh and blood He could see in Peter, but to the devil — the invisible foe Jesus could see — from whom Peter's suggestion came.

The forces we are to wrestle against are divided into four classes — four "againsts"

> Against Principalities
> Against Powers
> Against the rulers of the darkness of this word
> Against spiritual wickedness in high places (Ephesians 6:12, 13)

These beleaguering forces surround the believer who must carry on a truceless war against them. Even when he meets hostility or the actual cruelty of men, the believer's conflict is with the darker and deeper powers behind them. Satan has control over nations and men, and also a vast host of demons and evil spirits. And this satanic wrestler knows all the holds and falls, and spiritual wrestlers — all who are in Christ Jesus — must not be ignorant of the foe's devices (II Corinthians 2:11). What the Christian must remember in the conflict is that he does not wrestle against hellish forces to gain a position. Already

Christ in His wrestle with principalities and powers, spoiled them completely (Colossians 2:15); and because He has lifted us up into Himself, trusting in the power of His Resurrection, we are more than conquerors. We can stand against all the devil represents as we stand where God has put us, namely, in Christ Jesus (Ephesians 1:3). It is only thus at the end we shall be able to confess with Paul, "I have struggled the good contest" (II Timothy 4:7; See I Timothy 6:12; Revelation 2:10).

The Writer

It is somewhat interesting to find that "writing" and its cognates appear over 400 times in the Bible. The invention and development of writing, occasioning writers, is a fascinating subject and is fully dealt with under this caption in a reliable commentary or dictionary such as the *Zondervan Pictorial Bible Dictionary*. It is a known fact that men wrote on tablets of clay before the Flood. The Arabs believe that Enoch was the inventor of writing, while the Jews believed Enoch left a number of writings. Jude refers to *The Book of Enoch*. Pre-Flood writings have been found and are known as *Pre-Flood Seals* seeing that the earliest form of writing was by a seal made of a small piece of stone or metal. Each person had his own seal with which to stamp his name on letters, contracts and documents. Inscriptions made on soft clay remained indelible as the clay hardened. This is the form of writing found in prehistoric cities.

Halley remarks that "writing began when God put a 'mark' or 'sign' on Cain. That mark stood for an idea, and those around knew what it meant. Thus 'signs' or 'marks' came to be used to record ideas, words or combinations

of words." Such sign language is still used in some countries like China and Japan. Behind all crude attempts to record events and facts, there was the overruling providence of God, instructing men to write so that His Word could be preserved. Original truth could not be retained in any other way. At the beginning, marks stood for part of words, or syllables, but about 1500 B.C. a simplified form of writing was invented, and twenty-six different marks were made to express different words it had taken 500 marks to express. Thus alphabetic writing was born.

There was what *The International Standard Bible Encyclopaedia* calls "Inward Writing." By this form of writing is "commonly meant the inward image or counterpart of visual or tangible handwriting as distinguished from the inward records of the sound of words, but the term fairly belongs to all inward word records. We meet this kind of writing in the Bible in the writing upon the tablets of the heart (Proverbs 3:3; 7:3; Jeremiah 17:1; II Corinthians 3:3), which is thus not a mere figure of speech but a proper description of that effort to fix in memory which some effect by means of sound symbols and by the sight symbols of ordinary handwriting." A voice is heard, and a vision and even handwriting is seen (Exodus 19:19; Numbers 7:8, 9; Isaiah 6; Amos 7:1-9; Revelation 17:5; 19:1, 2).

The chief Hebrew words used for writer are *sopher* and *shoter*, and correspond to Assyrian words for "writing" and are used also for kindred officers. *Sopher* is connected with *sepher*, meaning a book, and with the idea of numbering, the writer being an enrolling, or census officer, or a royal secretary (Judges 5:14; II Samuel 8:17; II Chronicles 26:11; Isaiah 33:18).

"Writer" and "scribe" are used interchangeably (See under THE SCRIBE). Back in Deborah's time we read of those who were able to "handle the pen of the writer" (Judges 5:14). The psalmist could speak of his tongue as "the pen of a ready writer" (Psalm 45:1). To be a scribe or writer was the ambition of every poor boy with initiative.

The first definite reference to writing is in the divine command to Moses, "Write this for a memorial in a book" (Exodus 17:14). After the revelation was received from God on Sinai, Moses acted as the Spirit-inspired historian. "The Lord spake by Moses" (Exodus 32:16). Thus Moses was divinely prepared to embody in tangible form the first 2,500 years of human history (Hebrews 11:24-29). The Spirit of wisdom and revelation possessed his mind, enabling him to remember the necessary facts, and likewise guided Moses to record the same. The Bible offers clear, unmistakable evidence of holy men of old being divinely inspired to record a divinely-given message (Exodus 24:3; II Samuel 23:1-3; Luke 1:1-14; I Peter 1:12; II Peter 1:21; Revelation 1:1-19). Christ constantly referred to recorded Old Testament truths under the authoritative caption, "It is written." God made known His will verbally, in a direct and personal way, and Spirit-inspired writers recorded for posterity the divine revelation. It was thus that the Bible came into being.

As to writing materials, stone, clay, wax, bricks, metal and boards were used. Early Egyptians wrote on soft clay with a three-cornered stylus, or pen of iron, tracing characters with precision. Papyrus, made from marsh reeds, and used as early as 2,500 B.C. in Egypt was the forerunner of our writing paper. The term Bible is from *biblos,* named after the inner bark of the papyrus. One reason why the original manuscripts of the Bible have been lost is because of the perishable nature of the material used. As old copies wore out, fresh ones were made. Although the Ten Commandments were written on stone or clay, they were transferred to papyrus or leather, along with other divine words for "the books" (Exodus 17:14). The exploits of Thothmese III in Palestine 1500 B.C. were written in rolls of very fine vellum. Blotting out names from a book (Numbers 5:23) implies a material from which the writing could be expunged by washing. Such a material was manufactured out of the skins of animals. Skins were rolled on a stick and fastened with a thread with ends which were sealed (Isaiah 29:11; Daniel 12:4; II Corinthians 3:3; Revelation 5:1; 6:14). Doubtless the skins of sheep or goats became the parchments we read of (II Timothy 4:13).

As to pens, the same were originally from reeds from which the pith had been extracted. Jeremiah speaks of writing with "a pen of iron, and with the point of a diamond" (17:1, See Job 19:23, 24). The stylus used by the Egyptians was made of hard metal, ivory or bone, sharpened at one end for the purpose of writing, smooth at the other, so that whenever it was necessary to make erasures, the writer had only to turn the broad end of the pencil, smooth the wax, and renew the writing. Probably the apostles used quills (II John 12; III John 13). "Write with a man's pen" (Isaiah 8:1).

In ancient times, the ink used was dry ink and moistened when required. Manufactured from lampblack or carbon, it was dissolved in gall nut or acid. The Egyptians used a red ink made from cinnabar (Numbers 5:23;

Jeremiah 36:18; II Corinthians 3:3). The inkhorn or inkpot (Ezekiel 9:2, 3, 11), came to be a necessary instrument of the writer and was usually attached to the girdle. The inkhorn had a long shaft which held the reeds, with a container for ink at one end. Before the days of fountain, or ball pens, I can remember as a boy seeing rent collectors going from house to house signing rent books with a quill they dipped into an ink bottle attached to their vest. Reed pens, inkhorn and scribes are sculptured on the tombs of Ghizeh, contemporaneous with the Pyramids.

The only record we have of Jesus writing anything is when He stooped down, and with His finger wrote on the ground (John 8:6). What He wrote we are not told. It must have been convicting because of its effect. Writing in dust was by no means unusual in the East. Jeremiah says that "they that depart from me [the Lord] shall be written in the earth" (17:13) — as soon be blotted out and forgotten as the writing of a child upon the sand. Is it not blessed and comforting to know that if our names are written in the Lamb's Book of Life, that no one and nothing can ever erase them?

MALE OCCUPATIONS

MALE OCCUPATIONS

IN THE SPIRITUAL REALM

Dividing the occupations of the Bible, as we have, into the two sections of secular and spiritual, we yet recognize that a good many of the occupations we have included under the former group would, perhaps, have been more fitting under the latter. Some of the occupations associated with the secular realm are equally applicable to the spiritual realm and have, in fact, a fuller connotation when treated as spiritual occupations — an aspect we have not neglected. Take, for instance, secular occupations such as THE ADVOCATE — THE BONDSMAN — THE COMFORTER — THE DAYSMAN — THE DELIVERER — THE KING — THE REDEEMER, to choose a few, the same are more widely used from the divine standpoint than the human. Such occupations have a double application as we have shown, whereas those we have brought under Spiritual Occupations are definitely spiritual or related specifically to the religious sphere.

A striking feature, however, of many who followed their own particular trade or craft was the ambition not only to satisfy themselves as craftsmen or to give good service to those who employed them but to labor for the glory of Him who gave them their ability to follow their own particular craft. They served their masters according to the flesh, not merely as men-pleasers, but as God's servants doing His will from the heart (Ephesians 6:5-7; Colossians 3:17, 22). "Whatsoever ye do — whatever the legitimate occupation be — do all to the glory of God" (I Corinthians 10: 31. "Whatever ye do — whether painter or preacher, carpenter or curate, mason or missionary — do it heartily, as to the Lord, and not unto men" (I Corinthians 10:31; Colossians 3:23).

In the vision Ezekiel, the prophet-priest had of the glory of the Lord in which there was a mystic unfolding of the splendor of the four living creatures, or *The Cherubim,* Ezekiel noticed that "they had the hands of a man under their wings" (1:8). Is this description not suggestive? Wings and hands! Wings suggest vision, worship, ascent Godward. Hands represent toil and trade, secular occupations of any kind. Yet over the hands the wings were spread. Eloquent, surely, of the truth that our vocation must be inspired by vision; that a believer no matter what his or her secular occupation may be, must see to it that work and worship are combined. The spiritual should pervade the secular. In fact, to the Christian nothing is merely secular. Whatever we may earn our daily bread doing, we must labor not as men-pleasers but with the glory of God as our goal. Such an incentive constrains us to give of our best whether we push a pen, sell goods, or minister exclusively in holy things. One has read of a godly man who earned a living making and mending shoes and who had over the outside of his shop, "John Bradford — Shoemaker to the glory of God." And we can depend upon it that his shoes were the best in the town, just as the farm implements Jesus the Carpenter made were of the highest quality.

Sir Robert Peel, renowned English statesman is best remembered as the creator of the modern police force. At one time, while in the presence of several great men, some of whom were rank unbelievers, the name and fame of the Saviour was assailed. Peel rose to his feet, drew all eyes to himself, and quietly but effectively said, "I would have you know that I am Christ's servant still." Statesman of the country he loved — servant of Christ whom he loved with a more intense love. Overshadowing the brain and hands of the statesman were the wings of affection and adoration for the Master.

We now come to those occupations expressly spiritual because of their relationship to full service for the Lord: and as with the secular occupations dealt with, so with the following spiritual occupations, the alphabetical order is employed.

The Apostle

Occurring seventy-eight times in the New Testament, and in the majority of cases used of The Twelve, apostle means one who is fully authorized to represent the person whose message he bears. From the Greek definitions of this significant title we have first "one dispatched or sent forth": secondly, "the actual delegate of the one sending him." A renowned Greek authority says that, "In classical Greek the word was almost entirely restricted to the meaning of a "naval expedition," a fleet dispatched on foreign service. An "apostle" implies "one sent forth," see I Kings 14:6 and John 13:16 where the same word is rendered "He that is sent." Four times we have apostleship (Acts 1:25; Romans 1:5; I Corinthians 9:2; Galatians 2:8). There is one reference to "false apostles" (II Corinthians 11:13) where the original word is *pseudapostolos*. It is from *pseud* that we have "pseudo" meaning "sham" or "spurious."

It was after a night in prayer, early in His Galilean ministry, that Jesus selected from His many disciples the twelve He Himself named apostles (Luke 6:12, 13). They, themselves, had nothing whatsoever to do with the choice. The selection was of Christ's own sovereign will and plan (John 13:18; Acts 1:2). Four records are given of the names of those He chose, namely, Matthew 10:2-4; Mark 3:16-19; Luke 6:14-16; Acts 1:13. A brief historical sketch of each may suffice. For a fuller treatment see the author's *All The Men of the Bible* and *The Twelve Who Changed the World*.

1. Simon

This leader and spokesman of the apostolic band was surnamed "Peter" by Jesus, who also called him Cephas (Matthew 10:2; Mark 3:16; Luke 6: 14; John 1:42). He is elsewhere referred to as Simeon (Acts 15:14). Peter was the son of Jona (Jonas, John 1:42), a native of Bethsaida and a fisherman by trade (John 1:44).

2. James

Commonly called James "The Great" to distinguish from the other James in the list, this apostle was the son of Zebedee and Salome, and was surnamed by Christ, with John, *Boanerges* (Matthew 27:56; Mark 3:17; 15:40), and was likewise a fisherman.

3. John

With his brother James above, John was surnamed by Christ, *Boanerges* meaning "Sons of thunder." Possibly these brothers were so named because of their fiery zeal (Mark 3:17; 9:38; 10:37; Luke 9:54). John, too, was a fisherman, and became the writer of the fourth gospel, three epistles and Revelation.

4. Andrew

The brother of Peter, and former disciple of John the Baptist, Andrew, a native of Bethsaida, was the spiritual father of Peter. What a trophy Andrew secured for Jesus that day he brought his brother to Him! (Matthew 4:18; John 1:40, 44).

5. *Philip*

Also of Bethsaida, Philip was one of the earliest of the disciples, and was wonderfully used of the Spirit (John 1:43).

6. *Bartholomew*

The best and most trustworthy commentators identify the man Nathanael, to whom Christ paid a striking tribute (John 1:47), with Bartholomew, whose name in the lists comes next to Philip. It was no unusual thing for an apostle to possess two names. Simon was also called Peter; Levi was known to the rest as Matthew, while one of the twelve rejoiced in the threefold appellation of Lebbaeus, Thaddaeus and Jude. Bartholomew, like Bar-Jona was a surname.

7. *Matthew*

This son of Alphaeus was a publican or tax-gatherer, and was known as Levi. He became the writer of the gospel bearing his other name, Matthew (Matthew 10:3; Mark 2:14; Luke 5:27).

8. *Thomas*

A twin, Thomas is also called Didymus. Because he was given to doubt and despondency, we came to speak of "Doubting Thomas." Dr. Alexander Whyte says, "If to say man is to say melancholy, then to say Thomas, who is called Didymus, is to say *religious* melancholy" (John 11:16; 14:5; 20:25; 21:2).

9. *James*

This son of Alphaeus is called "James the Less." Less implies that he was not as well known or as prominent as the other James. It is affirmed by many Bible scholars that he was not the Lord's brother and writer of James (Mark 15:40; Galatians 1:19).

10. *Thaddaeus*

Possibly a son of James, Thaddaeus was also called Lebbaeus, and surnamed Thaddaeus. He is the Judas — not Iscariot — of John 14:22. It is believed that he was the bishop of Jerusalem (Acts 1:13).

11. *Simon the Canaanite*

This Cananean was also called "The Zealot" (Matthew 10:4; Mark 3:18; Luke 6:15; Acts 1:13). The epithet Cananean has no connection with the geographical "Canaan." The word comes from a root meaning "to be ardent or zealous," which the English word "zealot" represents. We have no record of this apostle of an ardent enthusiastic spirit.

12. *Judas Iscariot*

Mentioned last in all the lists of the twelve, Judas is sometimes called the son of Simon. It is likely that he was a native of Kerioth, a small village in the tribe of Judah (Joshua 15:25; Jeremiah 48:24; John 6:71; 13:2, 26). Whenever mentioned, it is always with the tragic label — "which also betrayed him." His name and fearful sin are inseparably coupled together.

Why did Jesus choose twelve — no more, no less? Evidently there were others eligible for the high dignity of apostle. It is used of Barnabas (Acts 14:4, 14), of Andronicus (Romans 16:7), of two unnamed brethren (II Corinthians 8:23, ASV margin), of Epaphroditus (Philippians 2:25, ASV margin), of Silas and of Timothy (I Thessalonians 2:6) to define their relation to Christ. Apostle is also used vaguely of the messengers commissioned by the churches (II Corinthians 8:23; Philippians 2:25). Paul likewise was an apostle (I Thessalonians 2:6), being chosen directly by Christ Himself, after His ascension, to carry the Gospel to the Gentiles. Like the original twelve apostles, Paul was also *called* and then *sent*. Yet, with those we have just mentioned, Paul was not in the apostolate unless we hold that he was the true substitute for Judas Iscariot. Why then did Christ deliberately choose The Twelve? Let another answer —

> Christ appointed twelve in clear allusion to the tribes of a new Israel, a spiritual circumcision, another peculiar people, and by such a choice did two things. He made a stupendous claim for Himself. Every Jew knew in a moment what that choice of twelve implied. It implied that Jesus was the promised and long-expected Messiah. It meant that He was the fulfillment of prophecy. . . . This further thing the choice of this number *twelve* did. It provided the apostles themselves with a constant stimulus to devotion and support of faith. The number *twelve* would carry their minds back to the promises, to that word of the Lord which standeth sure. It would be to them what the figurative names of their children were to the prophets, what the bones of Joseph were to the enslaved Israelites, a stimulus to their drooping and halting faith.

Although all the Twelve were on an equal footing, three of them mentioned together, namely, Peter and James and John, seemed to have been closer to Jesus than the other nine. These three witnessed the raising of Jairus' daughter, the transfiguration of Christ, and His agony in Gethsemane. What is known as the "apostolic age" was the period of the history of the Christian church during the lifetime of the apostles from Pentecost to the death of John, near the end of the first century. John was the last of the Twelve to die, and with him the apostolate died or ended.

The office and commission of the apostles was remarkable because of the essentials Peter stated before the election of Judas' successor. The outstanding qualifications for apostleship were —

1. They were all required to have been eye-and-ear witnesses of what they testified of, especially of the resurrection of Christ (John 15:27; Acts 1:21; I Corinthians 9:1, 15; I Corinthians 15).

2. They were all called and chosen by Christ Himself that they might be His companions and helpers, and continue His ministry after His ascension. Thus He gave much attention to their spiritual equipment as Dr. A. B. Bruce proves in his volume *The Training of the Twelve* (Luke 6:13; 9:10; Galatians 1:1).

3. They were all divinely inspired. All the Twelve spoke and wrote with a consciousness that they had been especially commissioned by the One who had called them. Mysteries were revealed to them yet they were slow to apprehend the spiritual nature of Christ's kingdom, with His death and resurrection as the necessary preliminary to same (John 16:13).

4. They had power to perform miracles (Mark 16:20; Acts 2:43; I Corinthians 9:2; II Corinthians 12:12). Their miracles were the credentials marking them as the extraordinary, not permanent ministers, and because of these signs of apostleship they could have strictly no successors. Commissioned immediately by Christ Himself, independent of any other, and having an office that was unique it could not be passed on to others. Apostolic succession has no warrant from Scripture. Christ Himself gave no hint to the Twelve that they were empowered to elect others whether to apostleship or to any other ministerial office. That the apostles made a mistake in regard to Matthias as a succes-

sor to Judas Iscariot is proven by the inspired records themselves.

The apostles had no "successors," as that word is ordinarily understood. They were appointed by Christ for a special ministry which would never need to be repeated, namely to witness the Resurrection, and to lay the foundations of the Christian church for which they were endowed with large and altogether peculiar gifts. Unusual miraculous power and remarkable, inspired enlightenment were theirs as long as their office lasted. When the office ceased, so did the gifts and powers accompanying it cease. As Professor Wm. Townsend expresses it —

> Equally unscriptural is the theory of apostolic succession which is urged by Romish and Anglican writers. This teaches that no ordinations to the ministry of the church are valid, save those which come through bishops, and by bishops only who can claim unbroken descent from the bishops of Rome since the days of the apostles. This claim is grounded upon the commission given by Christ to His disciples (John 20:21-22; Matthew 28:19-20). But the office of an apostle was not a permanent one, and ceased with the apostles. In their writings there is not a trace of evidence that they ordained successors to themselves, nor is there any proof that an order of bishops was appointed in the apostolic churches, with the exclusive right to ordain.

If there are any real successors of the apostles they are not popes, archbishops, bishops and ministers, by virtue of their office, but all bornagain religious leaders, and equally all non-official believers, insofar as they know Christ as Saviour, have His mind, bear true witness for Him, and are thereby sharers in the zeal, devotion and sanctified purpose of the Twelve.

As of old Apostles heard it
By the Galilean lake,
Turned from home and toil and kindred
Leaving all for His dear sake.

Jesus calls us from the worship
Of the vain world's golden store:
From each idol that would keep us,
Saying, "Christian, love Me more."

All that remains to be said is that the title, apostle, is applied to our Lord Himself, and that as used of Him, expresses His relationship to God, as His sent One, the Ambassador from heaven to man to prepare man to go to heaven. "The Apostle and High Priest of our confessions, Christ Jesus" (Hebrews 3:1). As the Apostle, Christ pleads God's cause with us: as High Priest, He pleads our cause to God (See John 17:3, 18).

The Bishop

Bishop, meaning, "overseer" or "superintendent" (see under same) is an Old Testament Gentile term describing a secular occupation but taken over by the apostles and christianized. It is employed of sundry municipal and military officers and of taskmasters (Numbers 4:16; 31:14; Judges 9:26, 28, 35; II Kings 12:11; II Chronicles 2:8, 18; 34:12; Nehemiah 11:9). In classical Greek, Homer and Plutarch applied the same word to the gods, while in Athens the governors of conquered states were likewise called "bishops." In early Old Testament times "elders" represented an official class having both civil and religious duties — the elders of a city functioning as the elders of the synagogue. When the church came into existence, "elder" was used exclusively in a religious sense.

The actual word "bishop" occurs five times in the epistles (Philippians 1:1; I Timothy 3:1, 2; Titus 2:7; I Peter 2:25). A cognate term, "oversight," another Old Testament term the apostles adopted (Genesis 43:12; Numbers 3:32, etc.), is used by Peter when describing the solemn responsibility of the bishop or elder of a church (I Peter 5:2). Paul employs the same word when exhorting the leaders in the church at Ephesus to grasp the unspeakable honor of being set as an "overseer" by the Holy Spirit in — not over — a church.

Bishops, elders, pastors were practically interchangeable or synonymous terms, with a plurality of them in a church as the will of God (Acts 14:23; 20:17; Philippians 1:1). Eldership in the apostolic local church was always plural. There is no instance of one elder in a local church. That renowned Greek authority, Bishop J. B. Lightfoot says, "It is a fact now generally recognized by the theologians of all shades of opinion that in the language of the New Testament the same office in the church is called indifferently bishop — elder, or presbyter." Both Irenaeus and Jerome declared the two offices to be identical.

Although the duties of a bishop are not clearly refined we know that his was a "good work," and demanded holiness of life. His was the responsibility of guarding revealed truth from perversion and error, to oversee the spiritual life of a flock. As the church grew it was necessary to have those who were qualified by divine unction to expound the Scriptures and shepherd the sheep. As an overseer, then, the bishop's main duty was to teach the Word. In church life today the office of bishop or elder with the attachment of authority from above, the guardianship of truth, the general supervision of the flock, along with the gift of teaching is still necessary. Let it be made clear, however, that any one occupying such an office today does so not by any human ordination

but by recognition and appointment (John 21:16; Acts 20:28; I Timothy 3:1, 2; Titus 1:5, 7, 9).

The word "rule" in connection with a bishopric must not be misunderstood (I Timothy 3:4, 5; 5:17). It means "to stand before," "take the lead." To serve, then, and not to lord it over God's heritage, had to be the object of a bishop. He was a spiritual shepherd and any authority he had was not humanly conferred. There was no official appointment of bishops. The committal Paul speaks of (II Timothy 2:2) refers to the impartation of instruction, not to the conferring of office, or of gift. It is the teaching, not ordination that was to be handed down. Bishops or elders were appointed by the Holy Spirit, which appointment or ordination was recognized by the designation of the hand, and the language used indicates the reception of a spiritual gift, not the impartation of an official status (Acts 13:3; 14:25, 26; 15:40; 20:28; I Timothy 1:6; Titus 1:5).

As a distinctive term for one particular class of minister the word "bishop" or *episcopos* is not to be found in the New Testament. In Paul's time, the church was unaware of any distinction between "elder" or "bishop" (Philippians 1:1). Ignatius, about A.D. 115, was the first writer who made a single bishop a ruler in a church, but confessed that he had no apostolic authority for such a change. From then on there developed a hierarchy of bishops and archbishops. By a gradual process bishops became an august body within monarchial episcopacy with the concentration of a community's authority in the hands of a single bishop. Such an office, however, was more moral than official. Bishops were not ordained by the power and unction of the Holy Spirit to be a sacerdotal caste or priestly order, but God-chosen administrators whose life and conduct and ability was to be worthy of all honor amongst their fellow saints.

It is affirmed that apostolic succession was an effort to keep heresy out of the church, and that, therefore, a bishop was the only church official qualified to baptize or administer the Lord's Supper excluding thereby all heretics from the ordinances. Thus, any bishop able to trace his succession through previous bishops of his See back to the apostles was in a position to claim validity for his acts. Today, episcopacy is governed by the bishops and the consecration of other bishops, and the ordination of priests and deacons can only be by a bishop who along with other bishops claims historic descent from apostolic or sub-apostolic times. But such preeminence above other pastors in the church has no foundation in the oracles of God. Bishops and elders were set aside by the apostles or apostolic delegates, but as we have neither of these, ordination to such an office is not Scriptural. As one writer expresses it, "When you provide apostles to choose elders for us, we shall be exceedingly obliged for both. How can we have elders appointed according to Scripture unless we have apostles or their delegates?"

Bishops and Elders are not mentioned among the gifts to the church, but were spiritually-minded men set apart by the apostles. It is, therefore, only logical to conclude that with the cessation of the ordaining authorities there was also the cessation of the office. But from the second century on, the office of bishop advanced its claims until from this divergence from apostolic usage there developed the whole system of episcopacy with its assumptions of autocratic rule and worldly estate. Distinctive dress for

bishops came into being around the third century.

Before leaving this particular office, a word may be necessary as to the present unscriptural distinction between clergy and laity. The New Testament speaks of the whole true church as the clergy of God. The word "heritage" is *kleros,* from which we have "clergy." Apostolic teaching forbids official superiority on the part of one member of a church over other members (I Peter 5:3). Bishop Handley Moule affirms that "the deepest principles of Christianity preclude the idea of an ultimately indispensable ministry. The primary and ruling idea of the Church is that of a body whose every member, by the Spirit, lives directly by his Head, and any ministerial claim is foreign to such a concept. It is interesting to note that a Christian minister is never called *sacerdos.* As one of 'the true Israel of God,' he is a 'king and a priest,' just as every other believer is."

The Deacon

In the early days of the church the apostles were its sole administrators of its affairs, but soon the work became too great for them, and provision had to be made for the discharge of duties of a secular or inferior nature. Thus the office of deacon came into being and the apostles were freed from practical administration and thus able to give themselves continually to prayer and to the ministry of the Word. The cause and manner of the appointment of deacons are clearly recorded by Luke (Acts 6:1-6). The so-called seven deacons are not spoken of by that title, though the service they were to render is specified, namely, the administering of funds and property given on behalf of the needy. The office of a deacon was not so prominent as that of the bishop or elder, for a deacon would assist.

The word deacon itself means "servant" or "minister," and any service rendered was known as "deaconing." The importance and serious nature of deaconing can be gathered from the qualifications necessary for the office. Deacons were a definite class of men of high Christian character (Philippians 1:1; I Timothy 3:12, 13). After proving their fitness and readiness for deaconing they were appointed by choice of the assembly, the free-working Spirit overruling the choice and authority of the apostles (Acts 6:3). While popularly elected deacons were set apart for one limited function, namely, the administration of the poor funds, God inspired some of them with higher gifts as for example, Stephen and Philip, two of the "seven" who became fruitful evangelists (Acts 6:8; 8:4, 26). Deacons are represented as distributing to those present at the Lord's Table, the bread and wine, and also conveyed portions to the absent. They also baptized new converts, as well as cared for temporalities.

The word minister means "to act as a deacon," or "to serve" (Matthew 20:28). Jesus is declared to be a deacon — as the term "minister" implies — of the circumcision (Romans 15:8). Paul called himself and his fellow-laborers in the Gospel, the Lord's deacons (I Corinthians 3:5; II Corinthians 6:4; Ephesians 3:7; Colossians 1:2). "If any man serve — act as a deacon for — me" (John 12:26). Household servants were to be a good *diakonos* from which we have "diaconate." Under THE SERVANT — which see — we pointed out that the English word "servant" is represented by two Greek words — *diakonos* and *doulos*. The former describes a servant in relation

to his work, and the latter term, his relation to his master.

Gradually the churches in Christendom gave different meanings to the position and functions of deacons. Among Roman, Greek and Anglican Churches, deacon is the title of an assistant clergyman or chaplain of subordinate rank. In other denominations, deacons are more allied to spiritual than to pecuniary matters. Deacons are considered to be an order in the ministry and elected by annual conference and ordained by the bishop as in the Methodist Episcopal Church for the threefold ministry of

1. Administering baptism and solemnizing marriages.
2. Assisting elders in the administering of the Lord's Supper.
3. Ministering as a traveling preacher.

The Elder

Like its interchangeable term, bishop, that of elder is a predominantly Jewish title taken over from the Old Testament and given a Christian significance. In the New Testament the various terms for the office of elder — bishop, pastor, teacher, minister, preacher, steward, angel or messenger — describe different aspects of the ministry rendered. The Greek word for "elder," *presbuteros*, from which we have "presbyterian," means senior or elder, grayheaded or bearded and is frequently used in the Greek translation of the Old Testament to signify a ruler or governor — one chosen not so much for his age, as for his merits and wisdom. As a title it was extensively used both among Hebrews and surrounding nations (Genesis 24:2; 50:7; II Samuel 12:17; Ezekiel 27:9).

In ancient times, older men in a community functioned as elders in civic affairs. For instance, they served as local magistrates in bringing murderers to trial (Deuteronomy 19:12; 21:3; Joshua 20:4), punished the disobedient (Deuteronomy 21:19), passing penalty for slander (Deuteronomy 22:15), judgment in marriage matters (Deuteronomy 25:7), and in questions relating to the Law (Leviticus 4: 15; Deuteronomy 27:1). These elders governed a community and made all major decisions. Elders shared the responsibilities of Moses (Exodus 3:16; 12:21; 24:9; Numbers 11:25). When Israel became a monarchy, elders still functioned. They were a separate class from the heads of tribes and the princes of the fathers' houses (I Kings 8: 3). Each town had its group of elders, as Bethlehem did (I Samuel 16:4). The elders made up the Sanhedrin, the governing council of the Jews. Both in the Psalms and in the prophets, the elders are frequently spoken of as a distinct class, bearing an official character, and occupying to a certain extent a separate position (Psalm 107:32; Lamentations 2:10; Ezekiel 14:1; 20:1).

Taken over from the Sanhedrin, the office of elder came to represent the oversight of all spiritual affairs in a church (Acts 20:17-28; I Timothy 3: 2-5; 5:17). In fact, the word is used in four principal ways in the New Testament —

1. The Jewish elders spoken of throughout the gospels, and who joined with the scribes and Pharisees against Jesus (Matthew 27:12).

2. The Christian elders or bishops when the church came into being (Acts 14:23). The terms bishop and elder are used interchangeably (See THE BISHOP). The elders of Acts 20: 17 are called "bishop" in 20:27, see Titus 1:5-7. When elder is used it is not in respect to position so much as seniority of age, maturity, dignity, and spiritual experience and wisdom. Bishop on the other hand, meaning overseer, shepherd, denotes the character of the work he was called upon to do, or, the function of the office. A present-day local church corresponds to a New Testament assembly when it consists of "saints, bishops or elders, and deacons" (Philippians 1:1).

3. Those advanced in years. "Ye younger, submit yourselves unto the elder" (I Peter 5:5). There may be the double application here of age and position. Laying hands suddenly on no man (I Timothy 5:22-25) is used in connection with appointment to fellowship. Precipitate action might turn out to be association with other men's sins. As a rule the apostles never appointed persons as elders soon after conversion. Time must elapse for the Spirit of God to work in the soul and discipline them. Capabilities and moral and spiritual qualities must be manifest if an elder was to be respected and valued. "Not a novice," or one newly-planted (I Timothy 3:6). Elders, manifesting divinely-given qualification, were to be highly esteemed in love for their work's sake (I Thessalonians 5:12, 13). Watching for souls as those that must give account, they had to be obeyed (Hebrews 13:17). Their fatherly instructions had to be followed, and no accusation was to be received against them but before reliable witnesses (I Timothy 5:1, 19). At all times they had to keep before them the judgment seat of Christ with its full reward (II John 8).

4. The twenty-four enthroned elders (Revelation 4). These elders in heaven around the throne of God typify the heavenly saints in their character of the royal priesthood of twenty-four courses — "governors of the sanctuary and governors of God"

(I Chronicles 24:5; 25:31). What perfect, unending service the saints will then offer!

The Evangelist

Occurring thrice in Scripture, the name evangelist implies one who announces or proclaims good tidings. Each time (Acts 21:8; Ephesians 4:11; II Timothy 4:5), the reference is to the publishing of the Christian Gospel, with its emphasis on the death and resurrection of Christ, and of His power to save sinners thereby. While Paul does not mention bishop and elders as gifts to the church, he does include evangelists which is more of a work than an office. The ministry, not the office, was a divine gift (Ephesians 4:11). Says Professor A. M. Renwick in his *Story of the Church* —

> From a Scriptural point of view, the evangelist was temporary in the sense that he preached the Gospel to those outside the church and planted churches where they did not previously exist. He differed from an apostle in not possessing of necessity any supernatural powers. He traveled about, and his duties were mainly conversion of sinners and the building up of a congregation which he left afterwards to a settled ministry. Throughout the ages evangelists have done a great work in times of moral darkness and spiritual decline by acting as auxiliaries to the regular ministry.

God Himself was an evangelist for He "preached before the gospel to Abraham" (Galatians 3:8). Christ was also an evangelist for He came to "preach the gospel" (Luke 20:1) which His finished work at Calvary made possible. Two persons are specifically mentioned as evangelists, namely, Philip and Timothy. Philip had a wonderful fitness as an evangelist to proclaim in an impressive and convincing manner Christ's redeeming (Acts 8; 21:8). At Samaria, supernatural manifestations accompanied his evangelism (8:5-8). It was after the martyrdom of Stephen that Philip went forth and "preached the gospel." Timothy is the other named evangelist (II Timothy 4:5). As the travel companion of Paul in an evangelistic ministry, the young evangelist had great opportunities (Acts 16:1; 19:22; 20:4; Romans 16:2). Yet Timothy was exhorted to engage in tasks of moral supervision and patient doctrinal instruction, suggestive of the ministry of a settled pastorate. Not only was he to win outsiders but also to establish them in the faith. As an evangelist, he founded churches — as a teacher he built them up in the faith.

Titus at Crete was likewise fruitful in pioneer work of evangelism. Early disciples were all evangelists for they "went everywhere preaching the Word" (Acts 8:4). There were many evangelists who were not apostles. As for Paul, although not referred to as an "evangelist," he was the prince of evangelists in the early church. What a mighty ingathering of souls was his! Did he not refer to the prophetical agency of evangelists when he spoke of the church being "built upon the foundation of apostles and prophets"? (Ephesians 2:20; II Corinthians 8:18, 19). Barnabas, the companion of Paul in his evangelistic labors, also played an important part in the early extension of the Gospel (I Corinthians 9:5, 6; Galatians 2:9). A good man, and "full of the Holy Ghost and faith" wherever he went "much people was added to the lord" (Acts 11:22; 13: 2-4; 14:14). The name evangelist was given to the writers of the four gospels because they tell the story of the Gospel and because the effect of their message was very much like the work of the preaching evangelist. Says Dr.

James M. Gray — "In character, the gospels bear something of the same relation to the epistles as evangelists bear to pastor and teacher."

Eternity alone will reveal what the church owes to Spirit-filled evangelists. J. R. Green in *The History of the English People* declared that John Wesley's revival-ministry saved England from a bloody revolution. The present writer owes his life in Christ, under God, to a traveling evangelist who had a deep passion for lost souls and preached the message of a Saviour's love and grace. Because, essentially, an evangelist is a winner of souls, every believer can and should evangelize. In the economy of God every Christian should function as a soulwinner. Burdened with the need and peril of souls Paul cried, "Woe is me, if I preach not the Gospel."

Seek the souls around to win them,
Seek to Jesus Christ to bring them —
Seek this first!

The Minister

As the common New Testament term for minister is the same as deacon — *diakonos* — much we have written under THE DEACON (which see) is applicable here. "There shall also my servant be — my *diakonos* be" (John 12:26). Of the two other words used for minister the first implies "one who discharged a public service at his own expense," then, in general "a public servant, administrator or magistrate" (Romans 13:4; 15:16; Philippians 2:25; Hebrews 1:7; 8:2). The further Greek word means, "a rower under the steersman" and came to denote any subordinate acting under another's direction (Luke 4:20, ASV "attendant"; Acts 13:5; 26:16; I Corinthians 4:1). Minister, then, strictly means "one who serves or waits upon another" (Exodus 24:13). Thus the term is used in a variety of ways both in the spiritual and secular realms. We do a disservice to the essential meaning of ministry if we limit the word to a separate ministerial order. Ministry is now restricted in a way unknown in Scripture. All the saints are ministers, or at least they should be.

Diakonos covers "the diversities of ministries" (I Corinthians 12:5). It applies —

1. To angels (Psalm 104:4; Hebrews 1:4).
2. To the Lord Jesus Christ (Matthew 20:28).
3. To the apostleship (Acts 1:7; 20:24; 21:19; Romans 11:13, etc.).
4. To pastors and teachers and all ministers of the Word (I Corinthians 3:8; 4:1; Ephesians 4:12).
5. To disciples in general (John 12:26; See Stephenas, I Corinthians 16:15; Archippus, Colossians 4:17; Tychicus, Ephesians 6:21; Colossians 4:7, etc.).
6. To service rendered to the church because of "gifts" bestowed (Romans 12:7; I Corinthians 12:5 — hence all kinds of service, Matthew 20:26; Acts 6:2).
7. To assisting and feeding the poor among the saints (Acts 6:1; 11:29; 12:25; Romans 15:25; II Corinthians 8:4, 19).

We must always remember that all believers are "The ministers and stewards of thy mysteries." May we render our service in the light of the judgment seat of Christ! (I Corinthians 3:13).

The Pastor

Pastors and teachers were given to the church for its enlightenment and edification. It is their responsibility to care for the flock of God, not their flock (Ephesians 4:11). While the pastor must function as a teacher, perhaps the former gift has a wider significance than the latter, seeing that the work of the pastor includes much general godly care that would not come under the head of the teacher. Pastoring was probably the service to bishops, or overseers, and was an office involving tender care and vigilance. The flock must be fed and tended — the tending including feeding and folding, guiding and guarding (Acts 20:17, 28; I Corinthians 12:11; I Peter 5).

Pastor, meaning "feeder of sheep," is identified with pasture of a right and wrong kind. Paul's word about the doctrine of false pastors and teachers is that they act as a "gangrene" (II Timothy 2:17. See John 10:9). The counsels of true pastors were to be obeyed (Hebrews 13:17) — held in reputation and honor, to be highly esteemed because of the resemblance they bear in their shepherding to the Chief Shepherd Himself (Philippians 2:29; I Thessalonians 5:12, 13; Hebrews 13:20; I Peter 2:25; 5:4). Jeremiah has some caustic words about unfaithful pastors (Jeremiah 2:8; 10:21; 12:16; 22:22; 23:1, 2). Are not these whom Shakespeare describes in *Hamlet?*

> Do not, as some ungracious pastors do,
> Show me the steep and thorny way to heaven,
> Whiles, like a puffed and reckless libertine,
> Himself the primrose path of dalliance treads,
> And recks not his own rede.

Yet the prophet describes the true pastors as being according to God's heart, living and laboring to feed His people with knowledge and understanding (Jeremiah 3:15). These are they who follow the Lord and whether the truth they declare is glad or sad

they are true to their commission (Jeremiah 17:16). In Anglican circles, the bishop's official emblem is a shepherd's gold, bejeweled crook, symbol of his pastoral authority of the flock.

The Preacher

As "preacher" and its cognates occur some 150 times in the Bible, such an occupation must be an important one. The first to be described as a preacher, or herald, proclaimer, as the term implies was Noah who preached righteousness to those before the Flood (II Peter 2:5). Jonah's preaching resulted in a national revival, even though the message he proclaimed was only an eight-word sentence — "Yet forty days and Nineveh shall be overthrown." But it was effective because it was the preaching God commanded (Jonah 3:1-4). The Hebrew prophets had a message derived from God, hence the oft-repeated phrase emphasizing divine authority and inspiration, "the word of the Lord." Any true preacher must be a man with a divine message. "Every living preacher must receive his communication direct from God, and the constant purpose of his life must be to receive it uncorrupted, and to deliver it without addition or subtraction" (Revelation 22:18, 19).

Whether we think of Moses, whose proclaimed messages were "imbued with power, sublimity and pathos" more than any other Old Testament preacher, Deborah and Barak, Samuel and others were raised up by God, and they presented His truth in simplicity and with conviction. With the advent of John the Baptist there was a revival of prophetic preaching, so productive of moral and spiritual results. As a whole the preaching of the prophets consisted in the delivery of a divine message in song, in accusations, in rebuke, pleading and exhortation, prophecy and promise.

One of the common words describing a preacher means a crier or herald (Matthew 3:1; Romans 10:14). Bible preachers were heralds of God, to whom preaching meant the proclamation of divine truth or "the fulfillment of a divinely instituted ambassadorship" (II Corinthians 5:20). Their responsibility was to declare a divine revelation, not human opinion, theories or speculations. The Greek word here suggests not only the herald himself but the substance as well as the act of preaching. Another expressive word for preaching is *evangelidzo*, meaning "to announce good news" (Psalm 40:9; Isaiah 61:1). This term is akin to THE EVANGELIST (which see).

The prince of preachers was Jesus Himself who came as a herald proclaiming the glad tidings of God's love (John 3:16). Constantly He preached and taught in the synagogues (Matthew 4:17, 23; Mark 1:41; 6:2; Luke 4:16; John 6:59; 18:30), and gave to "preaching a spiritual depth and practical range which it never had before." He was more concerned with the heart of preaching than its art. With Him, as with the prophets before Him, He only proclaimed what God inspired Him to herald forth (John 17:8, 14). What impressive words for any preacher ever to have before him — "the words thou gavest me!"

Christ's preaching was "in power, insistent for attention, directive for conduct, and creative of character because He thought of Himself as a Messenger delivering a message from above. Certainly such a message, like a diamond, had many facets, but He brought to each occasion the type of message required. Powerfully, He preached about 'The Kingdom of God,' 'The Fatherhood of God' — a Fatherhood not extending to all men without regard to character, but only to those who were in fellowship with Himself as Saviour. Sin and righteousness, eternal life and death, pardon and power, conduct and character were fully expounded. Christ's preaching was never reduced to trifles of thought. He always had a powerful message for those who faced Him. His preaching was always dignified in character, harmonious with His mission of salvation, indicative of His own outlook upon life, and suggestive of His unique homiletical methods." Because preaching is divine truth communicated through personality, through His themes Christ expressed His personality and style.

While the Master preached His death and resurrection in their divine perspective, His disciples were slow in grasping the truth of His Saviourhood. But after the resurrection and ascension, what mighty preachers some of the apostles became as they witnessed to all Jesus had said and done. Ponder their reported sermons in Acts 2; 7; 8; 10; I Corinthians 15:15. Those early preachers knew that there must be an organic union between the word in the text and the sermon (I Corinthians 12:8; II Timothy 4:2). They preached under divine compulsion as Richard Baxter, of Kidderminster did, of whom it was said that he always preached as a dying man to dying men and women. Martin Luther is reputed to have said, "The devil does not mind the written word, but he is put to flight whenever it is preached aloud." When a man has the inner call of the Holy Spirit to preach, whether or not he receives the external call from a denomination, like Jeremiah God's word will be in his heart a burning fire shut up in his bones, and weary with forbearing, he must herald it forth (Jeremiah 20:9).

The Priest

An examination of the original words used of any Bible theme often enables one to understand the full import of the theme. At times, however, the derivation of words does not shed much light upon Biblical usage, as in the case of the word "priest" which scholars affirm to be of uncertain origin. Priesthood in one form or another appears to have existed from the beginning of the history of our race. Cain and Abel presented their respective offerings to God.

The Hebrew *Cohen,* for "priest" — a common surname among Jews — means "to draw near" and aptly expresses the function of a priest as a mediator between God and man. *Cahan* means "to present" (Exodus 19:22; 30:20, 21). This word originally meant a "seer" (Compare THE SEER), as well as one who had to do with divine things. A priest is a minister of any religion, whether heathen (Genesis 41:45; Acts 14:13) or Biblical (Matthew 8:4; I Peter 2:5, 9). The Greek word for "priest," *hiereus,* is related to *hieros,* meaning "holy" and describes one set apart to, and engaged in holy matters. The Latin is *sacredos,* or saved in the sense of being devoted to a god. Says Fausset, "Priest, our only word for *hiereus,* comes from *presbuteros,* the word chosen because it excluded a sacerdotal character." *Presbyteros,* derived from "elder" suggests the priestly function of counsel. If priest is associated with the term meaning "to preside," then Aristotle's definition of a priest, namely, one presiding over the things relating to the gods may fit in with Hebrews 5:1 — "Every high

priest taken from among men is ordained for men in things pertaining to God, that he may offer both gifts and sacrifices for sins."

The New Testament never uses *hiereus* as a title of a Christian minister. The only Christian application of this particular word is

1. To the unique high priesthood of Christ.
2. To the common priesthood of all believers.

All who are saved by grace, whether men or women, are priests, although many of them are not called to be public ministers of the Word. Priestly acts are never restricted to any one class in the Christian community. When an altar, with its official priest, and not the pulpit occupy the central place in a church, the New Testament teaching of the priesthood of all believers is not recognized therein. Approaching the subject of priesthood itself we can only give an outline of its functions. For a comprehensive and complete study the reader is referred to the exhaustive treatment of such a theme in Fairbairn's *Bible Encyclopaedia* or in Fausset's *Bible Encyclopaedia and Dictionary.*

1. Heathen Priesthood

The term *cohen* or *cahanim* used in the Old Testament for religious priests is also used of pagan priests. *Chemarim* represents idolatrous priests and in the Syraic signifies priests in general. Roman poets speak of Egyptian priests as the *linigiri* — from which we have "lingerie" — the wearers of linen. Many Egyptian bas-reliefs depict ancient high priests and priestesses in a variety of dress. In Gentile priesthood we have "the priest of Jupiter" (Genesis 41:45, 46; I Samuel 5:5; Acts 14: 13). In Ur of the Chaldees Abraham would be familiar with the gods and goddesses, priests and priestesses of the temples of the Sumerians, with the chief temple belonging to the moon god Nannar.

Writing on the institution of the high priesthood, James Josiah Reeve in a remarkable survey of the subject in *The International Standard Bible Encyclopaedia*, reminds us that —

> Temples with an elaborate ritual, a priesthood and a high priest were familiar to Moses. For a millennium or two before his time these had flourished in Egypt. Each temple had its priest or priests, the larger temples and centers having a high priest. For centuries the high priest of Amon at Thebes stood next to the king in power and influence. Many other high-priesthoods of less importance existed. Moses' father-in-law was priest of Midian, doubtless the chief or high priest. In founding a nation and establishing an ecclesiastical system, nothing would be more natural and proper for him than to institute a priestly system with a high priest at the head. The records give a fairly full account of the institution of the high-priesthood.

But as far as the priesthood of Israel is concerned there is no trace of Egyptian influence. True, Joseph married the daughter of the priest of On, On being the center of the cult of Ra, and its priests held in the highest possible respect. Thus Pharaoh could confer no greater social honor on Joseph than to give him as wife the priest's daughter (Genesis 41:45). This fact, however, had no bearing on the introduction of Israel's priestly family which took little or nothing of its powers and functions from Egyptian sources. The Aaronic priesthood had nothing in common with that of Egypt. Such a priesthood was of divine origin, and its duties, functions and powers in no way contradict the claim.

Professor M. G. Kyle, the eminent Egyptian archaeologist, writing on one essential element in the duties of the priestly office, namely, sacrifice, makes this pertinent observation —

> The entire absence from the offerings of old Egyptian religion of any of the great Pentateuchal ideas of sacrifice, substitution, atonement, dedication, fellowship, and indeed of almost every essential idea of real sacrifice, as clearly established by recent very exhaustive examination of the offering scenes, makes for the element of revelation in the Mosaic system by delimiting the field of rationalistic speculation on the Egyptian side. Egypt gave nothing to that system, for it had nothing to give.

2. Patriarchal Priesthood

As far back as Cain and Abel, man was his own priest (Genesis 4:1-7). The entrance of sin into humanity necessitated a priest. God's law had been broken, and a mediator was necessary whose primary function was to bring man to God, and God to man — "to propitiate God and to present the worship due to Him; on the other hand, to afford the worshiper the assurance of forgiveness and absolution." Fausset says that this idea between God and the people is expressed by "the presenting the atonement for the congregation, and the gifts of a reconciled people (Leviticus 21:7; Numbers 16:5; 17:5). Again, he brings back from God's presence the blessing of grace, mercy and peace (Numbers 6:22-27). This calling of the priest as representative mediator of the people is intimated in the term priest, a root of which means either to present one's self, or to present something or some one else. A priest would, therefore, be one who presents himself as a representative of another."

In the days of the patriarchs, the head of each family acted as the household priest. Noah offered representatively on behalf of those who were saved in the Ark (Genesis 8:20). Abraham, Isaac, Jacob and others built altars and offered sacrifices to God. Job, as the family priest, offered regular sacrifices for his sons (Job 1:5). When Israel became a people, priestly authority and activities were centralized in the person of one man, Moses. "The hereditary priesthood of the heads of families was not abolished, but, at the request of the people — and with divine approval — their duties were transferred to Moses" (Exodus 20:19; 24:6).

At Sinai God instructed Moses to tell His chosen people that He had chosen them to be "a kingdom of priests, and an holy nation" (Exodus 19:6), but afraid of close nearness to God, Israel renounced such a high calling, and God accepted their renunciation of priestly obligations. Thus Moses became the mediator for the nation, and the Aaronic priesthood became the temporary depository of all Israel's priesthood, until Christ the antitypical High Priest came. The "everlasting priesthood" Moses speaks of simply means "entailed upon posterity" (Numbers 25:13).

Under Jewish law the characteristics of a priest were —

1. He was chosen of God.
2. He was the property of God.
3. He had to be holy unto God.
4. He offered sacrifices and gifts to God, and took back gifts from God (Hebrews 5:1-4).
5. He taught the people about God.
6. He prayed for the people of God. "Offering incense," symbolizing prayer was exclusively the priest's duty (Numbers 16:5, 30; II Chronicles 26:18; Psalm 14:2; Revelation 8:3).

The divine institution of the Aaronic priesthood culminated in the high priest, the first being Aaron, the brother of Moses (Leviticus 4:15, 16). For further characteristics of Aaronic high priests see Deuteronomy 10:8; 17:10, 12; 18:5; 21:5; 24:8; 31:9; 33:10; I Samuel 2:28; Hebrews 8:3; 9:7, 25; 10:11, ASV margin; 13:11. In the original, the term for high priest means, "the great priest" (Numbers 35:28) or "the head priest" (II Kings 25:18; II Chronicles 19:11; 24:4; Ezra 7:5). He was the priest, greater than his brethren-priests, upon whose head the anointing oil was poured and who was consecrated to put on garments. For a fuller study of all matters relating to the consecration, dress, duties, and emoluments of the Aaronic priesthood, the reader is advised to consult comprehensive articles under "Priesthood" in a reliable Bible dictionary or encyclopedia.

According to Hosea's prophecy, priesthood was to cease in Israel, as it did (3:4, *Amplified Bible*). Today, the Jewish people have their rabbi but no priest. When Christ came, He united in Himself the three offices of prophet, priest and king, terminating thereby these offices in Judaism. When He returns, however, to usher in His millennial reign Israel will resume her priesthood and "shall be priests of Jehovah, the ministers of our God," to the Gentile nations in Christ's millennial kingdom (Isaiah 61:6; 66:21).

3. *Divine Priesthood*

Christ is our great High Priest, not after the order of Aaron, but of Melchizedek (Psalm 110), whose sacerdotal functions in going forth to bless Abraham, He will exercise when He returns to bless Abraham's children. Now, while hidden in the holiest of all, Christ is exercising the functions of Aaron in appearing in the presence of God for us. Our Lord superseded the Levitical priesthood by offering Himself once for all. There were two requisites which Aaron did not possess but which were essentially necessary to the true High Priest, namely —

A. The possession of a sinless nature, symbolized by the wailings and offerings for sin.

B. The possession of the divine nature, typified by the anointing and the investment of the holy garments. Both of the conditions were fulfilled in Christ (Hebrews 7:26), whose priesthood furnished the substance of which the Aaronic priesthood was the shadow and symbol (Hebrews 5:1-10).

Because Christ completed and superseded the Aaronic priesthood, His eternal priesthood is the central theme of the Epistle to the Hebrews, whereas "our Redeemer He executeth the offices of prophet, priest and king both in His estate of humiliation and exaltation." W. E. Vine indicates the following seven outstanding features of His priesthood —

1. Its Character (5:6, 10).
2. His Commission (5:4, 5).
3. His Preparations (2:17; 10:5).
4. His Sacrifice (8:3; 9:2, 14, 27, 28).
5. His Sanctuary (4:14; 8:2; 9:11, 12, 24; 10:12, 19).
6. His Ministry (2:18; 4:15; 7:25; 8:6; 9:15, 24).
7. Its Effects (2:15; 4:16; 6:19, 20; 7:16, 25; 9:14, 28; 10:14-17, 22, 39; 12:1; 13:13-17).

Christ is referred to in these different ways throughout Hebrews —

As a priest (5:6; 7:11, 15, 17, 21; 8: 4).
As a high priest (4:15; 5:5, 16; 6: 20; 7:26; 8:1, 3 asv).
As a great high priest (4:14).
As a great priest (10:21).

As a merciful and faithful high priest (2:7).
As the Apostle and High Priest of our profession (3:1 asv).
As the High Priest after the order of Melchizedek (5:10).

Every holder of the sacerdotal had to have very definite qualifications —

The priest had to be capable of sympathizing with others in their infirmities.
The priest must be called of God and not self-appointed.
The priest must naturally have something to offer (Hebrews 4: 15; 5:2, 4; 8:3).

While Aaron perfectly satisfied these qualifications, in a fuller measure our great High Priest fulfils such conditions (Hebrews 2:17; 5:5). Thus, the superiority of Christ's priesthood over that of the past is given prominence in Hebrews. The present intercession of Christ as our Advocate who watches over us and counsels and guides us is also clearly taught by Paul (Romans 8:26, 27; Hebrews 7: 25).

4. Christian Priesthood

In the early church the priesthood of all believers was a tremendous reality. Actually, this corporate priesthood is of two orders, answering in some degree to the double character of the high priesthood of old. All who are the Lord's in this dispensation of grace are "holy" priests to offer up spiritual sacrifices resembling, thereby, the Aaronic order. They are also "royal" priests to show forth the virtues of Him who called them out of darkness into His marvelous light (Colossians 1:13, 14; I Peter 2:9, 10), herein resembling the Melchizedek functions, which Christ Himself will exercise when He reigns as the Priest-

King. It must not be lost sight of that all believers, men and women, are priests, and are all responsible to offer up the sacrifices of praise, almsgiving and devotion (Romans 12:1; Philippians 2:17; 4:18; Hebrews 13:15, 16; I Peter 2:5). Regenerated Jews and Gentiles constitute "a kingdom of priests," "a holy and royal priesthood" (I Peter 2:5, 9; Revelation 1:6; 5:10; 20:6).

Paul used symbols of priestly ritual in connection with his own sacrificial ministry (Romans 15:16; Philippians 2:17; II Timothy 4:6). Although believers will not function as kings until the King of kings Himself comes to reign (Matthew 19:28; Luke 22:18, 20:30; I Corinthians 4:8), yet they do presently serve as priests as they bring the Word of God to men, and lead men to Christ. "By virtue of their relation to Christ all believers have direct approach to God," says David Foster Estes, "and consequently, as this right of approach was formerly a priestly privilege, priesthood may now be predicated of every Christian. That none needs another to intervene between his soul and God; that none can thus intervene for another; that every soul may and must stand for itself in personal relation to God — such are the simple elements of the New Testament doctrine of the priesthood of all believers."

Christianity recognizes no special, distinctive priesthood. All Christians have an equal right and privilege to draw near to God in and through the merits and work of the great High Priest Himself. Under the Aaronic priesthood, only those of that priesthood could draw nigh to God. No other Israelite had such a privileged position. But now all believers by virtue of their union with Christ, as a spiritual people, are a continual priesthood. Every member of His body should function as a priest. Thomas Aquinas wrote that, "the righteous layman is united to Christ in a spiritual union by faith and love, and therefore hath a spiritual priesthood for the offering of spiritual sacrifices." What a mighty force the church would be if only every Christian practiced the priesthood! Having the right of immediate access to God, which is characteristic of priesthood, may we be found exercising our privilege and prerogatives as priests.

5. Ecclesiastical Priesthood

This unscriptural aspect arises out of what we have just referred to. The testimony of the early fathers against a special sacerdotal caste is most emphatic. Justin Martyr, for instance, spoke of all believers as "the high priestly race of God." Irenaeus wrote of "every just man of the priestly order." Tertullian asked: "Are not we laymen also priests?" and also maintained that "the laity also have a right to administer the sacraments and to teach in the church." In no sense has the church or any church an official priesthood. It was around the second century that Cyprian of Carthage, who was made a bishop by popular acclaim, insisted on the high place of the episcopate, making stupendous claims for the absolute supremacy of the bishop as a God-appointed ruler of the church. Cyprian also conceived the idea of the clergy as sacrificing priests, who, when they officiated at the Lord's Supper, offered up on the altar the very body and blood of Christ. Before Cyprian's time, however, the church constantly affirmed in its dealing with the heathen world that it had neither altar, sacrifice or priest. But with Cyprian's departure from the divine order there gradually developed a distinct order separating themselves from secular employment to assume "the office of priest as the dispenser of grace — conferring rituals and as the custodian of the kingdom of heaven entrusted with the dread power of the keys." To affirm, as Rome does, that no one can be saved or benefit by the grace of God except through participation in the rituals of the church, is absolutely foreign to the teaching of the New Testament. A sinner can only be saved by grace, and grace alone; and once saved becomes a priest with the privilege of offering up spiritual sacrifices. We cannot do better than quote the summary Professor A. M. Renwick gives us in his excellent work on *The Story of the Church*. Dealing with the changing face of the church from A.D. 604, the writer, dealing with the priesthood says —

> As sacerdotalism increased, the altar, which formerly had no place in the Christian Church, became of greater and greater importance. This led to drastic alterations which extended even to the architectural design of churches. The priesthood of all believers was wellnigh forgotten. The priest was now regarded as of a different order from the laity and as having a special grace and divine authority by reason of his ordination. He became indispensable in the Christian's approach to God. He handled divine mysteries and his work was regarded as a species of magic, like the work of heathen priests. The altar at which he officiated, and upon which he offered again the sacrifice of the body and blood of Christ, came to be regarded as the most sacred place in the building and was railed from the nave of the church. There thus grew up a priestly caste separated from the people.

But as we have already pointed out Christian ministers are never in the New Testament called by the name "priests" *(hierlis)*. Paul does not mention the term in the Spirit's gifts to the church. *Hierlis* is applied only to the Aaronic priests, to Christ, and to all Christians. While this would have been the most natural word for Jewish writers to have used, the Holy Spirit restrained them from employing it to describe those who minister the Word — who are called bishop, deacons, elders, ministers, but never sacerdotal, sacrificing priests. Fausset reminds us that the synagogue, not the temple, was the model for organizing the church, and that Korah's punishment for usurping the sacerdotal priesthood should act as a warning to all Christian ministers who not content with the ministry, usurp Christ's intransmittable priesthood (Numbers 16:9, 10; Hebrews 7:24).

With the development of sacerdotalism around the sixth century, vestments were introduced as being an essential part of the priest's equipment. Why, by the end of the fourth century the bishops were discussing the propriety of different colors for their robes! Then with the introduction of the Mass, a wardrobe of vestments for High and Low Mass was designed. But up to this time ministers wore no distinctive dress. The amount of money spent today on priestly attire must be enormous.

6. Millennial Priesthood

Christ will realize to the full the prophecy of Zechariah and reign as "a priest upon his throne" (Isaiah 4:2; Jeremiah 23:5, 6; Zechariah 6:13). In the glorious millennial age, Christ is to sit upon the throne of Israel as King and Priest, the perfect antitype of the king-priest, Melchizedek. Then the divine purpose for Israel will be fulfilled and as God's earthly people they shall be named "the priests of the Lord" and the Gentile nations shall call them "the Ministers of our God" (Isaiah 61:

6; 66:21). The priestly function of believers continues through the millennial reign of the Lord. As the heavenly people of God, and presently "a royal priesthood" they shall be priests of God and of Christ and shall reign with Him (Revelation 20:6), assisting Him in His governmental control of all things.

So there will be a blessed and holy series: Christ the royal High Priest, the glorified saints as kings and priests, and Israel in the flesh as king-priest to the nations in the flesh. As Dr. F. A. Tatford expresses it —

> The whole universe will be bound together by golden sacerdotal chains; on earth, the priests of Israel — a whole priestly nation functioning for others; over the earth, the priest of this age, reigning with their Lord in glory, and supreme above all, the Sovereign Priest after the order of Melchizedek.

The Prophet

Egypt may have had its autocratic Pharaohs — Greece its famous poets, philosophers and painters — Rome its renowned soldiers, statesmen and Legislators, but Israel is conspicuous for her mighty prophets. The importance of the office of a prophet can be gleaned from the fact that it is mentioned over 400 times in the Bible, and its cognates some 150 times. Abraham is the first to be named a "prophet" (Genesis 20:7), who became prominent as the recipient of divine revelations (Psalm 105:15). It would seem, however, as if Enoch preceded him by centuries for he, too, was a prophet who prophesied of the future (Jude 14). Isaiah is the first prophet to be quoted in the New Testament (Isaiah 7:14; Matthew 1:22).

When the priest failed as God's medium of revelation and expression, He raised up a new order to witness for Him in plainer warnings, namely, the prophets. The priests were Israel's first teachers of God's law. By types, acts and words they conveyed to Israel the divine mind and message, but the nation repeatedly rejected the divine voice through the priest. With the advent of Samuel the great prophet, the priesthood was reformed and the order of the prophets was established. He, it was, who established theological schools for prophets and their sons (I Samuel 19:12, 20; II Kings 2:3, 5; 4:38). The prophets were distinguishable by their hairy garments with leathern girdle and simple diet — a virtual protest against abounding luxury (I Kings 19:6; II Kings 4:10, 38; Isaiah 10:2; Zechariah 13:4; Matthew 3:4).

One of the Old Testament words for prophet means "to bubble forth as a fountain," and is equivalent to the inspiration of the Holy Spirit (Job 32:8-20; II Peter 1:19-21). "My heart is bubbling up a good matter" (Psalm 45:1). Generally the term implies a "public expounder" just as prophecy indicates "public exposition" (Matthew 13:14; Romans 16:26). A divinely chosen prophet was a speaker for, or of, God — "the mouth of the Lord" (Ezekiel 7:1). He was one speaking forth truth for another, as Aaron was Moses' prophet or spokesman of God's will (Exodus 7:1). Augustine says, "The prophet of God is nothing else but the teller forth of the words of God to men."

Occasionally "prophet" is synonymous with "seer" (Compare THE SEER), that is one who "sees" truth with his inner eyes (I Samuel 9:9; Isaiah 2:1). He was a gazer upon the spiritual world (I Chronicles 29:9). "Samuel the seer, Nathan the prophet, Gad the gazer." Fausset comments that "As the seer beheld the visions of God, so the prophet proclaimed the divine truth revealed to him as one of an official order in a more direct way. God Himself states the different modes of His revealing Himself and His truth" (Numbers 12:6, 8). The two main characteristics of a true prophet then, were that of seer and speaker — "the spiritual vision which gave him the knowledge, and the power of utterance which enabled him to declare his message with power."

The divinely chosen prophet (Deuteronomy 18:15, 18) differed from a self-chosen one (Jeremiah 23:16; 29:26, 27), in that he did not utter a production of his own spirit. His utterances did not originate in his own reflection or calculation (Ezekiel 13:2, 3). The true prophet, like his Antitype, Jesus Christ, spake not of himself (John 7:17, 18; Numbers 11:17, 25, 29; 12:6-8; I Samuel 10:6; 19:20). Professional prophets, of whom there were many, trained to exercise prophetic functions, practiced them as a profession — exciting themselves with music and wild dances. Because this class were not divinely inspired they were often directly opposed to the mind and will of God. Often the true prophets denounced the professional prophets, and the latter persecuted the former. This professional order gradually degenerated until it became a base organ for the flattery of king and court. The true prophet, on the other hand, possessed by the Spirit, spake in the Spirit and declared what he intuitively and directly saw and heard (Isaiah 6:1; Micah 1:1; Habakkuk 1:1; Zechariah 2:1; Acts 10:1; 22:18; Revelation 1:12). They were thus compelled to announce the divine message, which was as a fire in their bones before release (Jeremiah 20:7, 9). Further, the Spirit who inspired was not confined to any priestly class but selected at will from among

every station of life, age or sex (Numbers 24:2).

Scripture leaves us in no doubt as to the exact function of true prophets. They were God's remembrancers; watchmen and guardians of the people. Patriots as well as prophets, they warned their nation of approaching dangers and judgments, and pleaded for or against the people (I Kings 17; 18:36, 37; Romans 11:2, 3; James 5:16, 18; Revelation 11:6). "The priests were Israel's regular teachers; the prophets extraordinary, to rouse and excite." Fairbairn points out that there were three essential qualifications for the true prophets of old —

1. *Theirs had to be a personal communication direct from heaven.*

God's prophets occupied a special and peculiar position of intercommunion between heaven and earth. They were men of God, who entered into God's mind, breathed God's Spirit, and proclaimed a message which had first imparted light to their own eyes and awakened a response in the sanctuary of their own bosom.

2. *Theirs had to be a communication befitting supernatural agency.*

Prophecy, which was a history of events before they came to pass, had to disclose the fundamental truths and principles of God's righteous government as the moral hinges on which the events of the time and the issues of eternity perpetually turn.

3. *Theirs had to be a faithful delivery of divine communications.*

Whether the message was pleasant or otherwise there had to be the faithful announcement of it. Often the prophets had to suffer in the fulfillment of their office. Sometimes the boldest of them quailed in their task or experienced a temporary eclipse of faith, as in the expressed reluctance of Moses, "Behold they will not believe me, nor hearken to my voice," or when Elijah requested that he might die (II Kings 9:1-5; Jeremiah 21:7; Acts 27:24; Galatians 1:16). They were men of like passions as we are. For the sake of clarity and convenience we classify Bible prophets in this fourfold way —

PAGAN PROPHETS

All heathen systems of religion had their so-called prophets. There were the 450 of Baal whom Elijah challenged, ridiculed and exposed (I Kings 18:17-41). Babylon was the headquarters of the art of soothsaying, which was a form of prophecy in its endeavor to probe the future. As we previously indicated (See THE SOOTHSAYER), God condemned this art (Leviticus 19:31; 20:6, 27; Deuteronomy 18:9, 16). Soothsayers represented a part of the web of superstition so characteristic of the ancient world. In Canaan, Israel found a people professing to unveil the future and discover the will of their gods by various arts the Bible calls "abominations" — which abominations constituted a danger to God's people (Deuteronomy 18:15). These so-called prophets of antiquity however, are clearly distinguished from those of divine origin (Deuteronomy 18:15-18). Ancient Greece, as with Mesopotamian countries, had its god, oracle, prophet and people. Israel, however, had only one intermediary between God and the people, namely, the prophet who received the very words of God Himself, and faithfully declared them.

HEBREW PROPHETS

The period of Old Testament history, when the nation had the specific and special ministry of God-selected prophets, lasted about 500 years, from the ninth to the beginning of the fourth century B.C. That there were occasional prophets before their period can be gathered from Peter's saying, "All the prophets from Samuel." What an important part these men of God played in Hebrew history! Raised up by God these patriot-prophets were the authoritative voice dictating terms to kings, upbraiding the disobedient people, and indicating what their true line of policy and activity should be. During the Monarchy, the prophetic office was born, and God spoke to the people, not through kings nor priests, but by His servants the prophets, whose messages were given the imperative of revelation and duty, by the usual preface, "Thus saith the Lord."

The two general periods when the prophets exercised their political, moral and predictive ministry are as follows —

The First Period

This stretched from the time of Samuel (1050 B.C.) to the time of Jeremiah (629 B.C.), and included the ministries of Samuel, Elijah, Elisha, Obadiah, Joel, Jonah, Amos, Hosea, Isaiah, Micah, Jeremiah, and others less prominent.

The Second Period

This ran from the Exile (605 B.C.) to the close of the prophetic office (433 B.C.) and embraced the works of Daniel, Ezekiel, Haggai, Zechariah and Malachi. Then there followed the four hundred years of silence, unbroken by a single prophetic voice until the coming of John the Baptist.

In the historical development of the prophetic office Abraham is prominent among the first to become recipients of divine revelations (Genesis 20:7; Psalm 105:15). The intercourse between God and Moses was always of a particular nature. They spoke together "face to face" (Exodus 33:11; Numbers 12:6). The song of Moses (Deuteronomy 32) has been called, "The Magna Charter of Prophecy." With Samuel, there began the official prophetic order of the Old Testament. Of the hundreds trained in "the school of the prophets," only a few find mention. The bulk of prophetic writings are to be found in the utterances of the sixteen named prophets from Isaiah to Malachi. Their books are known as the major prophets — Hosea to Daniel; the minor prophets — Hosea to Malachi. The only sense in which the latter are minor is in respect to the size of the book. They are not less in importance than the former.

A true prophet was the declarer and interpreter of the divine will respecting the past, present and future. While some of the prophets were closely associated with literature, compiling historical records and preserving national chronicles (I Chronicles 29:29), their great work was not of a literary nature. They were rather men of action, exercising the twofold ministry of forthtelling and foretelling. While much of Old Testament prophecy was of a predictive nature, it was not necessarily, nor even, primarily, foretelling, that is, telling beforehand what would happen in the future (Micah 5:2; John 11:51). It also included forthtelling which means the telling forth of truths concerning the will and purpose of God which could not be known by natural means, whether such truth was related to the past, present, or future (Genesis 20:7; Deuteronomy 18:18; Revelation 10:11; 11:3).

The Prophet as a Forthteller.

Nothing in literature is more scathing than the denunciations of the prophets against the injustices of their own times. Isaiah, Jeremiah, Hosea, Amos and Micah — how these mighty patriots could arouse the conscience of the nation as they presented God in His august holiness, ranged on the side of the poor and the oppressed against those who were guilty of exploitation, self-indulgence, and greed! Times may have changed but the principles declared by the prophets have not changed. How they need a reemphasis today by another army of God's inspired messengers!

Those ancient prophets were not simply nor chiefly "seers," meaning those able to see into the future (I Samuel 9:9), they were also heralds of God inspired to understand God's will for their own age, and, irrespective of any reaction, to declare it. As critics and censors of private and public morals, they kept before the nation the high ideal of its true life as a divinely chosen nation. Although seemingly austere, they had hearts of compassion as they stood out as the national conscience incarnate, as the voice of God pleading with His people. They were not afraid to call surrounding evils by plain names, and denounce them in uncompromising terms. As God's remembrancers they pleaded for, or against, the nation (I Kings 17; 18). The moral teaching, outstanding in their public ministry, is sorely needed in our day of abounding iniquity (Isaiah 1; 58; Ezekiel 18; Micah 6). Our nation's greatest need is that of prophets, not politicians.

The Prophet as a Foreteller.

The ministry of a true prophet was predictive and Messianic, as well as political and moral. Out of the midst of existing conditions the prophets were always looking forward, foretelling both the failure and restoration of the chosen people, and the coming of the Messiah in and through whom the purpose of God on earth would be realized for His people. Thus, the Messianic (future), as well as the moral (present) were combined in many prophetic utterances. Predictions, as to Israel, surrounding nations, and the Messiah must be given their place in any estimation of Hebrew prophecy, with such a predictive element being far removed from that of a "fortunetelling" order. This prophetic thread is woven into the texture of inspired history with God Himself as the first Prophet (Genesis 3:15; Deuteronomy 18:21, 22; I Samuel 2:27; Jeremiah 28:9; Acts 2:36; I Peter 1:10; II Peter 3:2).

The fulfillment of prophecy constituted an integral part of genuine prophecy, and is an evidence of divine inspiration. Prophecy remains an empty word and falls to the ground, if it is not raised up or fulfilled. Predictions fulfilled established a prophet's authority (I Samuel 3:19; Jeremiah 22:11, 12; Ezekiel 12:12, 13). Predictions of future, and even remote events, proved that such predictive prophecy was from a divine source, thereby removing it from human ignorance and error. "To see and foretell future events may be called a miracle of knowledge, as properly as to raise the dead may be called a miracle of power."

In spite of the professed ability of astrologists to read the future, man with all his talents, sciences and desire cannot penetrate the unseen. The future is known only to Him who knows the end from the beginning. One design of the prophetic dispensation in the Old Testament was to give a striking manifestation of the omniscient, true God, as distinguished from all idols and lying vanities (Isaiah 41:21-27; 42:8, 9; 44:6, 7; 45:20, 21). Just as the working of miracles is beyond human power, so to predict

the distant contingencies of futurity is beyond the reach of human sagacity. The Holy Spirit alone can show us things to come (John 16:13).

The bulk of Old Testament prophecy is associated with the coming of Christ as the Messiah, and this predicted One for whom Israel wistfully waited is the Saviour we worship and serve. Further, as all who bore testimony to Jesus before His birth were preachers of righteousness, so all who testify that Christ came in the flesh, exercise the same prophetic function. A further design of prophecy was to "testify beforehand the sufferings of Christ, and the glory that should follow" (I Peter 1:10, 11); and it was to these predictions that both Christ and the apostles appealed (Luke 24:26, 27, 44; Acts 3:22-25; 26:22, 23). It is because the great design of prophecy was to bear testimony to Christ that "the testimony of Jesus is the spirit of prophecy" (Revelation 19:10). Most striking and affecting pictures of the spirit and behavior of the Messiah amidst the most distressing and humiliating experiences are portrayed by the prophets (Psalm 22; Isaiah 53; Zechariah 12:10). Professor W. T. Davison reminds us that —

> In the Person, life, sufferings, death and resurrection of Jesus the Christ, and in the establishment of His Kingdom on the earth, is to be found the fullest realization of the glowing words of the prophets who prepared the way for His coming. For a still more complete fulfillment of their highest hopes and fairest visions the world still waits.

Concerning all the prophets wrote of Him, we can rest in His own words, "Till heaven and earth pass away, one jot or one tittle shall in no wise pass away from the prophets, till all things shall be accomplished." All Messianic prophecy is but the development of the primary one about the appearance of the Saviour "the woman's seed" (Genesis 3:15). The Messianic Psalms are rich in this line of prophecy. While the prophets who gave witness to Jesus did not understand the full depth of their prophetic messages, taken in their entirety they present a unified picture of the work of Him whose day they saw when they spoke of Him. Matthew quotes from Hosea, "Out of Egypt have I called my son" (Hosea 11:1; Matthew 2:15). Israel, naturally a "son" (Exodus 4:22) whom God brought out of Egypt; and Christ, the greater Son, was also taken out of Egypt. These passages illustrate how many prophetic utterances often had a deeper meaning than at first appears. When, as the Son, Christ appeared, He could expound in all Old Testament Scripture the things concerning Himself (Luke 24:27, 44, 45).

CHRISTIAN PROPHETS

In the New Testament, prophets are placed next to apostles (I Corinthians 12:28; Ephesians 2:20). Bishop F. J. A. Hort aptly sums up some of the gifts to the church in this way — "The two types of exceptional and temporary functions — apostles and prophets; and two corresponding types of ordinary and permanent functions — evangelist, pastor and teacher." Vine reminds us that the Prophets mentioned by Paul are not the prophets of Israel, but the gifts of the ascended Lord whose ministry it was to edify and encourage believers (I Corinthians 14:3), and to prove to unbelievers that the secrets of a man's heart are known to God who, by His Spirit convicts of sin and constrains to worship (I Corinthians 14:24, 25). These prophets exercised an important function in the early church before there was a trained ministry and before the canon of the New Testament was completed. They were the Spirit-inspired announcers of truth whether dealing with past, present or prospective aspects of it; and corresponded to the place and authority of the ancient description of prophets (II Kings 17: 13). Ordinarily, New Testament prophets were forthtellers rather than foretellers — those whose gift enabled them to speak to edification, exhortation and comfort (I Corinthians 12: 9, 28; 14:3). Prophecy, as used by Paul, is to be understood in the general, in the sense of one functioning as the Lord's mouthpiece to His people. Neither in the Old or New Testament is prophecy confined to the foretelling of future events. It also includes a voice from God through His servant to the conscience of those near present events as the prophecies of Jeremiah abundantly prove (I Corinthians 12:31; 14:22, 25, 39, ASV).

Discussing the specific New Testament prophet as one to be distinguished from others who "speak the word of God," Dr. J. C. Lambert gives us this distinction —

The apostle was a missionary to the unbelieving (Galatians 2:7, 8).

The prophet was a messenger to the Church (I Corinthians 14:4, 22).

The teacher explained or enforced truth that was already possessed (Hebrews 5:12).

The prophet was recognized by the spiritual discernment of his hearers (I Corinthians 2:15; 14:29; I John 4:1), as the divine medium of fresh revelation (I Corinthians 14:15, 30, 31; Ephesians 3:5).

Among the prophets of the New Testament who continued the Old Testament spirit of prophecy we have —

Anna the prophetess (Luke 2:36).

Zacharias, who is expressly said to have prophesied (Luke 1:6).

Simeon, whose adoration was of an unmistakeably prophetic nature (Luke 2:25).

John the Baptist, successor to Malachi who was a prophet predicted the coming of the Lord Jesus Christ. Not only did the people recognize him as a great prophet, but Jesus spoke of him as the greatest prophet of the former dispensation (Matthew 11:9; 14:5; 21:26; Mark 11:32; Luke 7:26; 20:6).

The Lord Jesus Christ was a prophet. He was recognized by the people and His disciples as a prophet (Matthew 13:57; Luke 13:33, 34). With no uncertainty He Himself assumed this role (Luke 4:24). He was the Prophet who came into the world (Deuteronomy 18:15-18; Isaiah 61:1; John 6:14; Acts 3:22, 26). The prophetic office reached its highest stage of development in Him because He stood in a more intimate relation to God than any other previous prophet. Christ excelled both as a forthteller and foreteller. He resembled the prophets of old in His appeal to His own generation, and likewise gave much attention to the prediction of future events in His oral ministry. He departed, however, from the prophetic custom in the use of the formula, "Thus saith the Lord." He never used it, or appealed to a higher source for the confirmation of His utterances. As "very God of very God" He had the authority to say, "Verily, verily, *I* say unto you."

Caiaphas, the high priest, functioned as a prophet when he predicted the substitutionary aspect of Christ's death (John 11:47, 51; 18:13).

Agabus provides us with a rare instance of the prediction of a future event (Acts 11:28; 21:4, 10). Agabus is grouped with other prophets from Jerusalem (Acts 11:27; 21:10).

Judas and Silas were prophets at Antioch (Acts 13:1).

Philip had four daughters who prophesied (Acts 5:9).

Paul himself is described as a prophet long after he had become an apostle (Acts 13:1; 16:6; 18:9; 22:17; 27:23). All who proclaimed the Word of God were prophets (Hebrews 13:7). In the public service of the church, prophecy occupied a prominent position (I Corinthians 12:28; 14; Ephesians 2:20; 3:5; 4:11). A single assembly might possess several prophets (I Corinthians 14:29). To quote Dr. Lambert again, "Certain of them, possessed no doubt of conspicuous gifts, moved about from Church to Church (Matthew 10:41; Acts 11:27; 21:10). Others, endowed with literary powers, would commit their 'visions and revelations' to writing, just as some prophet of the Old Testament had done, though of this literary type of prophecy we have only one example in the New Testament — the Book of Revelation" (Revelation 1:3; 22:7, 9, 10, 19).

John the apostle gave us the most outstanding prophetical book in the Bible. But with John and the completion of the canon of Scripture, prophecy apparently passed away (I Corinthians 13:8, 9). As Vine puts it, "In his measure the teacher has taken the place of the prophet — compare the significant change in II Peter 2:1. The difference is that, whereas the message of the prophet was a direct revelation of the mind of God for the occasion, the message of the teacher is gathered from the completed revelation contained in the Scriptures." God has no new truth to reveal. By the Spirit, however, we can gain fresh insight into truth already given (John

16:7, 13). The Apostle John was the last of the prophetic order.

> The harp of prophecy, so long
> By sacred impulse fired,
> Had breathed its last entrancing song,
> And with the seer died.

FALSE PROPHETS

While the term "false prophets" does not occur in the Hebrew text, all that it implies is evident (Luke 6:26; II Peter 2:1). The line between the true and the false, and the tests by which the true can be separated in practice is marked. From the beginning of time, the true has been plagued by the false. God, His Son, and His Servants have had their imitators (I Kings 22:22; Isaiah 28:7; Jeremiah 23:16; 28:1; Ezekiel 13:14; Zephaniah 3:4). Departure from truth on the part of those prophets connected with idolatrous worship was obvious (Deuteronomy 13:4, 5; I Kings 18). Sometimes the high prophetic gift was perverted for selfish advancement or for mere financial gain (Micah 3:5; Zechariah 13:4). Those given to false prophesying spoke after "the deceit of their own heart" (Jeremiah 14:13, 14). Others, destitute of any real prophetic gift aped the role of the prophet (Jeremiah 23:28, 31). It was against all the self-deceived prophets that the true prophets had to contend. C. E. Schenk writes —

> The only test here was the spiritual character of the utterance, and this test demanded a certain moral or spiritual sense which the people did not always possess. Consequently, in times of moral darkness the false prophets, predicting smooth things for the nation, independent of repentance, consecration and the pursuit of spiritual ideals, were honored above the true prophets who emphasized the moral greatness of Jehovah and the necessity of righteousness for the nation.

Following the career of Old Testament prophets we discern how far their character bore out their profession, "what motives actuated them — whether crooked policy, immediate expediency, or high, self-denying principles." Thus in the centuries before Christ, or afterwards, one of the best criteria was, "By their fruits ye shall know them." False prophecy, it has been said, is best conceived as a degeneration of the true.

Coming to the New Testament we are exhorted to "beware of false prophets," and to turn away from them and their pernicious teaching. The early church suffered much from false prophecy. The term for "false prophet" is *pseudoprophetes* — "pseudo," meaning sham or false, and is used of false prophets in the present period since Pentecost (Matthew 7: 15; 24:11, 24; Mark 13:22; Acts 13:6; I John 4:1). Any religious teacher or minister, irrespective of his denominational label, who denies the fundamentals of the faith is a false prophet. It is because of the open denial of the faith once delivered to the saints by many theological training centers and pulpits today that we face the growing apostasy the apostles predicted.

All false prophets are to reach a dread climax in "the false prophet," co-supporter of "the Beast" in the Tribulation (Revelation 16:13; 19:20; 20:10) — himself described as "another beast" (Revelation 13:11). These two beasts are to be the tools and instruments of Satan for the planned destruction of God's people. The lake of fire is to be their final and eternal abode (Revelation 20:10). With Christ as our Prophet, and the Holy Spirit to teach us what is true, we can be kept from all that is false (I John 2:27; 4:1-3). Compare THE TEACHER.

For those desiring a more comprehensive study of the prophetical aspect of the Bible we recommend the most exhaustive treatment to be found in Fairbairn's *Bible Encyclopaedia* under "Prophecy" which concludes with the observation, "The range of prophetical literature is so extensive that no one can master all that has been written on the subject."

The Saviour

In the Old Testament Scriptures "saviour" is used in a subordinate sense of God's servants sent to deliver, by displays of miraculous power, His chosen people from their enemies. These human instruments were saviours who secured a national salvation for Israel (Judges 3:9, 15; II Samuel 3: 18; II Kings 13:5; 14:27; Nehemiah 9: 27; Obadiah 21). The Greeks applied *soter* — the Greek for "saviour" — to their gods. Cicero arraigned Verres for using it: "Soter . . . How much does this imply? So much that it cannot be expressed in one word in Latin." It was used of the philosopher Epicurus; of rulers like Ptolemy I and Nero; of men who had conferred signal benefits upon the country. Thus, "the adoption of *Soter* by Christianity was most natural, the word seemed ready-made," but in the New Testament it is a strictly Christian term and is never applied to a mere man.

In the Old Testament "Saviour" is used of God some thirteen times, seven of which are to be found in Isaiah 43 - 63, and carries the basic concept of Him as the Deliverer of His people. Man had no power in himself to save himself (Job 40:14; Psalms 33:16; 44:3, 7). He must look to God alone for salvation whether spiritual, physical or material (Isaiah 43:11; 45:22; Hosea 13:4, 10). The New Testament also refers to God as

a Saviour, Deliverer, Preserver. As the latter, He gives "to all life and breath and all things" (Luke 1:47; I Timothy 1:1; 2:3; 4:10; Titus 1:3; 2:10; 3:4; Jude 25).

Generally, however, the term is appropriated to the Messiah, all past saviours of Israel prefigured. *Soter* is the comprehensive term for the spiritual and eternal blessings brought to men by Christ's appearance and redeeming work. Used of Him twenty-four times, two thirds of which are in the epistles, His mission is resident in His name — "Jesus who shall save his people from their sins" (Matthew 1: 21). He possesses many titles, but Saviour is above them all because it speaks of His mighty love, His infinite sacrifice, His perfect obedience, His life of suffering, His death of shame, His glorious resurrection and all the glories circling around such a name (Philippians 2:10). "Saviour" is preeminently the title of Him who came to seek and save lost sinners (Luke 1:47; 2:11; 19:10; Acts 5:31; Romans 5:9, 10; Ephesians 5:23; I Timothy 1: 1; 2:3; 4:10; Titus 1:4; 2:13; 3:6; I John 4:10, 14).

The epithet "Saviour" was given to Christ as a title of honor, it being the mark of Christians that they look for Him to return as a Saviour from heaven (Ephesians 5:20; Philippians 3:3). Dealing with the elaborate designations Peter uses in speaking of Christ, Benjamin B. Warfield says that, "two things that are notable in Peter's list of designations are the repeated use of Saviour of our Lord, and the clear note of Deity which is struck in their ascriptions. Saviour itself is a divine appellation transferred to Christ. . . . In II Peter it occurs five times, always of Christ, and never alone, but always coupled under a single article with another designation, and so forming a solemn formula" (II Peter 1:11; 2:20; 3:2, 18). To fully expound the significance of the term Saviour would be to expound the whole contents of the Gospel (Ephesians 1:3). To quote Warfield again, "The whole New Testament may be said to be an exposition and enforcement of the announcement — 'The Saviour, who is Christ the Lord' (Luke 2:11); and in the course of this exposition and enforcement it teaches us many things."

Born a Saviour, Christ knew Himself to be the Saviour-Messiah. "The declaration of His Saviourhood was inseparable from His Messianic consciousness." The world to which He came needed a Saviour, and He never forgot His prime purpose to die for man's salvation. From beginning to end His life was committed to this inflexible purpose. "To reach this goal He must become the Evangelist of His own evangel." Now His cross is the symbol of salvation for a world of sinners lost and ruined by the fall. No matter what we may think of Christ, unless we know Him, experimentally, as the Saviour from sin, we have missed God's purpose in sending Him from heaven to earth (Luke 2:11; I Timothy 1:15).

FEMALE OCCUPATIONS

FEMALE OCCUPATIONS

Women in the Bible

Without woman there would never have been the human race. This is why Eve, the first woman, and earth's first sinner, is called "the mother of all living" (Genesis 3:20), meaning that along with Adam she was the fountainhead of humanity. The Hebrew word for "woman," *ishshah* asserts her full humanity (Genesis 1:26, 27). The significance of the English term has been defined as being made up of *woe* and *man,* and called, "Man's woe" because Eve tempted Adam to eat of the forbidden fruit whereby both became sinners and the source of original sin. But such an explanation is untenable in spite of the woe Eve brought into the world.

"Woman" is a contraction of "womb-man" Taken out of Adam, he said she shall be called *ishshah,* that is "womb-man," or "female-man" (Genesis 2:23). *Ish* is the Hebrew for "man." The Vulgate version gives us *vigaro* for woman which is a feminine form of *vir,* a man. The generic term for man includes woman. "Male and female created he them.... God said, Let us make man ... and let them" — the "them" being synonymous with "him" (Genesis 1:26, 27). Thus *Ish* (man) and *Ishshah* (woman) emphasize the spiritual relationship which existed between Adam and Eve. They were one flesh (Genesis 2:24).

Although woman's position was to be one of inferiority and subjection to man (Genesis 3:16), yet she was never meant to be treated as a mere drudge, or chattel or plaything, but as man's "help meet" or companion, or helper (Genesis 2:18-24). As part of his inmost body Eve was to possess an intimate relationship to Adam, which the indissoluble nature of marriage illustrates (Genesis 2:24; Matthew 19:5; I Corinthians 6:16; Ephesians 5:31). Coming out of Adam as Eve did there was of necessity the inseparable unity and fellowship of the woman's life with man. She was Adam's complement, essential to the perfection of his being. God made man and woman to be mutually interdependent.

It was Eve's supremacy of influence and stronger personality that led Adam to disobey God's command (Genesis 3:16), and the penalty of her ill-fated leadership was subjection to her husband. As humanity developed this subjection became more marked and severe, but under the Law, Hebrew women enjoyed a much higher status and a greater degree of equality than did the women of surrounding nations. Their liberties were more evident, their employments more varied and important, and their social standing more respectful and commanding. Hebrew women played only a minor part in the religious services of ancient Israel. As their value gradually decreased an Israelite could fervently thank God that he was not born a woman who found herself excluded from participation in synagogue services, permitted only to witness the services from the galleries or behind curtains. They were only granted extremely restricted access to the Temple. With the advent of Christianity women were liberated religiously as well as socially. But in matters of ruling and teaching in the house of God they were never to usurp authority over man and thereby reverse the divine order (I Corinthians 11:5, 13; 14:34, 35; I Timothy 2:11; I Peter 3:1).

Under the Mosaic Law many provisions were applicable to women and vice versa, but in general the sexes were treated as equals in their relation to God and in religious matters. While there were no women priests there were women prophets (I Samuel 1; 2; Luke 2:37). Miriam shared the leadership of the Exodus with her brothers, Moses and Aaron, and, Deborah was an outstanding deliverer of Israel. (For other aspects of religious equality see Genesis 16:7; 21:17; Numbers 6:2; Deuteronomy 12:18; Judges 13:13, 14; Psalm 68:25; Jeremiah 9:17-20; Mark 5:38). Under grace there is neither male nor female (Galatians 3:28).

As paganism developed the social condition of women went backward. The practice of polygamy cheapened womanhood and brought about much animosity and separation (Genesis 31: 32; I Kings 2:19; 7:8; 15:13; Esther 2:3, 9). Women suffered enslavement and debasement in numerous cults of Oriental paganism. Under Mohammedanism women became degraded, endured rigid seclusion, were shut out of ordinary society, and forced to conceal their features in any public place. Israelitish women, however, went about with their faces exposed to public view, the veil being used only on certain occasions (Genesis 12: 14; 24:64, 65; 29:10, 11; 38:14). In Assyria a man could mock his wife and say to her, "Thou art not my wife"; which freed him from her. If a woman repudiated her husband she could be drowned. Under Roman law, the woman had little freedom. On her marriage her property became her husband's and all her earnings were his. Christianity, however, restored women's rights and also the sacredness of marriage.

Because the modern position of women in Christendom is due directly to the influence of Christ, who *is* Christianity, it is necessary to observe His understanding of, and sympathy with women which set a pattern not only for Christian living but also for the treatment of women. He was indeed as A. R. Bond describes Him, "The Knight of Womanhood." Through tradition women were not given the place of honor and consideration she presently has in civilized lands. As the slave of her husband, she could be set aside at his pleasure. But Jesus elevated her to man's side and fixed a standard of ethics for both.

In the authoritative character of the words, works and attitude of Christ we have emphasized the original nature of marriage: an obligation of purity towards women; mutual social intercourse; just treatment of women whether pure or otherwise (Matthew 5:27-32; 9:18-26; 19:3; Luke 8:2, 3; 10:38-42; John 4). From the first, women were responsive to His teachings and devoted to His person. Mary and Martha, the sisters of Lazarus, gave Him His favorite earthly "home." Mothers rejoiced in His blessing upon their children, and in His raising of their dead (Matthew 19:13-15; Luke 7:12-15). Women in turn cared for His dead body (Luke 23:55, 56), and became the first heralds of His resurrection (Luke 24:9, 10, 22). To quote A. R. Bond again —

The home at Bethany, the women upon whom miracles were wrought, the tearful and womanly preparations of His body for the tomb, the eager visitors to His open sepulchre — all these testify to the Gentle Knight, who willingly braved the censure of His fellow religious workers in order that He might rescue woman from her serfdom of ignominy, sin and inferiority. His lance of truth broke His enemies' lances of error and conceit. The rights of the kingdom could not distinguish between the masculine and the feminine.

Further, women were prominent from the first in the activities of the fast growing early church, and the apostles gave full dignity to women, and set high standards for wives of church leaders and for women in official positions (I Timothy 3:11; Titus 2:3-5). Paul saw in marriage a type of the union between Christ and His true Church (Ephesians 5:22, 23). Sharing in the gifts of Pentecost women are found engaged in official and unofficial ministry (Acts 1:14; 2:1, 17; Romans 16:1; Philippians 4:2; I Timothy 5:3).

The only chapter in the Bible written by a woman about women is that in which King Lemuel's mother taught her son the virtues of what Tennyson called, "The Miracle of Noble Womanhood" (Proverbs 31). The only woman to be called "great" is the unnamed woman of Shunem who was so kind to Elisha the prophet (II Kings 4:8). Two features worth mentioning are these. First, the interchange of dress between man and woman was forbidden (Deuteronomy 22:5). Doubtless it was this law that influenced Paul, a strict Jew, in declaring it improper for women to imitate men in worshiping with uncovered heads (I Corinthians 11:3-16). The second interesting feature is that even in Biblical times there was a tendency to silence relative to the age of women. The proverb has it, "Women's Hell is old age." The exact age of one woman is given. Sarah was ninety years old when she bore Isaac, and 127 years old when she died (Genesis 17:17; 23:1). We are given the approximate age of Anna (Luke 2:36, 37), and of the daughter of Jairus (Luke 8:42).

As to the duties and employments of women, where Christ is not known, they still have an undue share of hard, laborious work. Charles Kingsley wrote, "men must work, and women must weep," but through the centuries women have had more than their share of both working and weeping, especially in those lands where a wife was reckoned to be a co-partner with her husband. Seneca remarked that, "Women are born to suffer," and in the capacity to endure ill-treatment sorrow and pain, woman has proved herself superior to man. Further, how great is her capacity for work. Mothers do not agitate for a forty-hour week.

Man's work lasts till set of sun,
Women's work is never done.

Have you come across *The Tired Woman's Epitaph* which belongs to the eighteenth century and reads? —

Here lies a poor woman who was always tired;
She lived in a house where help was not hired.
Her last words on earth were, "Dear friends, I am going
Where washing ain't done, nor sweeping, nor sewing;
But everything there is exact to my wishes;
For where they don't eat there's no washing of dishes.
I'll be where loud anthems will always be ringing,
But, having no voice, I'll be clear of the singing.
Don't mourn for me now; — don't mourn for me never —
I'm going to do nothing for ever and ever."

In these modern days when much is said and written about the equality of the sexes, and women vie with men in almost all professions and occupations, it is profitable to go back to ancient times and discover how women were employed. In many beneficial ways, women have been emancipated from much of the drudgery and hardships of everyday tasks, yet so many of the old-time employments remain. As we come, then, to female occupations, let us classify them as we did with male occupations, namely, secular and spiritual.

IN THE SECULAR REALM

While the number and variety of female occupations was considerably less than those of men, nevertheless, they were vitally important in the economy of home and nation. In the everyday life of Bible women, tasks were often onerous because in addition to the constant responsibilities of motherhood, all the household cares devolved upon them. Rising before dawn, they would grind flour and cook the day's bread, secure water and wood, undertake household chores, supervise the children, prepare meals, help in the fields, go to the market and sell garden produce, and when at home they had to find time to sew, weave cloth, or plait straw. For Hebrew women there was little ease. Let us enumerate some of the female occupations the Bible mentions.

The Cook

Women, as well as men, were employed as cooks. Female cooks existed in royal courts (I Samuel 8:13; 9:23, 24). Compare material in "Male Occupations" under THE COOK *and* THE BAKER. Generally, public cooks and bakers were men — for the household, in a more private capacity, the cooks were women. When strangers came to visit Abraham he hurried to Sarah's tent, and said, "Make ready quickly three measures of meal, knead it, and make cakes upon the hearth" (Genesis 18:6). It has been affirmed that in a Jewish home where there were daughters the oldest did the cooking. This may be why Leah was tender-eyed — inflammation was caused by the heat of the oven.

Until He left home Jesus must have daily watched His mother preparing bread for the day, and observed that she always set aside a bit of the dough. Then when the next baking day came round she took this bit of old, sour dough and mixed it with the new. That was the leaven. Remembering this homely practice, He turned it into a forceful illustration, "The kingdom of heaven is like unto leaven, which a woman took, and hid in three measures of meal, till the whole was leavened" (Matthew 13:33).

Ordinarily, Jewish women were not afflicted with too much cooking seeing the meals of the Jews were neither numerous nor so substantial and varied as ours. Usually the people ate twice a day — about noon and in the evening. We have instances of a special midday meal (Genesis 18:1; 19: 1-3; 43:15, 16; Ruth 2:14; John 21:4, 12). Among the women's cooking utensils she would use an iron baking pan (Leviticus 2:5, ASV) or shallow iron plate (Ezekiel 4:3); frying pan (Leviticus 2:7); flint knife for cutting up meat to be cooked and a fork or fleshhook for lifting it out of the fleshpot (Leviticus 22:6, 10; Judges 19:29; I Samuel 2:13). An important phase of the cook's work was that of buttermaking. Curdled milk was poured into a goatskin bag, and a woman seated would subject it to many well-aimed punches. This punching or thumping process was the "churning" (Proverbs 30:33). After being continually shaken up and thumped the milk became butter. By separating the water from the milk, cheese was produced (Job 10:10). If "the greatest animal in creation is the animal who cooks," and humans are the only ones in God's creation who can cook, how constantly gratified we should be to those who prepare and cook our necessary meals. It would be interesting to discover how many meals a mother cooks for her household in the course of her life.

The Dressmaker

While the word "dress" is never used in the Bible in respect to clothes, yet its equivalent is found in the synonyms "apparel," "attire," "vesture," "clothes," "garment," "raiment," and any garment mentioned testifies to the diligent needlework of women. Deborah gives us a list of an ancient dressmaker's art (Judges 5:30 ASV. See Exodus 26:36; Isaiah 3:18-26). The preparation of domestic fabrics and the different articles of clothing were chiefly supplied by the skill and industry of women. Ancient people had no knowledge of the mass production of clothes or of buying them off the rack ready to wear. Clothes, then, represented hours of laborious female effort as Solomon describes in his portrait of the prudent housewife (Proverbs 31:19; Psalm 45:14). The historian refers to certain "families of the house of them that wrought fine linen" (I Chronicles 4:21). There is also the "little coat" which Hannah made for Samuel (I Samuel 2:19). All articles of women's clothing would naturally be the fruit of her own hands. The ideal woman is one who "seeketh wool and flax, and worketh willingly with her hands" (Proverbs 31:13). Our Lord's illustration about sewing new cloth to an old garment suggests His power of observation. Perhaps He had seen His mother attempt such a hopeless task.

The Bible, anthropology and archaeology all witness to the early use of skins of animals and dress material, ready at hand and requiring little preparation. "They went about in sheepskins, in goatskins" (Hebrews 11:37). God was the first Dressmaker

seeing He made coats of skin and clothed Adam and Eve (Genesis 3:7). Skin was superseded by wool as sheep-shearing implies (Genesis 31:19; 38:12). Linens from flax is first mentioned in Exodus 9:31. References to clothing are of an incidental nature. For a full description of Eastern dress, with its common usages, the reader is directed to any Bible dictionary article under "Dress."

While we have many figurative modes of expression derived from different articles of dress, none is so much used by sacred writers as that of the girdle. Fitting the body for active service, and acting as a binding attachment, the girdle is an arrestive simile (Isaiah 11:5; Jeremiah 13:11; I Peter 1:13). The rending of garments was regarded as a common symbol of mourning (Joel 2:13).

The Embroiderer

This occupation is in the same category as the one just considered. To embroider, means "to interweave," or "to weave with a diaper," implying that the tissues of threads were diapered in checkers or small figures. An equivalent term is "needlework," designs being woven into the cloth by a needle or hook (Exodus 26:36; Judges 5:30; Psalm 45:14; Ezekiel 16:16-18; 26:16). Embroidery, then, was the art of working patterns or designs on textile fabrics with wool, linen, silk or golden thread by means of a needle. This checkered weaving composing the tabernacle curtains with cherubim traced in variegated colours represented the work of a skilful weaver (Exodus 26:1, 36; 35:25; 38:23).

Embroidery was commonly practiced and highly prized by ancient Orientals. We read of "broidered work from Egypt." Bas-reliefs of the clothes of kings of Assyria and Babylonia display luxurious colors. Babylon was famed for its garments of varied colors, attracting the eye, such as Achan coveted with disastrous results (Joshua 7:21; Ezekiel 27:7, 23, 24). Mummy clothes are still preserved revealing such an art as practiced by the Egyptians. The Romans described embroidery as painting with a needle. Sisera enjoyed embroidery in bright colors (Judges 5:30). Much of Israel's skill in this direction was the result of divine direction. That men, as well as women, embroidered is evidenced by the fact that Aholiab was an embroiderer (Exodus 28:39; 35:5; 38:23). Clothes of gold were reserved for God's house and royalty (Exodus 39:3; Psalm 45:13). Many of the priest's robes must have been impressive drapery. Secrets of the rich and gorgeously colored character of embroidery such as was used to adorn royal robes have been lost. Medieval and modern methods of the weaving of cloth of different colors have produced specimens of beautiful embroidery. Nature, however, outstrips any design of variegated colors on both sides of many of her plants and flowers as John Milton hinted in the lines —

> Cowslips wan, that hang the pensive head,
> And every flower that sad embroidery wears.

The Gleaner

Under the Mosaic Law the gleanings of the vineyard, cornfield, and the oliveyard had to be left for the poor, orphans, widows and strangers (Leviticus 19:9; Deuteronomy 24:19-22; Judges 20:45). Early agricultural laws in Jewish legislation displayed a very humane spirit, and so the needy had the right to glean what was left by the reapers for them. It was laid down that the reapers must not harvest to the extreme limits of a field but to leave for the poor and fatherless the forgotten sheaves (Deuteronomy 24:19). That the generosity of the master determined the amount and value of the gleanings of the harvest is illustrated in the liberality of Boaz (Ruth 2:16).

How this merciful provision of the law of Moses was carried out by the better part of God's covenant people is beautifully demonstrated in the history of Ruth, the most celebrated gleaner in the Bible, who became the ancestress of our blessed Lord. If it be true that "Poverty is the discoverer of all the arts," then the penury of Ruth became the door of wealth and honor. Thomas Hood in his lines *Ruth* wrote —

> Sure, I said, Heaven did not mean,
> Where I reap thou shouldst but glean,
> Lay thy sheaf a-down and come,
> Share my harvest and my home.

The Bible uses "gleaning" in a figurative sense. Gideon praised the pride of the Ephraimites when he said that the glory of their conquest surpassed his, as the gleanings of their vineyards did the whole crop of Abiezer (Judges 8:2). The captured Benjamites were looked upon as the conquerors' gleanings (Judges 20:45). Because of her wickedness, Israel was to be utterly destroyed, even to a thorough gleaning and destruction of those who first escaped (Jeremiah 6:9). The prophet gives us the same picture of Israel's complete annihilation later on in his prophecy (49:9, 10).

The Grinder

The duty of grinding grain and of baking generally devolved upon the female members of a family. Where female slaves were kept the domestic art of grinding was their task. Hence the deep degradation of a captive young man being forced to grind (Lamentations 5:13), and the insulting humiliation for a man to be found undertaking this prerogative of women (Judges 9:53). That grinding was of a menial nature can be gathered from phrases like, "the first-born of the maid-servant that is behind the mill," and "Take the millstone and grind" (Exodus 11:5; Isaiah 47:1, 2).

There were two primitive methods of grinding grain. It could be pounded in a stone mortar with a pestle (Leviticus 2:14), or in the indispensable handmill which the Law forbade a debtor to remove. Take not "the nether or the upper millstone to pledge: for he taketh a man's life to pledge" (Deuteronomy 24:6). Such a mill consisted of a fixed base stone, known as the "nether," or understone; and of the upper stone which was lighter than the nether stone, and which because of its position was called "the rider." It was the upper stone, being hear at hand, that the women cast at Abimelech (Judges 9: 53; II Samuel 11:21). A small hole was bored near the edge of the upper stone into which a wooden pin was inserted so that the women could revolve the stone. Into another hole in the center of the upper stone the grain was poured and was ground or rubbed between the stones.

The mill was daily used for grinding corn and other food (Numbers 11:8) required for immediate consumption. The grinding would take place at night or at daybreak, and only enough would be ground to last one day (Proverbs 31:15). Our Lord referred to the general practice of grinding when in describing the separations taking place at His return, He said, "Two women shall be grinding at the mill, the one shall be taken and the other left" (Matthew 24:41; Luke 17:

35). It was usual for the women to be alone and seated over against each other, with the millstones between them. What a shock for the woman left as she sees her fellow-grinder taken! Grinding is used in a figurative sense of firmness and of undaunted courage (Job 41:24); of cruelty to the poor (Isaiah 3:15); of utter desolation and ruin (Jeremiah 25:10; Matthew 21:44). Grinders describe molar teeth (Job 29:17; Ecclesiastes 12:3, 4). Pliny speaks of "The great grinders which stand beyond the eyeteeth and in no way whatsoever do they fall out themselves."

The Handmaid

A handmaid was a young unmarried female always at hand to do the bidding of those who owned her. Usually slaves, handmaids were daughters sold by their fathers into such bondage (Exodus 21:7). Chaste women, when given up to the will of others as the property of masters, often became their concubines. Appearing often then in the Old Testament but seldom in the New, handmaid normally means a female slave (Genesis 16: 6; 25:12; 29:24, 29; Proverbs 30:23; Jeremiah 34:11, etc.). It was the custom for a mother to give her daughter a handmaid on marriage (Genesis 29: 24).

In a good household a maidservant would be well taken care of, and sometimes became the heir of her mistress (Proverbs 30:23; 31:15). While Hagar's mistress was not as kind to her handmaid as she might have been, the wife of Naaman was very kind to the little Hebrew captive who served in her house. Anxious about her master, she became the means of his recovery from leprosy and must have been rewarded by him. Under ordinary circumstances release was not permitted (Exodus 21:7). They could not leave when they liked because they were not their own. But when the year of jubilee came around God said they could have their liberty if they wished it, and if they decided to go they were not to be sent away empty. If they decided to stay, a handmaid saying, "I love my mistress, I do not wish to go free," was then taken to a door, the soft part of her ear was laid against the wall, and a little hole pierced through it. By that pierced ear, she became a servant for ever. It was her badge of willing, contented servitude.

The term handmaid likewise indicates humility, and self-depreciation in the presence of superiors (Ruth 2: 13; 3:9; I Samuel 1:11; Psalms 86:16; 116:16). Ruth's approach to Boaz, Hannah praying unto the Lord and addressing Eli (I Samuel 1:16) reminds us of Wordsworth's lines —

> Give unto. me, made lowly wise
> The spirit of self-sacrifice;
> The confidence of reason give;
> And in the light of truth thy
> Bondsman let me live!

The term also expresses a sense of religious humility (I Samuel 1:11; Psalms 86:16; 116:16) and thus occurs four times in the New Testament. Mary, when speaking to Gabriel and in her "Magnificat" called herself, "the female slave of the Lord" (Luke 1:38, 45. See Acts 2:18; Galatians 4:22, 23).

The relationship of servant to master is a favorite of our relationship to God. Attendance with eyes fixed on the mistress ready to obey her slightest gesture, and strict ownership are used to describe our unfailing loyalty to our heavenly Master (Psalm 132:12; Isaiah 41:8; 42:1-4; 49:1-6; 53:12, etc.). Compare material under THE BONDSERVANT, THE SERVANT, THE SLAVE.

The Harlot

As these lines are being written in my London home, our English papers — and those abroad — are giving much space to the *Ward* case with its revelation of prostitution, sex orgies and vice, and of the downfall of a prominent cabinet minister because of his association with one of the young prostitutes. Local authorities in all large cities are concerned about the growing army of callgirls, or prostitutes, ready for the degrading hire of their bodies. It may surprise some people, however, to learn that the Bible has a great deal to say about harlotry or whoredom.

Prostitution, growing out of universal sexual and social conditions, is first referred to in Genesis 38. By Solomon's time, owing to foreign influences, prostitution with its seductive arts and voluptuous songs reached a fuller shamelessness (Proverbs 6:24; Isaiah 27:11). Because of the money lavished upon women of this class, the weak and unwary easily succumbed and thus gave themselves over to such a dissolute life for gain. The blighting influence of harlotry is vividly pictured and strongly denounced by the prophets (Deuteronomy 23:17; Proverbs 29:3; Isaiah 23:16; Jeremiah 5:7; Ezekiel 16:25; Amos 7:17; Nahum 3: 4). While harlot, prostitute and whore are equivalent terms and designate an unchaste woman, married or unmarried — one guilty of sexual immorality (Matthew 5:32; 19:9) — it is as well to fully understand the Bible words employed to describe illicit sexual intercourse.

There is the regular word for "harlot" — *Gonah* — which is the one most frequently used for female licentiousness.

Then there is a special kind of harlot — a religious prostitute or harlot-priestess of a heathen religion in which fornication was a part of worship (Genesis 38:21, 22; Deuteronomy 23:17).

Further, "the strange woman" occurring only in the Book of Proverbs is used in contrast to a man's rightful wife (I Kings 11:1; Proverbs 5:17-20).

Another term "foreign woman" also confined to Proverbs describes one outside the nation of Israel guilty of prostitution. The word "prostitute" occurs once in KJV. (Leviticus 19:29), although other versions translate it "harlot," just as they give "prostitute" for "whore" in other passages (Deuteronomy 23:17). The masculine *quadesh* or "Sodomites" implies male prostitution in the same vile, heathen worship that *quadeesh* or harlot-priestesses indulged in Deuteronomy 23: 17; I Kings 14:24; 15:12; 22:46; II Kings 23:7; Job 26:14). *Porne,* the New Testament word for a harlot is from a root meaning "to sell" and is used literally of those who were the objects of Christ's mercy (Matthew 21:31, 32); of those the prodigal son spent his substance on (Luke 15: 30); of the prevailing licentiousness in Corinth which made it a byword (I Corinthians 6:15, 16); of Rahab (Hebrews 11:31; James 2:25). The term is likewise used symbolically as we shall presently discover of mystic Babylon (Revelation 17:1, 5; 15, 16; 19:2).

Elucidation may be necessary regarding those who were given over to immoral service in heathen sanctuaries who, although the term *quedeeshah* describing them means "consecrated women," they were yet engaged in the abominable worship of heathen deities by prostitution. "The men of Babylon made Succoth Benoth" their idol in Samaria (II Kings 17:30). This idol's name means, "booths for

their daughters," referring to their prostitution in this degrading and detestable worship. "Tamar veiled herself and sat by the wayside as a consecrated harlot under a vow, and was so regarded by Judah." Whore implies one consecrated to an idol.

Harlotry prevailed in Egyptian cults. Soon after Israel settled in Canaan the purity both of their morality and their religion was endangered by the contaminating influences of heathen rites in which supposedly consecrated harlots played a part. The prophets give us a glimpse of the prevalence of prostitution, religious and otherwise, in their day (Jeremiah 5:7; Hosea 4:14). One of the blessings of the Exile was the extinction of idolatry and religious prostitution. We learn from the Apocrypha that the continuance of common harlotry prevailed after Malachi with harlots haunting the streets, and singing their seductive songs — the badge of a harlot (Isaiah 23:16). In the time of "The Maccabees," the Gentiles of Palestine countenanced harlotry and had traffic with "women within the circuit of holy places" (II Maccabees 6:4. See Proverbs 7:10). Harlotry then represents the habitual notorious practice of unchastity, whether by the public known women of the street or the professional devotée in pagan temples who was invested with sanctity as a member of a religious caste and who prostituted herself to the service of her gods. That there was a true and holy dedication of oneself to the service of the only living God, is seen in Samuel's ministry in the sanctuary at Shiloh as the principal priest and keeper of the house of God (I Samuel 1-3; See Exodus 33:11).

The divine attitude toward fornication is clearly defined. Adultery was unchastity before marriage but detected later in the case of a woman with someone other than her betrothed (Leviticus 20:10; Deuteronomy 22:21-23). Immoral relations between sexes were deemed to be a venial sin (Deuteronomy 22:28). The unholy trade of prostitution is condemned in no uncertain terms (Proverbs 23:27; Romans 1:24; I Corinthians 6:9; Galatians 5:19, etc). A priest was not allowed to marry a prostitute (Leviticus 19:29; 21:7, 14). One chief concern of a father in Israel was to "keep his son from the evil woman" who "hunteth for the precious life" (Proverbs 6:24, 26). A father was forbidden to compel his daughter to become a harlot although apparently she was free to take her own way (Genesis 38; Leviticus 19:29; 21:7, 14). No part of a common harlot's gain could be accepted for God's work (Deuteronomy 23:18). The children of a harlot were outlawed and the harlot herself brought under the sternest social ban (Deuteronomy 23:2; Matthew 21:31, 32).

While Hebrew legislation condemned prostitution there was no legal penalty against such except in special cases. A priest's daughter becoming a harlot could be burned with fire (Leviticus 21:9). Judah ordered Tamar to be burned (Genesis 38:24). A bride, guilty of harlotry was stoned to death (Exodus 19:13; Deuteronomy 22:21; Luke 20:6). Because of the moral abomination involved in prostitution, the harlot, dying in her sin, is excluded from heaven (I Corinthians 6:9 - 20; Revelation 22:8, 15). Fornication was not regarded by the heathen as being very wrong hence it is classed with things which Gentile usage allowed but Jewish law forbade (Acts 15). There were times when Israel was contaminated by so-called sacred prostitution, which the Law

and the prophets decried (Deuteronomy 22:5; I Kings 14:24; 15:12; Hosea 4:14). Such a form of prostitution was almost swept away by Josiah's reform (I Kings 15:22; 22:46; II Kings 23:7; Amos 2:7).

Because "lax views of sexual morality were widely prevalent in the generation in which Christ lived evident both from His casual references to the subject and from His specific teaching in answer to questions concerning adultery and divorce," His followers especially in Greece and Asia Minor were exposed to the danger of harlotry (Acts 15:26, 29; Romans 1:24; I Corinthians 6:9; Galatians 5:19). Dealing with fornication Christ went to "the root of the matter, making this sin to consist in 'looking on a woman to lust after her.'" In contact with erring women, He endeavored to bring them within the pale of mercy and redemption. The Pharisaic tribunal might forbid His speaking to a sinful woman like the one of Samaria (John 4), but she had a soul that was worth saving through the revelation of the water of life, and He thus leaned on the side of mercy (Matthew 21:31, 32; John 8:11). Women of the streets found in Him a Knight who would bring them divine forgiveness and acceptance. In his illuminating volume, *Stand up and Praise God,* Dr. Paul Rees tells of a prominent Hindu woman who came to a Christian worker in India, bringing with her a *devidasi,* a poor, bedraggled, abused temple girl. "I bring this girl to you to be saved," said the Hindu to the Christian. Then she explained, "I once heard my husband read a chapter from your Sacred Book of a woman in adultery and how Jesus spoke to her and how He saved her. We have no such story in our books, so I brought the girl to you." Dr. Rees comments,

"How we bless God for the record of Jesus loving even harlots out of their sin into His own priceless salvation, and for the fact that in His human genealogy harlots are mentioned." Grace gives the lie to the proverb that "Once a whore always a whore." His blood can make the vilest clean.

As Rahab finds honorable mention in the New Testament (Joshua 2:1-24; Matthew 1:5; Hebrews 11:31; James 2:25), as one who came to be saved by faith, it is questioned by some writers whether she was actually a harlot, seeing that *Gonah* can mean either a "harlot" or an "innkeeper." For instance *The Bible Companion* argues, "The spies Joshua sent to spy out the land were undoubtedly the most confidential persons he could select for the purpose, and their errand involved the greatest consequences. How could they therefore go to lodge with a woman of ill-fame? No; they went to a tavern kept by her. A further proof is that Rahab was actually married to Salmon, a Jewish prince (Matthew 1:5). And is it probable that a prince of Judah would have married a prostitute (Deuteronomy 23:17, 18; Hebrews 11:31)?" We incline to the interpretation however, that Rahab was a harlot whether or not she was the hostess of the family inn. But she repented of her shameful life and became a trophy of divine grace, and that her faith was richly rewarded in that she became the mother of Boaz, and an ancestress of the Messiah (Ruth 4:21).

Female adultery and every form of unchastity is used figuratively throughout Scripture. The Jewish people regarded as the spouse of Jehovah became guilty of spiritual harlotry or whoredom (II Chronicles 21: 11; Isaiah 23:16, 17; Ezekiel 16:26). Idolatry, or any defection from the divine covenant, was looked upon as harlotry (Isaiah 1:21; Jeremiah 2:20; Ezekiel 16; 23; Nahum 3:4). God's heart as the Husband of Israel (Jeremiah 3:20) was grieved when His people "played the harlot with other gods." Says the *Zondervan Pictorial Bible Dictionary* "the two words 'adultery' and 'idolatry' can be identically defined as taking the love which belongs to one and giving it to another. In the former case the one wronged is the wife or husband who has been deserted; in the latter it is God." The apostate church of the Great Tribulation is described as a whore (Revelation 17:1, 5, 15, 16; 19:2). Walter Scott in his renowned *Exposition of Revelation* comments, "The great whore is not only Satan's counterfeit of the true church, but is the concentrated expression of every anti-christian movement and sect then in existence, consolidated and controlled by Satan. . . . This gigantic system of spiritual whoredom is, without doubt, Satan's masterpiece, and the vilest thing beneath the sun." The mystic "Babylon the Great" is spoken of as "the mother of harlots" because her offspring are numerous. "She is the parent, the source of each and every religious system which courts the world." The great harlot (Revelation 19:2) is to meet her deserved doom and become an everlasting witness to the religious judgment of God (Isaiah 34:10).

The Maidservant

Occurring some twenty-five times in the Bible, this term is identical with handmaid — which see (Genesis 12: 16; 24:35; 30:43; Job 31:13). Today, because of more lucrative employment for women, households requiring maidservants find it very difficult to secure them. Such an occupation is deemed to be too confining and poorly paid.

The Midwife

The word midwife means "to help to bear," the "with-wife" or "with the woman," and was used of those women who gave skillful assistance to other women in labor and childbirth. the LXX version has *obstatrix* from which we have "obstetrics." The Hebrew word *ïalad* is a common one covering many English words in the KJV in connection with childbirth. In many cases these female attendants at birth would likely be the female relatives or friends of the mother. In condemning the spiritual harlotry of Jerusalem, the prophet Ezekiel enumerates the duties of a midwife at birth, namely, the cutting of the navel cord, washing the infant in water, and swathing in swaddling clothes. That ancient midwives had considerable skill is seen in a case like that of Tamar who evidently required some amount of operative manipulation to relieve her of her twins by Judah (Ezekiel 16:4; Genesis 38:28). That they were also comforting and assuring can be gathered from the midwife who assisted at the birth of Benjamin and witnessed his mother's travail and death in childbirth; and also from the midwives who consoled the wife of Phinehas in the hour of the premature birth of her son (Genesis 35:17; I Samuel 4:20).

Midwife help at delivery would include the placement of the mother in a kneeling posture, leaning on somebody's knees, or seated on a labor-stool or birth-seat (Exodus 1:16). Described on the walls of the palace of Luxor, in Upper Egypt, is a chair of peculiar form with a mother-to-be seated on it. Normally, Hebrew women required no midwives seeing they gave birth to children with great facility and delivery was quickly over. "Lively" expresses the ease with which they gave birth to their children, and of their ability to look after themselves. The exceptional cases of childbearing referred to in Scripture emphasize the sorrow of conception as a penalty of Eve's transgression (Genesis 3:16). There are two cases of twins in which the mothers suffered much — Esau and Jacob (Genesis 25:22), and Perez and Zarah (Genesis 38:29). Rachel's case was one of fatal *dystocia* (Genesis 35:18, see Genesis 31:35). The shock of Phinehas' death resulted in premature and fatal labor for his wife (I Samuel 4:19).

The two named midwives of the Bible are Shiphrah and Puah. Fausset contends that they were Egyptian for Pharaoh would not employ Hebrew women to destroy the males of their own nation. The answer of these midwives implies they were used to attend Egyptian women (Exodus 1:19), in difficult cases. Aben Ezra speaks of these two as "chiefs over all the midwives who were more than 500." When it is said that God dealt well with the midwives because they obeyed God rather than Pharaoh, it may mean that He blessed them both in regards to the members of their families and their substance. Or the phrase "making them houses" as a reward may imply that they married Hebrews and became mothers in Israel (Exodus 1:21). Jewish legend says that Shiphrah and Puah had different duties. The former dressed the infants and the latter whispered to them or used artificial respiration by blowing into the child's mouth, somewhat akin to "the kiss of life" method used today.

Because labor pain is so uniquely severe, nine-tenths of the more than forty uses of the word "travail" in the Bible — as of a woman in travail is employed as a figure of intense suffering (Isaiah 53:11; Jeremiah 13:21; Romans 8:22; Galatians 4:19). Socrates spoke of himself as "a midwife of men's thoughts," and an ancient writer said of him that "no other man ever struck out of others so many sparks to set light to original thoughts." Out of the intellectual school of Socrates came Plato, Euclid and others. His influence on the minds of others was unique. The greatest philosopher, however, cannot compare to Him who spake as no other man. His life and teachings gave birth to an unending, universal influence.

The Mourner

Because the ancient Hebrews placed a much greater emphasis on external symbolic acts than we do, we may have a tendency to deem their public expression of grief somewhat artificial or hypocritical. But such acts were natural, and were valid manifestations of sorrow in Hebrew life and culture. Thus it was deemed fitting to employ professional female mourners at the burial of the dead. The prophets speak of "the mourning women that were come," and of "such as were skillful of lamentation to wailing" (Jeremiah 9:17; Amos 5:16). An Egyptian bas-relief illustrates part of a scene at a burial with a group of mourning women carrying out their lamentations. These wailers were for the most part females (Ecclesiastes 12:5; Jeremiah 9:17, 18; Matthew 9:23), although men followed the same occupation (II Chronicles 35:24). Bishop Lightfoot, commenting on "the minstrels" in the house of Jairus says that even "the poorest Israelite, his wife being dead, would hire at least two pipers and one mourning woman to make lamentation. The rich prided themselves on swelling the number of paid mourners."

Gradually, mourning for the dead became a profession, learned and paid for like any other occupation. Probably at first they were hired to swell the tide of real sorrow but their services became "a mere formal pageant, demanded by pride and custom, rather than sorrow." This Oriental expression of grief had a twofold seemingly contradictory manifestation — toward those around there were the wails and repeated shrieks, as an evidence of grief for the departed, but the immediate relatives of the dead assumed a silent and reverent submission to the will of God symbolized by placing the hand on the mouth. "I was dumb . . . because thou didst it" (Job 1:21; Psalm 39:9).

Arranged around the bier the hired mourners would shed copious tears. Ashes were sprinkled on their heads, and hands would be on their heads as they wailed. Jeremiah said to Israel under punishment, "Thou shalt go forth from the Lord, and thine hands upon thine head" (Jeremiah 2:37). Tamar put ashes on her head and "laid her hand on her head and went on crying" (II Samuel 12:20; 13:19). Beating of the breast, tearing of the garments, wearing sackloth and fasting were other accompaniments of grief (I Samuel 31:13; II Samuel 3:31, 35; 12:20; Isaiah 32:12).

Between the interval of death and burial then, professional mourners were hired to lament the dead. A traveler, giving a vivid account of the first experience with such mourning wrote — "It rose like the far-off wavering sound of many owls. It shrilled, wavered, dropped, and then died away, like the moaning of the wind at sea. We never heard anything so wild and plaintive." When it came to the funeral procession, the mourners moved swiftly because of a Jewish legend that innumerable evil spirits were hovering around to attack the soul which was deemed to be in the body until interment took place and the body was actually buried. At funeral feasts the hired mourners would sing elegies. The weeping prophet, Jeremiah, is said to have taught the mourning women their dirge (Jeremiah 16:7, 8). Food eaten at the time of mourning was considered impure (Deuteronomy 9:17-22; 26:16; Hosea 9:4).

A great company of devout women bewailed and lamented Jesus as He was led away to be crucified. Characteristic of the tenderness of His sympathy, He turned and said to the mourners, "Daughters of Jerusalem, weep not for me, but weep for yourselves, and for your children" (Luke 23:28). Who were these sorrowing "daughters of Jerusalem" whose wailing was loud and bitter? One commentator suggests that perhaps they were "one of the sisterhoods which were formed in that city for mitigating the sufferings of condemned criminals by narcotic drinks." More accustomed to pain than men, women have mastered the art of weeping with those that weep.

Not she with trait'rous kiss her Saviour
   stung,
Not she denied Him with unholy tongue;
She, while Apostles shrank, could danger
   brave,
Last at His cross, and earliest at His grave.

In the New Testament, words denoting grief are not so frequent as in the Old Testament, which is as it should be seeing Christ came to comfort all who mourn by remitting all their sins and imparting peace to their souls (Matthew 5:4). From the first burial in Eden until now this earth has been a vale of tears, but the promise is that all sorrow and sighing are to flee away. No eyes are wet with tears

in Gloryland (Isaiah 25:8; 35:10; Revelation 7:17; 21:4).

The Nurse

The Hebrew term for nurse is used both in the masculine and feminine, and is a word denoting anyone who sustains and nourishes another. In some cases nurse represents the foster-mother, just as Moses' mother was "a nurse of the Hebrew women," and became the foster-mother of the foundling (Exodus 2:7). At other times nurse represents a lady's maid or tire-woman, one who supports or nourishes another woman (Numbers 11:12; Deuteronomy 4:16; II Samuel 4:4; Isaiah 49:23; 60:4). Moses applied the designation to himself in relation to Israel — "as a nursing father bearing the sucking child" (Numbers 11:12). The same word is translated "them that brought up" (II Kings 10:15), which is applied to the guardians of the sons of Ahab. We have it again in "Mordecai brought up Esther" (Esther 2:7). In Bible times, nurses held a position of honor, and were treated with great kindness and respect (Genesis 24:59; Exodus 2:7; II Kings 11:2).

Healthy Hebrew women cared for their own children, giving suck for as long as three years (Genesis 21:7; I Samuel 1:23). There were families, however, that employed professional nurses of the same sex as the infant — male nurses being described as "nursing fathers" (Numbers 11:12; Isaiah 49:23). Children were carried by their mothers or nurses, not in arms, but on the shoulders, seated astride, and sometimes, for a short distance on the hip. "The daughters shall be carried upon the shoulders" (Isaiah 49:22, 23) — a prophecy of the time when because of the exalted position of Israel, foreign kings and queens will offer their services and wait upon the chosen people of God. "Ye shall be borne upon her sides" (Isaiah 66:12). Among the notable nurses of the Bible we have the best nurse Moses could have had — and hired and paid at that — his own mother. Miriam the sister of Moses said to Pharaoh's daughter when she rescued the baby from the Nile, "Shall I go and call to thee a nurse of the Hebrew women that she may nurse the child for thee?"

Deborah was a family nurse who attended Rebekah when she was a child and followed her through the years. She went to her new home when Rebekah and Isaac were married, and became the nurse of their children, Jacob and Esau. When this faithful nurse died there was great lamentation and Jacob called the place where she was buried near Bethel, "The Oak of Weeping" (Genesis 35:8). Naomi became the nurse of her grandchild, Obed (Ruth 4:16). It was a nurse who saved the young prince Joash from slaughter by his cruel grandmother, Athaliah, and cared for him six years (II Kings 11:2; II Chronicles 22:11). Another nurse fled to a place of safety carrying a boy of five, Mephibosheth, Jonathan's son. Unfortunately, in the flight she let the boy fall and he became lame on both feet for the rest of his life (II Samuel 4:4).

Paul, in writing to the saints at Thessalonica, speaks of himself as their nurse, "We were gentle among you as a nurse cherisheth her own children" (I Thessalonians 2:7). The apostle reminded the Corinthians that as babes he had fed them with milk (I Corinthians 3:2). The word Paul used for "nurse" was not that of a hired nurse, but of a mother who nurses her own children. His converts were his spiritual children, and with the tenderness and patience of a mother nursing her own children, Paul nourished them on the milk and strong meat of the Word of God.

Today, nurses represent the most noble, honorable and sacrificial of occupations. What else can we do but admire them as they care for the needy, watch the sick, dress wounds and carry out a doctor's orders? One of the most famous of nurses was Florence Nightingale, "The Lady of the Lamp." Born in wealth she became a brilliant scholar, but it was as a nurse when in 1854 she went to the Crimean War and found thousands of men in hospitals where more died than in battle. She would stand for twenty-four hours without a rest directing arrangements and binding wounds. Countless young women have been influenced by her devotion to the sick and diseased. Another renowned nurse was Edith Cavell — a Christian woman — falsely accused of spying and shot. Good Lord Shaftesbury said he owed more to his nurse than to his mother. When the nurse died she left Shaftesbury her watch, which he always wore. Often he would say of it: "That was given me by the best friend I ever had in the world." Robert Louis Stevenson was another who owed so much as a child to his faithful nurse. How beautiful is his "Dedication" to her in one of his books —

To Alison Cunningham
From Her Boy

For the long nights you lay awake
And watched for my unworthy sake;
For your most comfortable hand
That led me through the uneven land:
For all the story-books you read:
For all the pains you comforted:
For all you pitied, all you bore,
In sad and happy days of yore: —
My second Mother, my first Wife,
The angel of my infant life —

From the sick child, now well and old,
Take, nurse, the little book you hold.

The Queen

While not conspicuous in Scripture, princesses (I Kings 11:3; Lamentations 1:1) and queens find a place therein. In our companion volume entitled *All the Kings and Queens of the Bible,* a full classification of the latter will be found. Princesses is translated as "ladies" (Judges 5:29) — "queens" (Isaiah 49:23). The new name of Abraham's wife, Sarah, means a "princess" (Genesis 15:15, ASV margin). A princess was the wife of a prince (Esther 1:18); and also the daughter of a prince of Midian (Numbers 25:18). Solomon had 700 princesses as wives (I Kings 11:3 — where the word "princess" represents consort of the king in contrast to the concubines). "Princess" is used metaphorically of a city (Lamentations 1:1).

As to the queens adorning the portrait gallery of the Bible, they are few in number, evidenced by the fact that king occurs over 2,000 times, but Queen only 50 times, and in the majority of cases only incidentally. Three words for "queen" are to be distinguished.

1. The queen *regnant* (I Kings 10: 1; Esther 1:9; Daniel 5:10).
2. The queen *consort* (Psalm 45:9; Daniel 5:2, 3).
3. The queen *mother,* or "powerful mistress," who commanded great influence and enjoyed a position of fixed dignity, as for example, Bathsheba, Jezebel and Athaliah (I Kings 2:19; 15:13; II Kings 10:13). The functions of a queen reigning in her own right would be identical with those of a king. As a wife of a reigning monarch, a queen held a position of comparatively little importance. In fact, in the majority of named kings in the Bible,

little or nothing is recorded of their wives. Figuratively, queen is applied to a heathen deity (Jeremiah 7:18; 44:17), and to the city of Babylon where the term is used as an expression denoting sovereign contempt and imaginary dignity and power (Revelation 18:7).

The Saleswoman

Although there are numerous references in the Bible to merchant princes (Isaiah 23:8), merchants, buyers, and sellers (Compare THE BUYER, THE MERCHANT), Lydia is the only named female buyer and seller the Bible mentions (Acts 16:14). Solomon speaks of the prudent, industrious wife who "maketh fine linen, and selleth it" (Proverbs 31:24); and the prophet told the distressed widow to sell her surplus oil to pay her debt (II Kings 4:7). But Lydia is conspicuous as an astute, successful business woman. Luke reminds us that among Paul's converts there were "chief women not a few" (Acts 17:4). Here "chief" implies women of high estate — refined, cultured and well-to-do — of whom Lydia was one whose prominence in business circles reminds us of the comparatively independent position of women in Asia Minor and Macedonia at that time.

Inscriptions and scrolls preserved from apostolic days mention the existence of a guild or corporation of purple-sellers, or traders in purple-dyed cloth or garments. These fine wares are repeatedly mentioned in Scripture for purple was the raiment worn by kings and nobles (Judges 8:26; II Chronicles 2:14). It was as "The King of the Jews" that our Lord was derisively robed in a purple robe (Mark 15: 17; John 19:2). (See also Luke 16:19; Revelation 18:12). As for the purple dye itself, it was manufactured by the

Phoenicians from a marine mollusk, the shell of which was broken in order to extract a small gland which, when removed and crushed, produced a milky fluid that became red or purple on exposure to the air. Quantities of these broken shells still remain on the coasts at Tyre and Sidon.

Lydia, who was likely a member of the purple-sellers guild must have had a prosperous business in Thyatira. Her large-hearted hospitality indicates a certain measure of wealth. Considerable capital would be required to buy the expensive products she dealt in. The fact that she carried on the business by herself is an evidence that she was either a spinster or a widow. As there is no evidence that she was married with a family of her own, we must assume that her household consisted of her staff of female slaves and freed-women who assisted her in business.

Because Lydia is represented as bearing the name of the city in which she lived, some scholars question Lydia as being her actual name. Those born in Lydia were known as "Lydians." Sir William Ramsey says that perhaps her actual name was either Euodius or Syntyche (Philippians 4:2). This we do know that she was an educated proselyte drawn to Judaism by its high ethical and spiritual teaching. Although sincerely religious she did not know the Gospel of redeeming love and grace and was led, through Paul's preaching of divine grace, into the consciousness of a new life and became the first member of a church which quickly developed great vigor(Acts 16:14-40). We have the dual action resulting in the conversation of this renowned saleswoman. "The Lord opened her heart that she attended unto the things spoken by Paul" (See Psalm 119:18, 130; Luke 24:45). Chrysostom says of this dou-

ble action, "To open is the part of God, to pay attention that of the woman."

Lydia became Paul's first convert in Europe. As soon as she believed, she led those around her to Christ, and her eagerness to serve the Lord with her substance is seen in her loving care for Paul and Silas. Lydia may have been one of those women who labored with Paul in the Gospel (Philippians 4:3) with her large home probably becoming the center for the church at Philippi (Acts 16:14, 15, 20). Her love for her newly-found Saviour evidenced itself in bountiful hospitality. Money made in business was used to care for God's saints and the extension of the Gospel through their ministry (I Timothy 1:10; Hebrews 13:2; I Peter 4:9).

The Spinner

"Let every girl attend to her spinning," said Cervantes, the Spanish novelist, and truly every girl in early Bible times had to attend to her spinning because there were no mills then to mass produce linen both for general and personal use. As spinning and weaving were kindred employments generally assigned to females (Compare THE WEAVER in male section) we group them together under this cameo. Tapestries for the Tabernacle were spun by wise and willinghearted women (Exodus 35:25, 26; Proverbs 31:13, 19). The first mention of linen cloth as an article of dress is in the account of Joseph's apparel which Pharaoh provided him (Genesis 41:42). Solomon refers to "the spindle," and in paintings on ancient tombs spinners are represented as using this most ancient instrument. With great dexterity spinners could use two spindles, weighted with stone balances, at once. This implement was about eight to twelve inches long, with the rope of carded fiber or wool attached to one end and the spindle rotated by hand. The left leg was elevated to enable the spinners to give the circular motion to the spindle by rolling it rapidly along the thigh. Until recently Arab women twisted the spindle in this same manner (See Exodus 35:25, 26; II Kings 23:7; Matthew 6:28 — where Christ in this famous verse uses the work of the spinner to illustrate His message).

The main raw materials used by the Egyptians and Hebrews were wool, goat's or camel's hair and flax (Exodus 35:26; 36:14; Joshua 2:6; II Kings 1: 8; Job 31:19; Matthew 3:4). Evidently there was a thriving flax industry on the banks of the Nile (Isaiah 19:9). As to the preparation of materials before spinning or weaving, wool before being spun was thoroughly scoured and carded by means of a bow-string; and the stalks of flax were riffled and exposed to the sun till thoroughly dry (Joshua 2:6). Once dry there came the repeated processes of steeping, drying and heating until the fibers were ready for the "heckling" or combing. "Let women spin, not preach," says an old proverb. The wonderful fabric Hebrew women produced reveals that their time was fully occupied in spinning, not preaching.

The Water Carrier

As the Hebrews were an agricultural people many chores around the farm fell to the women. Ancient murals depict women in white headdress with a pitcher of water poised on the head. They had been to the well and were carrying water home for household needs (Genesis 24; John 4). Another use of water was that of feetwashing — the servant's task (Genesis 18:4; 24:32; Luke 7:36-50; John 13: 4-8; I Timothy 5:10). The water thus secured was the living water, the fresh water from bubbling springs and streams (Song of Solomon 4:15; John 4:14). Another female chore was that of carrying on the head a load of fuel made up of dried, flat cakes of dung and straw for baking purposes.

The Winnower

Egyptian bas-reliefs depict winnowing women wearing headcloths and loincloths holding winnowing scoops with which they toss the corn into the air, and other women sweeping up the grain with a brush of switches. We have several references to winnowing tools and necessities (Ruth 3:2; Psalm 1:4; Isaiah 30:24; 41:16; Jeremiah 4: 11; Matthew 3:12; Luke 3:17). The shovel, fan and fork was used for tossing the grain into the air — the broom for sweeping the floor before threshing and for collecting the wheat after winnowing. The mixture of chaff and grain must be winnowed or separated and this is done by tossing it in the air so the wind may blow away the chaff. Our Lord used this process with great effect in warning Peter of the satanic sifting or winnowing he was about to experience (Luke 22:31). The same is figuratively employed to describe the discriminating judgment of God between the godly and the ungodly together with the destruction of the latter (Isaiah 30:28; Amos 9:9; [Moffat]; Luke 3:17). The winnowing which followed the threshing has been expressed thus: "A sieve of fine mesh retaining the grain is lifted slightly away from the female winnower who adroitly throws the contents in the air. Meantime, blowing as hard as she can into the descending mass, the clean corn is caught without losing a single grain."

The Witch

A witch was the female counterpart of a wizard or soothsayer (Acts 16:16.

Compare THE SOOTHSAYER, THE WIZ-ARD under the male section). The degraded occupation of witchcraft or sorcery is strongly condemned by God. "Witchcraft which sought to injure others by magical arts, has always been regarded as evil and worthy of punishment among nations" (Exodus 22:18; Deuteronomy 18:9-14; I Samuel 15:23; II Kings 9:22; 23:24; II Chronicles 33:6; Isaiah 8:19; Micah 5:12; Nahum 3:4; Acts 19:18, 19; Galatians 5:20). A witch was one in league with evil spirits, and one who was able to "bewitch" or "to use an evil eye" or mesmerize (Acts 8:9-11; Galatians 3:1). Shakespeare who wrote of the "witching time of night" also gave us the lines —

> The greatest curse brave men can labour
> under
> Is the strong witchcraft of a woman's
> eye.

But the voice as well as the eye was used to beguile unwary souls. Acquainted with the art of ventriloquism, wizards and witches were able to make the sound of their voice to be heard as if it issued from their belly of from the ground; and thus pretend that it was an evil spirit speaking (Isaiah 8:19; 29:4). While "the Witch of Endor" (I Samuel 28:7) is not named a witch in the Bible, but "a woman that hath a familiar spirit," meaning, the equivalent of a medium, she was yet "the mistress of a spirit by which the dead was conjured up."

Witchcraft raged from the fourteenth through the seventeenth centuries. *Hammer for Witches* was a treatise drawn up systematizing the tenets of witchcraft, laying down a regular form of trial and examination. The celebrated Bull of Innocent VIII issued in 1484 sentenced to death all who practiced witchcraft and other diabolical arts. It has been estimated that nine million suffered death for witchcraft as the result of the Bull of Innocent. As late as 1705 two women were executed at Northampton for witchcraft.

There is a legend to the effect that if you drew the blood of a witch you deprived her of her power of sorcery. Shakespeare in *King Henry VI 1. 5*, has the line —

> "Blood will I draw on thee: thou
> art a witch."

Witchhazel is supposed to be a shrub efficacious in discovering witches — a forked twig of the hazel made into a divining rod for the purpose. As for "The Witches' Sabbath," it was reckoned to be night-time when witches and demons gathered to plan mischief. Tradition has it that a witch first anointed her feet and shoulders with the fat of a murdered babe, then, mounting a broomstick, or rake, made her exit by the chimney and rode through the air to the place of rendezvous where the assembled witches feasted together, and concluded with a dance, in which they all turned their backs to each other. Our Lord declared that one evidence of His return would be that of "abounding iniquity." Is not the revival of "black magic" one aspect of our iniquitous time?

FEMALE OCCUPATIONS

FEMALE OCCUPATIONS

IN THE SPIRITUAL REALM

It was divinely ordained that women should be "keepers at home," caring for all that concerns husband and children; and as "discreet, chaste, and good" (Titus 2:4, 5) making the home a bulwark against the evil world outside. As we have indicated there were those noble, necessary arts which women became proficient in, all of which were related to family life. That there were career women is proven by the occupation of Lydia. Generally speaking, however, business women were few and far between; and even in the religious sphere they were not prominent. In public gatherings of the church their attitude had to be one of quietness with the recognition of the leadership of godly men. There was, of course, opportunity for capable women in their own area as one can gather from a few glimpses in the New Testament of women at work. In the church today can be found female pastors, deacons and elders which are foreign to the New Testament order. There were no women among the apostles and elders of apostolic times. While, as we shall see, there were a few prophetesses there were no priestesses save in heathen religions. Does the apostle's command about women speaking in public forbid their ministry as pastors and teachers (I Corinthians 14:34)? What are the proper religious functions of women in the ministry of the church? If there be neither male nor female in Christ, have both males and females the right to hold office in the church? Dr. Samuel Johnson who was a bigot in many ways says that — "A woman preaching is like a dog's walking on his hind legs. It is not done well; but you are surprised to find it done at all." Quite recently the convocation of Canterbury decided to license women to preach in the churches of any Church of England diocese. A few Congregational and Methodist Churches have paid women ministers. But the Southern Baptists in America, as well as the Plymouth or Christian Brethren, and many others exclude women as preachers from pulpits.

What is the exact position as to female ministry? Since woman gave to the world the Founder of Christianity countless women have been drawn into its fold. In the days of His flesh, women ministered unto Jesus (Luke 8:2, 3). They were the last at His cross and the first at His tomb on the resurrection morn. Paul acknowledged the services of those women who labored with him in the Gospel (Philippians 4:3). We shall never know what the cause of Christ owes to womanhood. One wonders what the church would do today without religiously-inclined women. Look around any Sunday congregation today and you will find that women predominate.

For the well-being and progress of the early church female service was necessary. The need was felt for a class of women to assist, in particular, those of their own sex. Thus a wide range of spiritual and practical activities presented themselves to Christian women and today consecrated women are accomplishing more than we realize for the cause of Christ among women and children both at home and abroad. In Paul's day the seclusion of women from men necessitated the services of godly women to care for those of their own sex in spiritual matters. In the Bible two female religious occupations are mentioned:

The Deaconess

Phoebe, meaning "pure," and sometimes spelled Phebe, is the first to be mentioned as a female-deacon, and appears first in a long list of Christian men and women who had some contact with Paul in his apostolic labors, and whom he was anxious to commend (Romans 16:1). The apostle spoke of Phoebe as a sister, which denotes a spiritual relationship and a Christian status. Then he went on to describe her as a servant, which is a term implying a position. The Greek word is *e diakonos,* and is related to deacon or helper. The idea of helper goes back to the beginning when the first woman was called by the noblest of titles "a help." The ASV margin at Romans 16:1 gives us "deaconess" for "servant," a translation with which Bible scholars agree.

The fact that Phoebe is spoken of as a deaconess in the church at Cenchrea — one of the ports of Corinth — implies the existence of some kind of a female "diaconate" in apostolic times (See THE DEACON). We cannot infer from this isolated reference, however, that there was an order of deaconesses ordained for service in the church. As there is no historical record of such an order, and no recognition of such an official position in the epistles we may conclude that the service Phoebe rendered was occasional or temporary. It is not said that she held office in the church, but that she exercised a gracious yet unofficial ministry among the saints at Cenchrea as an active member of the assembly there. We have little information as to the institution of deaconesses simply because, in Paul's day, a deaconess was not yet a question of office. As such she does not appear in gifts to the church, unless we include her under "helps." It is noticeable, however, that in the middle of a passage devoted to deacons that Paul makes a transition from one class to another, namely, deacons to deaconesses — not "women" in general, but a special category (I Timothy 3:11) and that the same qualifications were required in both with such modification as the difference of sex required.

The details regarding widows does not imply an order of deaconesses (I Timothy 5:9, 10). Of these W. Corswant says —

> There is the question of the registration of widows over sixty years of age who enjoyed a good reputation. Would they alone have the right to receive help from the Church? It has been thought that they constituted a sort of college or order called to render important service to the community, but it does not appear that they were "deaconesses" so called; holding an office which related them to the clergy.

Fausset's comment on these widows is that they formed an "ecclesiastical order of widowhood, a female presbytery . . . standing in the same relation to the deaconesses of younger age (I Timothy 5:9-11) that the male presbyters did to the deacons." Pliny in his letter to Trajan spoke of "two slave women called ministers." An insight into the nature of the ministry of the women who knew the apostle and labored with him can be gathered from the description he gives us of Phoebe — "a *succourer* of many, and of myself also." In the exercise of her position as a deaconess she manifested kindness, generosity and benevolence. The word "succor" means a protectress or patroness, and is the feminine form of "prostates," the title of a citizen in Athens, who had the responsibility of seeing to the welfare of resident aliens who were without civic rights. Among the Jews it signified a wealthy patron of the community. Applied to Phoebe, succorer denoted a term of dignity, evidently chosen instead of others which might have been used, such as "Helper," an indication as Vine further suggests "the high esteem with which she was regarded, as one who had been a protectress of many." It may be that she succorred Paul during illnesses.

What is clearly evident is the fact that Phoebe was going to Rome on some important business the nature of which is not disclosed, and that Paul commended her to the Christians there asking them to receive her in the Lord, and assist her in whatever business she had need of them. Because of all she had been to the saints she was worthy of a kind reception. Perhaps she was the bearer of Paul's letter to Rome, where she may have combined business with her particular ministry. We can imagine how the duties of deaconesses increased with the rapid spread of the church. There would be female and youthful inquirers in the doctrines of the church to instruct, female baptisms to assist at, visitation of those imprisoned for their faith, and especially the comfort of those soon to receive the martyr's crown, regular systematic church visitation bringing consolation and encouragement to the sick and needy. For their spiritual ministry there was likely the laying-on of the hands of a bishop, which was more of a benediction than an ordination.

By the fourth century, deaconesses were numerous. Chrysostom was deeply interested in such a sisterhood and had many devoted friends among them. Among his writings are seventeen letters addressed to Olympias, a lady of wealth and rank, who for many years was a deaconess in Constantinople, where one church had, at one time, forty deaconesses engaged in its work. But as the spirit of Monasticism invaded the church, the order declined and under the Romish system there appeared the nunneries with their artificial channel of separate female service. After a lapse of about a thousand years, the German divine, Theodore Fliedmer, restored the primitive order of deaconesses. Earnestly believing in the scripturalness of the Order, and perceiving that godly women had a special gift for service, he inaugurated the Kaiserswerth Deaconess System from which the ever-increasing demand for trained women was met. Florence Nightingale received much of her training at Kaiserswerth though she became a nurse and not a deaconess. In Britain, around 1875, William Pennefather, founded the celebrated Deaconess House at Mildmay, and thereafter several deaconess institutions came into being both in Britain and America. Now, almost all denominations have their deaconesses or sisters with uniforms in different color and style, whose work it is to supplement the work of the pastor, active in "whatsoever their hands find to do."

The Prophetess

The lofty vocation represented by the prophetic office was not confined to men (Compare THE PROPHET). It was shared by women, the prophetess being the female counterpart of the prophet. Both were inspired by the Spirit to forthtell and foretell, and shared the same gifts and powers, not only to give divine instruction in religious and moral truth but also to announce predictions as to the future. Both functioned as the Lord's mouthpiece and messenger to the people for the purpose of enlightenment and edification. The Hebrew word for prophetess is *nebiah,* meaning, a female preacher or herald; while the

Greek word was *prophetis,* the feminine form of *prophetes,* a proclaimer of a divine message. Thus the description of a true prophet of God applied equally to the prophetess. Words placed in the mouth by God had to be repeated without addition or subtraction (Deuteronomy 18:18; Revelation 22:18, 19).

The declaration of the psalmist was fulfilled in those godly women who became renowned as prophetesses —

The Lord giveth the Word;
The women that publish the tidings are a great host (Psalm 68:11, ASV).

The Amplified Bible reads —

The Lord gives the Word of power;
The women who bear and publish the news are a great host.

Among Old Testament named women who exercised the function of a prophet we have —

1. *Miriam* (Exodus 15:20).

With this sister of Aaron and Moses, we have the first of that long series of Bible women who were not only pious and God-fearing, but who exercised a quasi-ministerial office. Miriam heralded forth the victory of the Lord over Pharaoh and his host. Other proclamations and prophecies of hers are not recorded.

2. *Deborah* (Judges 2:18; 4:4).

This valiant woman was both judge and prophetess. She is the only one to be named a judge in Israel. Her "Song" (Judges 5) was one of great fervor and dignity. As a warrior, Deborah inspired a somewhat timid Barak to plan and execute the campaign that resulted in the defeat of the Canaanites at Keshon. Ellicott has this profitable comment on Deborah, a prophetess —

She is the only judge to whom the title "prophet" is expressly given. "Prophetess" implies the possession of poetic as well as of prophetic gifts (Exodus 15:20); and we see her right to such a title, both in her predictions (4:9), her lofty courage (5:7), and the splendor of her inspired song (5). She has modern parallels in the Teutonic prophetesses, Veleda and Alaurinia, and Joan of Arc, the "Inspired Maid of Domremi." Among the Jews prophetesses were the exception; among the ancient Germans they were the rule.

Because Lapidoth, the husband of Deborah, means "flames," "lamps" or "splendors," she has been called "a woman of lamps," a reference to her shining gifts and fiery spirit.

3. *Huldah* (II Kings 22:14; II Chronicles 34:22).

This wife of Shallum "dwelt in Jerusalem in the college" where Hilkiah the priest and his associates gathered for mutual fellowship. The question might be asked, Why did Hilkiah not consult contemporary prophets like Jeremiah or Zephaniah? The simple answer is that Huldah was the nearest at hand seeing she lived in Jerusalem. Anathoth in Benjamin was Jeremiah's home town. That Huldah had a high reputation as a prophetess is gathered from the fact that she must have been included among "the prophets" who appeared before the king (II Kings 23:2). Her prophecy was a combination of warning and forecast (II Kings 22:15-20).

4. *Noadiah* (Nehemiah 6:14).

From Nehemiah's prophetic prayer, we gather that Noadiah, named with Tobiah and Sanballat, enemies of Nehemiah, was a false prophetess who with others had tried to terrorize Nehemiah. She is grouped with "the rest of the prophets" all of whom prophesied about Nehemiah.

5. *Isaiah's Wife* (Isaiah 8:3).

The unnamed wife of the prophet received the title "the prophetess" as a courtesy title just as Areshah, the wife of Mohammed was known as the "prophetess." The same title of honor is comparable to "Sultana" for the wife of the Sultan. Evidently Isaiah and his wife shared prophetic gifts. They were "drawn together by united thoughts and counsels, in contrast with the celibate life of Jeremiah (Jeremiah 16:2), the miseries of Hosea's marriage (Hosea 1; 2), and the sudden bereavement of Ezekiel (Ezekiel 24:16-18)."

The prophetess wife of Isaiah bore him children with prophetic names, so that in the future when "anyone should call these children by name he would necessarily remind everyone of the political prophecies which called forth and explained the names." Shear-jasbub (7:3) means, "the remnant shall return." Maher-shalal-hash-baz (8:3, 4) implies, "Seeding-in-the-spoil, hastening-in-the-prey." Both Hosea and Isaiah gave their children names which were hopefully significant. Each child was a sign and portent (see Isaiah 7:14). The fact that the mother of Isaiah's children was herself a prophetess, sharing her husband's hopes and fears, gives a yet deeper interest to the choice of names.

The bestowal of the prophetic gift continued in the New Testament. At Pentecost, the differentiation between the sexes in respect to prophetic gifts was removed (Acts 2:19, see Joel 2:28). Paul groups men and women together as being able to pray and prophesy (I Corinthians 11:4, 5). Here prophesy means the gift to teach the truth of God, and does not actually contradict Paul's later instruction that women were to be silent and not teach (I Corinthians 14:34; I Timothy 2:12). These injunctions covered public gatherings when the whole church met, whereas the ordinances of chapter eleven refer to the private devotions of individuals (See Romans 14:6; Colossians 4:5; Philemon 2).

1. *Anna* (Luke 2:36)

It was doubtless on the long flight of the fifteen steps of Herod's temple that Anna the prophetess praised the Lord and prophesied. The mention of Anna as a prophetess is all the more remarkable when we remember that as a woman she was recognized as such at a time when no man was recognized as a prophet. Certainly, her contemporary Simeon functioned as a prophet although he is not named as one (Luke 2:25-35). Anna bore the name of the mother (Hannah) of the founder (Samuel) of the school of the prophets, and was immersed in Old Testament prophecies of the Messiah. She was born more than one hundred years before Christ was born. If she married at fifteen years of age and had been a widow for eighty-four years (2:37) when she "spake of Christ to all them that looked for redemption in Israel," then she was about 106 years old when she testified to the Redeemer.

As a reputed prophetess a chamber was assigned to her within the precincts of the temple where "her form, bent and worn, we may believe, with age and fastings, had become familiar to all worshipers at the temple." She was one of the devout circle who cherished expectations of Christ's advent and, when He appeared, instantly recognized Him as the sent One of God.

2. *Philip's Daughters* (Acts 21:8, 9)

Although the four daughters of the evangelist are not specifically referred to as prophetesses it is declared that they "prophesied," or had the gift of inspired teaching. Dr. Merrill F. Unger says that "women prophets are attested in Phrygia at a later period. Two of these who remained single are traditionally claimed to be buried in Hierapolis, while a third who later married was said to have been buried at Ephesus." All four of Philip's daughters were "virgins" and Ellicott suggests that this word not only indicates that they were chaste, unmarried women but that "they had devoted themselves, if not by irrevocable vows, yet by a steadfast purpose to that form of service they represented."

As to their "prophesying" such a term includes prediction of the future and the proclamation of a Spirit-inspired message for those the daughters preached to. The question can be asked, When and where did they preach? Female preaching in the church had been forbidden (I Corinthians 14:34; I Timothy 2:12). Perhaps they confined their ministrations to those of their own sex, and, accompanying their evangelist-father in his missionary journeys, were able to influence their own sex among Jews and Gentiles for their Lord, and then assist, as a matter of decorum, in the baptism of female converts.

3. *Jezebel* (Revelation 2:20)

To this temptress of Christians at Thyatira was given the name of Israel's infamous queen, Jezebel. The only other woman, apart from Anna mentioned as a "prophetess," was a self-styled one. Although Ahab was king of Israel, he was but a puppet in the hands of Jezebel who was the idolatrous, virtual ruler of the nation (I Kings 18 - 21). The Jezebel John describes eclipsed her Old Testament counterpart in sin, cruelty and idolatry. Arrogantly assuming the honored title of "prophetess" she professes to "teach with authority. Combined with teaching she can employ all the arts and seductions of minds specially trained to effect her fell purpose." Many prophetic students hold that Jezebel is here used figuratively of the Popish system (Revelation 17; 18) which affirms that it cannot err in faith and morals. The dogma of Rome is that "her teachings and seductions, however contrary to Scripture and repellent to human understanding, must be acceptable as authoritative and infallible," says Walter Scott. But a deserved and terrible end awaits the corrupt Jezebel and all those who have imbibed her principles and teachings. Impressive, is it not, that self-confessed, deluded prophetesses were the founders of some of the false cults flourishing today, whose representatives creep into houses and lead silly women astray (II Timothy 3:5)? How we all need spiritual intuition whereby we can detect immediately that which is not an authoritative message from God!

EPILOGUE

Now that the profitable and pleasurable task of gathering together, alphabetically, all the occupations of the Bible is completed, will you suffer a word of practical exhortation? Returning to the question on the title page of this volume may we ask you the question, "What is *thine* occupation?" What *you* do for a living may be similar or different from friends of yours. But whether you are a parson or postman, duchess or dressmaker, teacher or toolmaker, archbishop or artist, is yours a vocation with a vision? Do you enjoy your living, as well as earn it? Thomas Carlyle is credited with the saying, "Give me the man who sings at his work," which expresses the philosophy that if a person delights in his labor it will not be a drudgery. Absorbed in work, whether it represents brain or brawn, or both, the worker will give of his best for the remuneration received. Toil will not be a treadmill if our eyes are on Him who, as a carpenter, lived with men who worked.

This for the day of life I ask:
Some all-absorbing, useful task:
And when 'tis wholly, truly done,
A tranquil rest at set of sun.

It matters little whether our niche in life is high or humble, so long as we labor not only to please those who employ and pay us, but for the praise of Him who gives us ability and strength to labor for our daily bread.

Whatever dies, or is forgot —
Work done for God, it dieth not.

To quote Carlyle again, "The wages of very noble work do yet lie in heaven or else nowhere." Thomas W. Treckelton writes —

The toil of brain, or heart, or hand,
  Is man's appointed lot;
He who God's call can understand
  Will work and murmur not.
Toil is no thorny crown of pain,
  Bound round man's brow for sin;
True souls, from it, all strength may gain,
  High manliness may win.

BIBLIOGRAPHY

Angus, Joseph, *The Bible Handbook* (London: The Religious Tract Society, 1862).

Bailey, Albert E., *Daily Life in Bible Times* (New York: Charles Scribner, 1943).

Bouquet, A. C., *Early Days in the New Testament* (London: B. T. Batsford Ltd. 1959).

Corswant, W., *A Dictionary of Life in Bible Times* (New York: Oxford University Press, 1960).

Davidson, Donald, *The Workmen of the Bible* (London: James Clarke & Co., 1937).

Ellicott, Charles, *Commentary on the Whole Bible* (Grand Rapids: Zondervan Publishing House, 1954).

Fairbairn, Patrick. *Fairbairn's Bible Encyclopedia* (Grand Rapids: Zondervan Publishing House, 1957).

Fausset, A. R. *Bible Encyclopedia and Dictionary* (Grand Rapids: Zondervan Publishing House, n.d.).

Hastings, James, *Dictionary of the Bible* (Edinburgh: T. and T. Clark, 1909).

Heaton, E. W., *Early Days in the Old Testament* (London: B. T. Batsford Ltd. 1959).

Nicholson, Wm., *The Bible Companion* (Glasgow: Pickering and Inglis, n.d.).

Orr, James (edited by), *The International Standard Bible Encyclopedia* (Grand Rapids: Wm. B. Eerdmans, 1939).

Shipley, Joseph T., *Dictionary of Word Origins* (New York: The Philosophical Library, 1945).

Sinclair, George, *Bible Occupations* (2 volumes) (Glasgow: John Smith & Son Ltd. 1913).

Smith, Elsdon C., *The Story of Our Names* (New York: Harper & Brothers, 1950).

Tenney, Merrill C., (edited by), *Zondervan Pictorial Bible Dictionary* (Grand Rapids: Zondervan Publishing House, 1963).

Thomson, W. M., *The Land and the Book* (New York: T. Nelson, 1891).

Unger, Merrill W., *Archaeology and the Old Testament* (Grand Rapids: Zondervan Publishing House, 1954).

————, *Archaeology and the New Testament* (Grand Rapids: Zondervan Publishing House, 1962).

Van Deursen, A., *Bible Manners and Customs* (London: Marshall, Morgan & Scott, 1958).

Vine, W. E., *Expository Dictionary of New Testament Words* (London: Oliphants Ltd. 1958).

————, *Scripture Manners and Customs* (London: Society for Promoting Christian Knowledge, 1895).

SCRIPTURE INDEX